C0-DMS-693

MID-AMERICAN
★ FRONTIER ★

This is a volume in the Arno Press collection

MID-AMERICAN
★ FRONTIER ★

Advisory Editor
Jerome O. Steffen

Editorial Board
Richard S. Brownlee
William W. Savage, Jr.

*See last pages of this volume
for a complete list of titles*

The Black Hills Trails

Jesse Brown and A. M. Willard

ARNO PRESS
A New York Times Company
New York — 1975

Editorial Supervision: ANDREA HICKS

———◆———

Reprint Edition 1975 by Arno Press Inc.

Reprinted from a copy in
 The University of Illinois Library

THE MID-AMERICAN FRONTIER
ISBN for complete set: 0-405-06845-X
See last pages of this volume for titles.

Manufactured in the United States of America

———◆———

Library of Congress Cataloging in Publication Data

Brown, Jesse, 1844-
  The Black Hills trails.

  (The Mid-American frontier)
  Reprint of the ed. published by Rapid City Journal
Co., Rapid City, S. D.
  1. Frontier and pioneer life--Black Hills, S. D.
and Wyo. 2. Black Hills, S. D. and Wyo.--History.
3. Little Big Horn, Battle of the, 1876. I. Willard, A. M., 1847-1921, joint author. II. Title.
III. Series.
F657.B6B8 1975   978.3'9   75-83
ISBN 0-405-06852-2

The Black Hills Trails

Jesse Brown and A. M. Willard

The Black Hills Trails

A History of the Struggles of the Pioneers

in the

Winning of the Black Hills

By

Jesse Brown and A. M. Willard

Edited by John T. Milek

Rapid City Journal Company
Rapid City, South Dakota
1924

Copyright 1924
by
Jesse Brown
and
W. B. Willard

DEDICATION

To the fearless shot gun messengers, whose courage and steadfast devotion to duty on the frontier, won for all future generations the rich heritage of the Black Hills, this book is gratefully dedicated.

Men of the Gordon Party

From left to right, top row: Tommy Quinner, David Aken, Angus McDonald, Lyman Lamb, Red Dan McDonald, and John Boyle
Lower row: Jim Dempster, Dempster McDonald, R. R. Whitney and B .B. Logan

FOREWORD

The Black Hills of South Dakota comprise the battle ground of the last pioneer conquest in America. They were the last real frontier border on the continent, and while Alaska was later exploited, that territory did not present all of the problems and difficulties that constituted the elemental struggle of man with nature and man that entered into the genuine frontier as it existed in the first years of the rush to the Hills.

The complete and true story of the pioneer days has never been written and it is proper at this time after the passing of almost fifty years, and while a few men of that great army of adventurers that flocked to the Hills, are still alive, that some of the incidents of those days may be recorded in the words of those who were either the actors or witnesses. This book does not claim to be a history, but is a collection of tales by many authors who know whereof they write and thus presents a reliable source book to which he, who would in the future, write the history of the Hills, may resort to find the true and correct story of the pioneers. No doubt readers will find many of the accounts at variance with their accepted versions of the several incidents, but this will be found true of every event in life, even of this day, where there is more than one witness. But most of the tales have been checked up through newspaper accounts, private diaries, public records and eye witnesses, and are as accurate as may be made. And in the years that are now dawning, when the last soldier in that mighty army of sturdy nation builders shall have answered final roll call, the stirring scenes of the past may arise again before the mind of the reader, though the voice of the actor may have long been silenced.

To the territory of the Black Hills, the lure of gold led men and women from every walk in life, and in the shadows of the pine clad mountains, some of the most romantic incidents and great dramas of human life were enacted. Along the trails and freight roads leading into those Hills are many graves, some unknown, where ended forever, fond hopes and dreams of those who fell by the wayside. The day of the road agent and highwayman has passed forever. The old freight trains and heavy wagons that slowly rumbled over hill and dale of long ago, are now mere memories, but they were advance guards of the great unconquered force that drove the savages from the Hills and made there a fit habitation for the men and women of today.

The period of time covered in this book is approximately the last quarter of the 19th century, a time when the Hills were truly western and still under the spell of frontier enchantment. Great changes have taken place since those years. Over the trails of the pioneers where men toiled and battled with mud and storms and drove the long ox teams, today people hurl their high powered autos along graded and paved highways at the speed of the wind. In the gulches that once rang with the war whoop of the red man, there now echoes the merry laughter of little children. Beneath the shade of a giant oak or lofty pine, whose roots perchance entwine the dreamless head of some forgotten pioneer, today the tourist joyfully plucks the wild flowers, or entranced, looks upon the magnificent panorama of the Hills.

That the story of how this change was wrought, that the picture of those turbulent years may not entirely fade away, that the names of the intrepid and heroic men who ventured forth into the uncharted wilds and fought the good fight, might be preserved, is the purpose of this book and the hope of its authors, Jesse Brown and A. M. Willard. To their long and untiring efforts, overcoming great obstacles, is due this work. Especial mention is made of Joseph Gossage, pioneer newspaper man of the west, to whom is due the preservation of many tales from the Sidney Telegraph, then owned by him. To Mrs. Alice Gossage, his versatile wife, fell the task of superintending the printing of this book and at the same time keeping the big newspaper office of the Rapid City Journal in full swing. The gratitude of the authors is expressed to the several writers who have contributed the accounts and articles credited to them in the pages of this book. The spirit of the pioneer comradeship so abundantly displayed by them, has made the assembling of the stories for this book, a labor of love.

A Black Hills Hunter

TABLE OF CONTENTS

CHAPTER I.
THE BLACK HILLS

The Badlands—Legend of the Rose—Early Explorers—The First Prospectors—The Custer Expedition—Gold First Discovered—The Collins and Russell Party—The Beginning of Custer—The Prospector 17

CHAPTER II.
THE TRAILS

An Incident in the Story of the Pony Express—Red Cloud Opposed the Invasion of the Territory—Jesse Brown at Fort Kearney—The Black Hills Distances—Transportation, etc.—Experiences of Early Day Gold Seekers, 1875—A Freighting Outfit—The Freighter—The Freighter's Unwelcome Guests—From Cheyenne to Custer in June, '76—When Fate Saved a Party of Pioneers—Montana Party—The First Trail Makers—The Deadwood Trail 47

CHAPTER III.
INDIAN RAIDS AND BATTLES

Pioneer Days were Stirring—The First Miner Killed by Indians in 1875—California Joe—First Death in Custer—Wood Choppers Fall to Indian Bullets—The tragedy of Pino Springs—The Pony Express Rider—Murder of the Metz Family—Battle of the Springs on the Hill—The Wagner Family—The Killing of "Jimmy Iron"—The Mexican and the Indian Head—Holland and Brown—Death of Charles Mason—Rapid City Founders Fight Indians—The Killing of Leggett and Hayward—Death of Wilson and Abernathy, 1877—The Indian Trouble Near Rapid City—The Messiah Craze—Death of Sitting Bull—The Battle of Wounded Knee—The Murder of Few Tails—The Romance of the Big Horn—The Song of the Vanished West 83

CHAPTER IV.
BATTLE OF THE BIG HORN

The Indian Account of the Battle—The Burial of the Dead—The Sole Survivor—News of the Custer Massacre Received in the Black Hills—Crook's March from the Yellowstone—The Battle of Slim Butte—The Treaty.... 132

CHAPTER V.
HIGHWAYMEN AND ROBBERS

The Program of a Holdup of 1876—The Killing of "Stuttering Brown"—The Killing of Johnny Slaughter—Robbery of Union Pacific—Trail and Capture of Robbers—The Killing of Frank Towle—The Passing of a Mexi-

TABLE OF CONTENTS--Continued

can Robber's Spy—The Web-May Holdup—The Killing of Bob Castello—Wall and Blackburn Holdup—The Robbers' Roost Holdup—The Canyon Springs Stage Robbery—Sidney, Nebraska, the Scene of a Three Hundred Thousand Dollar Theft—The Death of Curley Grimes, 1879—Holdup of Homestake Pay Train 240

CHAPTER VI.
NECKTIE PARTIES, FORMAL AND INFORMAL

Swift Justice—The First Hanging in the Black Hills—The Rapid City Necktie Party—Two Butchers who Became Prosperous—Lame Johnny—The Capture of Tom Price and his Band of Agents—The Hanging of Fly Specked Billy—The Stoneville Battle—Tuthill—Fiddler—The Assassination of Dr. H. P. Lynch—Negro Infantry Runs Amuck—The First Legal Hanging—The Hanging of Hicks—Chief Two-Sticks Paid the Penalty—Hanging of Negro Charles Brown—Brutal Double Murder 287

CHAPTER VII.
LAW AND ORDER ESTABLISHED

First Efforts to Establish Law and Order—The Duel of Tom Moore and Shannon—The Hinch Murder—A Duel in Deadwood—The Killing of Ed Shaunessy by Dick Brown—Experiences of a Pioneer Lawyer—The Killing of Brodovitch by Sam May (Turkey Sam) and Blair (Darby)—Black Hills Organized—Court Business on the Frontier—Chinatown in 1877—The Killing of Kitty Leroy—A Fatal Quarrel—Aurora Mine, 1877—First Political Campaign in Lawrence County—The Case of Martin Couck—The "Pagan" Jury—Crow Dog and Spotted Tail—The Struggle Between Father DeSmet and Homestake Mine—He Carries Nine Buck Shots—Buffalo Gap—Stole Borger's Team—Our Horse Thieves Return, One of them has a few Wounds in a Tender Place, but the other Feels Fine—Attempted Jail Delivery—Circuit Court—Everybody Pleads Guilty or Gets it in the Neck 341

CHAPTER VIII.
FOUR FAMOUS PIONEER NAMES

Father DeSmet—Preacher Smith—The Old Hunter's Reverie —"Wild Bill"—Calamity Jane 390

CHAPTER IX.
FRONTIER SKETCHES

Life in Deadwood in '76 and '77—Celebration of July 4th in the Centennial Year—How Pactola was Given that

TABLE OF CONTENTS--Continued

Name—The Illicit Still in Early Days—Black Hills Salt Springs—A Cargo of Cats—A Bear Story—The Great Snow Storm—Great Fire in Deadwood in 1879—The Hunting Party—The Pierre Trail—The Death Dealing Blizzard of 1896—The Story of Black Hills Gold Jewelry—Language of the Roundup 419

CHAPTER X.
TRANSPORTATION

The Story of the Cities—Deadwood—Directory of 1878 of Deadwood—Lead City—Towns of the Past—Fort Meade—Sturgis—Rapid City—Spearfish—The Livestock Industry—The Black Hills Newspapers—The Tin Industry—The Story of Gold—The Gold Industry in 1877—The Romance of Alfalfa—The Tale of the Hills 458

APPENDIX
BIOGRAPHICAL SKETCHES

Captain Willard—Jesse Brown—Scott Davis—George V. Ayres—W. J. Thornby—C. V. Gardner—Richard B. Hughes—W. H. Bonham—Capt. Jack Crawford—Jean P. Decker—Major A. J. Simmons—Joseph B. Gossage—Lee R. Baxter—Jack Langrishe—Thomas Cooper—John Manning—H. O. Alexander—Ellis T. Peirce—John D. Hale—Galen E. Hill—Joe E. Cook—Anna Donna Tallent—Horatio N. Ross 513

ILLUSTRATIONS

Men of the Gordon Party	8
A Black Hills Hunter	12
Bear Butte	19
The Badlands	22
Custer Train	34
Gordon Stockade	42
Treasure Coach at Canyon Springs	49
The Evans Bull Train	65
Wounded Knee Battlefield	121
Custer's Monument	219
Stage Team Running Away	246
Gang of Outlaws	253
Sitting Bull	254
Capt. Davis Behind a Pine Tree	265
Harney Peak Above the Clouds	286
Historic Hangman's Hill	295
Hanging of Ernest Loveswar	337
In the Black Hills	389
Badlands	393
Rev. H. W. Smith's Monument	399
Wild Bill's Grave	411
Deadwood in the Early Days	421

TABLE OF CONTENTS--Concluded

Cheyenne and Black Hills Stage	459
Hill City Before Stampede to Deadwood	462
Deadwood, 1876	464
Scene on Main Street, Rapid City, 1877	480
Scene in Rapid City, 1880	480
Homestake at Lead	502
Scott Davis, Jesse Brown and A. M. Willard at Canyon Springs	512
Frontispiece	
John R. Brennan	107
Sam Scott	108
W. A. Remer	116
General Custer and Lieutenant Cook	162
General G. A. Crook	225
Chief Red Cloud	236
Gail Hill	266
Billy Sample	275
Archie Riordan	380
James Butler Hickock (Wild Bill)	404
Seth Bullock	507
Jesse Brown and Scott Davis	523
George V. Ayres	524
W. J. Thornby	525
Capt. C. V. Gardner	527
R. B. Hughes	529
Jean P. Decker	536
Joseph B. Gossage	542
Tom Cooper	548
John Manning	551
H. O. Alexander	552
E. T. Peirce	553
John D. Hale	555
Anna Donna Tallent	566
Horatio N. Ross	572

CHAPTER I.

THE BLACK HILLS

High above the prairies of western South Dakota and eastern Wyoming there rises a series of rocky crests whose rugged peaks greet the traveler long before he stands enchanted at their feet. To the wanderer who journeys toward them, they first appear as a great black cloud on the distant horizon, and then when the long rolling prairies are passed, they stand forth in their mighty majesty and grandeur, the highest peaks in America east of the Rocky Mountains. They are the Black Hills, the land of the golden fleece to whose shores the argonauts of the seventies sailed over the vast oceans of the prairies, many to perish on the voyage and others to die in the cruel clutch of the monster, Avarice, that lay waiting them at the goal.

In the days when the world was young, a great crumpling of the surface took place and the western area of South Dakota was thrust upwards until the innermost depths of the earth were pushed out to the blaze of the sun once more. Broad streams of water coursed along and over the newly made mountains, carrying away the crushed and broken surface and sent the boulders, rocks and earth tumbling towards the sea. The waters then sought a new ocean bed and left the area high and dry pointing with giant fingers towards the skies and thrusting its majestic peaks among the clouds. The Black Hills then, present the remains of moutains from whose tops and sides have been carried away, the debris of their making and we see today the fresh and sharp crests and gulches left when the titanic struggle of force and mass ended. They cover an area of about one hundred miles square in which gold and silver, tin and lead, iron and coal, gas and oil have been found in paying quantities.

Within the broad expanse of the Black Hills are majestic mountains piercing the clouds seven thousand two hundred feet above the sea, or deep underground caverns where one may wander for a hundred miles in darkness where no ray of sunshine has ever reached and sound is unknown. Beautiful dales nestle among the hills, and noisy brooks go tumbling down the gulches. Dark green pines, silvery birch, and stately oak vie with the roses, lilies and flowers in great profusion to paint the landscape with a lavish display of color. Numerous and pretty birds flit among the trees and shrubs and mingle their cheery songs with the babbling of the rippling waters where the swift going trout makes his home. Deer and elk once held sway within their borders, and bears and cougars joined with wolves in their cruel mission.

This region had long been the favorite hunting ground of the Indians where they could always find game in plenty. Here they could secure lodge poles for their tepees and flints for their arrows. Among the plants they obtained medicinal herbs and in the hot springs they found healing waters. Naturally the Indian mind associated many of the peaks and gulches with stories and legends and gave their names to the several places. To the northwest part of the Hills rises a huge, fluted column of volcanic origin, having much the appearance of a tepee and this the Indians called Mato Tepee, or Bear Lodge. Its height of 5117 feet is really imposing. It was also known as Devil's Tower, a name given to it by the Indians. To the northeast of the Hills, arises another lofty peak looming far above the prairies in its height of 4422 feet. This was known as Mato Paha, or Bear Butte. To the name of this peak is associated the Indian legend to the effect that many moons ago, when the red men were camped near the base of the great hill, and the braves were far away on their hunting trip, a hungry bear sneaked into the camp. The squaws were busy with their labors of tanning skins and preparing for their lord's return, and did not notice the stealthy approach of the animal who entered a tepee and there finding a sleeping papoose grabbed him in his mouth and ran from the place with the baby within his jaws. The cries of the little one aroused the women who hurried, terror stricken, to the rescue of the babe, but the swift moving bear gained the fastness of the lone mountain and never again was heard the cry of the little one. And ever afterwards the hill was known as the bear hill and Indian mothers stilled their prairie babes with the story of the Mato Paha.

Bear Butte

A detailed description of the various wonders and beauties of the Black Hills will not be given here for the reason that there are so many booklets and writings setting them forth that the reader may be loath to tarry herein to read them if we should presume to attempt that task. However, there is a region near the Hills of which little is known by the majority of readers and which by its forbidding appearance, is not commonly explored, and that is the Bad Lands, a short description of which may prove of interest.

THE BAD LANDS

In western South Dakota there lies a large area of practically useless land that in formation and general topography is not equaled by any other spot on the face of the globe. This area has long been known by the very appropriate name of the "Bad Lands." It is almost impossible to cross it either on foot or horseback and this country in the early years was the abode of deer and mountain sheep which grazed upon the little valleys interspersed among the buttes and ridges. The general appearance of the Bad Lands to one who approaches it from a distance is that of a wonderful city composed of great towers, domes, minarets and castles and as one gets into the tumbled ruins he sees about him a most fantastic and wondrous creation of the Architect of the universe. Long sharp ridges of stone, gravel and clay point toward the sky while here and there from every towering hill the wind and rains of centuries have eroded and carried away the lower portion leaving enormous rocks projecting over the base and beneath which the swallows, by thousands, have built their mud nests and made their noisy homes.

From the standpoint of the geologist the Bad Lands present a spot of the greatest interest and date back to the time when the Continent of America was in its infancy. In the beginning of its creation the vast prairies of the west were then great undulating plains through which the rivers and creeks quietly and peacefully flowed. Along their banks were the tropical growths and the luxuriant vegetation of the primeval days. Over the prairie scampered the ancestors of the many of the fauna of this day. The deer, then the size of the jackrabbit, flitted over the hills and perchance played hide and seek with the little three toed horse whose spreading hoofs enabled him to travel over boggy places. In the trees squirrels chattered back and forth or perhaps sought to flee from their enemy, the terrible sabertooth cat. Giant hogs uprooted the luscious growing plants, tapirs browsed beneath the leafy trees, camels and rhinoceroses wended their way over the parched hillsides. Here and there a crocodile bathed in the mud, while multitudes of turtles sunned themselves on the boggy creek banks. Although some of the forms of animal life of that day were much smaller than now, we do find that other forms were much larger than their descendants at the present. Some of the turtles have never been equaled in size by any that are in existence today, but master of the animal world of the west, and lord over all was the giant brontotherium or thunderbeast, elephantine in size and appearance.

The world in those times was in rapid process of formation and great cataclysms took place. The Rocky Mountains were thrust up through the plains, old Harney Peak pushed through the crevices and the Black Hills were born. Vast numbers of animal life were destroyed. Great streams of water rushed through the new born mountains and carried with them all kinds of animals and deposited them in the lower depressions toward which the water hurried. Then came another mighty upheaval and a change in the western hemisphere took place. Extensive deposits of coarse gravel are found upon the preceding deep sea mud, finer and finer grows the deposits of gravel to be followed by deep sea mud and the sand and silt. A third time the Bad Lands tell us that old Mother Earth was wrenched and torn and the waters rushing down toward the plains carried with them the broken fragments of the Rocky Mountains and the rent and crushed peaks of the Black Hills. Again the troubled waters became quiet. Fine gravel was piled upon coarse, sand and silt upon the smaller gravel and deep sea mud and more recent deposits pressed down the coarser layers. Then the continued upthrust of the Black Hills raised the former lake bed of the Bad Lands, and the streams which forged their way out from the canyons and fissures of the mountains as they grew old, once again tore through the broad lake deposits and marked the course of the White River and Cheyenne for the future generations. Through this soft sand and gravel mixed with clay which during millions of years had been deposited in the former low lands, the rushing waters plowed and dug their way until today the temples, pyramids, castles and domes of the Bad Lands stand forth in their variant forms and sizes. Here indeed is the graveyard of the dawn of the American Continent. Row upon row, shelf upon shelf are deposited the bones of the creatures of long ago. The great and the small, the slow and the quick, the fierce and the timid alike have lain down to-

The Badlands

gether and out from the silent walls of the past their skulls and grinning jaws look down upon the visitor whose irreverent feet crush the bones of the dead and disturb the deep silence of their tombs.

A visit to the Bad Lands of today is indeed to turn back the pages of history and look at the wonders of life as it existed millions of years ago. It is fitting and proper that so wonderful and marvelous an area should be at the very door step of the Black Hills country about which the tales and stories that are set forth in this book have been created and made a matter of history. To this region have come the geologists and men of science from all parts of the world and in all the great museums of America, England and Europe fossils and skulls from the Black Hills of South Dakota look upon the curious visitor who little dreams and realizes that through the silent and bleached masses, once rushed the warm blood of sensient beings whose forms laid down to never ending sleep ages before the soul of man had been breathed into the dust of earth.

The Black Hills country did not always belong to the Sioux, the tribes, from whom the pioneers wrested the golden empire. Their occupancy of the territory was about two hundred years, prior to which time it belonged to the Crows, who had in their turn driven older tribes therefrom. The wars between the Sioux and Crows closed about the time the weaker nation was driven south and was compelled to forsake forever, their ancient hunting grounds. It is said their last stand was taken on the top of a high flat topped butte in western Nebraska south of the Hills where they had been driven by the conquering tribes, who surrounded them on this peak. The place was impregnable to the attacking forces, and they began a siege knowing that the Crows must soon starve or surrender. However, the Crows outwitted their enemies and by taking the skins of their ponies and tying them together, they lowered the whole band, except one old man, to the bottom of the steep bluff opposite the camp of the Sioux. The lone Indian kept the camp fires burning until his fellows had made good their escape and then came down to the Sioux to submit to his fate. This hill is known today as Crow Peak.

As the Sioux had driven forth their predecessors in title and occupancy, so likewise in the course of time, it was decreed that they should go forth and forsake the gem of the American Continent. And to this sad event with all its woeful consequences, there comes a pretty story, the Legend of the Rose.

LEGEND OF THE ROSE

The wild rose grows in great profusion throughout the Black Hills. It is found on the banks of every stream, in every grassy part and on every mountain side, attaining a depth of coloring that is denied the rose of the plain. The Legend of the Rose was first published in the Deadwood Pioneer in 1878, by John M. Whitten, City Auditor, into whose hands the manuscript had fallen by accident. It is probable that no copy of the paper containing the Legend is now in existence as the files of the Pioneer were burned in the great fire of 1879, but R. B. Hughes has attempted to reproduce it from memory and has written it as follows:

Long, long ago, when the oldest man now living had not yet been born there came from the land of the morning sun a band of white men in search of gold. For many moons they had traveled by day through dense forests and over wide prairies and by night their camp fires shone upon the streams. At last from a high place they beheld before them the valley of the Beautiful River, while beyond, the peaks of the Paha Sapa (Black Hills) glistened in the sun. Then were their hearts made glad for this was the land of their desire. Descending to the valley they found a village of the red men. But no smoke arose from the lodges, no children played about the doors of the wigwams. From all sides came the sounds of mourning, for the people had been stricken by a deadly sickness. Many already had died, while of those who yet lived none were able to gather fuel to keep the fires burning.

Famine, too, was there, for though there were buffalo on all sides of the hills no warrior had strength to draw the bow strings that his woman and children might have food.

Now were the hearts of the white men melted with pity. They gathered and heaped the fuel for the tepee fires, and hunted the buffalo until every want for food was supplied. But better than all there was among the pale faces a great medicine man. So powerful was his medicine to cure, that those who received it at once felt the stagnant blood leap in their veins. This man ministered to the sick by night and by day, that all who were yet alive at his coming stood upon their feet strong and well. Then the white men went upon their way to the land of gold and the red men gave thanks to the Great Spirit who had sent them help in time of need. But there was one among the red men whose heart was bad. The Medicine man whose medicine was of no avail against the sickness was filled with anger because that of the white men was more powerful. He whispered into the ears of his people that if the pale faces were allowed to go back to the land of the Morning Sun with gold they would return in numbers so great that the red men would be driven from their hunting grounds, and the buffalo and elk and deer and antelope would be destroyed. Thus he wrought upon their fears until they sought out the camp of the pale faces where they delved in the earth and labored in the streams of the mountains. In the early light of the morning while the men slept they came upon them with tomahawk and knife until not one was left living. And built fires that consumed the bodies of the dead to ashes that no trace of them might remain. Then was the Great Spirit angry. His voice was heard in thunder tones in the gorges, clouds blacker than the darkest night rolled over the mountain tops and from them came lightnings, blasting and withering all they touched. The winds rose, and catching up the ashes of the white men carried them upon their wings far and wide. The red men now knowing that their work had been evil fled from the wrath of the Great Spirit, fled from the mountains to the plains. To them henceforth were forbidden the delights of Paha Sapa. Nevermore might the Indian hunter pursue the elk and deer in their fastnesses, never again build his camp fires in the beautiful parks or trap the beaver along the clear rippling waters. To the place of the sinking of the waters he might go, but no farther. Thus the Paha Sapa became to the red man a land of dread. The wrath of the Great Spirit having been appeased he caused his rains to fall upon the earth, and wherever the ashes of the pale faces had found a resting place there sprang up a blossom in beauty, the Wild Rose.

EARLY EXPLORERS

A region so rich in mineral wealth, so adorned with the beauties of nature and so stamped with the sublimity of its Maker, as the Black Hills, could not escape being early and widely known. We find that this country had long been the favorite hunting place for Indians, and that white men first saw its shadows in the days when this republic had not been even dreamed of as a possibility. In the year 1743, on the first day of January, Louis-Joseph Verendrye and Francis Verendrye, two sons of a great French explorer, came within sight of the Black Hills, while wandering westward with a band of Indians. Soon after this they proceeded into the Hills from the northeastern corner, probably in the neighborhood of Sturgis and on into the park country near the upper hills where they found that their enemy whom they sought had left camp. The Indians beat a hasty retreat back to the camp site in the northeast and the Verendrye brothers went with them. They then wandered on towards the east and on a hill near the present site of Ft. Pierre and overlooking the Missouri river, they planted a leaden plate in commemoration of the discovery of the country and its claim by the King of France. This was done on the 30th day of March, 1743, and there it remained throughout the years until on the 16th day of February, 1913, a school girl noticed the ancient plate of lead and brought it to light once more, thereby corroborating a tale that had been the source of much discussion among historians.

From that year, the Black Hills remained a sealed book to the white men and we read nothing more of them until the coming of Lewis and Clark in 1804, who crossed the plains in their great journey of exploration to the coast. They did not vary from their route to visit the Hills but heard of them at the time, from the French traders under the name of Black Mountains. While in this account they are referred to as Black Mountains, we find that in a statement made by Prince Maximilian from Germany, who was at the mouth of Bad river in June, 1833, he calls them Black Hills, evidently using the name common to the people to whom he spoke at that place.

The success of the Lewis and Clark expedition put a great impetus to the fur trade and in 1811, we find the Astor party pushing for the coast and passing to the north of the Hills, in a country now known as Harding and Perkins counties. Bonneville, in 1831, came nearer to the region, but did not enter the rough country, coming up from the southwest and when directly west of the city of Edgemont, turning west and continuing into Wyoming. In 1848, we find the intrepid missionary, Father DeSmet with the Indians in the Black Hills, for a few months and for several years later his work among the red men carried him all over the country around the region where he from his knowledge of minerals and association with the Indians, knew of the presence of gold, but the secret of which he carefully guarded until the existence of gold became a published fact.

The traders and trappers who had visited the Black Hills country brought back not alone specimens of gold, but also petrified bones and teeth of strange and unknown animals. A description of these bones in 1847, aroused so much interest among scientists, that in 1849 Dr. John Evans visited the Bad Lands and obtained such specimens and a general knowledge of the country as to furnish the material for a most valuable book published by Dr. Leidy. Thaddeus A. Culbertson in 1850 also made a journey to the region for the Smithsonian Institution, and F. V. Hayden spent much time and labor among the clay hills and buttes in 1853, '55 and '57, despite the hardships and the great danger from the Indians. In 1855 he even reached Bear Butte which he ascended at that time. Thus through the enthusiasm of the men of science, the Bad Lands part of the Hills were more throughly known than the mineral bearing portion, many years before the advent of Custer.

General Harney in 1855 skirted the southern and southeastern border of the Hills, passing from Ft. Laramie through northern Nebraska and out into Dakota, through the vicinity of present Scenic and Wall. To Lieutenant Warren, however, is due the credit of a first extended exploration of the Black Hills. In 1857, he went northward from Ft. Laramie, to the west of the Hills, where at a point known as Inyan Kara, he was so strenuously opposed by the Indians, that he decided to retreat and turned back, but instead of abandoning his journey, he swung off to the east passing through Custer county, and thence northward through the heart of the Hills and coming out to Bear Butte in the northeast. From this point he travelled in a southeasterly direction over the foot hills and out in the Pine Ridge country. In 1859 Captain Reynolds journeyed westward reaching the Hills near Bear Butte on the northeast and thence passing westward along the foot hills, directed his course northward into Montana.

THE FIRST PROSPECTORS

While the instances set forth were the recorded events of the white man's knowledge of the Hills, we find that within the valleys and gulches of the Hills were left mute proofs of the occupancy by men at a time long prior to those noted. Here and there a pick and shovel, an abandoned shaft or primitive sluice box all buried beneath the accumulated drift of years were found by the pioneers of the early seventies, indicating that other men had preceded them in the search for gold many years before.

In the month of March, 1887, a small gulley near the foot of Lookout mountain near the city of Spearfish, gave up the last message from a party of gold seekers long forgotten. Louis Thoen was hauling rock for the foundation of a building and while prying up a large flat rock, noticed that it had beneath it, a smaller flat rock with certain markings upon it which attracted further attention. He picked up the rock and brushed the dirt from it and upon the smooth surface there stood forth the rough characters inscribed by a pen knife. He carried the rock home with him and after cleaning it, there appeared inscriptions on each side, one of which read, "Came to these Hills in 1833, seven of us De Lacompt Ezra Kind G. W. Wood T Brown R. Kent Wm. King Indian Crow all ded but me Ezra Kind killed by Indians beyond the high hill got our gold June, 1834." On the reverse side is the farewell message of this first historian of the Hills "Got all the gold we could carry our ponys all got by the Indians I have lost my gun and nothing to eat and Indians hunting me." The draw in which this simple record of a tragedy destined to be the first in a long series, was penned, was six or eight feet deep at point of discovery and well covered with brush woods. R. H Evans, who was one of the first settlers in the valley, found upon his first coming, camp utensils secreted upon Lookout mountain not far from the draw, and showing by the rust that they had long been resting there.

The report of the discovery of the inscribed stone reached far and wide and attracted much attention in the newspapers throughout the nation. John Cashner, in whose possession the stone was held for some years, received letters from several parties inquiring about it, and one was from Troy, Missouri, stating that an uncle of the writer, T. Brown, left the country there in 1832 in company with a man named Kent on a trip to the west and was never heard from again. Another person, claiming to be a relative of Ezra Kind, wrote for further information and claimed that such a person had left with a party of good seekers and entered the Hills but was never seen again. All of the circumstances surrounding the discovery and the testimony of the letters would seem to sufficiently corroborate the words scratched upon the stone, but who the men were, from whence they came and what the final scene of the adventure must forever remain unknown. Be that as it may, however, in the swift flight of years, this rudely inscribed piece of sandstone must stand in mute testimony of the melancholy fate that became the lot of many a brave pathfinder in the wilds of the West and also a pathetic effort of the human mind to reach beyond the grave to loved ones far away.

That the presence of gold in the Black Hills was known to a few of the people of the frontier long before the adventures of Custer or his expedition were known is clearly evident in history by the finding of the rock or stone hereto described, but also by an instance that is set forth in the Black Hills Telegraphic Herald, a newspaper established in May in the year 1878, and which is set forth as follows:

"Every few months the miner or the adventurous prospector brings to light some fresh evidences of early mining operations in the Hills. These operations must have been carried on by quite a number of men but their names and where they came from are matters of conjecture and will probably remain so until the end of time. Mining implements have been unearthed, buried many feet below the surface of the old mining claim. A chain was found partially imbedded in a large tree where it had probably hung for many years. The old tools and shack found last winter are also another evidence of early visits of miners to this country. We have now discovered another link in the unwritten history. Last Friday there arrived in Lead two hunters Frenchmen, Le Fevre, who will be remembered by old residents of Battle Creek as being there in the year '76. These men had been hunting and trapping in the vicinity of Bear Lodge Mountains. They report that one day last January while tracking the wounded deer they shot, they came across the skeletons of two men. They were found on top of rather a peculiar knoll and rocks, earth and pieces of trees formed a sort of rough breastwork behind which their remains were found. The skulls of both men were in a fairly good state of preservation and through one of the skulls was a large hole evidently made by a bullet and the second victim, scarcely more than ten feet away, had the iron head of an arrow firmly imbedded in the thigh bone, the wooden part was evidently broken off and only a portion could be located which was wrapped in rawhide. The wood of the arrow was considerably warped and showed signs of being exposed to the weather for many years. They also found part of an old iron camp kettle, a broken stock of an old rifle made of fancy knotted wood, which was filled with bullets showing that a fight for life must have been long and bitter. No clothing of any kind could be found in the vicinity except the heel and counter of an old boot. The enemy evidently stripped the bodies entirely naked.

"The hunters in their search for something that could lead to the identity of the parties tore down part of the breastwork and were rewarded by the discovery of what was a cover of a leather memorandum book. There had been considerable writing on this cover but all they could make out were the figures '1-2-52' which probably was '1852.' The bones were found much scattered out as though wild animals had eaten part of them after they had been killed. The hunters collected what they could find and buried them under the breastwork which they had so gallantly defended. The inscription on this book and the inscription on the wall of the old tunnel discovered last winter are the same.

"All evidence so far discovered goes to show that these early pioneers of the Hills had many fights with the Indians, who at that time occupied this country. And it may be possible that if these men belonged to the party who ran the old tunnel near Rutabaga Gulch, that the party escaped from the tunnel and were fighting their way to Montana, or the old overland trail through that country. One by one the merciless savages picked them off, until only two remained, and these two seeing escape was impossible, selected the spot where the hunters found their bones, and fought their savage foes until by starvation, or the entire consumption of their ammunition, they became an easy prey for their unrelenting foes.. The theory that their surrender was caused by their ammunition giving out, seems to be confirmed by the finding of the broken gun stock, which had probably been used as a last weapon of defense."

THE CUSTER EXPEDITION

The stories that were continually coming from traders and trappers who had dealt with Indians in the Black Hills country were published throughout the United States and people began to become more and more excited over the reported presence of gold in the mountains. So persistent were the rumors of the presence of the valuable mineral and so great was the interest shown throughout the region that finally the attention of the United States Government was directed to the matter and an expedition under the command of General George Custer was fitted out in the year 1874 for the purpose of exploring the Black Hills region. There were two objects to be attained by this expedition. One of them was to ascertain the feasibility of the possible location of a military post to command the region between Fort Laramie and the Montana forts and the other object was to learn about the mineral resources and general geological nature of the Black Hills country.

The expedition left Fort Abraham Lincoln July 2, 1874, and consisted of ten companies of Cavalry, two of Infantry, white and Indian scouts, interpreters, miners, teamsters, geologists and college professors, totaling about one thousand men. This large expedition with the big, heavy, cumberson army transport wagons slowly wended its way over hill and dale, creeks and rivers and travelled in a southeasterly direction for the then little known region of the Black Hills. As the long line of wagons and cavalry trailed, it left deep marks which can yet, after the passing of almost half a century, be found in some places. The incidents of the journey are recorded in the diary of the officers and the reports made to the War Department by the several men in charge of the different departments represented in the expedition. The trip from Fort Lincoln to the Black Hills carried them over a dry, barren and desolate region but when they came to the Black Hills the wonderful foliage and vegetation with the clear rippling mountain brooks was so vastly different to what the men had seen along the road that they became very profuse in their praise of the new found country. The expedition entered the Black Hills country on the northwest corner near the peak known as Inyan Kara and from there it proceeded in a southeasterly direction in an effort to penetrate the fastness of the Black Hills. On July 24 the expedition camped in a valley which they called "Floral Valley." General Forsythe describing this valley says, "The whole valley is carpeted with flowers. I have gathered twenty-seven varieties within twenty square feet and the view along the valley as it first widened, then contracted and then widened again, with the sound of the brook murmuring constantly at our feet has been exceedingly pleasant and attractive." Professor Donaldson describes it in these words, "The floral decoration is the very richest. Every order and species seem to vie with every other in giving brilliancy to the display. The gaudy sun-flower and the delicate hare-bell, the fair lily and the bright blue daisy, the coarse eglantine and the modest violet, the gay larkspur and the fragrant peppermint, roses and pinks, asters and phlox, bell-flower and calliopsis, geraniums, goldenrod, purple cone-flower, are part of Flora's contribution to these lovely dells."

The journey to the hills was not without its dark side and the first trouble that occurred to mar the memory of the expedition was that on the night of July 21st, when on their camp in Red Water Valley,

Custer Train

Private John Cunningham died from chronic diarrhoea combined with pleurisy. On the morning of the next day two privates, Joseph Turned and William Roller, of the same troop M, engaged in a quarrel about 4 o'clock with the result that Turner was shot. These two men had joined the cavalry four years before at the same time and the question arose as to who was the best man. At the time they had their first fight, Roller, who was whipped, gave up and admitted that the other fellow was the winner but Turner appeared to be a man of overbearing qualities and took advantage at every opportunity thereafter to annoy and harass his weaker comrade. It appears that several days before this incident he had tied the two front feet of the horse which Roller was riding together with a rope with the result that in the morning the legs had been so badly burned that the Captain would not permit the Private to ride his mount. He was compelled throughout the day to walk and lead his horse. To a cavalry man this is the highest insult possible and this greatly angered the man Roller, and the next morning while he was bending over his little camp fire cooking his morning meal, his comrade, Turner, approached and when opposite the fire, Roller denounced him and declared that he who would treat a poor dumb beast in such a manner was no better than a dog. Whereupon Turner made a grab for his pistol with his right hand but unfortunately for him he reached to his right hip where the cowboys carry their pistols. The cavalry man carries his pistol on the left hip. Roller noticing the movement of Turner immediately reached for his pistol but on the left side and from his crouching position fired a ball through the body of Turner who fell mortally wounded. Turner was placed in the ambulance and rode all that day over a journey of 23 miles, but died that evening when they entered camp. There were now two dead soldiers in the camp and it became necessary to halt to prepare for their burial and on this day, the 23rd day of July, 1874, on the western slope of the Black Hills occurred the first military funeral and the first recorded funeral of a white man in the Black Hills, which Professor Donaldson describes as follows: "Upon a little knoll within the limits of the camp, a broad grave was dug. In the evening, at a quarter to nine o'clock the whole regiment, by companies, was called into line to attend the burial.

"1st in the procession was the band.

"2nd, an ambulance bearing the two dead.

"3rd, the companies of which the deceased were members.

"4th, other companies.

"5th, Regimental and staff officers and civilians.

"As the solemn cortege marched across the campus the band played a mournful dirge. A hollow square was formed about the grave. Side by side the two bodies were lowered into the vault. By the light of a lantern the funeral service was read. A platoon of soldiers then stepped to the end of the grave and fired three successive volleys The dead heeded not. A trumpeter then came up, and blew loud and long. No response came. He then blew the call, 'Day is closed, light put out!' The grave was then filled. As the placid moon and twinkling stars looked down upon the solemn scene, slowly and sadly we left the dead alone, 'to sleep the sleep that knows no waking.' To hide the grave from the desecrating savage, who would soon come prowling around, its surface was leveled off and a fire was kept burning on it all the next day.

Private Roller was placed under arrest immediately after the shooting and under order of General Custer was compelled to walk thenceforth throughout the rest of his expedition until the return to Fort Lincoln. He was then turned over to the civil authorities on the charge of murder, at Yankton, but was eventually turned loose and returned to his command where he served out his enlistment.

From this point the expedition proceeded up along Floral Valley over the crest of the divide and down Castle Creek so named by Custer because of the rugged and castellated hills that bordered the valley. On this creek they camped for one day, on July 27th, where the miners were given an opportunity to prospect. Colonel Ludlow, who was chief engineer, in his report made in April, 1875, states, "The gold hunters were busy all day with shovel and pan exploring the streams." But nothing further is said about gold. In his report made to General Sheridan on August 15, 1874, from Bear Butte, referring to July 27, he said, "Miners with the party report indications of silver in quartz rock, along the banks of the creek." The march was again taken up and proceeded out over Elk Horn prairie but the command was compelled to retreat and camped in the evening of July 2th, on Castle Creek at a point four miles below the last camp.

GOLD FIRST DISCOVERED

The botanist of the expedition was Prof. A. B. Donaldson, of the University of Minnesota, and in his report to the St. Paul Pioneer under date of July 28th, he states, "Neither gold nor silver have been found, but the miners report the indications more promising." On the 29th of July they left the Castle Creek country, went over the ridge and down a stream that flowed to the southeast which was followed for several miles but left on account of the difficulty of moving the wagon train over the winding and narrow valley. This brought the expedition out on the high rolling prairie and along the old Indian trail, and onto a stream where the camp for the night was made. At seven o'clock in the morning of July 30th the march was resumed, three hours later than usual owing to the fact that all of the train had not arrived in camp until after four o'clock in the morning. The afternoon of July 30 found the expedition along the head waters of French Creek where camp was made at three o'clock and held all the next day while parties were sent out in all directions and Harney Peak was climbed by Custer and officers with him. And in this camp on July 30, 1874, on the head of Castle Creek in the afternoon, gold was first discovered. Prof. N. H. Winchell, the official geologist of the expedition, in his general report, dated February 22, 1875, referring to events of July 30, states, "The gold seekers who accompany the expedition report the finding of gold in the gravel and sand along this valley." Colonel Ludlow, the engineer, under his entry of July 31st, referring to this same camp, reports, "The command remained in camp while surveying parties were sent out, and the gold hunters redoubled their efforts."

On August 1st, the camp was moved down the creek three and a half miles to afford fresh pasture for the livestock where they remained until August 6. Under date of August 2nd, Colonel Ludlow states, "There is much talk of gold and industrious search for it is being made. I saw in General Custer's tent, what the miner said he had obtained during the day. Under a strong reading glass it resembled small pinheads of fine scales and irregular shape, perhaps thirty in number." The reports of General Custer and Prof. Donaldson, under date of August 2nd, each refer to the discovery of gold. In their camp of August 1st to 5th, where the City of Custer now stands, the first deep prospect holes were dug and here the presence of gold in paying quantities was demonstrated.

From the above official reports it will be concluded that gold under the Custer expedition was not discovered at any time prior to the 30th day of July, 1874, and that the place where the eager eyes of the miner as he scanned the bottom of his pan were brightened by the golden lustre, was at a point three and a half miles west of the present city of Custer. With the expedition were two practical miners, H. N. Ross and William T. McKay, who are the miners referred to in the several reports. Both of these men are now dead, but Ross, who outlived his companion for many years, claimed to be the one who first panned the yellow dust and to him we leave the honor of the discovery. He also fixed July 27th as the date of discovery, and the corporate limits of the present city of Custer, as the exact location, a large sign to that effect being now placed there to mark the spot. It is self evident that his memory of dates is in error, for he was twenty-eight miles away and a three days' march from that point on the 27th day of July. He first saw French Creek after the hour of three o'clock in the afternoon of July 30th, and no doubt proceeded to examine the sand and gravel near the camp, in which Prof. Winchell says, the miners claimed to have found gold, on that afternoon. This location for the discovery of gold further up French Creek and without the corporate limits of Custer City, and at a point known as discovery rock, has long been known to pioneers as the place where Ross told them he first discovered gold. The spot within the city of Custer now marked as point of discovery is probably the place where the first prospect hold was dug and gold was revealed in paying quantities.

McKay, the companion of Ross in the gold searching of the expedition asserted that gold was first discovered upon the tributary of Castle Creek, which he called Gold Run Creek. If this statement be true, it would fix July 27th as the correct date for discovery of gold, for on that day the miners were camped near the head waters of Castle Creek and had plenty of time in which to find the golden particles for they were afterwards found there in abundance. The failure of the officers of the expedition to note this place and date, may be due to the fact that Prof. Winchell had not been called upon to decide the nature of the metals supposed by the privates in the command to be gold, and felt somewhat piqued. He did not state that he saw any gold at any time in the course of the trip, but this was due to his refusal to see the gold as explained by Custer. The claim of Ross that he first discovered gold within the corporate limits of Custer City, if in fact he did so claim, would tend to destroy his credibility as to the matter of time and place, for we know that gold was found before Custer camped upon or permitted any of his men to explore the present site of Custer.

However, in commemoration of the discovery of gold and the work of Ross in those early years, the pioneers of the Black Hills, on July 27th, 1922, caused to be erected within the city of Custer, a beautiful monument built from rocks and minerals gathered from far and near in the Black Hills and dedicated it with appropriate exercises, to the memory of the hardy miner. On that day, the people of Custer received the thousands of guests with true western hospitality, and feasted them upon several barbecued oxen.

Professor Winchell, an expert geologist whose duty it was to examine and ascertain the geological formation and mineral deposits in the Black Hills, did not have much respect for the opinion of the common, uneducated, practical miners with the expedition and accordingly did not give any weight to their work. He declared that he saw no gold in the Hills but General Custer in his report states that if he really did not see any gold it was because he refused to look at it because there were numerous specimens of gold in the possessioin of the soldiers during the trip through the Hills. After the discovery of gold on French Creek, the presence of valuable minerals was found in numerous other places and creeks in various parts of the Hills which were examined. However, Custer's time in which to make the exploration of the Hills was limited and he hastened on his way, circling around from the southern portion of the Hills up toward the northeastern corner and skirting the hills from Elk Creek north to Bear Butte which he ascended and then bade good-bye to the Black Hills country.

The dispute that arose between General Custer and Professor Winchell over the presence of gold in the Hills caused another expedition under the jurisdiction of the United States geological survey directed by Professors Newton and Jenny to be sent into the hills with orders to make a more detailed and careful examination. This expedition made a definite report as to the presence of gold and other valuable minerals throughout the Hills. They arrived in June, 1875, and spent over four months in their work which covered the whole rugged portion of the region. There

were some four hundred men with this command and
they found miners already in the Hills.

THE COLLINS AND RUSSELL PARTY

When General Custer was in his camp at Custer
Park near Harney Peak in August, 1874, he dispatched Charlie Reynolds, the scout who later was killed
in the battle of the Big Horn, with his preliminary
report to Fort Laramie. Before preparing for this
journey, Dan Newell, the blacksmith with the expedition, shod the horse that Reynolds was to ride by
placing the shoes on the horse's feet backwards with
the purpose of deceiving the Indians as to the direction the rider was proceeding. After enduring great
hardships, the scout reached his destination and soon
the world was apprised of the fact that Custer had
discovered gold in the Black Hills. So much notoriety had been given to the reports of the miners and
traders from the hills that when it became definitely
known that there really was gold in the mountains,
in every large city men were ready to rush to the new
gold fields. The intense interest of the people and
the wide publicity given to their plans caused the
United States Government to make it very plain that
any attempt on the part of the gold seekers to tresspass upon the lands of the Indians in the Black Hills
would be promptly dealt with by the military and
this had the effect of discouraging and disbanding
many of the groups who had gathered for the purpose of making the trip across the prairie. However,
there was one group of people, who, despite the warnings of the Government, determined to make the perilous trip and see for themselves the gold of the mountains. This group was commonly known as the Gordon party, but in fact it should be more properly
known as the Collins and Russell party because Collins and Russell were the first leaders and instigators
of the expedition and Gordon was the man who was
chosen as Captain of the band when they proceeded
on their way.

The names of the members of the party were:

Gordon Stockade

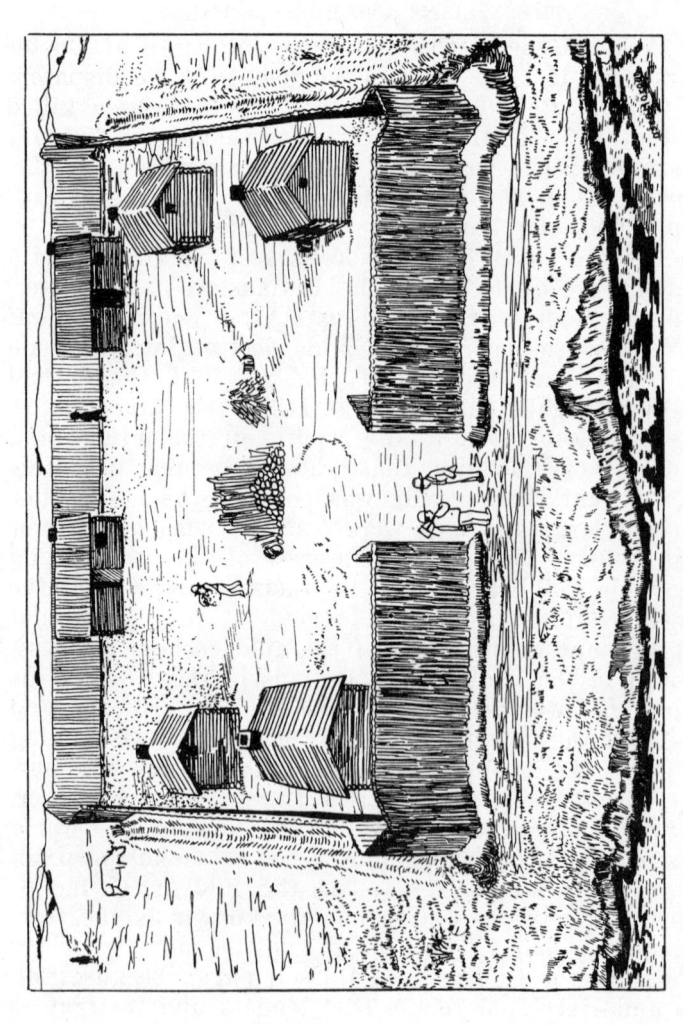

T. H. Russell, Lyman Lamb, Eaf Witcher, Angus McDonald, B. B. Logan, Red Dan McDonald, Black Dan McDonald, James Dempster, James Powers, J. J. Williams, Quiner, John Gordon, J. W. Brockett, Newton Warren, H. Bishop, Chas. Long, Chas. Cordeiro, Moses Aron, R. Whitney, Harry Cooper, David Akin, John Boyle, Chas. Blackwell, Thomas McClaren, Henry Shannon, D. G. Tallent, Robert E. Tallent and Annie D. Tallent, there being twenty-eight persons all told. This party, after passing through great hardships and escaping many dangers in the long journey across the wild and unknown prairies, reached French Creek on the 23rd of December, 1874, at a point two and one-half miles below the city of Custer. They built a very fine stockade and called it the "Gordon Stockade" where they remaineed all winter and in March they laid out and surveyed the townsite which they called "Harney City." Howver, before the work of the organization could be completed the United States army came upon the scene and the whole party were put under arrest in the month of April and taken out of the Hills. Among these intrepid pioneers was the first white woman to enter the Black Hills, Mrs. Annie D. Tallent, who later wrote a very interesting account of her experiences in her book known as "The Black Hills, or the Last Hunting Grounds of the Dakotahs," and she thus became known as one of the early historians of the Black Hills country.

THE BEGINNING OF CUSTER

Before the coming of the army these first comers had likewise succeeded in finding the golden particles on French Creek and although they were removed from the scenes of their labors, the knowledge of their success spread far and near and created intense excitement throughout the whole region. From the east and west, the north and south little bands of gold seekers were plodding their way toward the new Eldrado and the spring of 1875 found Custer on French Creek, again the scene of a gold digging operation, but in the summer of 1875 the Government again sent military details to the Hills to remove all gold seekers who had succeeded in escaping the military guards that had been sent out to turn the miners back from their journey to the Hills. Accordingly this expedition proceeded down the various gulches and coming upon miners read the formal order of the War Department of the Government and notified the men to congregate at Custer and be ready to depart by the tenth day of August. The miners worked with fever heat to recover as much gold as possible and when the day for departure approached they secreted their mining tools in various places, intending in due course of time to return and again take up the search for gold. In accordance with the order of the military commander, the miners began to gather at Custer Park and on the 10th day of August laid out the townsite. In order to establish the place the men all joined forces and built a log cabin in dimensions 16x24. It was proposed by a southerner and an admirer of the famous confederate general to call the new town or city Stonewall, but there happened to be by a majority of union sympathizers in the crowd and one man proposed that in view of the fact that Custer had camped there and was the first regular explorer of the country, that it would be proper to name the new city Custer and accordingly the men at that time decided on that name. In the matter of laying out the townsite a miner proposed to have the streets fifty feet wide as that distance was amply sufficient for a mining town but this proposition met with active opposition by an enthusiastic miner. In the meeting on the 9th, he arose and in a very eloquent speech declared that Custer was destined to become the metropolis of the Black Hills where the thousands of dwellers would need a city with streets one hundred feet in width. The spirit of the speaker caught the fancy of the crowd and it was unanimously decided to have the streets of that width. General Crook had informed the miners that if they would depart without force, they could have until the fifteenth of the month to go and after a guard of six people was left to protect the new townsite, every one knowing full well that the Indians must bid farewell to the new gold fields, the army marched out with most of the prospectors. But all of the prospectors did not leave the hills, partly because they were in such inaccessible places, that they could not be reached, and partly because they secreted themselves until the exit of the army. Soon the Hills were again resounding with the noise of miner's axes, picks and shovels for the spirit of the prospector is unconquerable and knows no end but death.

The prospector is splendidly pictured in the poem by F. J. Read which we herewith submit to the reader.

THE PROSPECTOR

He might have had the finest ranch in all this broad domain
its long stretches, remain in many places to this day.
With trees bowed down with golden fruit and fields of waiving grain.
He might have built a palace grand with walls of polished stone
With marble floors and frescoed walls and called them all his own,
But destiny has cast his lot in strange and far off lands.
His feet have trod the mountain's brown, and pressed the desert sands.
He's wandered where the canons dark uplift their walls so high
That twixt their summits only gleams a silver thread of sky.
He's camped in many a lonely place where men ne'er trod before,
And on the mountain's side he's made deep scars in search of ore,
He's traversed many a winding gulch and washed their golden sand
From the icy waves of the Yellowstone to the sunny Rio Grande.

He's climbed the highest towering peaks in all the rocky range
While clouds have rolled beneath his feet in shadows weird and strange,
He's laid him on the ground at night when hope of life was slim,
While flakes of snow have fallen white and drifted over him.
He's heard the warwhoop ring where now the farmer sows his grain,
He's heard the murderous arrows whiz where cities dot the plain.
He's seen the deadly avalanche crash down the mountain side
And heard the roaring waterspout burst on the great divide.
He's felt the simoon's scorching heat, the blizzard's icy breath
And seen the cyclone strew its path with ruin, wreck and death,
Yet still he climbs the rugged slopes in search of precious ore,
And persevering, he will search the hills for evermore.

—F. J. Read, in Saguache Crescent.

CHAPTER II.

THE TRAILS

To the land of the pine clad hills and the dancing waters came the prospectors to snatch from the sands the golden dust awaiting them. Over miles of prairies, past hostile red men, around awaiting military forces, they streamed, led on by the lure of gold and sustained by the fearless courage of the prospector. North, south, east and west each sent its quota to the fire line on the battle field of the wilderness. In course of time there came to be certain main roads and trails marked out and which we will describe for the reader.

The first and oldest trail was known as the Cheyenne trail. It began in Cheyenne, Wyoming Territory, and passing in a northeasterly direction held the following camp sites or stations on its line: Nine Mile, Pole Creek, Horse Creek, Bear Springs, Chug Water, Hunton, Chug Springs, Eagles Nest, Six Mile, Fort Laramie, Swing Station, Ten Mile, Government Farm, Rawhide Buttes, Running Water, Hat Creek, Old Woman, Lance Creek, Robbers Roost, Cheyenne River, Jenny's Stockade, Beaver Creek, Canyon Springs, Cold Springs, Little Meadow, Ten Mile, and Deadwood.

The drivers who piloted the stages along this line were Gene Barnett, Tom Cooper, George Drake, John Denny, Dave Greath, George Lathrop, Bugler John Nunen, John Bingham, George Graves, John Monroe, George Chapman, Cy Hawley, and Johnny Slaughter. Harry Hynds was the blacksmith for the line. Besides the regular run of passenger coaches, on this line, the importance of the gold shipments called for more careful protection and men who were especially brave, determined and reliable. These coaches were known as treasure coaches and were lined with heavy iron plates inside to protect from highwaymen's bullets. The original guards who accompanied these treasure laden coaches, and who were armed with pistols and shot guns, were Scott

Davis, Bill May, Boone May, Jesse Brown, Gale Hill, Billy Sample and John Cochran. These men became known as shot gun messengers and stood guard over hundreds of thousands of dollars worth of gold that went on the journey from Deadwood to Cheyenne. This trail became the scene of many bloody encounters and many of the tales set forth in this book were enacted along this route.

There soon sprung up another trail from the south which became known as the Sidney trail, commencing at Sidney, Nebraska, passing through Dry Creek, Greenwood, Clark's Bridge, Red Willow, Running Water, Hay Meadows, Deer Creek, White Earth, Red Cloud, Wells, Slate Springs, Cheyenne River, Lame Johnny Creek, French Creek, Sand Creek, Rapid City, Sturgis, Crook City and Deadwood. This trail likewise saw many a tragic end to golden dreams and became dotted here and there with spots where the grass grew taller and more green.

Those who came to the Hills more directly from the east, sought out a route from Ft. Pierre, which followed over the prairies directly west to the Hills through Willow Creek, Lance Creek, Plum Creek, Medicine Creek, Bad River, Box Elder, striking Rapid City as the first port of entry and thence following northward over the Sidney trail to Deadwood. This trail did not see so many fierce encounters with Indians and highway men as the other trails, but became the scene of tremendous freight transportation owing to the nearness of Ft. Pierre to the eastern homes of many pioneers who sought the Hills.

From the northeast, the trail left by Custer, furnished a known passage and the general direction for the Bismarck trail which starting from Bismarck, passed through Little Hart, Dog Tooth, Whitney Springs, Cannon Ball, Grand River, North Moreau, South Moreau, Antelope, Cedar Canyon, Elm Springs, Belle Fourche, Spring Creek, Crook City and Deadwood. This became a very important road and the deep ruts made by the heavy trains that rumbled over

From the northwest there also came a stream of

Treasure Coach at Canyon Springs

gold seekers and the Montana trail was established, beginning at Bozeman and angling southeasterly until Deadwood was reached. This trail was the least important of any of the routes to the Hills, but was the scene of many tragedies and Indian encounters.

These were the trails to the Black Hills and they embraced a territory including Montana, North and South Dakota, Nebraska and Wyoming, a veritable empire the conquering of which was indeed the winning of the West. Many thousands of adventurous men passed over them during the last century and to note the events that transpired along these trails would fill many volumes. However, it may be of interest to some readers to set forth some of the experiences of a few of the men who endured the trials of the times.

AN INCIDENT IN THE STORY OF THE PONY EXPRESS

As communication was kept up with those at home. the pony express system was inaugurated and the importance of this venture and some of the characters connected with its early conduct and incidents can be realized from the following article on the pony express written by J. K. Ellis, of Chicago.

Mr. Ellis is one of the noted writers from 1857 and was with General Albert Sydney Johnson's army at Fort Bridger. The Pony Express was established in the anti-railroad and telegraph days, on the plains as a medium of rapid communication between the Missouri River and the Pacific Coast. It carried a a light mail of important letters and valuable documents by relays of horses, twelve to fifteen miles each, running night and day at a rate of speed that was regulated by only the horse himself. It covered the distance of 2000 miles between St. Joseph and San Francisco on schedule time of eight days. This space in a number of instances was badly beaten, for on the occasion of Abe Lincoln's second election, the news was rushed through to the Coast in seven days, six hours and twenty minutes by the marvelous vehicle of horse flesh. A picture illustrative of the scene at-

THE BLACK HILLS TRAILS 51

tending the starting of the first pony out of St. Joe would aptly express the importance with which the event was hailed. Johnny Frye a noted jockey of the town was the first rider. He was taken bodily, horse and all, into the postoffice with doors closed. A vast crowd gathered along the street forming a long lane of human beings leading from the postoffice doorway to a distance of several blocks away. At a special time with the rider already mounted, a cannon was fired, the doors flew open and Johnny and his horse shot out of the building, and went flying away with their precious load amidst the cheer of the waiting thousands of humanity. And the first pony express like the spirit of empire of which it was an important factor westward took its way. It was run semi-weekly along with which was also run a weekly stage. It was the old Central, Overland, California and Pikes Peak Express Company, with old Billie Russell of the company of Majors Russell and Wadell at its head. This company had three hundred freight teams hauling supplies to all parts of the West. The terminus of the Pony Express was Salt Lake City. Wells Fargo conducted it from there to the Coast.

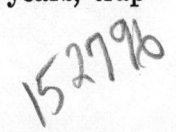

Two of the most prominent characters connected with the running of the road were J. A. Slade and Frank McCarthy. Slade was superintendent of a division extending from Julesburg on the South Platte to Sweet Water. McCarthy was in charge of a number of freight trains hauling grain to the different stations. Both of these men had already won distinction by use of their ready revolver. And it was an open secret that each one had slain his man. With regard, however, to the terrible slaughter by them while conducting the affairs of the road let it be said to whatever credit it may entitle them, that their numerous victims were all men as unscrupulous as themselves. Along the lines of the road quite a number of Indian traders had established themselves. They belonged to the worst type of Canadian French. Having Indian women and half breed families, they had dominated the old immigrant trail for years, trapping in the winter and trading or robbing immigrants in summer. There were legends of dark deeds being committed by them that were attributed to Indians, but nobody ever dared to raise a hand against them. It soon became apparent that the coming of the stage did not meet with their approval. In fact, they looked at it as a trespass on their hitherto domain, and in their unmitigated ignorance thought to drive it from the road. So they commenced to molest and harass it in various ways. Stock were chased away from the stations and mules were shot at night. Finally at Shoshay's ranch, on of the worst of the dens, a station keeper by the name of Robinson, was killed. This together with other atrocities which had been going on for sometime, had Slade and McCarthy worked up to a high pitch and caused them to commit one of the bloodiest deeds ever perpetrated by two men alone. Walking deliberately into the house they shot Shoshay, and two other men of the same stripe and also Shoshay's wife. She put up the worst fight of any and they were compelled to kill her. Shoshay and his Indian wife had two children about seven and eight years old, and when the shooting began they ran out of the house. This was about eight o'clock on a very dark night. The next morning the bones of the little girl were found picked clean by the wolves. An Indian found the boy in a most pitiful plight and took him into Horseshoe Station fifty miles from Ft. Laramie which was Slade's headquarters. Mrs. Slade who had no children of her own and hearing of the lost boy in distress went out and coaxed the Indian to let her have him. She knew nothing of the tragedy at the time and she worked for hours over the forlorn little boy picking the thorns out of his flesh. It was a week before she could get him into anything like a normal mental condition. He appeared to be frightened at every little noise and would hide from strangers.

  Years passed and still Mrs. Slade held to her bosom the little black eyed charge. The last time the writer saw her was in 1866 when she was on her way to the east with him after giving him a good education. From here Slade and McCarthy passed on east to a place kept by a Frenchman by the name, Tujuan, but before arriving there they met the stage and the driver told them that Tujuan was swearing vengeance against them. However, they paid no attention to what the driver had told them. They seemed to know no fear. Upon reaching this Frenchman's place they walked right into the house and there the first man they saw was another of the gang named Dubon, whom they shot. Later finding Tujuan they led him out and pointing to the mountains told him to go and never return. He asked permissioin to gather some of his effects and it was granted, but Slade stayed and saw him depart. McCarthy turned back west from here and Slade went on east of Julesburg and camped on the river where there were several others in camp. Among them was a Frenchman named Jule, who belonged to the same faction as Shoshay and who had heard of the high handed business up the country and had determined to kill Slade and McCarthy on sight. However, he was afraid to make any more while Slade had his gun strapped on him. One morning Slade walked around the corral unarmed and Jule, who was watching, followed and shot Slade three times in the body. Thinking he had killed Slade, Jule jumped on his horse and skipped out. Tom O'Brien, lately a citizen of Sturgis, South Dakota, then a stage driver on the Overland and Si Shury heard the shot and ran out and picked Slade up and carried him to the station. Slade asked them to take off his boots so that he might not die with them on as had been predicted. A ride to Ft. Laramie 200 miles away for a military surgeon was accomplished in eighteen hours and the surgeon with all possible speed was brought to the bedside of Slade where he did most excellent work, and finally brought him back to a perfect recovery.

    This shooting occurred about the first of April in 1860, and in July, 1861, fifteen months afterwards Slade and Jule had not met, and as far as Slade was concerned he did not know where Jule. was. One day Jule rode into Cold Springs Station about fifteen miles north of Julesburg. There he was met by three young men, Johnny Burnett, Mike Terry and Johnny Frye, the same fellow that had made the first ride on the Pony Express. These three men were chums of Slade, but unkown to Jule. Suddenly they pounced onto him and with a rope securely tied him to a post in the corral. It is probable that Slade had placed these men there for the purpose of capturing Jule, Anyhow, a short time afterwards the stage rolled up with Slade on board. On being informed that Jule was back of the house tied up, Slade walked out to where Jule was and drawing his revolver shoved it into Jule's face and fired. He aimed to kill Jule then and there and thought, as did all present that he had done so. The men went into the saloon. Later someone came in and told Slade that Jule was sitting up and asked to see him. So Slade went out and found Jule in a sad plight, blood running down over his chest from the wound in his cheek where the bullet had entered and passed back of his ear. Jule said, "I will give you a thousand dollars if you will send for my wife and let me see her before I die." Slade answered, "I don't want your money, although you owe me nearly a thousand dollars, and as to your wife, you did not think of mine when you cowardly shot me down unarmed. Now you've got to die." Then pulling his gun while Jule turned his face away Slade shot him through the back part of his head and Jule was no more.

About this time Slade became too notorious to suit the company and he was asked to resign which he did. He then went of Virginia City, Montana, where he took up a ranch and resided until his death. He became much addicted to drink and was wont to get on wild drunks and shoot up saloons, stores and terrorize people in general. On one of his sprees he entered a saloon and after loud and boisterous conduct he ordered the drinks for the whole crowd. However, there happened to be a young boy who remained back from the bar and did not take any part in the drinking. Slade noticed this and angrily commanded the boy to come up with the crowd and join in the drinking. The young fellow timidly replied that he never drank. This reply threw Slade into a raging fury and with an oath he pulled out his revolver and shot the boy dead. After a while one of the crowd sneaked out from the building, spread the report about the little town and in a short time about two hundred of the law respecting citizens seized upon Slade, carried him to the outskirts of the town where they had prepared a gallows for him and placed a rope around his neck. Slade now realized that his hour had come and like Jule begged to see his wife, whom he knew was the only person who might intercede and save his life, but in the midst of his appeals the trap was sprung, and when his wife arrived on the foaming black stallion she beheld a thing over which the ravens flap their wings.

RED CLOUD OPPOSED THE INVASION OF THE TERRITORY

To keep open the routes of travel in the region of the Black Hills trails called forth the use of the military as early as 1866, for we find General Carrington engaged in the work of establishing posts in the Wyoming and Montana country. That his task was no small one can be understood from the following account of some incidents of the time:

In 1866 General Carrington was instructed by the War Department to go out on the Montana road to rebuild and garrison Fort Reno on Powder River. After leaving Fort Laramie on this mission Carrington was met by Red Cloud who protested against him invading this famous hunting grounds of the Red Man. Of course Carrington was a soldier and paid no attention to the protest. Thereupon Red Cloud began a campaign of annoyance, and attacks upon the soldiers which rendered their mission very hazardous, and extremely difficult. After completing the reestablishment of Fort Reno and leaving a small garrison there, the main body proceeded on to the foot of the Big Horn mountains, where Fort Phil Kearney was built. There throughout the season while the soldiers were engaged in building Fort Phil Kearney and supplying it with fuel, Red Cloud kept up the most tantalizing tactics, and it was soon unsafe for any person to venture outside of the barracks unless protected by a detachment of military. General Carrington in his report to headquarters stated that a team could not be sent to the woodyard, nor for a load of hay to the meadows unless accompanied by a strong guard.

The first hunters sent out, came back themselves being hunted, and though game was abundant in close proximity no hunter dared try to obtain it. A reign of terror was up among the civilian teamsters so that no one of them would leave the stockade for wood or other supplies unless furnished with a sufficient guard.

Attacks upon the woodyard were of almost daily occurrence, and most always to the advantage of the Indians. Red Cloud by this time had assembled an army of about three thousand warriors, and this vast army were fed by their own resources while keeping the Fort in a state of siege.

Finally on the 21st day of December, 1866, a considerable force of Indians appeared between the Fort and the wood camp five miles away. Captain Fetterman with a force of 81 men was ordered out to drive them away and protect the wood camp. The savages retired without any show of fighting. They kept retiring on approach of the troops until they craftily led Fetterman into an ambush where he and his entire force was destroyed. Not a man escaped to tell the story. This left the Fort with a guard weakened to the limit. Every day and every hour Carrington expected an attack in force on the Fort, but it seems that Red Cloud did not know the condition there.

Throughout the following year, 1867, the Indians pursued the same mode of warfare, killing a soldier every time one ventured out, even fishing within three hundred yards of the stockade. And by their persistent conducting of war they were successful in preventing even one wagon from passing over this route, and the Montana road was never finished.

JESS BROWN AT FT. KEARNEY

On the first day of August, '67, another severe battle was fought between soldiers and civilians at the wood camp and Red Cloud's force, both sides lost heavily, but the Indians suffered far the greater loss. Porter and Gilmore were the contractors hauling wood for the winter's use at the Fort, they built a barricade of sod and logs for protection and had a guard of twenty-five soldiers. The Indians endeavored to capture it by storm. But the fire was so deadly and accurate that the enemy were forced to abandon the attempt.

I arrived there five days after this fight, skulls and other parts of dead Indians were lying where they fell, except where the wolves had carried them away. I was given charge of 24 teams belonging to John Y. Denny and McMichael and hauled saw logs for lumber to build dwellings and stables as the troops were living in tents and pine pole shacks at this time. We were not allowed to go anywhere without a strong guard. Red Cloud and his savages were on the lookout continually for an opportunity to pick off a man, and they could be seen at night dancing and pow-wowing around their camp fires.

One day a freight outfit came along from Fort C. F. Smith and went into camp not over three hundred yards from the stockade. Three day herders were sent a short distance to water their stock. Some of the cattle crossed over the creek and one of the men went to turn them back but he was shot and three scalps taken off his head, which was literally peeled.

The call to arms was sounded at the Fort and the soldiers did not take time to saddle their mounts but went on a run bareback buckling on their belts of cartridges. They got sight of the red skins but could not get close enough to get a shot.

Naturally in those days of intense interest in the

new gold fields, there should be sought information about the routes to follow, and the newspapers would endeavor to supply all data to their readers. We will herewith reproduce an account taken from the "Sidney Telegraph" of May 20, 1876, which paper then was under the control of Joseph B. Gossage of the present Rapid City Journal.

THE BLACK HILLS

In answer to the hundreds of communications we are in receipt of, we have compiled the budget of information herewith given, for the benefit of those who are afflicted with the Black Hills fever. While it is not as complete as we desire, we think it will answer most of the questions asked.

The first question propounded is whether we really believe there is gold in the Black Hills. This has been too well proven to admit of doubt. Gold is found in paying quantities in nearly all portions of the region, the richest discoveries having been of quite recent occurrence, on Deadwood and Whitewood creeks, some sixty miles from Custer City, which is now a large and flourishing town with regularly elected officers, a full complement of business houses, etc.

West and north of the Black Hills lie extensive mountain ranges of similar formation, which have been but little explored, but which are full of gold and silver, which latter metal has been discovered in large and rich veins, within thirty miles of Custer City. Good gold quartz mines have also been found in the Hills.

DISTANCES

Following we give the distance from Sidney to the Black Hills, the points mentioned being, as it will be seen, at convenient distances apart for camping and having accommodations for travelers:

Sidney to   Miles
Water Hole 12
Water Hole to Greenwood 12

THE BLACK HILLS TRAILS 59

Greenwood to Court House Rock 10
Court House Rock to North Platte
    River Crossing 8
Platte Crossing to Red Willow 10
Red Willow to Snake River 12
Snake River to Point of Rocks 8
Point of Rocks to Running Water 18
Running Water to Antelope Creek 10
Antelope Creek to Burdue Creek 7
Burdue Creek to White River 12
White River to Ten Buttes 8
Ten Buttes to Beaver Creek 20
Beaver Creek to Custer City 22

    Total distance 169

These distances are by the road now travelled between the two Agencies. The stage line leaves this route at Snake River, and running through Red Cloud. The distance by this route is 182 miles.

TRANSPORATION, ETC.

At present there is a stage line running between Sidney and Red Cloud. The fare to Red Cloud, first class is $12.50. The line will be extended on to Custer City by the first of April, running through in twenty-eight hours' actual travel.

It will cost less to outfit here than to bring outfits with you. Heavy stocks and hot competition cause this. All kinds of provisions and mining tools can be had cheap.

The following are the prices for mining tools, of which our merchants carry a large stock. Gold pans, $1.15 to $1.50; sluicing forks, $2; shovels, spring points, $1.40 to $1.50. Quick silver, per pound, $1.75 to $2.00; picks, $1.25 to $2.50. By outfitting elsewhere it will cost a man at least 25 per cent more than it would if purchased in Sidney.

EXPERIENCE OF EARLY DAY GOLD SEEKERS, 1875

In 1874 the Black Hills country belonged to the Sioux Indians and the white people had no rights in it whatever. The United States Government endeavored to protect the Indians in their hunting grounds and assisted them in trying to keep trespassers out of the hills, but despite the watchfulness and efforts of the United States troops, a great many people made an effort to go to the Black Hills. Very few succeeded in reaching the coveted region, many never even started. Some were intercepted enroute and forced to return under oath that they would not return to the Hills until a treaty was completed with the Sioux Nation. Some hardy travelers, however, evaded the troops and Indians and other obstructions and reached the Hills. In the following words we will relate the experiences of one of the men, John H. Brown, who overcame all difficulties and reached the Black Hills in his quest of gold.

"In the month of June, 1875, while engaged in the occupation of freighter and encamped at Sidney, Nebraska, I was made acquainted with the fact that a party was organizing for the purpose of starting on a prospective trip to the Black Hills, a distance of two hundred and fifty miles. I sent my name in requesting to become a member of the party, and was duly accepted at their next meeting. I was quietly informed that every move, act or word must be on the 'Q T.' Our party consisted of eleven men, ten on horseback and one driver of two mules, hitched to a wagon, loaded with oats for the mules, provisions and baggage for the men. The names of some of the party were: John Williams, driver of the team, John Gofler, George Johnson, Thomas Reed and a carpenter called Scotty, and Sam Jenkins. Taken altogether, these men were a formidable bunch, all old timers, acquainted with hardships, of great endurance, and ready for anything they might come up against. Before leaving Sidney, we all signed an article of agreement that would tend to hold the party together while enroute to their destination and even after arriving there. The article was worded that any man of the party getting cold feet and wanting to turn back at any time on the trip, should forfeit his horse, gun and ammunition and be without provisions or other means of sustenance. Every man signed without a whimper or objection and obeyed it to the letter. We made our preparations for departure, sent the man with the team ahead and told him to camp at Chalk Bluff, about fifty miles west and north, and to wait for the party. We left Sidney one at a time and it took four days before we were all together at the Bluffs. The next morning we broke camp early, turning directly north and struck out for the North Platte river, across country, through sage brush, prairie dog towns and rattlesnakes. On the afternoon of the second day, we reached the Platte, but to our great disappointment, we soon saw that the river was on a rampage and bank full of water caused by the melting snow from the mountains. Now the only thing to do was to go by way of Fort Laramie where there was a ferry owned by the Government. It was a forlorn hope that we could get across the river with soldiers right there watching for just such outfits as we were. But we pulled up the river within about three miles east of Fort Laramie and went into camp. The next day three of us rode into Fort Laramie unarmed. The soldiers seeing us on horseback with no equipment in sight paid little attention to us. The man Jenkins had formerly held the position as blacksmith at this place and was well acquainted with many of the soldiers, and especially the ferrymen. We were fortunate enough to make a deal with him to carry us across if we would get there before daylight.

"I pulled for camp in short order; everyone was in bed sound asleep and the rain was pouring in torrents. They all got out, mules were hitched to the wagon and by three o'clock in the morning we had crossed the river and travelled about fifteen miles before we camped for breakfast and a little rest, which we all needed after an all night session in the rain That night we camped at Rawhide Buttes, fifty miles from Laramie. Here one of our men took his gun and thought he would go up the creek and possibly find a deer, but in a short time he was back in camp out of breath and reported a band of Indians just east of the hill behind us and some of them on the hill watching our camp. Our stock was picketed right in the direction that the Indians were, so we figured that if we went out ofter our horses, we would be in close range of their guns, and if they came after the stock they would be in close range of our guns. We pretended that we were unconscious of their presence, got out our blankets and spread them down as if making preparations to sleep. We waited until dark, then every man gathered his gun and went for his horse, hitched up and drove nearly all night. We went into camp, staked our horses close by and put two men on guard in case the Indians had discovered our movements and followed, which they did. We had been in camp only a short time until they were on us, shooting and yelling and running into our horses in an effort to stampede them, but they were taken by surprise when they were received by two men on guard with repeating rifles. The rest of us were up in a moment as we were sleeping with our clothes on, and the Indians soon retreated to the hills where they kept up an intermittent firing until morning. We could not do much as they were concealed behind rocks and hills. As daylight came, the Indians were enabled to get our range and we soon realized that the fight would have to be brought to a finish, so we mounted and rode away in the opposite direction and riding around the hill, came upon the Indians in the rear. The Indians immediately retreated after losing a few ponies. We went back to camp and dug rifle pits and prepared for another attack, but they did not come. The next day we moved on and in due time reached Jenney's Stockade, which was located on the western side of the Black Hills. Here we had a good long rest and then broke camp and entered the hills proper, and travelled until well along in the afternoon, but we had no water and we were compelled to travel all day without water and go into camp that night almost famished from thirst. Early the next morning we were on the move again and after a short distance we came across an Indian trail leading down an incline and felt sure

THE BLACK HILLS TRAILS 63

it led to water. Here we waited while two followed the trail and soon returned with canteens filled with good, cold water. I do not believe that if we had found a mine of pure gold that we would have been more pleased than to find that spring of pure, cold water. We remained at this spring that day and in the evening, Jenkins and myself started out on a hunt for deer. After traveling for about two miles, we separated and planned to meet on the opposite side of a long ridge. I shot a deer, hung it to a tree and went to the other side to meet Jenkins. He was not there and I fired my gun but received no answer. I returned to camp and was surprised to learn that he had not been seen there. The next morning we mounted our horses and scouted over the country far and near but could find no trace of him. After a two days' wait, we moved on and made our permanent camp on French Creek, west of where Custer City is now located. We found bones almost everywhere and here in June, 1875, we erected a log cabin. After several weeks, we found that we would have to have more flour, bacon and coffee, and we sent two men to the Red Cloud Agency to buy them. When about fifteen miles from our camp, these two men caught sight of a man crouching in the bushes and to their great surprise, saw that is was Jenkins, as much astonished as they were to see him. During the three weeks that he had been lost, he had subsisted on turtle doves and rabbits, which he would kill with rocks, and a few berries, being afraid to fire his gun for fear of attracting Indians. He was taken back to camp and restored to his party and did not go hunting again as long as he remained there. The Indians were constantly on the move through the hills and we were compelled to keep guard day and night while the rest of us panned out the gold. They fired into our camp at various times, but did not come within close range. We were progressing in fine shape and had great hopes of a little fortune when we were suddenly approached by a troop of cavalry who notified us that they had come to take us out of the hills. The commander in charge gave us until the fifteenth to prepare to move out. The next morning we started and came up close to where Buffalo Gap is located and for two days travelled south until we reached the forks of the trail. Here the commander gave us our choice of going to Spotted Tail and be held there or taking an oath to stay out of the Hills until a treaty with the Indians was made to satisfy them. We chose the latter and were liberated and upon arriving at Sidney, Nebraska, we disbanded, shook hands and separated, and from that day to this, December, 1920, I have not met one of that party, and as far as I know, I am the only one living at this time.

A FREIGHTING OUTFIT

It might be interesting to some of our readers to have a description of what a pioneer freight train or outfit consisted and we accordingly note here the words of one of the old time and greatly experienced freighters—Jesse Brown. A freight team or bull team as they were called in the early days of freighting on the plains consisted of seven or eight yoke of oxen hitched to an old Murphy or Kern wagon made in St. Louis, Mo. The load generally weighed seventy-five to eighty hundred pounds. In yoking up or hitching the animals to the wagon, the wheelers or the pair that were immediately next to the tongue were yoked up first and fastened to the tongue of the wagon. The next pair to be yoked were the leaders and they were fastened to the wagon to which they belonged. The succeeding pairs of oxen were caught up in rotation until the entire team was completed. The first pair ahead of the wheelers were called first pointers, the third pair from the wagon were second pointers. The next two or three pairs were the wings, first, second and third. There were the right and left wings and each wing had a lead driver. The oxen in the wings were changed after every drive, that is, the right wing would lead on the morning drive and the left wing would lead in the afternoon drive. These lead teams would soon learn to turn out of the road and almost

The Evan's Bull Train. The last Bull Freight Train from Fort Pierre

make a circle to form the corral with very little assistance from the driver although the wagon master or assistant was always there to see that the two half circles were formed correctly. The term corral was used to describe the circle that was formed by the oxen and wagons as they came into camp, this plan being useful in the defensive tactics that had to be used against the Indians who were in the habit of making attacks on the freight trains by circling about them and attempting to shoot them from the rear.

In the regulation outfit there were four messes, about eight men to the mess and ordinarily there would be regular cooks who had no other duty to perform. They escaped the duty of the work of helping to grease the wagons or stand day herd or any extra work such as helping shoe the cattle when they became foot sore. There were no tents or cook stoves carried in the early days of freighting, so if it happened to be raining about meal time the men were compelled to fast until the storm was over. There was no wood along the line from the Missouri River to Fort Laramie, although there were some scattered green trees of cottonwood which were useless to the freighters. The food consisted of flour, bacon, beans, sugar, coffee, blackstrap molasses and dried apples but it was seldom that there was time for cooking beans unless the cook would stay up in the night to cook them. Accordingly, bread, bacon and coffee comprised the principal diet.

The whips used by the drivers were something wonderful. They were made by hand, generally by some of the old drivers. No one else ever need to try making a bull whip such as were used in those days unless they had been on the freight road and knew how to commence. Usually a piece of small rope, after being well tarred, was used for the foundation, at the butt or stock part of the whip. Then there would be a layer of buck-skin extending behind one another three or four feet until the whip when completed would measure some twenty feet or more.

An experienced and efficient driver would never

drag his whip after him but would carry it rolled up in his hand from which position it was quickly unlimbered when needed. Timber for whip stocks was very scarce. In fact, there was no material to be had only at the starting point on the journey. The stock was generally about four feet long but some stocks were used that were only two feet long where the driver had broken the original length of the stick in some manner or had been unable to get a longer piece for another one.

No driver was allowed to cut or draw blood from his cattle with his whip and was required to have a broad popper on the end which would make a report like a rifle shot but would not cut the hide of the oxen.

Majors Russell and Wadell, who owned the largest freighting outfits on the plains, consisting of three hundred teams, presented each driver with a Testament and requested each of them to read it each day, a request which very few complied with. Each man furnished his own bed or bedding and if there was no room for him in his wagon to sleep, he could spread them under his wagon or any place that suited him. Occasionally upon arising in the morning he would find that he had accommodated a partner in the shape of a rattle snake. The report was common that if a hair lariat rope circled around the sleeper at night it would prevent the snakes from passing over it but actual experience proved the story false.

Bull teams loaded, would average about one hundred miles per week. The wages of the drivers in the summer were around $50.00 per month with board and later in the season $75.00 was the figure. In winter camp, that is with the herd during the winter, $25.00 per month was paid but a man had an opportunity to make money on the side if he were experienced in trapping as beavers were plentiful in all of the streams. The men who were handling the teams were known commonly as "Bull Whackers." The above items present merely the ordinary run of the life of the freighter but he was not always in peace and plenty for many times men became sick and some of them died. Like all numbers of men who are gathered together, there were quarrels among them and they fought among themselves and sometimes died. They fought the Indians and were wounded and died and along the trail is many an unmarked grave where many a mother's son lies sleeping alone and forgotten.

THE FREIGHTER

No man bore a more important part in opening up to settlement and occupation of the Black Hills than the freighter. Indeed, upon him all others, of necessity, depended. What was true of the pioneering of this section was equally true of every military post, every frontier settlement, and every isolated mining camp of the west. All depended upon the freighter for the supplies necessary for their sustenance. Should he fail them, they too must fail. That he did not fail, though often called upon to surmount apparently mountainous obstacles, proves that he was a man of great courage, energy and resourcefulness.

Large amounts of money were ventured in purchasing, equipping and conducting the operation of the big freight outfits that travelled the roads between the Hills and the Union Pacific at Sidney and Cheyenne, the Northern Pacific at Bismarck, the steamboat landing at Ft. Pierre, and later, the Northwestern's terminus at Pierre. Numerous smaller but by no means insignificant trains there were from Yankton and other points. During the year of 1876 and the early part of 1877 all of the roads named were infested by hostile Indians, who took advantage of every opportunity to shoot the drivers from ambush, and kill or stampede the stock, whether mules or oxen. Bridges there were none. The streams, sometimes in flood, were forded, and a sight worth seeing and well remembered by the writer was that of three full ox teams of seven yoke in each team, twenty-one yoke in all, stretched out across the North Platte river on the old Sidney trail, attached to a single wagon loaded with supplies, hauling it through the stream in flood with a bottom of treacherous quicksand.

Time was ever of the essence of the freighter's contract. Whatever the difficulties encountered, whether by reason of high water, bad weather, bottomless gumbo or Indian depredations, the freight must be delivered, and even at this day the exhortation to "pull your freight" is understood by the old timer as a command to be obeyed, not questioned. Nothing short of an attack by an overwhelming force of Indians, causing a train to be held in "corral," would be accepted as a sufficient reason for serious delay. The efficiency of the service is attested by the fact that before the big outfits were organized in the spring of '76, flour commanded sixty dollars per hundred in Deadwood Gulch, while with the coming of summer and the freighter, the price dropped, and in the fall of that year it was plentiful at nine dollars per hundred, and only once afterwards during the time of dependance upon the mule and bull trains, and before the coming of the railroads, did the price go up to thirty-five dollars per hundred. This was for but a brief period in the spring of '77, when the roads were practically impassable.

The man in charge of the wagon train was known as the "wagon master," or more generally "wagon boss." With his outfit loaded and out upon the road he was in supreme command. His cargo always represented large values, and upon his shoulders rested a heavy weight of responsibility. The life of a "bull-whacker" or "mule-skinner" was not a picnic. He worked hard, often under wretched conditions of weather and roads; his pay was not munificent; his fare was of the roughest, often cooked over a fire of "chips," while his bed comprised a pair of blankets spread upon the ground under his wagon. Called upon to fight, he ever was compelled to fight in the open against a hidden enemy, the Indians always having choice of place and conditions. Attacked by Indians, the hunter or prospector or the light equipped pony express rider might have some chance of dodging, running or exercising some choice of ground on which to make a stand. Nothing of the kind was possible to the freighter. With his slow moving outfit, when attacked there was but one course to pursue. That was to "corral" the wagons in a circle with the stock inside, and prepare to "stand off" the enemy as well as possible from such shelter as the wagons afforded. Considerable time was required to prepare even this meagre protection, during which men and animals were exposed to the Indian bullets without a possibly of returning the fire.

Such a life, it may well be surmised, had little to attract the timid or effeminate. Naturally the men who engaged in it were men of courage and endurance, nor is it wonderful that among them were not a few turbulent spirits difficult of control. If their work was strenuous, they were inclined to take their pleasures no less strenuously, and with their wagons unloaded and their wages paid them in Deadwood or Lead, they usually made their presence known in the many saloons, gambling houses and dance halls open for the spending of their hard earned money. To keep a crew of such men under sufficient discipline to make their services reliable and efficient the wagon boss was of necessity a man of undoubted courage and tact. To him and to the men who with him toiled and fought over the various trails between "The States" and the Black Hills, that the pioneers might be sustained in their work of laying the foundations for the present prosperity of this region, this article is offered as a tribute too long delayed.

THE FREIGHTER'S UNWELCOME GUESTS

To better realize the task of the freighter and the problems that he had to solve, the following incidents in the life of Jesse Brown are given as he relates them.

In 1873 I was engaged in freighting for the Government to the different military posts, and the Indian agencies. In September of that year we made a trip to Fort Randall on the Missouri river. The Indians at that time were supposed to be peaceable as they had been gathered in by the U. S. army at Bordeaux Creek, east of where Chadron, Nebraska, is now, and called Spotted Tail agency. Notwithstanding the fact that while they were being fed and furnished everything in the way of provisions and clothing, the young bucks had killed their mail carrier and several others when caught alone. Neither the soldiers nor civilians were allowed to shoot at an Indian until the Indian got in the first shot, and the Indians knew this. Therefore they would ride right up to a man professing friendship and shoot him in the back. This happened frequently, and in passing through their reservation we were compelled to take chances in the pursuance of our duty. On many occasions I would not have given twenty-five cents for my chance.

One time when the bulls were brought in by the night herder, there were some of them missing. We were camped on a little stream east of the agency, enroute to Randall, so I went up the creek and the herder down. I had not gone over a mile when I found the trail of the cattle. I followed it up over a hill, and upon reaching the top of the hill I looked and saw the tops of some tepees. I stopped, hesitating and considering what best to do. But under the circumstances there was only one thing to do and that was to get those bulls. So I rode bravely right down by the tepees, the dogs coming out as if they would like to devour me on the spot, and the Indians following, some of them with their guns in their hands. I could talk a few words of their language and I said "Tokila tekleska" (meaning have you seen any cattle?) One old man pointed on up the creek. He proved to be the Chief Wounded Knee and a friend of the white man, and he got his pony and went with me and helped me drive the stock to camp. Of course he expected to get something for this and I gave him some sugar and bacon and he went away happy, but not anymore than I was at the result.

Upon reaching White River, close to where the Rosebud Agency is now situated we found the grass burned. The Sioux Indians had been down on the

Pawnee reservation and had a fight with the Pawnees and got the worst of the battle, and in making their get-away had fired the grass to prevent the Pawnees from following. The fire had swept clear to White River way ahead of the Sioux, but we did not know these circumstances at that time. So James M. Day and myself took saddle horses, after an understanding with Boone May, who was left in charge of the two outfits, that if we did not return that night, for him to start the next morning and follow up. If we found grass and water adjacent to each other we would put up a stake with a notice attached telling him which way to find grass. We rode two days along the road to Fort Randall and was satisfied that we could get through. On the evening of the second day having made up our minds to return to the wagons, we had stopped in a thick bunch of willows on Turtle Creek to make some coffee and broil some meat for supper. We had just about finished our repast when we heard the snapping of a dry willow and looking up there peeping at us was a big buck Indian. He says "How.' May says, "Hell, of course he wants something to eat." We gave him bread, bacon and coffee in a tomato can and packed up as soon as possible, because we knew that there more of his class around not far away. We saddled up and rode along as far as we could under the protection of a bank. I dismounted and peeped over the bank towards the road, and right in front of us was quite a body of red devils returning from the fight spoken of. We concluded to remain where we were until dark, which was only a short time. The next place west where water could be obtained was Rock Creek and that they would camp there we knew. So we calculated to pass around their camp and left the road going to the left or south, but on coming back into the road after crossing the creek on the west side ran into some of their ponies. The next moment we were surrounded by the bloodthirsty howling mob. Well, I thought sure our time had come for they were mad and craving revenge on account of the whipping they had received from the Pawnees. They took us into camp, where there were about one thousand warriors, and all the hubbub you ever heard was there. I know some of them wanted to shoot us from the way they looked and acted. Think of it "two pale faces" caught in their herd of horses at night. Heap Big Chief steal 'em ponies. But fortune is on the side of the brave. There happened to be a squawman there and he came up in the crowd, and we quickly explained to him who we were and our business; that we were trying to get through to Randall and were on our way to meet our outfit. That was all right and they motioned for us to go.

After riding some distance on the road towards our outfits we slacked up thinking probably that we were all right for the present at least, but upon listening for a moment we could hear the clatter of horses feet, they were following us. We speeded on again endeavoring to reach the camp which we expected to find at the next watering place about three miles ahead of us, and we did. They had just started fires for cooking supper, and having made a long drive were late in getting into camp. May told the cooks to put out their fires, then sent two men with our horses to the herd telling them to stay with the herd until morning, and every man to get his gun and get into his wagon and remain there unless called out in case of emergency. By this time the Indians were coming into the corral. They went around to every wagon trying to get some one up but that was just what we were trying to avoid, for we would have had to cook supper for the whole bunch of them and then suffer any depredation at their hands that they chose to commit. They prodded some of the men with their guns, and pulled the blankets off others, but not a word of protest was uttered by anyone. Finally giving up the idea of getting any of us up, they searched the grub wagons (we had two) and took all of our sugar, most of the bacon, and some coffee but did not disturb the flour, nor the beans. So we had bread and beans straight until we reached Fort Randall. It was our number that protested us from further damage at the hands of these renegades. We had thirty-three men and could have made a hard fight, but as I have stated before, the Government would not allow a white man to shoot an Indian until the white man was killed first. I have overlooked the fact that they also took Boone May's saddle and he swore vengence on the Indians right there, and future events have proven that he made good.

The next morning the same band of Indians on their way to the agency came upon a freighter by the name of Black Hawk in camp with his outfit. They were eating breakfast, when the reds charged upon them, dismounted and snatched the plates with the contents from the hands of the bull whackers and ate everything in sight that was cooked. Then ransacking their mess wagon, went to the herd, killed one of the fatest steers. Thus you can see the conditions and what the freighters had to contend with, without daring to dispute their rights or to make any resistance in the depredations of these pests.

TRIP FROM CHEYENNE TO CUSTER IN JUNE, '76

In April, 1876, I loaded up in Cheyenne for Custer in the Black Hills. I had twelve teams, Frank Whitney five, Matt Jobson two, Jim Clark two, Al Blye and Bill Edwards one each and John Dalzell two. Twenty-five all told. We organized and I was elected captain of the outfit. We expected to have to fight before we got through as the Indians were on the war path, and contesting the right of every one that sought to enter the hills. But there had been little trouble south of Hat Creek. I lost three horses at Niobrara but I always laid that to white men hangers-on at the ranch. The day before we reached Hat Creek there was an outfit attacked on Indian Creek and several men killed and a few Indians. They made a determined stand against the reds but really did not understand Indian mode of warfare The men were buried by the side of the road. We camped close by this place the next night, as that was the last watering place before reaching the Cheyenne river. Just before reaching this camp one of my men broke a tongue out of his lead wagon. After corralling I had taken one man, Louis Tadlock, with our guns and tools and went back and put in another tongue while the man stood guard. The next day we reached the Cheyenne river, and there we heard of the murder of the Metz family in Red Canyon. There was a spring there so we camped over night. I saw the tree where this family were sitting enjoying their dinner, when they were fired upon by their murderers. Metz and his wife were soon killed but a colored woman ran through the brush about a quarter of a mile when she was shot. This deed was blamed on the Indians but I am well satisfied that white men killed them for their money as it was very well known in Custer that Metz had sold his bakery there for a goodly sum of gold dust. I went up to the place where the persons had concealed themselves behind pine bushes that had been cut and planted in the ground and foot prints all showing boot or shoe tracks, besides their knee prints in the ground showed the weave of cloth.

The next morning when we yoked up there was one steer missing and it happened to be mine so rather than delay the outfit I told them to go ahead and I would look for the lost ox. Matt Jobson says, "Brown, if you are going to stay back, I will stay with you." We looked down the creek quite a ways and could see no trace of the animal. We went up farther towards the top of the hill. We saw a mule outfit passing and they had spied us. We searched the brush back and forth for a while and had about reached our camping place when we heard someone hallowing. We listened and found that they were calling first Brown and then Jobson. I called and asked what the matter was and Frank Whitney says, "Indians, that's what's the matter." The first thing that entered my mind was that our outfit had been attacked by Indians, but upon reaching the road we found that the mule train spoken of had overtaken our train and inquired if there was any men back in the canyon from the train. They were informed that there were two. They said that they discovered two men on one side of the hill and eleven Indians on top of the hill, and they had dismounted and were trying to get a shot at the two white men. It was Frank Whitney, Jim Clark and John Fleming that rode back to notify us of our danger.

We arrived at Custer City, unloaded and got the bill of lading signed, went out to May, Ward and Parshall's saw mill and selected the largest, clearest logs and had them sawed into boards. They measured from eighteen to twenty-four inches in width. I received sixty dollars per thousand in Cheyenne. Sold to Butler and Nealen to make wagon boxes.

While in Custer a government mule outfit came in and Calamity Jane was driving one of the teams, dressed in a buckskin suit with two Colts six shooters on a belt. She was about the roughest looking human that I ever saw. The first place that attracted her attention was a saloon, where she was soon made blind as a bat from looking through the bottom of a glass.

WHEN FATE SAVED A PARTY OF PIONEERS

With one other incident significant of the life of the trail we will complete the general account of the trails. Captain C. V. Gardner had come into Custer in March, 1876, and decided that it was a good place to locate, and although he went out of the city in company with a body of two hundred disgusted gold hunters and had seen much of the work of hostile Indians, he returned soon afterwards, having purchased some 60,000 pounds of merchandise and sent it forward by freight. On this trip he joined a party of gold seekers at the Platte and all progressed without trouble until they reached Hat Creek station, where in the morning the Indians made a raid upon their herd and tried to stampede the stock. The skirmish ended without damage to either side but prompted the outfit to send out a scouting party of six mounted men. All went well until "Down Indian Creek" was reached when the scouts came galloping back pursued by six warriors. After passing a knoll, they sought to stand off the savages until re-inforcements should come up, but the red fighters separated and part of them went around the knoll while the others passed over the top. The ones riding around the hill, ran right into the scouts and firing at them killed one man before they could get away. The remaining scouts fled at once to the corral that had been forming for the battle. Captain Gardner was between the scouts and the train when he saw the maneuver of the Indians and the death of the scout and became also a target but the bullets went wild and by dropping to the ground and crawling under cover of a coulee, he succeeded in reaching the corralled train just before the band of fifty Indians surrounded the camp and opened a vicious fire. For two hours they did their best to kill the white men, but finally retired without having done any more damage than to kill two horses of the train However, they took with them five good Indians as their share of the struggle. The besieged men did not know when the redmen would return to the fight and they were compelled to stand ready for battle at any moment. About two o'clock in the night volunteers went out to the scene of the tragedy of the day and Billy Wawn, picked up the body of the dead scout, now stark rigid and placing it upon his back carried it into camp like a cord wood stick.

This little battle cast deep despair over the party and after the burial of their unfortunate companion, they held a meeting and all voted to return to their homes, except Captain Gardner and five others. The majority vote prevailed and the train began its return journey, but was beset by Indians throughout the day. However, they met Hecht's and Street's and Thompson's freight outfits accompanied with thirty well armed men These men were the ones who were hauling the 60,000 pounds of freight into the Hills for Gardner and they were strong in favor of proceeding on with the journey, but Gardner informed them that they did so at their own peril and that he would hold them responsible for the loss of the goods entrusted to them, as the force of the Indians was too large to be driven off by the train. The next morning demonstrated the wisdom of Gardner's counsel, for after an unsuccessful attempt to stampede the stock, the train was surrounded by five hundred yelling and whooping savages, who sent a rain of leaden missiles over into the barricade of wagon and freight. There were one hundred eighty white men in the camp and they responded to the attack with such vigor as to cause the attacking fordes to withdraw after one hour of battle.

The leaders of the outfit were now convinced that with such determined and energetic opposition on the part of the Indians, assistance would be necessary and accordingly Captain Gardner and Billy Wawn, were chosen to ride to Laramie and seek aid from the troops at the fort. They mounted on two of the fleetest horses in the train, and set out on their long and perilous journey. But when they arrived at Raw Hide Buttes at three o'clock in the morning, they came upon the camp of Captain Egan, who when he learned that Gardner had been a captain in the civil war, received him quite cordially and promised to come to his rescue, stating that he was hunting Indians. Gardner and Wawn hurried to their companions near Hat Creek and led them to Indian Creek where they were joined by Captain Egan and his force. Here Captain Egan deposed the man who had been chosen captain of the train and placed Gardner in command stating that when he said "Go" they were to go and when he said "Halt", they were to stop. At this point Captain Egan posted his infantry and took his cavalry and scouted the country for Indians while the wagon train went onward. Fortune was kind to them, for after proceeding about eight miles a wagon broke and the train went into corral while the repairs were being made. The site of the break down being where they could go into this formation and at the foot of a long steep hill.

During the stop, Gardner was drafted as baker

and while busily engaged in kneading dough, the cry of Indians rang out and Gardner, without waiting to free his hands from the sticky mass, grabbed his gun and calling for volunteers, ran with the six men who responded, to the top of the knoll from where they could see the warriors in large numbers gathering to the attack. The scouts quickly returned to camp and Gardner called for a volunteer to send word to Egan for help. A young man stepped to the front and mounting a fleet horse, braved death from the red marauders and rushed away just as the Indians with wild yells and whoops came on to the attack. For three hours they sent the bullets whizzing into the barricades, but the defenders fought with the determination to sell their lives dearly. Suddenly the yells and crack of rifles ceased and over the hills came the white horse cavalry of Captain Egan with flowing manes and distended nostrils. The red scouts had seen his advance in time to save their hides and were soon out of range. Captain Egan had not been able to proceed on his trip owing to the miring of his mules and had returned to his post just in time to see the signal fires of the Indians and get the word from the besieged freighters. Thus fate had twice intervened to protect the gold seekers, first with breaking the axle before the train had entered upon the narrow hillside road where they could not have corralled in position to escape the bullets of the enemy, and second in the miring of the mules that held the military within easy riding distance. The soldiers escorted the train from here on into Custer, near which place they were met by a large body of men who had heard of the fighting and were coming out to the rescue. That night joy reigned supreme in Custer and dancing was the order of the day until the early morning hours, when Egan and Gardner were given the choicest room and couch of the town hotel, a front room parlor, with dirt floor and camp bed upon it. Ten o'clock in the forenoon saw the two army officers still calm and peaceful in sleep.

Thirty-five years later, when the Hills had become

the home of thousands of prosperous people and the war whoop a faint memory of the past, Captain Gardner in the course of business affairs happened to be detained out in the country near Buffalo Gap and was obliged to seek shelter for the night from one of the settlers. After the evening meal the genial captain and his kindly host were relating experiences of the days of long ago, and soon the clouds of smoke that they sent forth from their evening pipes were peopled with the ghosts of their younger days. And then there came the heroic story of the young lad who at the call of the intrepid captain, had rushed forth in view of the attacking force upon his perilous ride to save the one hunderd eighty of his embattled fellows from death and torture. And then these two gray haired boys grasped each other in joyful surprise, for one was Gardner, captain of the day, and the other Joe Marty, fearless rider to the rescue.

MONTANA PARTY.

The news of the discovery of gold in the Black Hills had spread far and near and gold seekers everywhere were planning to go there and seek their fortune. Accordingly in the territory of Montana in the month of March, 1876, the largest party of gold seekers that ever entered the Hills at one time was mustered together and broke for the south on the twentieth day of March. Bill Langston was appointed to act as leader of the expedition and Joseph Cook as his assistant. The expedition consisted of two hundred men, one hundred pack animals and a large wagon train. Among the men were expert miners, farmers and mechanics of all kinds and every man experienced on the western frontier. They struck the upper waters of the Belle Fourche river and while in camp on a creek west of Devils Tower they were attacked by the Indians and one man, named George Miller, was killed. The dead man was buried on this creek and to this day the stream is known as Miller Creek.

THE FIRST TRAIL MAKERS

Thus were the trails of the Black Hills blazed by

the struggling pioneers. However, the white men were not the original trail makers nor even were the Indian tribes that had fought and lost the Hills among themselves in the centuries of their warring. The genuine and first pathfinders to the Hills were the great herds of bison that were wont to resort to the foot hills in the fall when the prairie pastures became dry and parched. They sought out the easy grades over hills and through valleys, and located the watering places along their routes. Their tribes had for centuries marked out the gulches and gaps in the lofty ridges that encircled the hills of plenty and with with the coming of man there remained naught for him to do but follow the bison trail. The romance of the Black Hills Trails is fittingly sung in the poem by Richard E. Curran, of Ft. Pierre, South Dakota, which is herewith published that it may be more widely known and appreciated.

THE DEADWOOD TRAIL

An old trail, a bold trail,
    The old French trappers knew
A far trail and a war trail,
    Through the land of the fighting Sioux
A rough trail, once a tough trail,
    Where oft the war-whoop thrilled
The gold trail was a bold trail
    As it bore to the far Black Hills.

So long ago, that none may know,
    Not even the tribesmen red,
What time was first, to quench their thirst,
    The bison herd was led.
O'er hill and vale and wooded swale
    To the mighty river's shore,
On the ridge's crest, straight east and west,
    The bison's pathway bore.

At break of day on swift foray
    The red mass troopers sped
Fierce fighting clan of the Blackface band

By a wiley chieftan led.
By the ridge's crest, where the outlook's best,
    In the land of the dreaded Sioux.
On the bison's trail, hoofs left no tale,
    Well the raiding red men knew.

And all too soon for the red men's boon,
    The pale face trappers came,
Through summer glow and winter snow
    He followed the drifting game.
And ever best was the ridge's crest,
    With the lowlands spread to view
And there without fail was the bison trail,
    Through the land of the Teton Sioux,

From far to the west, mid mountain crest
    Came a tale of the glittering gold,
By word of mouth, both north and south,
    Of Deadwood Gulch men told.
And soon in view of the wondering Sioux
    Came the rush of the gold-mad throng.
And ever west by the ridge's crest
    Ran the bison's trail along.

Came a long draw train, through snow and rain
    In the height of the freighter's day,
And mighty loads o'er rutted roads
    Creaked slowly on their way.
By the ridge's crest came the stage express
    With keen-eyed shotgun guard
And the trail they knew through the land of the Sioux
    Was the trail of the bison herd.

An old trail, a bold trail,
    Let us mark it deep and well
And the bold tale of the gold trail
    To our wondering children tell.
'Tis a rough trail—wild enough trail,
    Yet I love this old trail best,
For the old trail, ye gold trail,
    You helped us win the west.

CHAPTER III.

THE INDIAN RAIDS AND BATTLES

The winning of the Hills was a conquest pure and simple and like all such movements in history, was paid for in a great toll of human blood. The white men were trespassers upon the most valued lands of the red men and the rightful owners vigorously resented the encroachment. The complete story of that struggle for empire between the white and the red men, would require many pages of tragic incidents and will not be attempted in this volume. We will relate some of the most important ones that the picture of the gory sacrifice of human life laid on the altar of gold may go down for the perusal of the coming generations, who may wish to know more in detail about the final chapters in the struggle that was waged for four centuries between the white trespassers and the red defenders in America. The account of the campaign of the Big Horn and the death of Custer, whom the Indians marked as the author of their troubles and the leader of the invaders, will be set forth in the chapter following this one.

PIONEER DAYS WERE STIRRING

In the early days of the settlement of the Black Hills, times were not in the least bit monotonous and would furnish ample and sufficient excitement to the most adventurous and restless spirits of these days of moving picture shows. In order to show the rapid sequence of these exciting events, through the kindness of George V. Ayres, the first mayor of the town of Custer and now a prominent and successful wholesale hardware merchant of Deadwood, South Dakota, we are permitted to use a few extracts from a diary that he made in the pioneer days. We quote as follows: "I arrived in Custer City, Saturday, March 25th, 1876, at three o'clock p. m. in a big snow storm, having been on the road from Cheyenne, Wyoming, seventeen days with snow ten days out of the seventeen.

At that time there was estimated that Custer City had a population from six to ten thousand but few buildings had been erected and completed. The people were camped everywhere in and around the town, in tents, covered wagons and brush houses to protect them from the weather. The principal business was general merchandise, saloons and gambling houses, hotels and restaurants, there being about one sack of flour to two barrels of whiskey. There was no organized government except a local organization called the 'Minute Men.' Captain Jack Crawford, the poet, was the Captain. The purpose of the organization was to repel the attacks of the Indians and prevent them running off the stock and after my arrival the Indians started trouble by massacreing the Metz party in Red Canyon." April 24th, Another party attacked by Indians in Red Canyon, one man killed but the Indians repulsed with a loss of five killed." April 26th. "A party attacked by Indians on Indian Creek. Stuttering Brown shot but not fatally. Report also came in of the killing of a man named Wood near Buffalo Gap." May 1st. "Report that three men had been killed by Indians near Mound City, near Castle Creek." May 2nd, "Two men reported killed by Indians on Slate Creek. Men sent down to bring in bodies. A party also sent out to bring in the party of men killed in Mound City near Castle Creek." May 3rd, "A party of sixty left for Cheyenne, scared out by the Indians." May 4th, "Indians came into town and ran off with twelve head of horses. A party came in from Cheyenne. They were attacked five miles this side of Red Canyon, by Indians, one man and two horses killed. About two hundred new arrivals today." May 5th, "The Indians came to town and ran off with sixteen more horses." May 6th, "Report from Hill City that the Indians ran off with eighteen head of horses from there." May 7th, "Reverend Smith held the first church services in the Hills. Congregation composed of thirty men and five women. I attended." May 8th, "Smoky Jones shot by Indians, just outside the city limits but not fatally." May 18th, "A party of six men who started for Cheyenne were attacked by Indians this side of Red Canyon, one killed and one seriously wounded. The others retreated to a better position and repulsed the Indians, killing three." May 20th, "Metropolitan Hotel and three other buildings burned. Captain Egan with two companies of cavalry arrived with a large train load of provisions. The safe in Stage Office robbed of $3000.00 in gold dust." July 14th, "Report came in that General Custer and his entire company had been defeated and killed by the Indians." August 7th, "Report came in that the outgoing stage for Cheyenne had been attacked by Indians on Indian Creek. The driver badly wounded and horses and mail were taken. Also report that General Crook had sent a dispatch from Fort Laramie that 800 Sioux warriors were headed for the Black Hills and to look out for them. A wagon train was attacked five miles out from Custer by the Indians but were repulsed without loss to the whites." August 23rd, "Four men killed about four miles from Custer City while putting up hay. One of them was a half brother to Tom Hooper. Report also came in from Deadwood that on Sunday, August 20th, the Indians had killed four men near Deadwood and ran off one hundred and ninety head of stock." This will serve as a sort of index to the events more fully described in the pages following, and arranged about in the order of their occurrence. The first account will give an idea of the first incidents in Custer, from an article written in December, 1875, from the Sidney Telegraph.

FIRST MINER KILLED BY INDIANS IN 1875

The fifteenth of last month was a gala day with the miners now in the Black Hills. Captain Pollock, of the 9th U. S. Infantry with much regret to himself, marched out of the hills and left Camp Collins, Custer City, with its comfortable quarters to the tender care of the poor, but honest miners, as he always styled them.

Custer City is looming up, a mere dot of her future greatness. It is a miner's town, in Custer's gulch.

The town was first laid out about August 10th, 1875, and now contains about thirty houses, and others are being erected as fast as the weather and other circumstances will permit. There are now three well travelled roads leading through the town, one to the north, one to the south, and one to the east. Custer trail, or the one leading north, traverses several noted mines.

On the 30th of November, there was a convention held by the miners in Custer City at which there were over two hundred and fifty miners present. The object of this convention was to establish a pony express from this point to the Spotted Tail Agency, and there is now such a conveyance running regularly every two weeks between these points. A carrier was appointed to carry the mail to and from the Hills at the rate of 25 cents per letter, and 10 cents per paper. Therefore, all mail directed to Spotted Tail Agency will get to us without delay. An express office has been established at Custer City with Mr. Dow as agent. It appears now that we have started well on the way to fortune, and if we only had a little more grub on hand we would be the happiest people on earth. It is through your columns that 1 wish to inform the miners that were here last summer, of the disposition of their "grub" that was left here in care of the party, who were left in charge of the property to go out. Some two or three of the party were away at the time, and did not get back for three or four days after the troops had left. When they returned they found most of the property had been taken away by the wretches. It is thought that one of the party by the name of Bob Kennon, could have saved much of the property, had he been so disposed, for he was in close proximity when the troops hurried out. Miners who had property here will not, therefore, depend on it.

We have had little snow so far this season and the weather continues to be fine. If this kind of weather will only continue, and we are left alone we can work all winter sluicing. The most unfortunate thing that has occurred here this winter was a miner killed by Indians, named Leroy Keis, which took place near the foothills, not far from what is known as Jenny's Camp, on Beaver Creek. Keis and a man named Jackson, started to Custer Park to see if the troops had gone out when they were ambushed, Jackson making his escape, but lost his horse. I am informed that the commanding officer of this garrison was told the above fact but declined to punish the Indians. We can expect nothing better from a man who has not lost any of the red devils, but who don't care a farthing for a poor honest man who is striving daily to make an honest dollar. Don't let the unfortunate death of the poor miner daunt any from coming, for the Indians who perpetrated the vile act were but a small band of fifteen or sixteen in number. It would be best for all who come to keep together as much as possible, as it is perfectly safe for a party of eight or ten to come through and after they are once in the Hills they are as safe as they were in Sidney. There are now a great many first class miners from Idaho and Montana here, and they are in good spirits over the prospects of the country.

A party returned a few days ago, from a trip to the north and west, about one hundred twenty-five miles where the finest coarse gold yet discovered in the Hills has been found. They found about fifty miners on those streams, all of them had from one to ten ounces of gold. While they were there one nugget was panned out weighing $22, at the rate of $16 per ounce, while nuggets from four to six dollars were very common.

I would advise all who contemplate coming to the Hills to lay in their supplies in Sidney. There is plenty of room in Custer City for immigration and comfortable quarters built for at least five hundred miners, so rush them along Mr. Telegraph for the more the merrier.

The most famous wretch that I know of, is the devil in disguise of Captain Pollock of the 9th U. S. Infantry who has repeatedly imposed upon the miners in every shape and form, has placed a blot on the good name of our army, by tying up miners by the thumbs for hours, and tantalizing them and then throw them in bull-pens, and leave them there to eke out an existence. Andersonville prison was an honor and a palace to this Pollock bull-pen, as it is known here by that name.

It is now growing late and as the pony express leaves in the morning I will bring this to a close by signing myself Old Pick.

CALIFORNIA JOE

About the 25th of April, 1876, I received a letter from California Joe, who had a ranch down on Rapid Creek and was trying to induce newcomers to settle there, and build a town to be called Rapid City. The note was written in lead pencil and ran thus:

My Dear Jack, if you can be spared for a week from Custer, come over and bring Jule and Antelope Frank with you. The reds have been raising merry old H--l and after wounding our leader ran off eight head of our horses including old Bally. The herder's name was Sherwood. There are only ten of us here all told and I think if you can come with two or three we can lay for them at the Lower Falls and gobble them next time. Answer by bearer if you can't come, and send me fifty rounds of cartridges for my fifty Sharps. Hope this will find your topnot still waving, I remain as ever, Joe.

I immediately went to see Major Wynkoop, commanding the Rangers and he gave me permission to go. I arrived at Rapid the next night with four comrades besides myself. After two days and nights watching, Jule Seminole, one of my scouts came in and reported that there were 25 or 30 Indians down Box Elder Creek about twenty miles, and that they were coming from the direction of the big Cheyenne, and would probably move up about Rapid that night. Jule could tell by watching their movements just about what they were going to do, and he was correct in this instance. About 3 o'clock in the morning Jule went up to his cabin and started a big fire in the fireplace, also done the same in two or three other cabins, to attract the attention of this thieving outfit. These cabins were over a mile from the place of ambush. Just as daylight was breaking, Frank Smith discovered one wading up the creek. Frank reported to Joe and I. Joe said "Let him alone he will signal to the others soon." In a few minutes the shrill bark of a coyote was heard proving Joe to be correct. Twenty-three well armed Indians rode up along the willow bank in Indian style, that is single file. We had been reinforced by two miners during this time making seventeen of us. We had six men on one side of the creek near an open space which we figured they would make a break for on receiving our fire from the opposite side. We took aim as best we could but it was a little dark yet to see the sights on our rifles. We gave them two volleys before they fully recovered from the surprise. We got fifteen ponies and eight scalps. Fifteen Indians escaped nearly all on foot. Joe killed three himself, the last one a long ways off. Joe rested his rifle on Frank Smith's shoulder, and killed Mr. Indian dead. There were three of our outfit wounded including myself, all slightly. But it had a wholesome effect on the Sioux, they did not venture back for some time.

FIRST DEATH IN CUSTER

Another incident of early days took place in Custer. The first death.

About eight o'clock in the winter of 1875, I was engaged in washing the supper dishes in my cabin. Two travelers entered, hungry, tired and footsore. After preparing supper for them and giving them a seat by the log fire they told me the following story:

The elder man, John A. Byers, formerly was a captain in a Maryland regiment during the Civil War, started from Sioux City on foot for the Hills, and was joined by the other, a boy about eighteen years old. They had travelled round five hundred miles carrying blankets and provisions and after escaping a hundred dangers, reached Custer in an almost exhausted condition. They stayed with me nearly a week when Byers went on to Deadwood. During this time Charley went to work to fix him a shelter. He dug into a bank about three feet and carried poles to raise it two feet above the ground. Covered it first with small poles and brush. The dirt, he put on too much dirt for the strength of the roof, and it broke in and killed him. There were no letters or papers to give us any idea who he was or where he belonged, and did not see Byers afterwards. Do not know anything more about him. On that day sitting on the green beside his demolished cabin I wrote these lines:

 Poor Charley braved the wintry storms
  And footed it all the way,
 And now he is a bleeding corpse
  He died at dawn today.
 His is the old, old story
  He saw bright prospects here
 He left his home, his friends, and all
  Perhaps a mother dear.

 If so, God pity that mother,
  Perhaps alone and poor,
 When someone breaks the blighting news
  Her heart will break I'm sure;
 To think she never, never more
  Will clasp him to her breast,
 Among the peaks in Custer Park
  Poor Charley now must rest.

 Down in the glade beside the brook
  Our boy shall sleep tomorrow,
 His weary march of life is o'er
  Now freed from care and sorrow.
 And while we think of home and love
  And better days in store,
 We humbly pray to Him above
  And bow to Heaven once more.
    —Jack Crawford, the Poet Scout.

WOOD CHOPPERS FALL TO INDIAN BULLETS

The town of Custer situated on French Creek in the southern part of the Black Hills was incubated in 1875 but did not show much animation until the following spring. The spirit of adventure was abroad in the land and men began pouring in by the hundreds with no other purpose than to chase the flimsy trail of fleeting fortune, far into the Indian country which was the forbidden land at that time. It was soon apparent that the camp was destined to become something of a town and that it was urgent on some body to go into the building business to provide shelter for the incoming hordes of anxious treasure seekers. Therefore men were employed by Mayor Farnem to list out the timber and cut logs from the ridges and snake them in for the construction of suitable cabins along French Creeek on which the embryonic city had squatted. The men engaged in the cutting of these logs were making great headway felling the gigantic pines that had never felt the stroke of a white man's axe till now. These men had not been on the job a fortnight until they were attacked by a band of the bloody Sioux Indians, and two of the timber men were killed. The survivors got into town and told their tale of woe. John Burroughs of Denver, Colorado, was serving as town marshal. He called a meeting that night which was held in Young and Gaylord's saloon to agree on some means of defense so that the log work could proceed. They organized the Custer City guards with forty-five expert shooters to stand off the Indians, and protect the town. The next morning, like the King's army, they marched out of town under the direct command of Captain Jack Crawford, the Poet Scout, with his long hair and fangled buskskin toggery. And this expedition by the way was his initiation into the mysteries of western craftiness. The scheme of protection worked fairly well and no more men were massacred on the job.

One evening while Crawford was coming alone on a good horse, musing to himself over some lines for a frontier ditty, such as he was apt to dash off at any old time, he was startled to come suddenly upon an Indian lying in the grass along the trail. Jack's first impulse was to shoot him on the spot but the buck made the peace sign and said he was sick and wounded, and so he was as the captain could see on closer observation. Crawford had just come out from Pennsylvania as a newspaper correspondent and his bug was to learn something more than James Fenimore Cooper ever knew about the inner workings of the noble red man. Believing that his hand was his own he got down and lifted the sick buck into the saddle and held him there as he led the horse to his cabin. They arrived after nightfall and to keep the matter away from the citizens who would stand for no friendly quarter to a savage, nothing was said by Crawford about his strange guest hidden away in his shack. One day when the Indian thought he was going to chip in for sure he asked to see Sam Young who he said he had known at Fort Laramie. Young went out to the cabin, took one look at the emaciated form of the invalid and said, "Well if it ain't Jules Seminole the meanest half breed in the whole tribe, and the only thing to do with this skunk is to put an end to him right now." Crawford was scared at this turn of affairs but begged for the buck's miserable life, which was not worth saving in any kind of weather. The appeal to Young carried and he promised to say nothing about it to the boys. And Jack Crawford was left in undisputed possession of his secret charge. He doctored him up and nursed him along through the convalescent stage. The readers of this, here in the west will know now just about what happened so it is scarcely necessary to add that one night when the host was absent, Jules Seminole flew the coop, like the villain with the smiling cheek. He took with him Crawford's good horse, a roll of blankets, some clothing and all the grub in the place to pay his benefactor for the kindness wasted upon his worthless carcass in the hour of great distress. All through his life he was worse than the serpent that slides along on the grassy sod, and stings the luckless foot.

The account was squared a short time later when he was lynched by some cow boys for killing a herder.

THE TRAGEDY OF PINO SPRINGS

J. S. McClintock, a pioneer of Deadwood, has written the following account of the killing of four men on the Pierre trail which is herewith submitted:

"Some time during the month of April, 1876, a freight train of horses was put on the road between Ft. Pierre and Rapid City by John Dillon, a wealthy merchant of Fort Pierre, for the purpose of furnishing supplies for the Black Hills trade. While on its first trip going west a camp was struck at a point on the road known as Pino Springs, and sometime during the night a valuable mare was crippled but was taken along four miles next day and left by the roadside, the train proceeding on its way to the Hills, where the freight was unloaded and the train started on its return trip to Pierre.

"On reaching the place where the animal was left, it was found to have so far recovered from its injury as to be able to travel, but for some reason, it was left behind and the train taken on to the Springs, where an early camp was made.

"John Harrison, the train master, then started back with two horses attached to a spring wagon, taking with him three others, one named Sadler, one known as Texas Jack, the name of the other man I have forgotten.

"It was found that they had caught the animal, and while returning to camp, in crossing a narrow valley along which ran a dry creek bed, skirted by small trees and underbrush, close to and paralleling the road for several hundred feet, they were fired on by a band of Indians at close range and literally shot to pieces. The horses, it appeared, had run in a circle and one running faster than the others, brought them back close to the starting point, where they stopped.

"As I remember it, the men were all found together on the wagon, where they had been stripped of their apparel and everything else was taken except the wagon and a song book, and it was believed that the boys were singing in a group when the volley was fired.

"A grave of sufficient width was dug and the bodies of the four unfortunate victims of red devils were shrouded in their blankets and placed side by side and covered with soil and left in that lonely spot, soon to be, with a few exceptions, forgotten by the world."

THE PONY EXPRESS RIDER

In the year 1876 Charley Nolin was a pony express rider carrying the United States mail from Sidney, Nebraska, through Rapid City on to Deadwood, Dakota Territory. In those day on account of the Indians being on the war path and hostile to the white riders it was necessary for the mail carriers to do their riding under cover of darkness as far as possible and rest in some secluded spot along the way during the bright sun light when the Indians would be roving about. At Rapid City he fell in on his last trip with a number of freighters and people who were coming to the Hills and he varied his usual rule of travelling by night and proceeded on his way for a while in company with the freighters known as the "Schofield Freighting Outfit." To the people with whom he conversed he stated that this was to be his last trip as a pony express rider and that he was anxious to complete it in order that he might return to his home in the States. He expressed the desire to hurry the journey toward its end that he might go home. When he reached the hill that lies southeast to the valley where Sturgis is now located and he was thus close to the wooded part of the Hills which would afford him more or less protection from the Indians he mounted his pony and stated to his companions that he would make a fast night ride and be able to get to Deadwood that night. He bade them goodbye and rode away. He had proceeded not much more than a mile, when Indians who were lying under the bank of a small creek fired three bullets into his body, killing him instantly. The savages stripped the body, took the revolver, belt, gun, saddle and pony, ripped open the mail bag, scattered the contents on the prairie, and cut three scalps from the head. The freighters in the Schofield outfit heard the firing and hurried toward the place. They found the young man lying dead beside the road and they buried him in a shallow grave near where he fell. Sometime later, E. L. Carl and Fred Dickenson passed by the grave and noticed that the coyotes had dug down to the feet of the dead mail carrier. They filled the hole with rocks and packed them down closely and there he rested until in 1880 when J. C. McMillan, Dan McMillan, John G. Wenke and Charles Francis of Sturgis purchased lot number ten in block number two of the Bear Butte Cemetery. There they reinterred the remains of the youth, high on the mountain side beneath the sighing pines and overlooking the valley whence the boy's spirit had been wafted home. The little creek still babbles along over its stony bed but thenceforth was known as Dead Man Creek and the gulch from whence it flows as Dead Man Gulch.

MURDER OF THE METZ FAMILY

The leading baker in Custer City in the year 1876 was known by the name of Metz. He had conducted a very prosperous business, for Custer in those days was the first town to be met on the trail from the south and the point to which the greatest number of gold seekers first directed their journey. When gold was discovered in Deadwood Gulch and the surrounding camps, the rush of gold seekers to the mining locations was so great that Metz foresaw that the days of Custer's prosperity were soon to pass and when he had an opportunity to sell his business and property at a good price he made the most of it and prepared to leave the Hills and return to Laramie City, Wyoming, from whence he had come. On the day that he had planned to leave the town of Custer, Scott Davis arrived with his mule outfit from Cheyenne and Metz inquired of him whether he had seen any Indians enroute. Davis informed him that he had seen none north of the Cheyenne river but advised Metz not to attempt to go out of the Hills alone but wait until the next day and go out with his outfit on their return trip as it would be much more safe. However, Metz decided to move out at once and go as far as Cheyenne River Ranch where he was to wait the coming of Davis. He had with him his wife, another man as the driver and a negro woman who had been their cook.

All went well with them and they arrived at the mouth of the Red Canyon where they camped for dinner, April 24th, 1876. They had prepared their meal and were unaware of any trouble or danger as they were seated beneath the large tree. It was a beautiful, bright summer day in June and peace appeared to be hovering over all nature, when suddenly the report of rifles rang out. Metz fell dead near the wagon with a bullet through his head and several others through his body. The driver of the party was found about a half mile from the wagon, and that of Mrs. Metz still farther away, shot through the heart. She had evidently made a wild race for life before the murderous bullet ended her terror. Robert Flormann was in charge of a party passing through the canyon the next morning and he found the victims mutilated and strewn along the gulch, but did not find the body of the negro woman. Mrs. Flormann assisted in the preparation of the dead for burial, her part being to clothe the body of Mrs. Metz, wash her face and brush back the disheveled hair. The three corpses were then sent back under escort to Cheyenne station where they were buried.

The wagons of the party had been ransacked, the trunks and boxes broken up and articles scattered all about, and much of the valuable things carried away. Search for the body of the negro woman failed to locate it, but several days later, Captain C. V. Gardner came out from Custer on his way to Cheyenne in company with several hundred disgruntled and discouraged gold seekers and made noon day camp in the canyon near the site of the murder. After camp was struck and the march began, Gardner took a tow path along the rivulet off the road and there he saw the body of the woman in a small ravine or draw, leaning face forward against the bank, in an upright position with her arms back of her neck, and with a single arrow piercing her back, as if she had been shot from behind while peeping over the top of the bank. He pulled the arrow from her body and sent the deadly weapon to Stebbin's & Post's Bank in Cheyenne for safe keeping.

In June, 1876, the Odd Fellows lodge of Cheyenne of which Metz was a member, called for volunteers to carry the body of their comrade back to his home. Six men volunteered, among whom was Herman Bischoff, now of Deadwood. Accordingly the men went out to the station and exhumed the bodies of Metz and his wife, already in advanced stages of decomposition and made the return trip to the Wyoming home. The journey was a most trying one and the men had to make frequent shifts to relieve each other from the terrible and sickening odors.

BATTLE OF THE SPRING ON THE HILL

In April, 1876, six men under the command of J. D. Hunter, left Custer City, early in the morning with several pack animals. They aimed to make their camp that night at a point in the Red Canyon called "The Spring on the Hill." It was about twenty miles from Custer City in a southwest direction. Although some of these men were old and experienced plainsmen, they were ambushed by about twenty-five Sioux Indians, while near the Spring. The Indians fired a volley at short range and Hunter was shot while he was dismounting, and died trying to tell the other boys a message for his wife.

John C. Coyer was wounded about the same time, and being in command, ordered the party to take to cover in the Coulee. While being dragged to cover by the men, Coyer killed an Indian himself, and though mortally wounded, kept command and encouraged the fighting boys. During this time the packhorses were wounded and in their mad stampede, rushed about and caused a great deal of confusion.

The Indians, after looting the packs, set the camp on fire to burn up the white men, but Coyer outwitted them again by having a back fire started. The fight continued until dark, and James Berry, moved by the piteous cries of Coyer for water, found a pony that had escaped the Indians and quietly went to the spring and obtained water for the wounded man, then slipped away to Custer, where he found Dr. Pierce, and reported the trouble. Three pistol shots from the gun of Pierce drew the whole town together at once, and twenty men with Mayor Bemis were soon on their way to Red Canyon where they arrived at daylight. The Indians, upon their arrival, skipped out.

The party buried Hunter on the knoll where he fell and Coyer, being still alive, was carried on a travois and brought back to Custer. An examination by Dr. Flick disclosed that his end was near. Coyer was given a pencil and paper, and while he was held up by his comrades, wrote a farewell letter to his wife, telling her to be brave, and directing what she was to do with the children. Then he laid down and died.

THE WAGNER FAMILY

Among the people who were gathered into the Hills in the 70's by the lure of gold long held in the mountain gulches there were some who could not get accustomed to the wild and boisterous times of those days and as soon as possible turned their faces toward their home country. There were streams of people coming in and also long trains going out. Among some of the people in the year 1877, who sought the eastern states from whence they had come was a family known as the "Wagner family" consisting of the two brothers and the wife of one of them. Becoming tired of the vain efforts to become rich in finding gold in the gulches of the mountains, in the month of July, 1877, they packed their household goods in a freighter's wagon, hitched up their team and left Crook City over the Bismarck Trail. This trail ran northeast over the Hills from the town of Crook City out east and north of Bear Butte. On the 17th day of July this party had passed Spring Creek at about noon and were hurrying rapidly to overtake the freighter by the name of Pete Oslund who was a countryman of theirs and who had preceded them along the trail. But when the incoming stage from Bismarck had arrived at a point on the school section northwest of Bear Butte they found that the Indians had waylaid the Wagner family. The ox team had been shot, one of the animals lying dead and the other standing by so badly wounded as to soon die. Along the road about twenty paces apart were found the bodies of the two men where they fell from the bullets of the savages, and stripped of their clothing but not scalped owing to their short hair. Near the wagon was found the woman whose body had been mutilated and the ox goad rammed into her abdomen. She had long beautiful golden hair and from her head was taken a scalp. The contents of the wagon, consisting of household goods, articles and supplies were broken and scattered about over the grass.

When the stage arrived on the scene the bodies were still warm but no Indians were to be seen. W. J. Thornby was on the stage that day and when he arrived at Crook City, hired a party to go out and haul the unfortunate family to that place where the two brothers and the wife with her unborn babe were buried. For many years there remained at the fatal spot a few broken pieces of dishes to mark the point where the cruel hand of fate had taken its tribute of blood and turned the morning of hope into the night of despair.

THE KILLING OF "JIMMY IRON"

Not all of the pioneers who were drawn to the Hills by the lure of gold devoted all of their time to the digging and washing of gold along the creek beds and hill sides of the new country. Some of them realized the futility of even trying to wrest the gold from the limited gravel beds in the gulches of the Hills and proceeded out to the rich and fertile plains where they resorted to farming and raising livestock. But the efforts of these early pioneer farmers and stock men were opposed by roving bands of Indians. It was necessary that some one be on guard at all times to watch out for Indians lest those who were in the valleys be fired upon by a red man from behind a small knoll or tree. One of the men who was thus employed in keeping guard over the valley while his companions were at work was a man known as "Jimmy Iron." This man during his life had many narrow escapes from death at the hands of Indians. One time when near Custer City on turning on a point overlooking a rock he met face to face an old Indian. They saw each other at the same time and the Indian with rare presence of mind advanced smilingly toward him and extended his hand with the usual greeting "How Kola How" but while shaking hands he fired a six shooter through his blanket. The bullet was not fatal and "Jimmy Iron's" enemy soon fell. Feeling himself wounded he examined the place where he felt a ball strike and found that the bullet had lodged in the sheets of a Bible which his mother gave him and which he carried in his vest pocket, the bullet having passed nearly through the book.

Besides the Indian's scalp he had the red man's pony and outfit to pay him for his escape, but Jimmy finally fell at the hands of his dreaded enemies and it occurred in the month of August, 1876, while he was guarding his fellow farmers who were engaged in the making of hay at the False Bottom at a point where the present town of St. Onge is situated. He had been going up to the top of a hill for several days in succession to look out over the valley for sight of Indians. One of his companions had advised him to seek a different route each day he would ascend to the hill for fear that the Indians observed his habits and learning that he was taking the same route would be enabled to ambush and kill him. Jimmy laughed at this advice but sure enough a few days after that when he was on his way to his lookout from the hill the Indians were lying in wait for him and fired upon him. He fell dead without any chance to defend himself. His companions buried him near where he was shot and years afterwards one of the men who had known and loved him in those days caused a monument to be placed over his grave in commemoration of the bravery of a pioneer scout and guard.

THE MEXICAN AND THE INDIAN HEAD

The herds of cattle and horses used by the miners and freighters to Deadwood in the early days were herded during the summer time in the fertile valleys of the foothills, owing to the great cost of feed and hay in the mining camps. Sometimes the stock would wander away from the vicinity of the herders and then a search for them would be made. Just such an incident in August, 1876, became the starting point for a most unusual event.

V. P. Shoun, the owner of the freighting outfit had several men in charge of his herd of cattle and horses in the foothills near Crook City and on August 1, 1876, his men were engaged in trying to recover some of the stock that had escaped from their control. While engaged in this work Brick Pomeroy found himself pursued by five Indians, but as he quickly took refuge in the underbrush, they were unable to shoot him but gave him quite a chase. However, before the race was ended, Pomeroy was enabled to tumble one of his antagonists to the ground by a well directed shot. The news of this attack so near to Crook City soon spread to the town and a Mexican in the camp conceived the idea of possessing himself of the scalp. He accordingly hurried out to the scene of the fight and finding the remains of the Indian, proceeded to try to remove the scalp lock. In this work he had never had any experience and failing to succeed, he hacked off the entire head and mounting a horse proceeded to Deadwood, which he entered, yelling and swinging the bloody head about as he held it by the long black hair. The sight of the yelling Mexican and the bloody head caused great commotion in the city and men ran to prepare for an Indian attack, thinking that a real battle was coming. At this moment, E. T. Peirce was completing his work of preparing the remains of Wild Bill for burial in the tent among the pines north of Main street in the afternoon of August second. He supposed that the uproar was caused by a band of Bill's friends gathered to lynch McCall for the murder of Wild Bill, and he hurried to the scene of action. There he saw the crowd about the wouldbe hero who claimed that the owner of the gory face had robbed him of his horse and he killed him and that he took along the head to prove his story. To kill an Indian in those riotous times was considered a worthy deed and some one perched upon a pile of lumber along the street, pulled out a pair of balance scales and called for contributions. Soon about sixty-six dollars were gathered in in the form of gold dust and presented to the Mexican.

Instead of purchasing another horse with the dust so freely bestowed upon him, the Mexican proceeded to gamble it away and in a quarrel that night at Crook City, he himself fell a victim to a loaded gun and the scant regard for human life. The gamblers of Crook City objected to the presence of the remains of the dead Mexican and hired Fred Coates of the town to place it out of sight, paying him therefor the sum of twenty dollars. He accordingly fastened a lariat rope about the corpse, and trying the other end to his saddle horn, dragged the erstwhile Indian fighter to a water worn draw beyond the town and there he piled loose rocks from the hillside over him.

And in the meanwhile, according to the statement of "Grasshopper Jim," the people of Crook City who came out to view the headless body of the Indian warrior who fell a victim to his thirst for blood, piled up a great quantity of dry pine branches and placing the remains upon it, set the mass afire and effectively erased any trace of them.

When V. P. Shoun arrived in town and heard what had happened he proceeded to try to locate the Indian head for the reason that his herder was entitled to the reward offered for Indian scalps at the time. He found that the head was in the possession of a saloon keeper and after some insistence, persuaded the bar keeper to go into the cellar and bring up the head. He then had Dr. Schultz remove the scalp for him and left the head with the doctor. The head was cut open and the brain weighed and found to be of unusual size.

HOLLAND AND BROWN

The gulches and hills about the mining camps in the northern hills did not furnish a supply of grass sufficient to care for the horses, mules and cattle belonging to the incoming miners and freighters and accordingly in order to meet this condition of affairs, Joe Burton and Joe Cook established a ranch out on Centennial Valley north of Deadwood where they built a large inclosure for the protection of the horses at night. To this beautiful valley under the care and protection of these men, the miners and pioneers would bring their horses and mules and thus escape the exhorbitant price of hay and grain that was charged in a mining camp at that time. This herd was known as the Montana herd and during the month of August, 1876, was composed of about 190 head of horses.

On the 19th of August, 1876, the herd had been placed in the stockade as usual for the night but the Indians after watching the action of the guards had proceeded to dig out several of the posts and make an opening large enough for the horses to escape. However, their plan failed and the next morning the herd was driven out to pasture. Cook who had gone down to Deadwood with the horses to be delivered at that time had not returned and Burton had started out with the quota to be delivered on that day when a rifle shot rang out and Burton looked back and saw a large band of Indians running and yelling toward the horses which fled in all directions. A great number of the horses rushed madly toward Deadwood from where they had been taken and rushed pell-mell excited and frightened into the city streets, thereby causing great consternation among the miners and settlers, resting easy and free from attacks by the Indians. Word of what had occurred out on the prairie reached the miners and the thought of the people out on the valley surrounded by Indians caused a large meeting of citizens to be held in Deadwood and various speeches were made urging the pioneers to rush out to rescue their comrades out on the plains. However, when the time came to assemble and proceed out on the prairie, very few of the men responded, it being claimed that they had no horses with which to make the journey. Nevertheless a small band of hardy men armed with various sorts of firearms took up the fight and went to the foothills where the Indians had made the attack upon the herd. When they arrived there they saw that the Indians had escaped with about one hundred head of horses and had proceeded on toward the eastern part of Spearfish with their booty. Accordingly they took up the trail and when riding down Spring Creek they saw near a ravine a lone Indian who opened fire upon them but without injury to the men. The rescuers held a council and decided not to make an immediate attack on the Indian on the theory that he might be a decoy to lead them into an ambush.

The Indian had disappeared behind a small knoll and the party cautiously stole up behind the hill as no further progress was seen on the part of the Indian. One of the leaders of the band, Isaac Brown, peeped over the edge of the hill to find out where the red men had gone when a crack of a rifle sounded and Brown fell dead. Charlie Holland, another one of the leaders, more brave than wise, after a short pause decided to attempt to learn the position of the enemy and thinking that he had located the Indian, fired his rifle and at the same time cried out, "Come on boys, I've got him," attempted to go forward but at the same moment he likewise fell dead from a bullet from the Indian's rifle.

All efforts on the part of the leaders remaining to put the Indian to flight proved unavailing and as night came on they realized the danger of trying to dislodge the Indian and accordingly retreated to Deadwood. The next day a larger and more wise crowd arrived at the scene of the tragedy and found the two dead men's bodies. An examination of the other side of the hill disclosed the fact that one lone Indian had taken a stand behind an oak tree and from this point had stood off the whole party and killed the two uncautious men. John T. Spaulding known as "Buckskin Johnny" was one of the rescue party and when aiding in the removal of the two dead men, he picked up a blood stained letter that belonged to Charlie Holland and read the address, "Sioux City, Iowa" and the last sentence, "My beloved husband, now Charlie for my sake don't expose yourself to the Indians, your loving wife, Mrs. Charlie Holland."

DEATH OF CHARLES MASON

While the stampeding of the Montana herd was on and the Indians were scattering through the gulches in their efforts to drive the horses to the prairies, Rev. Smith when at the point known as the "Rest" was murdered by one of the pursuers, and his body soon discovered by a rancher who lived near by, a more detailed account of which incident is set forth in a separate chapter. However, one of the red marauders did not fare very well for while on the trail his approach was heard by Dan Van Luvin and his companion who was skinning a deer that they had shot. Van Luvin opened fire upon the fellow and then galloped away to Deadwood for help, reporting the coming of a band of Indians. A small party set out and arrived upon the scene of the encounter but found the Indian much alive for before they awoke to the fact, Charles Mason fell dead from a rifle bullet.

The crowd responded and riddled the wounded warrior. It was found that the shot from Van Luvin's rifle, had killed the Indian's horse, and broken both legs and one arm of the red man who was compelled to rest his rifle over a log when he fired the fatal shot.

The bodies of Mason and Smith were both taken to Deadwood and buried in a common grave, side by side, but each in a rough board box, the body of Mason resting to the north of Smith. The bodies of Brown and Holland remained out on the prairie until the twenty-first, when the rescue party went out and brought them in. They were buried later in graves south of the one holding Smith and Mason, and this fact enabled the later location of the body of the minister when it was disinterred. Thus the twentieth day of August, 1876, went down in the annals of the pioneers of Deadwood as one of the most exciting of its time, the day being marked by the loss of over a hundred head of horses, the death of one Indian, and four of its citizens, one of whom was its first preacher.

RAPID CITY FOUNDERS FIGHT INDIANS

John R. Brennan was one of the founders of the City of Rapid City and its most loyal son. He wrote many years ago an account of several of the bloody fights that took place in that vicinity and we here reproduce the article as taken from the Pioneer of 1876, and written in August, 1876.

I send you a few items from this locality that may be of interest to the readers of your very excellent paper:

The red skins have made it hot for the boys in this vicinity for the past two weeks. On the 22nd inst. two of our citizens were building a cabin on a ranch two miles below town, when they were attacked by Indians. They made a running fight for a mile or more, when the Indians gave up the chase without capturing the men or horses. One of our citizens mounted a horse and started up the gulch to spread the alarm but the Indians were there before him, and had succeeded in murdering two men near where

John R. Brennan

Sam Scott

Bismarck saw mill used to stand, and about four miles from this city. On the same day, and about the same time four men on their way here from Deadwood, were attacked at Limestone springs on the Crook and Deadwood road and two of them murdered. The party consisted of Sam Scott, G. W. Jones, John Erquot, and L. S. Livermore. Jones and Erquot were killed, Scott and Livermore making their escape to the woods a half mile distant, where they lay until dark, and then started for this place, arriving here at about ten o'clock. Livermore received a shot in the arm just above the elbow. The next morning fifteen or twenty men started out to bring in the bodies. We went to the springs first and procured the bodies of Jones and Erquot, and then drove over to the old mill site after the other two. Arriving there we found one lying on his face in the creek, and the other on the trail about a hundred yards or so distant. They were placed in the wagon with the other two victims and taken into Rapid City. Four new coffins were made, graves dug and so forth, and the bodies laid about in their mother earth by kind and gentle hands. At the graves a short and appropriate funeral service was read for O. Patterson, George W. Jones, John Erquot, and Thos. E. Pendleton. Patterson was from Allegheny City, Pa., and was captain of a party of Pittsburghers who came to the hills early in the spring. Jones was from Boulder, Colorado. Erquot came to the hills a short time ago from Denver. He was well known in Kansas City, Mo., and in Fort Scott, Kansas. He held city offices in both places at different times. Pendleton was from New England, and was one of the New England Black Hills Mining Company, that arrived in the hills during the present summer. The bodies were terribly mutilated, shot almost to pieces, their ears cut off, etc. Next day, August 23rd, two men arrived from Spring Creek and reported finding a man murdered on the road seven or eight miles from here. Ten men went out and found the body as reported. A grave was dug, and the corpse buried where found. No one recognized the murdered man. He would weigh probably one hundred sixty pounds, dark hair, dark full whiskers. He wore, when found a pair of snuff colored overalls, and a blouse of the same material. He is buried eight miles from this place, on the road leading from here to Custer City.

All work for seven or eight miles up this creek has been stopped, owners of claims not considering it safe to work. I think they have good reason for caution, for we see Indians nearly every day on those prairies in the Hills and they seem to be drilling. Men have left the creek and come down to Rapid. The upper town (so-called) is entirely deserted, the few inhabitants it possessed having moved to this place. One hundred tons of hay which had been stacked there has also been moved here, and today they have commenced moving the houses. so that in a short time scarce a vestige will remain. We have a block house in the course of erection here which will be completed in two or three days. It is to be a two story structure twenty feet square, with two tiers of portholes in each story. We flatter ourselves now that we can stand off as many Indians as want to come around.

We have in the neighborhood of three hundred tons of hay stacked here, and are putting up more every day.

Dick Dunn's train left here two days ago for Fort Pierre. They saw no Indians on the way here from Deadwood.

KILLING OF LEGGETT AND HAYWARD

Mrs. Annie D. Tallent in her history of the Black Hills relates the incidents leading up to the death of two pioneers in 1876. Mrs. Tallent and her family returned to the Hills in 1876, although they had been taken out by the military the year before. After a most discouraging journey over the trail from Cheyenne, the party finally arrived in Custer in June, 1876. They discovered that one of the party was missing and upon going back over the trail the body of Leggett was found lying dead several miles from the town. His body had been stripped of clothing and a leather belt was found cut in two. Examination of the belt disclosed some three thousand dollars in greenbacks that had been overlooked by the murderers who left numerous moccasin tracks about their victim. Papers on his body gave the names and addresses of his relatives and revealed the fact that he had been a man of prominence in his home country. It was evident that the band that overcame him had followed the train and when he had tarried too far behind, shot him down without hindrance.

In the latter part of the same year, Mrs. Tallent also writes about one Hayward who had become obsessed with the fear that he was to be killed by Indians. He owned a team and wagon and was finally induced by a party of coal prospectors to haul them for a tempting compensation to the site of the coal beds some forty miles northwest of Deadwood. The outward journey was free from any Indian troubles, and after making their investigations, the miners began to return. But when they were between the camp and Spearfish, they discovered that a band of Indians were after them. A race for life began, but the red warriors were rapidly gaining upon the team hitched to the wagon and the driver turned off the trail to gain the protection of a draw or coulee nearby into which he ran the outfit. From below the banks of the draw they were enabled to stand off the red skins although they greatly exceeded their number. However, Hayward was beside himself with fear and despite the urgent warnings of his companions, persisted in standing up in the open to see whether or not the attacking forces had left. Finally a bullet found its mark and Hayward's body rolled into the ditch true to the fate which he had foretold. Towards night the Indians gave up the attack and the miners continued their journey home without further annoyance. They carried with them the body of the fated man and buried him in the cemetery at Spearfish in a plot reserved for Indian victims.

DEATH OF WILSON AND ABERNETHY, 1877

In July, 1877, a party of engineers were engaged in surveying the line between the Wyoming and Dakota Territory. They were escorted by a troop of United States Cavalry under the command of Lieutenant Lemley. While encamped on the banks of the Belle Fourche river, they were attacked by a party of Sioux Indians. Reports came into Deadwood that the soldiers were surrounded and were in danger of being annihilated. Deadwood went wild with excitement and speeches were made calling for volunteers to go out and rescue the soldiers. Lawyers, merchants, clerks, laboring men, miners, in fact every branch of business was represented in the lineup, some without fire arms and none prepared for a long trip. However, Captain Willard and Tom Hardwick in the absence of Sheriff Bullock and other men from the sheriff's office, gathered together a band of seven men of experience and struck out in the night for Spearfish Valley. When they arrived in the Valley, they could see the Indian signal fires way to the north and west and the next morning they met the soldiers who had managed to get away from the Indians without any loss of their men. However, they lost all their camp equipment consisting of three wagons and eighteen mules, also all their clothing and food. They proceeded to the place where the wagons were located, where they found one mule badly wounded and soon shot him. It was then learned that one of the teamsters was missing but a search of the river bottom found him nearly starved and his feet badly swollen from the cactus thorns. He was brought into camp and turned over to the surgeon and subsequently recovered. An effort was made to follow the Indians but they had too much of a start and the idea was given up by Willard who proceeded to return to Deadwood with three of the men who came out with him.

On their way to Deadwood they were passed several times by the Indians and had some narrow escapes, but managed to get away without any injury. It was planned to go out to the outfit known as the Pettigrew Camp where a great number of people were encamped with several women and children because the Indians were so numerous that they had decided to entrench themselves waiting for a more favorable opportunity to move.

While engaged in the work of scouting and trying to locate the Pettigrew outfit, Captain Willard heard a volley of shots up the creek and looking up over a knoll saw a large band of Indians chasing three white men. As there was no hope of giving assistance for there were so many Indians, Willard was compelled to remain there and see the Indians shoot down the fleeing men. After the Indians had left, Willard went to the bodies and discovered that one of the men was a man known as Billy Wilson and his friend Dave Abernethy who was scalped. It appeared that Billy Wilson had sold a wagon to a man who was trying to get out of the country without paying for the wagon and Wilson had warrants issued for the arrest of the man and had himself deputized to serve them. He had gone to the Pettigrew train and had left the train for the Hills when he was attacked by the Indians and killed. A man living near Spearfish had a yoke of oxen and an old fashioned, two wheel cart. He volunteered his services which were accepted and the bodies were loaded into the cart and started on the road to Spearfish where he arrived just before daylight.

Among the men who were with Willard was a young man named Thornby who was working for the "Deadwood Pioneer" and he immediately hurried on into Deadwood to get his story into the daily paper while Captain Willard tarried on behind. It appeared that the dead man, Wilson, greatly resembled Captain Willard and that some of the cow boys who had seen the dead man supposed him to be Captain Willard and when Willard later returned to Deadwood, he was met by Sheriff Bullock who said to him, "Cap, you are supposed to be dead now; why can't you remain dead? Your friends have made arrangements for a very fine funeral and here you come in and spoil it all. Go out on the street and show yourself!" And he did so. L. F. Whitbeck, a newspaper man, soon thereafter met Willard and expressed himself very much disgusted as he had given him a very fine obituary writeup and declared that Willard ought to go out now in justice to his friends and be killed for sure.

On this day two more men were killed on Crow Creek a few miles from where Wilson and the others were killed and in all there were ten men killed within the vicinity within a few days of each other.

THE INDIAN TROUBLE NEAR RAPID CITY

The report of the Indian attack on a freight train near Rapid City a few days ago has had a general circulation all over the country. The Telegraph is able to give the full and truthful version of the affair, in a letter from one of the men who were attacked. This is the first appearance of the hostile Indians on the Sidney route, and freighters inform us that the same gang of red desperadoes have been encamped on Hat Creek between Cheyenne and Deadwood for a long time past where they have been committing depredations on the stage and freight lines. This, with the additional inducement of a shorter route and better road, has driven the Cheyenne freighters to abandon the Hat Creek portion of the route and cross over to the Sidney trail. As a natural consequence, the Indians followed them.

The following letter from Mr. Streeter gives an accurate account of the disturbance:

"French Creek Ranch, Jan. 21, 1878.

"To the Editors of the Telegraph:

"About noon yesterday on our way coming from Deadwood to Sidney, and about seven miles southeast of Rapid City, our wagon train, known as the 'Colorado Boys' Outfit,' was attacked by Indians, seven in number. Three of them came out of a ravine and cut out all of our loose stock, twenty head in number, from behind the rear team and also cut off Mr. Chas. Reed, who was driving the herd. One of them took after the herd and the others tried their best to kill Mr. Reed, but as good luck would have it, in leaning over in the saddle to avoid the arrows being shot at him by the red skins the saddle turned with him and he fell to the ground but held on to the stirrup and was dragged out of the fight. But at that time we had, by dint of much labor (in turning over the bales of hay and sacks of grain), got our guns out of the wagons and went to work on the redskins, who 'got out of here' in a hurry. Four of the redskins had remained inactive watching proceedings and only firing an occasional shot, but when we had beaten off the three Indians who made the raid and had retaken the herd, they all went over the hill together on a full run, and attacked another train known as 'Curly's outfit,' and wounded Mr. H. D. Turman, I think mortally, and killed one mule, and wounded another. Mr. Turman was taken to Rapid City, and is now under the doctor's care but in a critical condition.

"Our outfit is composed of five, ten and eight mule teams and owned by Messrs. James Pollock, W F. Streeter, Fred Luttin, John Luttin, C. K. Reed, and J. T. Parrott and we were all engaged in the battle. Yours, etc.

Wm. Streeter."

THE MESSIAH CRAZE

The treaty of 1889 had been opposed by some of the chiefs of the Indian tribes who had foretold that the government would not keep its word and when in the year 1890, the Indian department began its policy of limiting the aid given to the Indians and to which they were entitled under the treaty of 1876, the opponents of the treaties were able to point to this move as proof of their prophecy. In addition to the lessened government ration there came the general drouth and crop failure of the year 1890 and with it much suffering and discontent among the various Sioux tribes. About this time there also came the strange story of the coming of a Messiah to avenge the wrongs of the Indians. The tale was an innocent conception arising from the fevered brain of a Piute Indian from Pyramid Lake in Nevada, which appealed to the imagination of the savage mind and with its passing

W. A. Remer

from mouth to mouth became distorted out of all semblance to the first dream.

The original idea was vastly different from the story that caused so much trouble and excitement, and we are indebted to W. A. Remer, sheriff of Lawrence County at the time, for the use of the following letter that came into his possession in Deadwood, through the mails. The men addressed were not then prisoners there, and the letter was never delivered. The identity of the writer was never learned, but the fact remains that it was a message sent to members of the Sioux tribes, and hence is of real historic interest. It is written in beautiful penmanship and has at the head of the first page, a woman's hand holding white birds and pansies, such brightly colored cut out pictures as were common on gift cards at that time. The words are as follows:

"Canton, S. Dak., 13th April, 1893.
"Buffalo Man, No Flash, Red Hill and Sun Flower, Indian Prisoners, Deadwood, S. Dak.

"My Brothers:—Twice I have been to Pine Ridge Agency, once to Rosebud, twice to Lower Brule and twice to Crow Creek, to see and talk with your people, and, with the pansy teach them its lesson of universal fellowship, culture and peace.

"Once I saw Two Strikes and Red Cloud and talked with them, telling them that I had been sent to them by The Great Spirit, with the flowers to teach them that only by following the example and teaching of the pansy, could they hope to survive; that war meant, for the Indians death and the destruction of their race; that peace and industry and good order meant life, prosperity and happiness.

"I was arrested almost at once and sent away for fear of creating excitement and more trouble. Again I went, when all was quiet, and again I was arrested and sent away, without being permitted to tell your people who I was or why I was there.

"Only yesterday I returned from Hot Springs where I went hoping to see some Indians from the reservation, whom I might teach the lesson and message of the pansy, and, through them, to all the tribes and all your people.

"But none were there or at Buffalo Gap, and I had no permission to go on the reservation, so that I had to return without seeing any of your race except some Indian police.

"I was sorry to hear, while in Washington, of the trouble concerning which you were arrested.

"I don't know who was most to blame for it, but I ask you again now, to see how little hope you have of helping yourselves by fighting. Your only chance is in being peaceable, united and helpful to each other.

"It is true that many white people are anxious to destroy you, but it is quite as true that the best white people are anxious to make it harder for them to do so, by continued disorder.

"Let me tell you, now and here, that it is only by peace and loving union with other flowers, that the wild violets, which you have all seen, grow larger, brighter and more beautiful and are called pansies; and now these pansies, which are only educated violets, lead the whole race of flowers, in their beauty and education, as you may, by following their example, lead all the races of men.

"It may be hard for you to believe that the smallest violets, even smaller than these little pictured flowers, grow to be the largest and brightest pansies, and in just the way that I tell you; by loving union with the other flowers, by which means they copy and learn all their brightness and beauty.

"I promise you and your people, from God, that if you will follow the example and teaching of the pansy, you shall, in two hundred years, lead the best progress of the world and be first in power, in America. This surely is worth striving for, and it is as sure, if you do your part, as the promise of God.

"I am, most truly,
"The Messiah."

Tribal councils were held, messengers sent from tribe to tribe, a new dance known as the ghost dance introduced. Religious fervour became intense, and the savage mind was stirred to the highest pitch of excitement. It was seen that the ghost dances carried the performers into ecstacies and efforts were made to stop the rites. This only added fuel to the fires and bands fled away to carry on the dancing. So universal became the disturbed condition of the western tribes, that it was finally decided to capture Sitting Bull in his camp on Grand River, since it was learned that he was preparing to join with his band the ghost dancers who had fled from the reservations to the Badlands, from which point, under his leadership, the movement would soon develop into a real Indian war of great extent.

DEATH OF SITTING BULL

Accordingly, the Indian police on the Grand River were ordered into action and a detachment of cavalry under Colonel Drum was sent to join in the task. The Indian police, loyal and prompt, after forced night rides, assembled to the number of forty-three at the home of Sitting Bull. Here they found at daybreak on the morning of December 15, 1890, that the soldiers of Sitting Bull who had been guarding him for just such an emergency, had failed in their task this one night and were away dancing. The police under the command of Lieut. Bull Head were enabled to enter the log hut of the chief without opposition and found him asleep on the floor. Upon being notified that he was under arrest, he agreed to go with the police and prepared to dress for the journey, having one of his wives go to the second of his cabins for some parts of his apparel. While engaged in this task, his young son, Little Crow, about seventeen years of age, upbraided him for so easily yielding to the commands of the police, and Sitting Bull balked at further progress. When he was outside of his cabin, he saw some one hundred fifty of his band excitedly gathering around, and he called upon them to rescue him. Thereupon Catch-the-Bear fired and shot Bull Head in the side, who from his position beside Sitting Bull, turned and shot Sitting Bull through the body, who also received a bullet through the head from Red Tomahawk, who was behind him. Sergeant Shave Head, the police on the opposite side of Sitting Bull was shot at the same moment by another supporter of Sitting Bull, and the three fell together. Catch-the-Bear, then fell a victim to Alone Man and the battle became a fierce hand to hand struggle. But the police soon drove their assailants into the timber and then carrying their wounded into the houses, held their position until Captain Fetchet of the military detachment arrived two hours later. The soldiers had a Hotchkiss gun with them and with this they fired two shells into the police camp before Red Tomahawk succeeded in showing them their error. The warriors of Sitting Bull were soon dispersed and fled from the camp.

In the short fight between the police and Bull's followers, four policemen were killed and eight of the enemy. The Indian women had joined in the attack, but the police simply disarmed them and thus acted quite differently from the manner in which we find the fully armed government troops performing a few weeks later at Wounded Knee. The body of Sitting Bull was taken to Ft. Yates and the two wounded police, Bull Head and Shave Head, died at the hospital later. And thus closed the final chapter in the life of the last and most unrelenting Indian foe of the West. Sitting Bull was not a warrior, but he was a most able strategist and held wonderful control over the tribes of the West because of his keen mind and appeal to their imagination as a medicine man. The buffalo head that he worshipped in his religious rites is now in the State Historical Society at Pierre.

THE BATTLE OF WOUNDED KNEE

The death of Sitting Bull created consternation in the minds of the Indians and some of his band soon joined the other forces in the Badlands. Wild were the rumors among the white settlers. Wild likewise were the stories of the intentions of the white soldiers. Peaceable Indians were driven to join the bands of hostiles as a means of self protection. Every day or two some tale of a fight with Indians would be reported. But most of the troubles were the acts of renegade and thieving Indians and many of the rumors of murders at the hands of red men were absolutely false. Unscrupulous white men took advantage of the general unsettled conditions and committed many crimes on the peaceful Indians. There was a general distrust and fear on the part of both white and

U. S. troops surrounding the Indians on Wounded Knee Creek 3 miles @ Miller

red men and most of it through misunderstandings and false rumors.

After the fall of Sitting Bull, the next most feared chiefs were Hump and Big Foot, but through careful management and the able work of Captain Ewers, Hump was finally induced to surrender and became a great aid in quieting the other leaders. Efforts to bring in Big Foot and his band were begun and finally this chief consented to surrender, which he did on the 21st of December, with 333 Indians. When the band arrived near their village, they declined to proceed further, stating they wished to remain at their homes. But Colonel Sumner informed them that they must proceed with him to the agency and sent them word that unless they did so, he would bring up his whole force and compel them to do so. The movement of the military frightened the Indians and they fled that night towards the Badlands. A general closing in of the circle of troops about the disturbed area was now ordered and the several bands were gradually taken under control. On the day of the 28th of December, 1890, Big Foot and his band were caught and they surrendered without trouble.

The band was met on Wounded Knee Creek and on the morning of December 29, 1890, in obedience to orders, they were encamped in an open plain near the banks of the creek and entirely surrounded by the soldiers, who had also posted Hotchkiss guns on the hills overlooking the plain. Big Foot, sick with pneumonia was in his tent which was being warmed by a camp stove under orders of Colonel Forsyth. Preparations were being made to disarm the Indians before taking them back to their reservation.

The prisoners had been guarded all night, and at eight o'clock in the morning, the soldiers deployed and entirely surrounded the Indian camp with a line of soldiers. This procedure caused much uneasiness among the Indians who were seen to move about among the tepees in a restless and nervous manner. When the cordon of troops was completed, all Indian men were ordered to come our from their tepees and gather in a group near by. They were commanded to sit down in a semi-circle and Major Whiteside proceeded to count them. He found that there were only ninety eight braves present and ordered some of the scouts to search the tents. Fifteen more were added to the circle. Colonel Forsyth then demanded the surrender of their guns and they replied that they had none. He told them that he knew they did have guns and repeated his demand, whereupon six of the men volunteered to go to the tents and get the arms. After some delay, they returned with only three guns, only one of which was useful. He then ordered a detail of soldiers to search the tents for arms, and they proceeded with the work, causing much disturbance among the women and children in the tepees as they tore up the layouts. This created some excitement among the braves and Captain Wallace moved the foot soldiers within twenty paces of their line. As the guns were taken from the tepees by the soldiers they were piled near the circle. During this work, an Indian dressed in a ghost shirt, was seen to arise and reaching his arms towards the skies, speak and gesticulate, and throw dust into the air. The officers did not understand him at first but when informed by an interpreter that the fellow was calling upon the earth to open up and swallow the soldiers, and telling the braves that soldiers' bullets would have no effect upon them and that they should arise and defend themselves and scatter the soldiers like dust, he was ordered to sit down. After the tepees had been searched, the soldiers were ordered to search each brave, and after six had been examined the ghost dancer suddenly jumped to his feet fired at the soldier who was guarding the guns, and the battle was on. From under their blankets the Indians drew their weapons and a most desperate close in struggle ensued. Captain Wallace was tomahawked, and each man fought for his life. The Hotchkiss guns opened fire upon the tepees, and the crazed soldiers pursued the fleeing men, women and children as they ran screaming for refuge, they knew not where. Many of the tepees were fired by the bullets and some of the wounded women and children were roasted alive.

When the carnage was over, thirty one soldiers were dead, thirty three wounded, and over two hundred Indians killed, among them Big Foot who was lying sick in his tent . The escaping Indians brought word of the terrible slaughter to the others coming in and soon they were on their way to the Badlands. Several light fights ensued and it looked like a general outbreak would occur, but the middle of winter was on and finally the Indians were convinced that their lives were not in peril and they returned to their reservations.

The dead and wounded soldiers were promptly taken from the field but no attention was paid to the Indian camp and the military forces were directed to the work of giving their attention to the red men who had not come in and were gathering for further defense. Three days elapsed before details were sent to the task of cleaning up the battle field, and in the meantime, a heavy snow storm had come followed by the icy blasts of a real Dakota blizzard. Many wounded Indian men, women and children lying helpless and exposed to the terrible sweep of the bitter cold wind as it hurled the icy darts of the snow drifts against them, perished and when the fury of the storm had ended, their stiffened forms told a terrible tale, of human suffering. But not all had died. Some there were who with frozen arms and legs were destined to endure the torture only to die soon after. Four babies, carefully wrapped, were still found alive beside the frozen bodies of their mothers, whose shawls had been used in the pathetic effort of the mother to shield her babe from winter's cruel and deadly grasp. Only one, however, lived, as the three days of suffering was too much for them.

A long trench was dug and from out of the snow drifts over a range of several miles, bodies of naked Indian men, women and children from whom the clothing had been robbed, were hauled like cord wood sticks and dumped therein. Torn and mangled bodies of little children, with the gory forms of women, glistening with the blood stained ice that clung to them, were flung into the common pit, and dirt and snow heaped upon them. Thus ended the final scene in the last Indian battle of the last century. A sad climax to a long series of wrongs on the part of both white and red men in their relations with each other. A forceful example of the innate savagery of man even though white, and the cruel, pitiless power of reason dethroned in the heat of fierce passion.

THE MURDER OF FEW TAILS

Of the many wrongs perpetrated upon the Indians by the white men in the west, one of the most dastardly crimes recorded is the murder of the Indian, Few Tails. This man with his squaw and another brave and his wife had been on a friendly visit to the Crows in the north and knew nothing of the troubles with the Indians in the Badlands and the Wounded Knee battle. He was returning to his reservation in the leisurely manner of the red man and had camped one night east of the Belle Fourche River in Meade County. While there he was visited by Pete Culbertson and another member of the family who could speak the Sioux language quite fluently, having associated with the Indians for many years.

Unfortunately for the Indians, They had with them some forty head of nice ponies which aroused the cupidity of Culbertson and before the end of the friendly pow wow with his hosts of the evening, he had conceived the plan of killing the whole group the next day and possessing himself of the ponies. Accordingly Pete Culbertson, Andrew Culbertson, Nelson Culbertson, James Juelfs, John Netland and Alva Martin knowing just what route the Indians would take on their journey, rode out around and ahead of them and secreted themselves at the mouth of the Alkali behind a deep cut bank. Here they awaited the approach of their victims who in due time came rumbling along in their several wagons and camping outfit, wholly unaware of the presence of the vipers who sought to sting them to death. When within about five rods of the steep bank, the rifle shots rang out and Few Tails dropped dead and one horse to his wagon. In the ensuing confusion of frightened horses the murderers were unable to inflict mortal wounds on the others and the Indian buck turned his team and fled up the divide. The white men ran to their horses and mounted them and galloped after the fleeing Indians, who fortunately escaped being killed by their volleys of bullets. He turned the reins of the team to his squaw and with a good Winchester rifle that he had, responded to the fire of his thieving guests with such accuracy as to compel them to remain beyond range and thus the fight continued on the run for several miles. The cowardly gang gave up the race here and hurried away for more help, well knowing that dead men tell no tales, and that they must wipe out the red man and his wife, or else they would lose the ponies and perhaps have to stand trial for their unwarranted acts. But by the time they had mustered a crowd under the false story of having been attacked by Indians escaped from the reservation, the lone fighter who had held the wolves at bay and saved the life of himself and wife, had reached Elk Creek where he abandoned his wagon outfit and mounting saddle horses, made a hurried ride to the reservation before the reinforced thieves could catch him and his squaw.

There happened to be at the home of Quinn near the scene of the fight, several soldiers at the time, and they sent a messenger to their comrade on the Cheyenne River and when he arrived at the Quinn home that evening, he directed one of the young Quinn boys to proceed to the scene of the attack and haul the wagon home. The young boy accordingly went to the wagon but noticed that the canvas had been tied to the front wagon wheels, which unusual position aroused his curiosity and he took the precaution to examine the interior of the wagon before moving it. Upon reaching his arm beneath the wagon cover, he was startled to feel the warm leg of a human being and he hurriedly left the scene of the tragedy. However, no further attention was paid to the incident until the next morning, but when the investigators arrived they found the wagon deserted and no one there except the dead Few Tails. A trail was found where a person had walked over the rough shaly hillsides towards the south, but it was lost as soon as the broad stretches of prairie with the tall grass upon them were reached, and the search was abandoned. It was the track of the wife of Few Tails who had been shot through the hip by one of the rifle balls and she had fallen to the bottom of the wagon box. She had remained in the wagon during the first shock of the battle, but when the hand of the boy had grasped her by the leg, she thought that the scoundrels were returning to complete their work of the morning. Finding herself alone once more and darkness coming, she painfully crawled from the wagon, bade farewell to the silent form of her brave and buoyed up by fear of the coming white men, painfully wandered on her way over hill and valley, across creek and gulch to the reservation, where she finally arrived and through the care of government surgeons, survived the harrowing experience.

The inhuman cruelty, the unjustified and treacherous crime called for investigation and when the woman had recovered, federal prosecution was instituted. However, the people had been wrought up to great heights of excitement by the wild rumors of Indian outrages, false stories of the Wounded Knee battle, and the act of renegade savages who had murdered four men in Ike Humphrey's cow camp on White River. So inflamed was the public mind that the trial became a mere travesty and the murderers were acquitted.

THE ROMANCE OF THE BIG HORN

Although preceding this event in point of time by many years, we will close this unhappy chapter by an account of an incident of 1877 taken from the files of the "Sidney Telegraph" then owned by Joe Gossage, and which so well portrays one of the many tragedies of those days:

"After leaving the mountains and striking into

the foot hills, we had travelled very slowly to let our horses pick up, and in fact we had no object in moving rapidly for we had formed no plans regarding our future movements. Some wanted to go one way, and others another. So, upon the whole, we concluded to keep on slowly in the direction we were then travelling for a few days, thinking we might run across the 'Roberts party,' who, we supposed were then in the mountains to the west of us. On the evening of the 25th, two of our party, who had been out hunting, came into camp and reported that they had heard firing all afternoon, and that they believed that someone was corraled by the hostiles, and also that they had struck two different trails leading in the direction of the firing, and that neither of them was apparently two hours old. Guards were posted and we turned in early fully expecting that our aid would be needed in the morning, and as fully determined that we would give it, and on the right side. Early morn found us in the saddle, moving as rapidly as our blundering guides permitted. About 9 o'clock we heard a number of shots to our right about a half mile distant. Putting our animals at their best speed we headed toward the point of a high bluff, on a dead run, and came immediately in view and in contact with about thirty-five Indians, some mounted and others on foot. We saw each other about the same moment, but the savages had a slight advantage, and got in the first fire, wounding one of our horses. The fight ended as suddenly as it was abruptly commenced—the Indians retiring in haste, as they usually do when getting the worst of it. Up to this time we had been unable to discover what had caused the firing. Moving to where we had first seen the redskins, we found five dead ponies, and in a little gully still further on, three dead Indians. Knowing that this was not our work, as the bodies were cold and had evidently been dead for hours, we commenced searching for the men, or man who had made such a desperate fight. Against the face of the bluffs, three hundred yards away, was a pile of rock, covering perhaps fifty or sixty yards in space, and as this seemed the most probable place for an attacked party to take shelter, we moved in that direction. When within twenty or thirty yards of the rocks we halted, and called to whoever might be there to come out, but receiving no answer, Mr. Travis and myself moved on the rocks in advance of the party.

Dismounting and hitching our horses to the brush we walked into the natural fortress. The first thing that attracted our attention was a dead horse with the saddle and bridle still on. Pausing only a moment we pressed on, looking for the rider. Ten or a dozen steps further on we found him—found him but that was all, for he was beyond all human aid. He bore upon every lineament of his countenance the appearance of rare intellectuality, and manhood.

The dead hero was about 26 or 27 years of age, of splendid physique, with dark hair and mustache, stained with his brain's blood. There he lay resting on his right side, with his head resting as though by chance upon a stone—as though God himself had laid him there in all his glory. There laid this silent hero, who for two eventful, desperate days, singlehanded had fought a band of desperate savages, and vainly scanned the plains and canyons for aid. God only knows what this silent western sentinel thought. He viewed death from the beginning as inevitable, for no man could withstand such an atttack and from the evidence before us we knew that the struggle had been as terrible as Custer's last fight on the Little Horn. Thirteen wounds proved it beyond all doubt. The right hand of this brave stranger held that which, in all probability, his gaze had rested upon when the dea'h rattle sounded in his throat—the picture of a very handsome young lady, taken by a Cottage Grove Avenue, Chicago, photographer. Attached •to this picture was a lock of light silky hair tied with a small piece of blue ribbon, and written upon the back was the following verse:

For deep in his heart where the shadows fall,
Is the grave of a love that is past recall,
And ever a face rose-wreathed and fair,
Will rise from the shadows to haunt him there.

Whether this lady was wife, sister or sweetheart, we could not tell but it was very evident that his last thoughts on earth were of her. Written at the bottom of the picture was the name, 'Mamie,' and again in a plain gold ring taken from his finger and engraved 'To Mamie' and opposite the word 'Mizpah.'

"We buried this stranger at sunrise the following morning, under the shade of a mountain pine, close to where he died. The picture and lock of hair were buried with him. No head-board marks his resting place, but before leaving the grave one of the party cut in deep letters on the tree,

MAMIE'S FRIEND,
Killed May 26, 1877

"He rests unwept in an unknown grave, like hundreds of other brave men who have died in the mountains, and whose relatives never knew their fate."

THE SONG OF THE VANISHED WEST

The Indians fought long and fiercely for their hunting grounds. The spirit of the struggle and the love of their broad prairies is much like the sentiments expressed by Charles Badger Clark, the poet of the Hills in his little poem to the cow boy of the west, which we are privileged to reprint here for our readers.

'Twas good to live when all the range
Without no fence or fuss
Belonged in partnership to God,
The Government and us.
With skyline bounds from east to west
And room to go and come;
I liked my fellowman the best
When he was scattered some.

When my old soul hunts range and rest
Beyond the last divide,
Just plant me in some strip of west
That's sunny, lone and wide.
Let cattle rub my headboard round
And coyotes wail their kin;
Let horses come and paw the mound
But don't you fence it in.

Peter Thompson

CHAPTER IV.

BATTLE OF THE BIG HORN

The year 1876 is one of the most eventful periods in the history of western events, for during this year occurred the Battle of the Big Horn, or what is sometimes called "Custer's Last Battle." There have been numerous varying accounts and stories told about this disastrous battle. Many of them are mere fairy tales and most of them are inaccurate and misleading. The present chapter will be devoted to an account of this great Indian fight, by one of the men who belonged to troops engaged, Peter Thompson, Troop C 7th U. S. Cavalry, commanded by Captain Tom Custer, a brother of General George A. Custer. Thompson was in his place with Troop C when Custer charged the Indians, but his horse gave out before the troop reached the main body of Indians and Thompson, with one other man was left behind From his position he could see his comrades in their struggle with the Indians, but was powerless to help them. After a perilous trip, he reached the Reno Command and remained with him through the rest of the battle, in which he distinguished himself for extraordinary bravery. He volunteered to get water for the wounded to relieve their terrible suffering, and was obliged to do this under fire from the Indians. In this dangerous work he was wounded severely, but despite his suffering and pain he made repeated trips to the river and brought water to his half-crazed wounded comrades. For this he was given a medal of honor for conspicuous bravery. Among his comrades he was regarded with the highest esteem and to his officers he was known as a good soldier. Today he is the only man living, who in fact, saw the dying struggles of the men of the 7th Cavalry. The account that is given here is absolutely true, and just as this man, this good soldier, the winner of the medal of honor, has related it in his own words.

"The headquarters of the 7th Cavalry was at Fort A. Lincoln. When we arrived at this place, General

Custer was absent, having been called to Washington, D. C., to give testimony in the famous Belknap case, and, to my mind, he was honest enough to tell the truth.

"General Grant was president of the United States at this time. After General Custer had given his testimony in the case, he was sent from Washington under arrest to report to the department commander of the Missouri, General A. Terry. Why this was done, none of us soldiers could understand, and neither did we believe that the real facts were made public. When the news came to Fort Lincoln that General Custer was under arrest it caused a great commotion among the soldiers. The various companies discussed the matter and all seemed to arrive at the same conclusion, namely, that it was spite on the part of President Grant. Two reasons were given for arriving at this conclusion, first, Grant's friendship for Belknap; second, Grant's desire to retaliate on Custer for his conduct to his son while on an expedition some time before. From what appeared to the men to be reliable information, Lieutenant Grant was continually getting under the influence of liquor, making it necessary for General Custer to place him under arrest, thus giving offense to the young man and also to his father who might not be fully informed as to the conduct of his son. But I only state the conclusions the men came to.

"During the absence of General Custer, Major Reno was in command at Fort Lincoln. While he was in command, our company suffered several severe reprimands. We were forced to the conclusion that his treatment of us was prompted by pure spite. Take a regiment of men isolated from civilization as we were, and there will always be found a number who will always show their animal spirits with singing, dancing, and shouting and having what they called a "general good time." This was the case in our company as well as the others. When our men were enjoying themselves in this manner, Reno would send his orderly to the orderly-sergeant of our company ordering him to stop the noise, whilst other companies were permitted to enjoy their hilarious fun. An order to the same effect was sent to us so frequently that our company longed for the return of General Custer. Whether it was a dislike to our company or to the Custers that made him cranky with us, I do not know, but the conclusion that the members of the company came to was that for the Custers, Major Reno had no love.

"Near the close of the month of March, our company was made happy by the return of Custer to his command. He had been released from his arrest at St. Paul, and made the journey from that place to Fort Lincoln by sled as the Northern Pacific railroad whose terminus at this time was Bismarck was blockaded with snow. Custer's first act on his return was to restore Frank Gerard to his old position as interpreter from which, during the commander's absence, he had been discharged by Major Reno.

"After Custer's return, we were not long in doubt as to our future plan of action. We were put to work and kept busy overhauling stores, sacking grain, etc. Wagon trains also began to arrive from other posts to be loaded with grain, food, ammunition, tents, packsaddles, and such other articles as are necssary for a campaign. The work was heavy, but we performed it cheerfully. The object of all this work and hurry was a matter of conjecture with us; we knew we were going to move, but in what direction was a secret to all but those in command. By the end of April everything was in order, preparations fully completed and the soldiers waiting for marching orders.

"On the fourth day of May, 1876, we moved out of our quarters and passed in review, marching around the post and thence towards our first camping place three miles below Fort Lincoln. We marched in the following order, cavalry first, artillery next, infantry next, the wagon train bringing up the rear.

"I might say that before we left the barracks, some of the members of our company formed in line one behind the other, and marched around and around inside the soldiers' quarters to the music of two bugles making noise enough to be heard by Major Reno. The object of this was to show that they held the former orders of the Major in contempt.

"All the companies of the 7th Cavalry converged at this point. While lying in camp here, we learned that the expedition formed, was against a large body of Indians which had left their different reservations stirred up and led by a turbulent warrior chief named Sitting Bull and other dissatisfied chiefs and squaw men.

"Our regiment was composed of twelve companies, about seventy men and officers composing a company. There were three majors, each commanding four companies. One colonel or general, as he is usually called, commanding the whole regiment. We were short two majors, several captains and lieutenants, the majors on sick leave namely, Majors Tilford and Merrill, the captains and lieutenants being on staff and other duties distant from this field of action. It is hardly possible to get the full strength of a regiment into the field as there is always some one on the sick list and others on detached service, and ours was no exception to the rule.

"On the 15th of May orders were given us to move to Hart River where we would meet the paymaster and receive our wages and all stragglers not going with the expedition would be cut off. But Oh! We here again met the blood sucking sutler with his vile whiskey, rotten tobacco, and high priced notions. It was plain to be seen that he would reap a rich harvest on this expedition.

"General Terry had joined us at Fort Lincoln, hence the expedition was under his command. Terry was a gentleman in every respect, he exercised very little of his authority on the march but let General Custer have charge of it.

"During the earlier part of the expedition, it rained quite often making the advance of the wagon train slow and tedious. The train was composed of about one hundred and sixty wagons, twenty of which belonged to citizens and some of their stock became so weak that it was all they could do to haul their empty wagons. When we came to a long hill, a muddy place, or a ford we had to get ropes and help them out of their difficulty. What a nuisance they were! A Government team consisted of six powerful mules to each wagon and they very seldom got into a place out of which they could not pull. There were places where we had to build bridges and grade approaches before we could cross, a work which ought to have been done by each company in turn. But this was not the case. The captain of our company, Tom Custer, was on his brother's staff. Lieutenant Calhoun was in command of Company E and this left Lieutenant Harrison in command of our company. He had us at nearly every bridge, building or road grading until we began to grumble and in no undertone either. Our dissatisfaction became so pronounced that one day Major Reno overheard us. The next time our company was brought up by Harrington, Major Reno ordered us to the rear. Were we sorry? Not much.

"As we travelled over the trackless prairie, we came across the trail made by Stanley when in conjunction with Custer in '73, he drove the Sioux across the Yellowstone River. We followed this trail until we came to the Little Missouri River where we camped some time for the purpose of constructing a crossing over the river and scouting up the river.

"Major Reno being the only officer of that rank in the expedition while on the march was in command of the right wing, and Captain Benteen who was senior captain was in charge of the left wing. Each wing camped in separate but parallel lines.

"It was about the 20th of May that we came to the Little Missouri River. While here Custer took Company C up the river to look for signs of Indians. We passed over a very rough country and were compelled on that account to cross the river many times, making it very hard on our horses. They had to clamber up the slippery banks and on recrossing to slide down into the river with their legs braced. The distance we travelled was 22 miles, the only sign of Indians we saw was a camp some months old. So we retraced our weary way and arrived in camp late at night with our horses completely tired out.

"We had along with our expedition two companies of Infantry and while crossing streams they would climb onto the wagons like bees on a hive. The poor fellows had a hard time of it when the days were hot or when it rained. General Terry suggested to Captain Sangers of one of the Infantry companies that when the ground was favorable he should allow his men to ride on the wagons. Captain Sangers replied that his men could walk thirty miles a day and run an antelope at night. But we all noticed that he clung close to his saddle during the march. It was all nice enough for a captain of Infantry on horseback with his men following behind him to speak thus. All the soldiers would like to have seen him on foot after making such a remark.

"The first day's march after leaving the river was very disagreeable for it rained all day. On the 22nd of May, we came in sight of the Badlands which at a distance presented a curious and pretty appearance. Some parts of them looked fiery red, others dark brown and black. What brought about this freak of nature, I cannot tell. There has been much speculation about it by travellers; some think that it was underlaid by a bed of coal, which in some way caught fire, burning, upheaving, and throwing the surface into all manner of shapes, but others think that it is of volcanic formation. Roads there were none and where water was found it was very bad on account of the alkali it contained. We were two days constructing a road for the passage of the wagons. While the rest of the regiment were busily engaged constructing the road, a company of infantry, for the country was almost impassable to horses, was deployed on both sides of us as skirmishers. We were very glad when we reached the open prairie. Timber is seldom seen in this country; a few cottonwoods along the streams and red pine on the bluffs being all there is and sometimes not even in these places was food to be found.

"The first camping place after leaving the Badlands found us without wood, but by dint of hard rustling and breaking up extra wagon tongues and such other odds and ends as we could find we managed to warm some coffee and cook some salt meat.

"As we approached the Powder River, the country began to be very rough and broken. When about 15 miles from the river, General Custer took half of our company and dashed off towards it. His object was to find as easy and direct a route as possible. We rode in this mad way for nearly an hour when we came to a halt. Riding up to one of our corporals named French, Custer told him to take a man and ride in a certain direction where he would find a spring of water and ascertain what condition it was in. Custer then wheeled his horse around and dashed away in a westerly direction, leaving us standing at our horses' heads until his return. Custer's brother, Tom, was the only one who went with him. This action would have seemed strange to us had it not been of almost daily occurrence. It seemed that the man was so full of nervous energy that it was impossible for him to move along patiently. Sometimes he was far in advance of all others, then back to his command; then he would dash off again followed by his orderly named Bishop, who tried in vain to keep Custer in sight. He would either return to us again or seek an elevation where he could catch a glimpse of the general dashing ahead over the country and try to intercept him on his way back. General Custer had two thorough-bred horses, one a sorrel and one a dark brown, and no common government plug had any show whatever to keep up with them when he was riding full speed. He also had a number of greyhounds for hunting purposes and many a chase he and his brother had when on this march. But after we crossed the Powder River hunting ceased.

"Corporal French soon returned looking very foolish. General Custer rode up to him and said, 'Did

you find the spring?' 'No, sir,' said French 'There is
no spring there.' 'You are a liar,' said Custer, 'If you
had gone to where I told you, you would have found
it.' He spoke in such a positive manner that we felt
sorry for poor Corporal French, for Custer knew the
country well, even better than the scouts, who were
hired by the government to guide the expedition. We
had two scouts along with us, one named Chas.
Reynolds, a quiet and dignified man. He led the
wagon train, piloting it and avoiding all bad places;
a better scout for a white man would be hard to find;
his mount was invariably a grey mule. The other one
was a half breed named Mich Burey who was well
informed regarding the country. He had crossed this
part of the country before, hiding during the daytime and travelling at night for fear of the Sioux
who were jealous of all strangers. With the expedition also were twenty-four Ree scouts, and a dirtier
set of rascals would be hard to find. Their interpreter was a half breed named Frank Gerard, and their
chief guide was Billy Jackson also of Indian extraction. But of these we will have more to say by and by.

"But to come back to the story. While we were
waiting and speculating as to our next move, Lieutenant Cook, adjutant of the 7th Cavalry and a member
of Custer's staff, rode up and said that it was General
Terry's desire that we should go into camp and not
attempt too long a march. So we went back and
found the regiment in its camping place for the night.

"On the following day we continued our march
and arrived at Powder River early in the forenoon.
Immediately a scouting party was formed composed
of the six companies B, C, E, F, G, and L, which was
all of the right wing. These were commanded by
Major Reno. Each company was provided with a
sufficient number of mules to carry the necessary provisions and ammunition. I do not think that there
were half a dozen men in the scouting party who knew
how to pack a mule without having its pack work
loose. But fortunately there were five citizens along
with us who knew the business and the boys soon

learned to lash a pack saddle and load securely. After two days of preparation, this scouting party started off in a northwesterly direction. The only wheeled affair we had was a large Gatling gun drawn by four horses.

"On this scout as well as on the expedition proper, we saw a great deal of game; such as antelope, rabbits and a few deer, the last named prefer to graze in the night time. The old soldiers remarked upon the absence of buffalo; but we arrived at the conclusion that the Indians, who were in the neighborhood had driven them into bunches farther west of our position. Our progress with mules was comparatively easy, but sometimes they became a little too sociable. One day we made our way through some pine covered hills; the trail was so narrow that the horses were jostling and jamming one another all the time. A mule, belonging to Company B, jammed the leg of one of our men between his saddle and a cracker box on its load. This hurt the man severely and in order to ease off the pressure he struck the mule on the nose, causing it to jump to one side. Captain McDugal of Company B, seeing this spurred forward and threatened to pull the man from his horse. It was well for him that he did not undertake to carry out his threat for there certainly would have been trouble.

"The third day after leaving Powder River, we came to Rosebud Creek. The first night here our company was fortunate enough to secure a good camping place. But our good fortune was of short duration for Major Reno sent orders for us to exchange places with Company F. We knew it was an outrage upon us, but Company F outranking us, their captain being with them, we had to comply. If Captain Custer had been with us it might have been different, but Lieutenant Harrington had more sense than grit.

"But so that I may be clearly understood, let me describe how we go into camp. Suppose Company C is next to headquarters; the other companies follow by twos. This is much better than by fours, as in the latter case the center horses are much worried by the outside ones. Company C would first be ordered to front into line, dismount, and unsaddle. Then the next company would pass by and take its position next to Company C and so on until at last the first company would finally become last and the last, first. When the march commenced again, Company C would be the last to start and the others following, all would regain their former positions. It is a recognized rule that when the regiment goes into camp, the companies take whatever position falls to them whether it be good or bad. When we exchanged places with Company F we got a poor camping place and a miserable sage brush to graze our horses on. You can imagine the feelings of our company when this exchange took place. The laws of the United States Army recognize in every commissioned officer, a gentleman; but all officers are not such. You cannot make a gentleman of a hog whether inside or out of the United States Army.

"Near the close of our first day's march up the Rosebud, we struck the trail of a large body of Indians, who seemed to be going in the same direction as ourselves. The trail was wide and so torn up by tepee poles that we found it a difficult matter to secure a good camping place for the night. This was especially so around watering places which were so necessary to us.

"On the 13th of June we commenced following the trail. Rosebud Creek undoubtedly derives its name from the fact that its banks are covered with rose bushes. At this season of the year, the air was laden with the odor of the roses and but for the fact that we were on business our march in its vicinity would have been pleasant.

"When the day's march was over, and we had moved into camp, orders were given that no bugles were to be blown, no loud noise was to be made, and double pickets were to be placed around our camp. Our scout which was Mich Burey was of the opinion that we could overtake the Indians in a day's march. We began to speculate as to what Major Reno would do. When morning dawned, all doubt regarding the Major's action disappeared; for he faced to the rear and began to march toward the Yellowstone River. When we reached it we found the water high and muddy; but we secured a very pretty camping place and plenty of grazing for our horses which they so badly needed. Our horses had become quite jaded; for our grain had all been consumed and the grazing had been poor; and the load that a cavalry horse has to carry is not light. Besides his rider and saddle, he has to carry an overcoat, extra blanket, one-half of a dog tent, one hundred rounds of ammunition, gun, pistol, and several days' ration. We had left our Gatling gun a few miles in the rear on a high, abrupt hill. We found it impossible to bring it down without the aid of ropes. Next day, a party of men were sent out with the necessary appliances to bring it in; a messenger was also dispatched to the headquarters of the 7th Cavalry, which was at this time at the mouth on Tongue River. Here also the wagon train was parked.

"Major Reno wished to receive instructions regarding his future actions. In due time, we received orders to remain where we were and that the headquarters would join us next day. Accordingly on June 20th the 7th Cavalry was united again. The wagon train was to remain where it was protected by two companies of infantry. The companies which had joined us brought pack mules. Our transportation facilities were very slim. We were to be supplied with fifteen days' rations from a steam boat named the 'Far West,' which was expected at our camping place on the 21st inst. The companies composing the left wing which had now joined us were A, D, H, I, K, and M. It was understood when the right wing left the Powder River for the scout under Reno that on its return the left wing was to take its turn on a scout providing we failed to discover anything. But the scouting trip under Reno had proven somewhat of a success. We now began to brace up for a rough trip; for all the men knew that General Custer if left to his own devices would soon end the campaign one way or another. Custer and some other of the officers were anxious to witness the opening of the Centennial Exposition at Philadelphia in July, 1876. It was reported among us that when General Terry and Custer joined us on the banks of the Yellowstone and confirmed by those in position to know that when Reno made his report concerning the discovery of the Indian trail and the supposed direction in which they were removing, General Custer upbraided him very bitterly for not finding out the exact number and the direction the Indians were taking instead of supposing and guessing. There were some sharp questions and short answers; but General Terry interposed and smoothed the matter over. The plan of action in this case seemed to be that General Custer was to take the 7th Cavalry and try to intercept the Indians and prevent them from going any further, while General Terry was to go up the Yellowstone to the place where Gillon's Infantry and part of the 2nd Cavalry were encamped, move them over to the west bank of the river and march to the assistance of Custer. What orders Custer received from Terry is merely a matter of speculation; but it seems to me that Custer was to use his own judgment as the case might require.

"On the forenoon of the 21st the 'Far West' arrived with our needed supplies and soon numbers of us were helping to unload them. But the article most anxiously inquired after was plug tobacco and with few exceptions all used it.

"On the afternoon of the 22nd the 7th Cavalry was ready to move. There were about 140 mules packed with 15 days' rations for the twelve companies. The Gatling gun which Major Reno had taken with him on the scout was placed on the steamboat. This was one of the first blunders of the expedition as later events proved.

"The whistle of the 'Far West' as it left the bank of the river brought forth a cheer from the throats of the 7th Cavalry. Custer rushed along the bank and motioned for the boat to put back to the landing. When this was done he leaped aboard and lugged Mich Burey ashore amid the cheers of our command. Mich was very popular, not only for his quiet demeanor but on account of his knowledge of the country He always inspired us with confidence.

During this exciting episode, many of the soldiers climbed up into the cottonwood trees which lined the bank of the river and placed their overcoats in convenient forks and crotches making them as secure as possible so that they would not be dislodged by the wind. They gave all manner of excuses for their conduct, namely, that they were going to travel so fast that it would take them all their time to keep their hats on, etc. But the true reason was to lessen the burden their horses had to carry. But I kept mine as I had grave doubts of our ever returning that way and future events proved my doubts to be correct.

The steamboat with General Terry on board had hardly started up the river again before we were on our way to victory or death. A very solemn feeling seemed to settle down upon the men from this time. Numbers of us felt that when Custer took active charge of the expedition there would be no more funny work. He meant business. Some of the men knew by previous experience that when General Custer turned himself loose, he made things hum. Some of our men had served under Custer in his Kansas campaign against the Indians.

In Colorado while lying in camp, numbers of cavalry men deserted, some in a sneaking way under the cover of night, others in broad day light. The latter would ride off with the government horses, until his strength was considerably depleated. Custer saw that the only way to stop this wholesale desertion was to use some harsh measures.

"One day it was reported to him that a few more men had deserted. He took a body guard, mounted on good horses and started in pursuit. The deserters were soon overhauled. Without words to the deserters he ordered his men to fire into them. They did so, killing some and wounding others. This had a tendency to stop desertion for some time.

"There is another story regarding him to the effect that when on the Black Hills expedition his brother, Tom, overslept himself and consequently failed to report his company. Presently Custer walked to his brother's tent and set fire to the high dry grass which surrounded it. It is needless to say that Captain Custer got out of his sleep and his tent in double quick time.

"These seemed harsh measures but we must remember that at that time the country was full of hostile Indians ever ready to take advantage of any slackness of discipline or to cut off any who had the misfortune to stray away from the command. But we do not approve of such extreme measures.

"As we are now approaching the most important period of the expedition, I will endeavor to give as accurate an account of it as possible.

"In the first place you will notice that we started from the Yellowstone River on the afternoon of the 22nd of June, General Custer in command of the 7th Cavalry, General Terry on board the steamer, the 'Far West;' the object of the latter's mission I have already stated.

"We travelled about fifteen miles that afternoon, then moved into camp. Orders were given that no bugles were to be blown; no firing of guns and no straggling were to be allowed. It may seem rather early for such precaution to be taken; we had not seen any Indians, and so far no settlers had put in their appearance. And all through that hard campaign the unbroken prairies and hills were as bare of human habitation as an iceberg is of grass.

"The only evidence we had that white men had ever been in that country was some pegs driven in the ground by Northern Pacific surveyors, which we found just before reaching the Yellowstone.

"On the 23rd of June we moved over a very rough piece of country. While moving along the ridge of an abrupt hill a laughable incident occurred. One of our men named Bennett was mounted on a bob-tailed horse which had proven to be very tricky. While crossing a shelving rock, overhanging a deep and rocky gorge, the horse stood stock still and lifting up the right hind foot began to scratch his ear. Bennett looked around helplessly; first down the rocky gorge and then at his laughing comrades. As soon as he could he induced his horse to stop combing his ear and edged away from that locality.

"Then one of our mules named Barnum, stumbled and fell, and went rolling down the hill with two boxes of ammunition on his back. As we watched him rolling we made some calculations as to how much mule would be left in case the ammunition exploded. But contrary to all, expectations, when he reached the bottom of the hill, he scrambled to his feet again with both boxes undisturbed and made his way up the hill again and took his place in the line as soberly and quietly as if nothing had happened.

"We camped that night on Beaver Creek where we found plenty of bad water, but good grazing for our horses. It kept them busy to fill themselves up after they were picketed out, for we made very long marches. Custer seemed tireless himself and seemed to think his men were made of the same stuff.

"It is a hard sight to see men, who have been roused out of their sleep at half past three in the morning; not only once but day after day, sleeping in their saddles; and lucky indeed was the man who had a quiet and steady horse that allowed the luxury of a sleep while travelling. I often took a nap in that way although my horse was a very restless brute.

"On June 24th we reached the Rosebud again where we moved into camp. There were numerous beaver dams in this stream and at this point the country was so flat that one of the dams would back the water for a considerable distance only to be succeeded by another of similar construction.

"We received orders in a quiet way to be ready to move that night at twelve o'clock, for the purpose of crossing the divide which separates the Rosebud from the Little Horn River.

"The men began to ask one another if they were going to travel all the time. We then made preparations for a short nap. No canvas was stretched; no mules were unpacked except those which were carrying the necessary supplies for supper.

"It was on this same stream (the Rosebud) that ten days before, General Crook had a slight skirmish with the Indians. It is said that he was driven from his camp leaving behind him two raw recruits who fell into the hands of the Indians. The poor fellows, thinking that mercy would be shown them, handed their arms to the Indians; but what mercy these savages have in their breasts has yet to be discovered. It is needless to say that the Indians killed them in a most shocking manner. This was done in sight of General Crook's command. It may seem strange to some that the command could see this outrage committed without trying to rescue them. But if we take General Crook's career as an Indian fighter we will be forced to the conclusion that he was a failure.

When midnight came you may be sure we moved promptly. Each company had to lead its own pack mules; it was too dark to see to drive; no moon; simply the faint starlight to guide us. We kept at a lively gait for three hours.

"As soon as the first faint streaks of daylight appeared we moved into a group where we were ordered to unsaddle and rest for several hours. A picket line was thrown out and each company detailed some of their own men for the purpose of guarding their own horses and pack mules. No canvas was stretched for shelter as we knew our stay would be comparatively short. Each man made a pillow of his saddle, and a mattress of his saddle blanket and overcoat, if he had an overcoat. As it was warm, covering was unnecessary. We laid as much as possible under trees and shrubbery, as a person always feels more secure under some sort of shelter. This probably arises from force of habit rather than from any real security.

"I will state here that I am too hard-headed to believe in dreams, but will here relate one which, in spite of my unbelief, disturbed me. I laid down under a tree and had fallen into a doze when I dreamed that the Indians attacked a small detachment of us soldiers. We were all dismounted and the Indians put us to flight. At this point I awoke expecting to find it real, but seeing the outstretched forms of my comrades, I composed myself and laid down to sleep again. But my dream instead of being cut off by my awaking began to run in the same channel, only this time I alone was the victim. An Indian with an uplifted axe came after me; there was no skulking but a fair and square race, and for the life of me I could not tell why I ran from the Indian. Just as the savage got close enough to me to strike I awoke only to find all vanish into thin air. But so profoundly had the dream impressed itself upon me that I could get no more sleep. Getting up I strolled through the camp looking at the horses and noting how poor and gaunt they were becoming. This was not to be wondered at when we take into account the long marches they had made without any grain to sustain their strength; nothing but dead grass or perhaps a little green grass which was very short at this season of the year.

I also noted the pickets that were thrown out to prevent a surprise. Of all duties picket guard is the most important and responsible while camping in an enemy's country. He has ever to be on the alert whether standing, sitting, or lying down. The latter position is the most preferable as he can see an object quicker and tell its character quicker than in either of the other positions.

"On this expedition the picket's orders were never to challenge anyone approaching from the outside as all such were considered enemies unless specially ordered. Picket duty is very lonesome, but as we said before, very responsible. He not only has his own personal safety to look after, but also the safety of hundreds of others. He has his regular beat to look after, the number of pickets being regulated by the distance they are removed from the command.

"There is also a guard placed over the horses whose duty it is to see that none are taken away by anyone without an order from the officers of the company, or should any break loose from their picket ropes, to secure them before guard is relieved, which change is made every two hours.

"This morning the soldiers were lying in every conceivable manner, when canvas was not stretched.

"Early as it was, General Custer and two of his staff, namely, Captain Custer and Lieutenant Cook, were in earnest conversation. What the subject of their conversation was no one will ever know, but it must have been of deep interest to them, for the interview lasted quite a long time.

"The mules were all unpacked and grazing at will. The water was very bad, being full of alkali. At half past six, the cook was awakened to prepare breakfast for the men, and that meal consisted simply of coffee, bacon, and hardtack; a kind of provision all old soldiers are well acquainted with.

It was half past eight o'clock when we moved out of camp. This was on the morning of the 25th of June, 1876, a day I will never forget as long as I live. Our gait was a lively walk. Having had a few hours sleep the men began to be talkative, and speculation ran high on how soon the campaign would end. One old soldier said that it would end just as soon as we could reach old Sitting Bull. Another said, 'If that is all, the campaign will soon be over, and Custer will take us with him to the Centennial.' 'Of course,' said a wag, 'we will take Sitting Bull with us.' This created a roar of laughter among those who heard him. The conversation continued; each one telling his neighbor what he would take when Sitting Bull's camp was captured.

"While still joking and laughing we came to one of the camping places of the Indians. Here we came to a halt for the purpose of noting the extent of the camp, and by this means to approximate the number of

Indians in the party. After wandering around we found that but a small party had made this their camping place, but from all appearances they must have had 'a high old time.'

"They had placed in the ground four upright posts upon which they had made a small platform of the limbs of trees. On this they had placed the heads of several buffaloes and from the appearance of the ground they must have had what is called a buffalo dance.

"A short distance from this place, one of the members of Company C found two scalps dangling from a short willow which had been stuck in the ground. From the appearance of the hair one scalp belonged to a man and the other a woman. The hair on both scalps was light in color.

"Our stay here was of short duration, and we began to follow what appeared to be a valley stretching out between two low lying ranges of hills, this dipped toward the Little Horn River. By following this valley, we were well protected by the hills on either side. Our progress was unhindered and we moved rapidly along feeling that there was something ahead of us that we must see.

"We had not travelled a very great distance before we came upon a large camping place which the Indians had evidently vacated but a few days before. While here, they had rounded up and slaughtered quite a number of buffalo, and then moved further down the valley.

"Our next resting place was in a deep depression of the valley. Custer rode some distance ahead of us and then turning to the right ascended to the highest point of the hills where he must have been able to see a long distance. He was not long in returning; and then the bugle was blown for the first time for a number of days. It was a call for the officers and they soon gathered around their chief. Frank Gerard so far forgot himself as to go and sit down near the place where the consulting officers were gathered. General Custer looked at him and said, 'Go where you belong, and stay there.' He did not wait for a second bidding. It was Custer's desire to keep every man in his proper place. This was perfectly right as in military life there must be discipline.

"Our company was resting quite close to the place where the officers sat in council. This resting place was on a piece of ground slightly elevated above the officers' position which, for the first time on the expedition, gave me an opportunity of seeing the officers all together and of noting their appearances. The most noticeable among them was Captain Benteen. He was senior captain of the regiment. There were also present, Yates, Kehoe, Custer, McDugal, Smith, Ware French, Moline, Lieutenant Cook, adjutant of the regiment on Custer's staff; Calhoun, MacIntosh, Varnum, Wallace, Harrington, Agerly, Sturgis, and other officers whose names I have entirely forgotten. It would be difficult to find a finer set of officers in the service of any country. From the manner of the conversation it would seem as though Custer had discovered something that was of great importance. We could not hear the conversation, but we could see that they were all deeply interested. The younger officers did not seem to take any part in the conversation but paid great attention while Custer and the more experienced officers were seeking to solve some difficult problem.

"In a short time the council broke up and once more we were on the move down the valley. As we proceeded the signs of Indians became more and more numerous. As these signs increased in numbers, Bloody Knife, one of the chiefs of the Ree Indians, became greatly excited, and his followers partook of his spirit and became excited also.

"While we were at the Yellowstone, six Crow Indians joined us, Half Yellow Face being their head man. The Sioux and Crows were bitter enemies and were continually fighting one another as opportunity offered. The Crows had held the country between the Big Missouri and the Yellowstone, but the restless Sioux had driven them slowly but surely back to the confines of the Yellowstone where they made their last stand and with the aid of the government kept the Sioux in check. The Crows, therefore, were ever ready to accompany any expedition that would afford them an opportunity to strike a blow at their old enemies. The government generally placed confidence in their friendship.

"Water was exceedingly scarce in the valley but as we knew that the latter was short we had hopes of something better when we got out of it.

"We found, as we proceeded, that the camping places of the Indians were but a short distance apart showing that they were travelling in a leisurely manner for the purpose of giving their ponies an opportunity to feed; or it might have been that each tribe camped by itself. But be that as it may, the ground was eaten quite bare in most places, showing that they must have had a great number of animals with them. One of their camps must have been broken up in confusion for numerous articles were left behind; such as coffee pots, tin plates, cups, axes, hatchets, and other articles that were good for further use. These articles were scattered about from one end of the camp to the other.

"The sight of these things puzzled us greatly. Was it for the purpose of lightening their burdens that they might travel the quicker, or for transporting the buffalo that they had slaughtered, or was it a hasty flight? These questions we could not answer.

"We had just passed through this camping ground when we discovered a single tepee standing near a large clump of cottonwood trees. The sight of this tepee caused a commotion among us. Lieutenant Cook rode rapidly up to Major Reno, giving him orders to take three companies of the left wing, cross the Little Horn River to its left bank and proceed down that stream. He then ordered a detail of Company F which was in advance with headquarters to investigate and find out the contents of the tepee. This left Captain Benteen with three companies of the left wing and one of the right, as Captain McDugal's company was rear guard and had charge of the pack train. General Custer then took Companies C, E, F, G, and L intending to go down the right bank of the stream, under cover if possible. We soon learned that a large band of Indians were in camp a short distance down the river. The plan marked out was to attack the Indians in the following manner: Major Reno was to cross the river to its left bank and proceed down until he struck their village and endeavor to keep the attention of the Indians until Custer had time to pass down the right bank and cross over and attack them in the rear.

"On the left side of the river the country was flat, on the right it was very rough and broken; there was a low range of hills cut up by numerous intersecting ravines.

"It was Custer's intention to keep out of sight of the Indians until he had time to cross over the river, three miles below. After Reno left us we commenced to travel in parallel lines with the Little Horn River, which was thickly screened by cottonwood trees and underbrush.

"We now left the valley in which we had been travelling and commenced to climb the bluffs overlooking the river and surrounding country. At this time our horses were in a trot. At our right, and on a slight elevation, sat General Custer and his brother, Tom, reviewing the companies as they passed by. This was the last review General Custer ever held. Cook, the adjutant, was giving orders wherever Custer deemed it necessary. When we reached the top of the hill, we were ordered to form into sets of fours which would make us a more solid and compact body. Each one was told to remember his number. Let me explain the meaning of numbers.

"In the morning before mounting the companies form in single lines. Each man, commencing at the head of the company, calls out in turn his number; one, two, three, four, and so these are repeated until the company is all numbered into sets of fours. Cavalry men dismount and fight on foot except when a charge is made, but when a dismount is ordered, number four remains on his horse; numbers one, two and three dismount and hand their bridle reins to number four who holds the horses, while they deploy as skirmishers or as otherwise directed. The men composing the four with myself were Fitzgerald, Brennan, and Watson, and although composing one of the sets of fours that entered into action with Custer, not one of us ever reached the battlefield which proved so fatal to Custer and his men. Both Brennan and Fitzgerald turned their horses toward the rear, when they had gone two miles beyond the lone tepee.

"We soon gained the top of the bluffs where a view of the surrounding country was obtained. The detail of Company F which was sent to investigate the tepee, now passed by us on their way to the front with the report that it contained a dead Indian and such articles as were deemed necessary for him on his journey to the 'Happy Hunting Grounds.'

"About a half a mile further on we came in sight of the Indian village, and it was a truly imposing sight to anyone who had not seen anything like it before. For about three miles on the left bank of the river the tepees were stretched, the white canvas gleaming in the sunlight. Beyond the village was a black mass of ponies grazing on the short green grass.

"When the companies came in sight if the village, they gave the regular charging yell and urged their horses into a gallop. At this time a detail of five men from Company F was sent ahead to reconnoiter and from this point I was gradually left behind in spite of all I could do to keep up with my company. There were others also in the same fix. All urging on my part was useless. Getting vexed I dismounted and begun to fasten on my spurs, when I heard my name called and, on looking up, I saw Brennan near me on horseback. He asked, 'What is the matter?' I told him that I was afraid my horse was entirely played out. 'Well,' said he, 'Let us keep together.' I straightened myself up and said, 'I tell you what I will do I will trade horses with you if you will.' He gave me a strange look and turned his horse around and rode towards the rear, leaving me to shift for myself. 'Well,' I thought, 'I will get along any way.' I finished putting on my spurs, mounted my horse again. and rode on after my company, but my progress was very slow.

"My spurs having been poorly fastened came off again, and seeing a pair lying on the trail, I got off my horse to secure them. Hearing an oath behind me, I looked back and saw my comrade Watson, trying to get his horse on its feet. The poor brute had fallen and was struggling to gain an upright position. Beside him, I saw Sergeant Finkle of our company sitting calmly on his horse looking on and making no effort to help Watson in his difficulty. But finally the poor animal gained his feet with a groan, and Finkle passed on with a rush to overtake our company.

"By this time the last of the companies had disappeared over the crest of the hill I was still tugging away at the spurs, when Watson came up and asked what the trouble was and then passed on in the trail of the soldiers. I mounted my horse again but found that a staggering walk was all I could get out of him.

"I then began to look around; everywhere the hurry and bustle of life had disappeared; the only evidence of life was a cloud of dust which was gradually disappearing.

"I then looked across the river at the Indian village; it was all in commotion. One party of Indians were dashing down the river; others were hurrying towards their ponies; others were rushing toward the upper end of the village. The cause of this commotion was Major Reno with three companies of men about a mile distant from the upper end of the village, dashing along in a gallop towards them. The officers were riding in order a little in advance of their respective companies. It was a grand sight to see those men charging down upon the village of their enemies, who outnumbered them many times. The well-trained horses were kept well in hand. There was no straggling; they went together, neck and neck, their tails streaming in the wind and the riders' arms gleaming in the sunlight. It was no wonder that the Indians were in great commotion when they beheld the bold front presented by the cavalry. But alas! how deceptive are appearances. The cavalry dashed into the village where one of the non-commissioned officers halted and struck up the company's guidon along side of a tepee before he was shot from his horse. The halt was but for a moment, for the Indians came rushing toward them in great numbers. At this juncture the dry grass caught on fire threatening the destruction of the village, but the squaws, fearless as the braves themselves, fought the fire and tore down the tepees which were in danger of burning. Major Reno seeing that he was greatly outnumbered ordered an immediate retreat to a grove of cottonwood trees, which stood on the bank of the river about half a mile from the upper end of the village, where they found shelter for their horses and protection for themselves.

"Major Reno dismounted his men in the usual manner; number four remaining on horseback to hold the horses of the others. A skirmish line was formed, which advanced to the edge of the timber, to await the enemy who soon appeared in great numbers. The shots exchanged were few, and here, to my mind, is where Major Reno made a blunder. Instead of secreting his men, as he should have done, he ordered them to mount their horses, and led a retreat which not only proved fatal to a number of his own men, but also to Custer. Had he remained where he was he would undoubtedly have held a great number of the Indians in check. Although his numbers were less his advantages were greater. The grove of timber was not so large but that his men could have defended all of it and by this means engaged a sufficient number of Indians to give General Custer an opportunity to cross over the river and come to his assistance by attacking the Indians in the rear. As I have before mentioned, Major Reno led the retreat toward the river and across it and up to the top of the bluff. In

THE BLACK HILLS TRAILS 157

crossing the river, there was great confusion; each man seemed to be for himself. Here Lieutenant MacIntosh and numbers of others were shot from their horses.

"After Major Reno gained the top of the hill, he was joined by Captain Benteen with his three companies; likewise by Captain McDugal with the pack train making seven companies besides twenty men of the right wing who had been detailed to attend to pack mules of the right wing.

"All the above transpired in a very short space of time.

"Meanwhile I was pursuing my way along the trail on foot leading my horse, for I was afraid he would fall down under me, so stumbling and staggering was his gait.

"After the disappearance of Custer and his men, I felt that I was in a terrible predicament to be left practically alone in an enemy's country, leading a horse practically useless.

"While meditating upon the combination of circumstances which had brought me into this unhappy condition, I looked ahead and saw Watson but was unable to overtake him slow as he was going. He suddently turned aside from the trail as if he wished to avoid some threatening danger. While I was wondering what it could be, I saw a small party of Indians, about thirty in number, driving a small bunch of ponies and mules, coming towards me. I thought my time had surely come as it was too late to retreat.

"While I was making calculations as to leaving my horse and trying my luck on foot, I thought I saw something familiar in their appearance. On coming close, I saw they were our Ree scouts and two Crow Indians, one of whom was Half Yellow Face or Two Bloody Hands. He had received this latter name from the fact that on the back of his buckskin shirt the print of two human hands was visible, either put there by red paint or blood.

"When close enough I gave them to understand the condition I was in and asked for an exchange of mount. Half Yellow Face only shook his head and said, 'Heap Sioux, heap Sioux, heap shoot, heap shoot, come," and motioned for me to go back with them. I shook my head and answered, 'No.' They made their way to the rear and I went on ahead. The animals the scouts had they had captured from the Sioux.

"I had lost sight of Watson and thinking that I could make my horse go faster by mounting him I did so. I had not gone far before I became aware of the fact that I had company. When I had nearly gained the top of the hill, I saw five Sioux Indians. We discovered each other about the same time. Three of them turned aside and rode toward my rear. The other two brought their guns to their shoulders and aimed at me. Almost instantly my carbine was at my shoulder, aiming at them; but it was empty; while in the ranks or on horse back, I made it a practice to carry it empty. There we sat aiming at one another; the Indians did not fire and I couldn't. True, my revolver was loaded, but I was not fool enough to take my chances, one against five.

"After aiming at me for a few seconds, they slid off their ponies and sneaked after the other three. I now looked around to see how I was going to make my escape, I knew I could not retreat; with five I could not cope, and within the last few moments a few more Indians had gained the trail ahead of me; and to make my way down the face of the bluff, I knew was nearly impossible, as the Indians were climbing up to gain the trail.

"Looking to my right, I saw a ravine and at the bottom of it a small clump of wild cherry bushes. But beyond and on a higher elevation than on which I stood was a pillar of rocks, which I thought might afford me a means of defense. I knew I would have to act quickly if I was to save my life, so dismounting from my horse, which had carried me so many miles, I dashed down into the ravine toward the bushes; but the sudden flight of a flock of birds from that point caused me to turn aside and I made a bee line for the pillar of rocks above me. After arriving there I took an inventory of my ammunition. My pistol contained five cartridges, my belt contained seventeen cartridges for my carbine, a very slim magazine as a means of defense. I had left nearly a hundred rounds in my saddle bags, but owing to the incomplete condition of my prairie belt I was unable to carry more with me.

"Belts for carrying ammunition were, at this time, just coming into use, and a great many of us had nothing but a small cartridge box as means of carrying our ammunition when away from our horses.

"I was disappointed with my place of defense, I found that the pillar was barely eighteen inches through; it was about seven feet high with a piece of rotten cottonwood on top. It had been built by Indians for some purpose or other.

"After completing my inventory, I sat down and began to reflect on my chances for life, if I remained where I was. I knew that if the cavalry drove the savages from their village, they would scatter in all directions, and if any of the straggling devils came across such an unfortunate as myself, I would stand a poor show. I looked back toward the trail where I left my horse; he was still in the same place with an Indian riding around him. I thought that if he was going to be stripped, it was a pity that the ammunition I had left should fall into the hands of an enemy.

"I thought that my time for action had again arrived and that I had better seek other quarters, so I determined that I would try to reach the trail where it made a turn toward the river. I began to make tracks once more in a lively manner, and in a short time reached the point I had started for. At this point the trail was washed very badly on both sides as it descended towards the river. I looked back and saw a mounted Indian coming full speed after me.

"When my thoughts wander back to that incident, I am led to believe that the bold front of an enemy sometimes puts a strong man to flight. Such was the case with me, at any rate, at this time. I am ashamed to say that I did run several hundred feet and then checked myself and began to walk very slowly, for I knew I had the advantage of the savage. If ever I wanted to kill anybody it was right then, but when the savage saw me slow up, he wheeled around and galloped back over the trail as fast as he could go, leaving me to pursue my way in peace as far as he was concerned, but I was badly disappointed for I wanted his pony and if necessary would have shed his blood to obtain it, but no such luck was for me.

"The trail I was on led directly to the river and thence into the village. The commotion in the village had subsided; the signs of life were few; it appeared to me that it was deserted, so quiet and deathlike was the stillness. But when I looked closer, I could see a few Indians sneaking around here and there, and every once and again an Indian would dash out of the village, as if anxious to get to some given point in the least possible time.

"While making these observations, I also made a pleasant discovery. Down at the foot of the hill which I was descending, I saw a white man riding in a slow, leisurely way. Suddenly he left the trail and made his way up the river. Wishing to have company I was about to call for him to stop, but happily for me I did not, for I saw the reason why Watson, for such he proved to be, turned aside. He was making his way towards a party of Indians who were standing close to the river bank near a clump of underbrush They were talking and gesticulating in a very earnest manner. The day was extremely warm, but for all that the Indians had their blankets wrapped around them. Some of the blankets were stamped with the large letters I. D. meaning Indian Department. I then knew they were some of the hostiles we were after.

Watson had evidently not made this discovery. I was anxious to save him and if I did I must act quickly. So leaving the trail I ran down the hill at full speed and came to a place where there was a deep cut with steep sides that I would not have dared to face had I been able to check myself in time. But I could not; so I gave a leap which landed me many feet below, and, strange to say, I did not lose my balance. Fortunately for me the soil was soft and loose to light upon.

"When I got close enough to Watson, I called to him in a guarded voice. On hearing me, he checked up his horse and looked around. I rushed up to him and asked him where he was going. He answered, 'To our scouts, of course.' 'I then told him when we passed our scouts on the trail above. 'Well,' he said, 'Who are these ahead of us?' I told him that I was under the impression that they were hostiles and that we had better keep clear of them. He came to the same conclusion. The problem that now perplexed us was what we were to do. We finally concluded to enter the village by way of the trail. 'And now, Watson,' said I, 'I will help myself along by hanging to your horse's tail, as I cannot otherwise keep up with you.' So we started in the proposed direction.

"We had not gone far, before we saw a sight that puzzled us very much. Coming out of the river was one of our Crow scouts, mounted on his horse with the end of a rawhide rope over his shoulder, which he held firmly in his right hand. At the other end of the rope, straining and tugging to get away, was a Sioux squaw. The rope was tied around both her hands, but, struggle as she might, she could not break away.

"While looking on and wondering where the Crow was going we were further astonished by seeing General Custer dash out of the fording place and ride rapidup up to the Crow and commence to talk to him. Custer was well versed in Indian languages. The conversation with the Indian did not last long, and what the nature of it was I do not know, but the Crow released the Sioux woman, and she seeming glad to be free came running towards us in a half stooping posture and in her hand was a long bladed knife of ugly dimensions. So fierce did she look that my hand involuntarily sought the handle of my revolver. She

General Custer and Lieutenant Cook in the Field in 1876

must have noticed the movement for she made a short circle around us, ran over the bank, crossed the river, and disappeared in the village.

"The Crow then left Custer and rode in a jog trot towards the river and disappeared.

"Custer was mounted on his sorrel horse and being a very hot day he was in his shirt sleeves; his buckskin pants were tucked into his boots; his buckskin shirt fastened to the rear of his saddle; and a broad brimmed, cream colored hat on his head, the brim of which was turned up on the right side and fastened by a small hook and eye to its crown. This gave him the opportunity to sight his rifle while riding. His rifle lay horizontally in front of him; when riding he leaned slightly forward. This was the appearance of Custer on the day that he entered his last battle, and just one half hour before the fight commenced between him and the Sioux. When the Crow scout left him, he wheeled around and made for the same point in the river where we had first seen him. When he was passing us he slightly checked his horse and waved his right hand twice for us to follow him. He pointed down the stream, put spurs to his horse and disappeared at the ford, never uttering a word That was the last I ever saw of Custer alive. He must have gone thence directly to his command. We wondered why none of his staff were with him. In all probability he had outrun them. His being all alone shows with what fearlessness he travelled about even in an enemy's country with hostiles all around him.

"We reached the fording place as soon as possible, but all signs of Custer were gone. Whether he had gone through the village or waded down the stream to reach his command is a question that cannot be answered; but as we had seen no signs of him crossing to the opposite side we naturally thought that he had made his way down the stream.

"When we came to the fording place, we found that the water was rushing very rapidly. Both banks were wet with the splashing made by the animals going to and from the village. We stopped a moment to consider the best way to proceed and how to act, when we looked into the village. We could see the guidon fluttering in the breeze. This was the flag which had been placed there by the corporal just before he was shot. The sight of this increased our courage.

"Our plan was for Watson to cross the river first to show how deep the water was. Being very thirsty I forgot every thing else, and stooping down, began to dip water from the river in my hands and drink. While I was thus engaged and when Watson had forded to the middle of the stream, I heard the crack of three rifles which caused me to straighten up quickly and look around to see what the trouble was. Standing on the opposite bank of the river and at the very point we wished to gain were three Indians, with their smoking rifles in their hands. Watson, looking around at me, said, 'What in thunder is the matter?' I answered, 'If you don't get off your horse at once, you will get shot.' He did not need a second bidding, neither did he dismount in military style, but more like a frog landing with feet and hands in the water at the same time. This ungainly dismount caused the water to fly in every direction. The Indians no doubt thought that they had finished him for two of them turned around and disappeared in the village.

"'The one that was left stood facing me, still disputing our passage across the river. From his decorations of paint and feathers, I judged he was a chief.

"Watson began to crawl out of the water. If he was as thirsty as I was before he dismounted, I will guarantee that he was in that condition no longer.

"I made up my mind to climb to the top of the bank and let drive at our painted friend. I called to Watson to keep quiet for a few moments, and began to walk backwards up the steep bank, keeping my eyes fixed on the Indian and watching his every movement. When he saw my maneuvers he took aim at me and shot. But the only result was that the lead lay buried in the red clay at my side. The bank being very wet my feet slipped from under me several times. The Indian without lowering his rifle blazed away a second time, with the same result as before. I began to get my dander up and climbed to the top of the bank in no dignified manner. The red devil still kept aiming at me; I was a better target for him now than before. When I thought it time for him to fire. I dropped on my left side; the bullet whistling over my head, buried itself in the bluff behind me. As this duel had been one sided so far, I determined to try my hand. So loading my carbine which was done in a moment, I took aim at him as he turned to go to his pony, which was about thirty feet back of him on a slight elevation, winding up his rawhide rope as he did so. I fired, but missed him, because Watson who was on a line with the Indian made a movement which distracted my aim. I threw open the breech lock of my carbine to throw the shell out, but it was stuck fast. Being afraid that the Indian would escape, I worked at it in a desperate manner and finally got it out far enough to use my thumb nail, which proved effective. The cartridge was very dirty, a nice predicament for a man to be in at close quarters with an enemy. I was careful to put in a clean one next time, and calling for Watson to remain quiet for a moment, I fired when the Indian was within three feet of his horse. The ball plowed through his body, and buried itself in the ground under the horse, throwing the dirt in every direction. The Indian threw up his hands and fell with his head between the legs of his pony. It may seem hard to take human life, but he had been trying to take mine, and self preservation is the first law of nature.

"When I fired this shot, Watson jumped to his feet and began to lead his horse out of the stream toward me. I asked him if his horse was not played out; he said it was. In that case I told him that he had better leave it as it would take us all our time to take care of ourselves. He studied for a moment and then waded out of the stream leaving his horse with everything on it as I had done.

"After he had joined me, we had a consultation as to the best course for us to pursue. It was clear that the Indians still held the village, and it would be foolish for us to again attempt to enter it. To wade down stream was an impossibility. We finally decided to go down the right bank of the stream and see if we could not get sight of Custer's command, and join our ranks where we were much needed.

"Watson cast a last fond look at his horse and then we started on our perilous journey. We saw plenty of Indians on our side of the stream; they seemed to get bolder and more numerous, but so far they were some distance away. We kept very close to the underbrush, which lined the bank of the river.

Suddenly a small band of Indians came up towards us on a jog trot, which made us seek the cover. When they had passed, we moved on our way. Again we were sent to cover by the approach of more Indians. No doubt they were coming this way in order to enter the village by the ford. We concluded to seek some sheltered nook to cover ourselves from the extreme heat of the sun, and to wait until the Indians had quieted down for they were beginning to be like a swarm of bees. They were coming from every direction; so unlike what they were a half hour previous, when they were first surprised by the Seventh Cavalry, for surprise it must have been to them. But now they were beginning to recover themselves. After they had driven Major Reno across the river we noticed that the village was beginning to teem with life; the herd of ponies which had been grazing at quite a distance were now rounded up close to the tepees, so that the Indians had available mounts; ponies were dashing here and there with their riders urging them on; the dust would rise and mingle with the smoke of the burning grass and brush. The squaws had got the fire under control and had it confined to a comparatively small space.

"We managed to secrete ourselves in a bend of the

river, which turned like the letter S, and gave us running water on three sides of us. In a clump of red berry bushes we found a log which made quite a comfortable seat for us. Peering through the brush I thought I recognized the horse which Billy Jackson our guide had ridden. One of its hind legs was fearfully gashed by a bullet. I called Watson"s attention to it, but he did not think that it was the same horse. He had met Jackson when on the trail on the top of the hill but a short distance from the place where it turns towards the village. He said Jackson was in a fearful state of mind. Watson asked him what was the matter. He replied, 'Have you seen Custer?' Watson, surprised answered 'No,' and again asked what was up. Then Jackson informed him that Custer had shot at him, cutting away the strap that connected his stirrup to the saddle, and in order to save his life he had ridden away. Jackson said Custer saw that the stirrup strap was broken off and cast fearful glances around him in a mortal terror. Suddenly he put spurs to his horse and rode away, his long hair streaming in the wind and looking right and left as if expecting his enemy to appear at any moment. 'And the strangest part of it,' added Watson, 'was that instead of taking the back trail, he struck straight from the river across the country and as far as he could see him, he was urging his pony to its utmost speed. I then asked Watson if that did not account for Custer's presence away from his command. He shook his head and said he did not know.

"We had scarcely been concealed ten minutes before we heard a heavy volley of rifle shots down the stream, followed by a scattering fire. I raised to my feet and parted the brush with my gun, the stalks being covered with long, sharp thorns, which made it quite disagreeable for a person's clothes and flesh. Looking through this opening down the stream. I could see Custer's command drawn up in battle line, two men deep in a half circle facing the Indians who were crossing the river both above and below them.

"The Indians while fighting remain mounted, the

cavalry dismounted. The horses were held back behind and inside of the circle of skirmishers. The odds were against the soldiers for they were greatly outnumbered, and fought at a great disadvantage. Their ammunition was limited. Each man was supposed to carry one hundred rounds of cartridges, but a great many had wasted them in firing at game along the route. It does not take very long to expend that amount of ammunition especially when fighting against great odds.

"Watson took hold of the sleeve of my coat and pulled me down urging me to be careful, as the Indians might see me and called my attention to the village which was in a perfect state of turmoil. Indians were leaving the village in all speed to assist in the fight against the cavalry; others arrived from the battlefield with double burdens of dead and wounded. Then commenced a perfect howl from one end of the village to the other, made by the squaws and papooses. The noise gradually became louder and louder until it became indescribable and almost unbearable to the ears of civilized persons. Then it would almost die out until some more dead or wounded were brought in; this would put fresh vigor into their lungs. I could not keep still and so got onto my feet again. The firing was continuous. I removed my hat so that I would not attract attention, and looked over the panorama, as it was spread out before me. I could see that the fight was well under way; hordes of savages had gained a footing on the right bank of the river and had driven the soldiers back a short distance.

"The Indians were riding around in a circle and when those who were nearest to the cavalry had fired their guns (riding at full speed) they would reload in turning the circle. The well formed ranks of the cavalry did fearful execution, for every time the soldiers fired I could see ponies and riders tumbling in the dust, I could also see riderless ponies running away in every direction as if anxious to get away from such a frightful scene. Cavalry men were also falling and the ranks gradually melting away, but they sternly and bravely faced their foes; the cavalry men fighting for $13 a month, Indians for their families, property, and glory. It seemed to be the desire of each to utterly exterminate the other.

"Round and round rode the savages in a seemingly tireless circle. When one fell either dead or wounded he was carried from the field; but still there remained plenty to take his place; but if a soldier fell there was no one to take his place, and if wounded there was no one to bring him water to quench his thirst; if dying, no one to close his eyes. It was a sad, sad, sight. Lucky indeed was that soldier who died when he was first shot, for what mercy could be expected from a Sioux. If their enemy fell into their hands wounded or dying, it was simply to be put to the worst torture possible. Being in our present predicament we were utterly powerless to help as we wished we could. We knew our duty, but to do it was beyond our power. Look where we would we saw Indians; we two on foot could not cope with scores of them on horseback.

"During the fight between Custer and the Sioux, scores of Indians had stationed themselves on the bluffs overlooking the village as far as we could see, so that any movement on our part would have led to our discovery; but nevertheless we made up our minds not to remain long in our present place of concealment. So we began to map out a course by which we could join our command, where we felt we were so much needed. We found that we had made a mistake and had taken a wrong trail. The trail we had followed had been made by buffalo, when going to and from the river.

"Both Watson and myself had failed to notice the trail made by the cavalry in making their efforts to reach the lower end of the village. And thus we were brought to the fording place near the center of the village. A person could easily be mistaken, for the road over which they passed was rocky and sandy and hard, consequently, the marks left by the horses' feet were very faint. Notwithstanding this mistake left us in a very critical condition.

"Looking in the direction of the battle, I saw that the cavalry was being driven towards the foot of a small hill; their number greatly reduced. The firing was growing less every minute, but the Indians still kept up their seemingly tireless circling, making a great cloud of dust.

"The Indians who seemed to be detailed to bring in the dead and wounded were continually coming into the village with double burdens, showing that the soldiers though greatly decreased in numbers were still doing effective work. The squaws and papooses now kept howling without intermission. The noise they made resembled the howling of a coyote and the squealing of a cat.

"Watson kept his seat during the time of our concealment buried in deep thought. He seemed to come to one conclusion, and that was that the 7th Cavalry was going to be whipped. He said, 'The Indians greatly outnumbered the soldiers; while we have been here, we have seen more Indians twice over than the combined strength of the Seventh.' I told him that I could not bring myself to believe such would be the case. But Watson persisted in his conviction and said, 'It's no use talking, they are going to get the worst of it.' But I was just as positive in my belief, that the Cavalry would win.

"The plan we had mapped out for ourselves was to climb the right bank of the river and gain the trail of the cavalry and then if possible join our company. It was a foolish undertaking, for, a short distance below us, the bluffs came close to the river and the water washing at the base for so long a time, had caused the bluff to cave in and for the distance of a hundred feet up was so steep that even a goat could not climb it. On the top of the bluff just where we desired to go, there were seated three Indians with their ponies but a short distance behind them. We did not feel any way alarmed on their account for we felt able to cope with that number. So we left our retreat and moved down as far as we could for the cut in the bank. I felt exceedingly thirsty and said to Watson, that I proposed to have a drink. So jumping from the bank I landed at the edge of the water, and I must say that the water tasted good. I asked Watson to hand me his hat and I would fill it with water for him and he did so. When I was handing his hat back to him I noticed that the three Indians had discovered us and were watching our every movement. But without fear we commenced our march up the hill, keeping as near to the cut bank as the nature of the ground would permit. When about half way up the bluff I noticed something that made me hesitate. Watson was a short distance behind me and was keeping watch on the flat below. What I discovered was several more Indians peering at us over the edge of the bluff; in all I counted eight and concluded they were too many for us, especially with an up hill pull on our side. While I looked at them one rose to his feet and beckoned for us in the most friendly manner to advance. But I knew he was a hostile and we stood no show whatever on foot with such a number against us. So I turned around and called to Watson to run for it, and I went after him full speed, but kept my eye on the movements and seeing that they were making preparations to fire at us, I called out, 'Stretch yourself, Watson.' And he did and gradually left me behind. The Indians let fly with their rifles with the usual result.

"One of the Indians mounted his pony and rode on the edge of the bluff abreast of us. Jerking off his blanket he waved it in a peculiar manner and shouted out some lingo to those in the village and then pointed toward us. We felt we were discovered.

"It was our intention to hide ourselves in our former place of concealment, but the Indians were watching us; so passing it we came back again to the fording place. We looked to see if the horse was still there but there was no trace of it; no doubt it had passed into the hands of the Indians. Passing the ford on the run, we came to some underbrush, when we slowed down to a walk, Watson still being some distance ahead of me.

"I now heard the clatter of hoofs behind me. On looking around, I saw a white man and what I supposed to be a Crow Indian. I called for Watson to stop and told him that we had friends coming. I turned around, intending to wait until they came up. No sooner had I faced them then they stopped, turned their horses across the trail, dismounted, threw their guns across their saddles, and took aim at us. To say that we were astonished would faintly express our feelings. There was nothing left for us to do but to run. The trail we were on ran through a thick clump of bushes, and we put our best foot first in order to gain its shelter. But before we could reach it, they fired at us, but as usual missed; but the twigs and leaves were cut by the bullets and we came to the conclusion that we were not to be killed by the Indians. But if we were not wounded in our bodies we were in our feelings.

"We determined to ambush them if they attempted to pursue us. We followed the trail for several hundred feet, then forced our way through the brush and with our revolvers cocked, lying at our feet and our guns in our hands we waited and watched for their appearance. But we waited in vain. They must have suspected our intentions. One thing we had made up our minds to do, that was to kill the white man even if the Indian escaped.

"We had been two hours and a half in our concealment in the bend of the river watching the fight between Custer and the Indians. It had taken us one-half hour to reach this place, making three hours in all. The firing in the direction of the battlefield had just now ceased showing this act of the tragedy was ended.

"The question may be asked why we attempted to join our command after two hours and a half. My answer is, a sense of duty, and love for our comrades in arms. Then others may ask why we did not go sooner. We were repulsed at the ford; we were surrounded by Indians on the bluffs; we were without horses; and when we did make the attempt we did so at nearly the cost of our lives.

"We were now undecided which way to go. We knew we were surrounded by Indians and we would be fortunate if we escaped at all. The noise in the village was as great as ever, which told us that the Indians still held it. We were ever on the alert, but could see very little on account of the underbrush. I ventured to raise myself and scanned the top of the bluffs to see if there were any Indians in sight. But I could not see any, and this puzzled me very much, but on looking down to the lower end of the bluffs, I could see a body of men on horseback mounting slowly up the trail on top of the bluffs. Then I saw several guidons fluttering in the breeze, which I knew as the ones which our cavalry carried on the march. I called Watson's attention to the approaching horsemen, but he was firmly convinced that they were Indians. I then drew his attention to the orderly manner in which they moved, and the guidons they carried and told him that we had better try to join them before they passed us. 'Well,' said he, 'Let's move.' So we started, following the trail until we were entirely clear of the brush and then began to climb the face of the bluff in order to reach the trail on which we saw the cavalry were moving.

"We had scarcely got clear of the underbrush before we became aware of the fact that we had run into a hot place. Before we reached the foot of the bluff we came upon an opening in the timber and brush with several large cottonwood trees lying upon the ground, stripped of their bark. They had undoubtedly been cut down by the Indians during some severe winter when the snow was very deep, and the ponies had to live upon the bark, not being able to get to the grass.

"Near the water's edge, some distance up the river, we saw a large body of Indians holding a council, and that we might avoid them we kept as close to the cover of the brush as possible and went as rapidly as we could toward the face of the bluff.

"So intent were we in our endeavor to escape the attention of the Indians by the river, that we did not perceive another party which was in the road we wished to take, until the gutteral language of the savages called our attention to them. I jumped behind one of the fallen cottonwood trees; where Watson went I could not at the time tell. I peeped over the fallen tree, and saw a group of mounted Indians, gesticulating, grunting out their words, and pointing towards the advancing cavalry. Suddenly they broke up and advanced toward my place of concealment. I began to think they had seen me and I crouched as close to the tree as possible. Drawing my revolver, I made ready to defend myself. I made up my mind that all but one shot should be fired at the Indians, and that one would go into my own head, for I had determined never to be taken alive. With open ears and eyes I awaited their coming. They passed my hiding place without seeing me and made their way toward the river. I jumped to my feet and started off once more, hardly caring whether the Indians saw me or not, for the presence of the cavalry had put fresh courage into me. I had not gone far before I heard my name called and on looking around I saw Watson coming after me at full speed. I was glad to see him safe, it gave me renewed courage, and we hoped that we would soon be entirely safe. After we began to climb the hill, I found my strength was giving out, and in spite of the fact that we were in full view of the Indians I laid down to rest and all my entreaties for Watson to go on and save himself were fruitless. He would not budge. But there was something that made us move sooner than I wished; a large body of Indians had crossed the river and were coming across the flat towards the hill we were climbing I struggled to my feet and staggered after Watson. The heat at this time seemed to me to be intense, but it might have been on account of my exhausted condition. Watson made no complaint, for like myself he knew it would do no good. After we had climbed nearly half way up the bluff, the Indians commenced to fire at us, but that did not trouble us, because we knew that the Indians when excited were very poor shots; and in our case the bullets went wide of the mark.

"We were becoming so tired that the presence of the Indians was no longer a terror to us. The hill we were climbing seemed very long; so much so to me that I fell down and lay there without any inclination to move again, until Watson called my attention to the head of the column of cavalry which now came into plain view. So with renewed energy we made our way up amid showers of lead. The savages seemed loath to let us go.

"When we stepped into the trail at the head of the advancing column, it was about five o'clock in the afternoon. The first man we recognized was Sergeant Knipe of our company. He had been sent back by Custer to hurry up the ammunition. He informed us that Sergeant Hanley, who had charge of our company's pack mules, had taken Barnum, one of our pack mules loaded with ammunition and drove it full speed toward the battlefield. He got as far as the pillar of rocks, which I have already mentioned, when the Indians opened fire on him. He quickly made up his mind to retreat as the Indians were too numerous to be dealt with single handed. So rapidly had they been moving that it was with great difficulty that he succeeded in turning the obstinate mule, which he finally did and drove it to the rear amid a shower of lead. The Indians made a desperate effort to cut him off, but he succeeded in returning to the pack train without any mishap. This was the only attempt made to take ammunition to Custer's command. There is no doubt that they needed it very badly Some one failed to do his duty. It may be out of place to criticize, but the duty that Major Reno owed to General Custer is too plain to be misunderstood. According to military rule it was Reno's duty to report to his superior officer, whether he had failed or succeeded in his mission; but instead of sending an escort with ammunition to Custer he simply allowed one man to take that dangerous journey alone. How much better it would have been had he with his seven companies gone to the assistance of Custer. He would no doubt have been successful and the loss of life would not have been so great.

"But here he was. Nearly three hours had elapsed since his retreat from the river bottom and during all this time Custer had been fighting against fearful odds; his men melting away; and his ammunition running shorter every moment until the last round was fired. And then who can conjecture the fate of the few that remained of that deserted band, slowly murdered at the leisure of the noble savage of the plains.

"The forces under Major Reno, at the time we stepped into the trail, were six companies of the left wing and one company of the right, namely, Company B under the command of Captain McDugal. Seven companies in all; and still Reno hesitated to act.

"No sooner had we made our appearance than the command came to a halt. We were questioned closely as to what we knew about Custer; as to where he was and what he was doing, etc. We answered all the questions as well as we could.

"Sergeant Knipe then told me that my horse had been found and was in charge of Fitzgerald, the horse farrier. Knipe added, 'We all thought you was a gonner.' This was good news to me.

"Just then the order was given to retreat and Reno's command began to march slowly to the rear. Of course we all wondered at this but said nothing. It was our duty not to question, but to obey. I made a dive through the retreating column in quest of my horse and found it in the center of the command led by Fitzgerald, who seemed greatly surprised at seeing me, saying, 'I thought the Indians had your scalp,' I told him I was too good a runner for that. On examining my saddle, I was glad to find everything as I had left it.

We did not retreat very far, for that was impossible. The Indians were closing in around us. Our retreat was covered by Company D commanded by Captain Weir. He was the only captain who wished to go to the relief of Custer. He had begged in vain to have Reno advance to Custer's relief. That being denied him he asked permission to take his company and ascertain Custer's position; but he was refused that privilege.

Major Reno moved to the left of the trail and went into a flat bottomed ravine. By this time the Indians were pouring a shower of lead into us that was galling in the extreme. Our horses and mules were cuddled together in one confused mass. The poor brutes were tired and hungry. Where we made our stand there was nothing but sand, gravel and a little sage brush. We were in a very precarious condition. Our means of defense were very poor. There were numerous ravines leading into the one which we occupied. This gave the savages a good opportunity to close in upon us and they were not long in doing so. Some of us unloaded the mules of the hard tack they were carrying and used the boxes for a breastwork. We knew if we did not do so we would be picked off one by one. We formed the cracker boxes into a half circle and kept them as close together as possible.

"By the time we had everything arranged the sun was going down. We all knew that the Indians never fought after night fall. We thought we would have time enough to fortify ourselves before the light of another day appeared. But in the meantime several accidents happened which helped to make it a serious matter for us. We saw that our horses and mules were beginning to drop quite fast, for they were in a more exposed position. This is very trying to a cavalry man, for next to himself, he loves his horse, especially on a campaign of this kind. A peculiar accident happened to a man lying next to me, sheltered by a cracker box and talking in a cheerful manner about the possibilities of us getting out of our present difficulty, when a ball came crashing through the box hitting him and killing him instantly. There was but one gasp and all was still. He had made the mistake of placing the box the wrong way the edge of the crackers toward the outside. While meditating on the uncertainty of life, a bullet struck the box behind which I laid, and as I heard the lead crashing through its contents, I wondered if the time had come for me to wear a pair of wings. But no, the ball stopped and I gave a sigh of relief, and I noted with great satisfaction that the night was closing in around us.

As soon as the fire of the Indians ceased we once more mingled with one another. In comparing notes we found that a few men had been killed and a number wounded but our stock had suffered the most. The men were greatly puzzled about the whereabouts of Custer and, as all the men loved their general, it was but natural that they should sneer at the idea of Custer getting the worst of any fight he might enter against the Indians. The story we told of Custer's battle they did not disbelieve but as to him getting the worst of the fight that was all bosh. For my part I deemed it best to say nothing further about it as contradiction was a thing I could not stand, when I knew I was right. There was no possibility for doubt that Reno's command heard the firing between Custer's men and the Indians. Besides, Custer had sent two messengers back, the first one Sergeant Knipe of Company C, the second one Bugler Martin from Company H to Captain Benteen; commanding him to bring his company to his assistance. I have not the least doubt but that Captain Benteen would have done so if he possibly could. But on his way to the river, he met Major Reno on his retreat and the result was that Reno assumed entire command of the forces.

"Let us now see what efforts were put forth by Reno to assist Custer. As I have said before, to my certain knowledge the battle lasted three hours The question is, What was he doing during this time? I was not with him so I can only tell what I heard from the members of the companies who were with him and they told me it was nothing but hesitancy what he should do. It is evident that he was no man for the position he occupied and seemed unable to act energetically in an emergency. If he had, things would have been very different. There is no excuse for Reno's remaining in ignorance of Custer's real position.

"After the firing of the Indians had ceased, I went where I had left my horse in charge of a man named McGuire. Here I saw something that under other conditions would have been laughable. McGuire had been given charge of five horses. When I left mine with him he was sitting on the ground, his head shrunk down between his shoulders, and his eyes bulged out to their fullest extent; and when I returned he was in exactly the same position, still holding the reins of the five horses in his hand, but three of them were lying dead. I asked him if he knew that three of the horses were dead; he mournfully shook his head, but, as one of the dead horses was mine, I left in disgust and began to figure on the possibilities of getting another. I was soon forced to the conclusion that my chances were very slim. As I strolled around I found everybody awake and talking with each other. The subjects of conversation were, the probability of getting out of our present fix and the whereabouts of Custer. The thought seemed to be that if Custer would only turn up our present difficulties would soon vanish. I was wise enough to hold my peace.

"I wandered to the edge of the bluff overlooking the village. By this time it was quite dark; I could plainly see several large fires which the Indians had built. There was a noise in the village which increased as night advanced. The deep voices of the braves, the howling of the squaws, the shrill piping of the children and the barking of the dogs made night hideous. But they appeared to enjoy it amazingly.

"Suddenly we heard, above all other sounds, the call of a bugle. The sound came from the direction of the village, and immediately following was the sound of two others. The officers hearing those bugle sounds ordered our buglers to sound certain calls and waited to see if they would be answered. The only answer was a long wailing blast; it was not what was expected. I now turned around and made my way to the place where my dead horse lay, and stripped the saddle of everything, then went and made my bed behind my cracker box. The last thing I heard as I lay down upon the ground was the howling of the Indians and the wailing of the bugles. I slept so soundly, that I heard and knew nothing until I felt some one kicking the soles of my boots. Jumping to my feet I saw Captain Benteen standing by my side When he saw that I was fully awake he told me I would have to render some assistance at the head of the ravine up which the Indians were trying to sneak. He added, 'If they do succeed, it will be all day with us'

"The Indians had been pouring in volleys upon us long before I had been awakened and they were still at it. Under the cover of darkness they had gained a foothold in some of the numerous ravines that sursounded us. It seemed as if it would be impossible to dislodge them. Some of them were so close to us that their fire was very effective. The ping of the bullets and the groaning and struggling of the wounded horses was oppressive. But my duty was plain. The way that I had to go to my post was up a short hill towards the edge of the bluff and the head of the ravine. While packing my ammunition in order to carry it easily, I glanced up in the direction I had to go, and for the life of me, I could not see how I could possibly get there alive for the bullets of the Indians were plowing up the sand and gravel in every direction; but it was my duty to obey.

"After getting everything in shape, I started on the run. The fire of the Indians seemed to come from three different directions and all exposed places were well riddled. Even as secure a place as where we had formed our breastwork was no longer safe. The red devils seemed determined to crush us. As I ran up the hill, which was but a short distance, I was seized with a tendency to shrink up and was under the impression that I was going to be struck in the legs or feet. I was not the only one to run for the head of the ravine. Captain Benteen was busily hunting up all the men he could to go to the same point, in order to keep the Indians in check and if possible to drive the Indians out of the ravine. It did not take me long to reach the top of the bluff, where I got a glimpse of the village, the river and the mouth of the ravine.

"I had gotten so far without being hit that I thought I was going to get through safe, but as I was entering the mouth of the ravine, a volley was fired by the Indians who occupied it and over I tumbled, shot through the right hand and arm. A short distance below I saw several cavalry men who were soon joined by others, eleven in all; a slim force indeed to clean out the ravine held by so many Indians, but they were resolute men. Captain Benteen soon joined them and made a short speech. He said, 'This is our only weak and unprotected point and should the Indians succeed in passing this in any force they would soon end the matter as far as we are concerned. And now' he asked, 'Are you ready?' They answered, 'Yes.' 'Then,' said he, 'charge down there and drive them out.' And with a cheer, away they dashed, their revolvers in one hand and their carbines in the other. Benteen turned around and walked away to the extreme left, seemingly tireless and unconscious of the hail of lead that was flying around him.

"Knowing that in my condition I was useless, I looked around to see if I could find anyone who could direct me to a surgeon. I knew that there were two with General Custer, but I was not sure whether we had one with us here or not.

"A short distance from me lay a wounded man, groaning and struggling in the agony of death. Just as I was thinking of getting up, I heard an order given by a Sioux chief A heavy volley of bullets was the result. My wounded neighbor gave a scream of agony and then was still. After the volley was past it was a wonder to me how I had escaped. I now struggled to my feet and found that I was weak and dizzy from loss of blood. I looked around me and saw what remained of those who had gone down the ravine against such fearful odds. Few of them returned but they had accomplished their object. We had men with us who seemed utterly fearless in the face of danger. One young man had the courage of a lion. Wherever duty called him, whatever the danger might be he was always found at his post.

"Going in the direction of the horses, I saw what suffering the poor brutes were enduring from thirst and hunger. But we ourselves were no better off. I found in the center of our place of defense that we had a surgeon busily attending to the wounded and dying. I asked him to attend to me when he had time to do so. He soon bandaged up my wounds and told me the only thing that could be done was to apply plenty of water. What mockery! Water was not to be had for love or money. Our way to the river was cut off excepting by the way of the ravine out of which the eleven brave men drove the Indians. But to attempt to get water by that route was too risky. I looked on while the doctor attended to the wounded that were brought in. Some of the poor fellows would never recover, others would be crippled for life and I would carry a broken hand.

"The sun reflecting on the sand and gravel made it very hot. The loss of blood and lack of water made me so dizzy that I reeled and fell and lay unheeded. But this was getting to be a common sight. I still clung to my carbine and revolver. When I fell I managed to roll over on my face and place my carbine under me. I knew that if anyone needed such an implement they were liable to take it. I do not know how long I lay there, but I have a faint recollection of being turned and my gun taken from me. This aroused me and I managed to struggle to a sitting posture, but the man and gun were gone. He had left his own in its place, but it was practically useless, the breech being broken.

"While I was meditating on the meanness of human nature, I saw Captain Benteen dash into the midst of our horses and drive out several men who were hiding and skulking among them. 'Get out of here,' he cried, 'and do your duty.'

"It soon became known that the Indians were concentrating for an attack upon our lines. They had closed in around us on three sides and so close were they, that we could hear them talking. Captain Benteen seemed to be aware of the impending danger, and was forming all the men he possibly could into line at the point where it was expected that the Indians would attack us.

"The heat of the day was oppressive and guns of the Indians were silent and these facts brought a feeling of depression over us. We all realized that our lives were not worth betting on, but the expression on the faces of the men was that of a dogged determination to sell them dearly.

"We only had two spades, the others having been either broken or lost, so our means of digging rifle pits were limited and natural defenses there were none. History hardly records a predicament such as we were in. It does mention the hardships of the soldiers of the late Civil War, but it was nothing to campaigning against Indians. A white man capturing an enemy usually spares his life but if captured by hostile Indians his days are numbered and he is known to men on earth no more.

"How were we going to transport our wounded? We had plenty of them and some of them very badly hurt. Look where you would, you could see either dead or wounded soldiers and the end not yet.

"The silence was suddenly broken by a loud command given by a hostile chief, which was followed by a terrific volley and a great many of our horses and mules passed over the range. Our men never wavered but hugged the grounds as close as possible and fired whenever they found the slightest opportunity to do execution. All realized that the less ammunition expended the better. Although the Indians outnumbered us many times, they lacked the courage and determination of the day previous when they fought Custer; they no doubt had been taught a bitter lesson. Had it not been for the watchfulness of our men, they certainly would have got the best of us. Whenever they attracted our men were always ready. While the hottest of the fight was going on and the tide of battle seemed to be against us, our doctor dropped his bandages, and grasping a gun, started toward the skirmish line. Some of the men seeing his action begged him to stay, telling him that it would be hard with the command if anything should go wrong with him, and to enforce their arguments a wounded man was brought in who needed his immediate attention. This for a time seemed to deter him for he laid down his gun and commenced work at his former occupation. He was kept very busy for some time.

"I made my way slowly over the small place in which we huddled together and was very much pleased to see some of the men stretching canvas over the wounded and dying. This canvas the officers had brought along for their own use, but it was given up by them for the humane purpose of sheltering the helpless. The canvas had to be stretched very close to the ground. The supports that were used were short pieces of wood of any kind that we could procure without risk.

"We had no use for firewood if we could have gotten it, as we had no water to cook with, hence our wounded were deprived of the comforts that a sick man needs. As I strolled around, I could see something of the horrors of our position. It was not a question of days but of hours. We could in all probability bury our unfortunate comrades who had fallen in battle, but it would be impossible for us to dispose of our dead horses and mules. The stench would become so great that it would drive us from our present position and where were we to go. It was utterly impossible to move our wounded, as we had no means at hand with which we could do so. We were quite willing to change our location if we could, but we hesitated for several reasons; we were separated from our leader and our forces were divided. The Indians seemed determined to exterminate us if possible. The only hope for us to accomplish our purpose was to make the effort after night came on. I wondered if any of the other members of Company C had been as unfortunate as myself. Although that company had entered the fight with General Custer, there were a few who had been detailed on the pack train. So I commenced to search around for them. I first found a man by the name of Bennett whom to know was to respect. I could see that his days were numbered. Kneeling down beside him I asked, 'Can I do you any service?' He grasped my hand and drew me closer to him and whispered, 'Water, Thompson, water, for God's sake!' Poor fellow, he was past speaking in his usual strong voice. I told him I would get him some if I lived. He released my hand and seemed satisfied and then I began to realize what the promise I had made meant. This was on the 26th day of June, a day long to be remembered by all who took an active part, in fact, a day never to be forgotten. As far as getting water was concerned it was a matter of the greatest difficulty. All routes to the river were cut off by the Indians, I was determined to make the effort nevertheless, and looked around for a canteen. I thought of the ravine which was cleared by the eleven brave men and hoped that I might be able to make my way to the river by that route. I made some inquiries of some skulkers whom I found in among the horses and from what they told me I concluded that the ravine route was the only safe one to take. In a short time I secured two canteens and a coffee kettle. I made my way to the head of the ravine which ran to the river. I found that very little change had taken place since the incident in the morning.

"The firing on the part of the Indians was rather dilatory. A person could make his way around with a little more comfort, but how long this would continue it was impossible to tell. As I gained the rise of ground that commanded a view of the village, river, and surrounding country, I saw a small group of men examining an object lying on the ground which I found to be an Indian bedecked in all his war paint, which goes to make up a part of their apparent courage and fierce appearance. He was found very close to our position which goes to show how closely we were confined. The Indians were able to occupy every available position afforded by nature on account of their numbers. If it had not been for the terrible position we were in we could have had a panaroma view of the snow capped hills of the Big Horn Mountains, which form the fountain heads of the Little and Big Horn Rivers.

"While wondering as to my next move, I was suddenly brought to myself with the question, 'Where are you going, and what are you going to do?' The questioner belonged to my own company, and I naturally expected him to sympathize with me in my errand of mercy. He not only tried to dissuade me, but called to Sergeant Knipe and told him of my intention of going to the river. The Sargeant told me of the hopelessness of the undertaking telling me that if I should ever attempt to make the trip I would never get back alive. I told him that as I could not carry a gun I thought I had better do something to help the wounded and the dying.

"Seeing that I was determined to go, they said no more, but one of the men of Company C, named Tim Jordan, gave me a large pocket handkerchief to make a sling for my wounded hand. I started down the ravine but I halted for I found I had not my belt in which I usually carried my pistol, having given it to one of my comrades. But on going back to the man and asking him for it he seemed to be confused and stated that he had lost it. So there was nothing for me to do but to console myself with the reflection that I had better have taken care of it myself. I turned around and made my way through the midst of several citizen packers who accompanied us on our expedition. No doubt they thought the position they occupied was the safest one to serve their country in. As I went down the ravine, I found it got narrower and deeper, and became more lonesome and naturally more depressing. I noticed numerous hoof prints showing that the Indians had made a desperate effort to make an opening through our place of defense by this route. But now it was deserted. After I had travelled a considerable distance I came to a turn in the ravine. Pausing for a moment I looked cautiously around the bend, and there before me was running water, the Little Horn River. On the opposite side was a thick cover of cottonwood timber, the sight of which made me hesitate for a moment. It was possible that some of the Indians were concealed in it to pick anyone off who was bold enough to approach the water; but I could see no signs of life and concluded to proceed. I made my way as rapidly as possible toward the bank of the river. I found the ground was very miry, so much so that I was afraid that I might get stuck in the mud. I concluded that there was nothing like trying. I laid down my canteens and took my kettle in my left hand and made several long leaps which landed me close to the water's edge. The water at this point ran very shallow over a sandbar. With a long sweep of my kettle up stream I succeeded in getting plenty of sand and a little water. Making my way back towards the mouth of the ravine a volley of half a score of rifle balls whistled past me and the lead buried itself in the bank beyond. I gained the shelter of the ravine without a scratch and I was thankful. I wondered whether it would be safe to stop long enough to put the water into the canteens, as the fire of the Indians seemed to come from a bend in the bank, a short distance from the mouth of the ravine on this side of the river. I was not sure but that the Indians might take a notion to follow me. Had I been armed I would have been more at my ease. I knew I could travel with greater ease if I left the kettle behind, so I placed it between my knees and soon transferred the water from it to the canteens. I started on looking back once in a while to see if the Indians were coming. I soon turned the bend of the ravine, but no signs of them did I see. Although my thirst was great I did not stop to take a drink until I landed amidst my fellow soldiers.

I offered to divide the water of one canteen with some of the men of Company C. They refused my offer when I told them that my effort was made in behalf of the wounded members of our company. On coming to Bennett I placed a canteen in his hand, but he was too weak to lift it to his lips. He was attended by John Mahoney of our company and I had no fear but that he would be well cared for. I skirmished around and found two more of my company slightly wounded. I gave them the other canteen and told them that if they should not require all the water that I would like to pass it around to some other wounded ones lying close by, which was so done. A man by the name of McVey, to whom I handed the canteen that he might drink seemed determined to keep it in his possession. I jerked it from his grasp and passed it on to the next. With a cry of rage he drew his revolver from beneath his overcoat and taking aim at me he told me to skip or he would put a hole through me. I was too much astonished for a moment to even move or speak, but when I did regain my speech, I used it to the best advantage as that was all the weapon I had. Fortunately I was not armed or I would have committed an act that I would have been sorry for afterwards. My action would have been justified by the law, as it would have been an act of self defense. The offers of money by the wounded for a drink of water were painful to hear. 'Ten dollars for a drink,' said one. 'Fifteen dollars for a canteen of water.' said a second. 'Twenty dollars,' said a third, and so the bidding went on as at an auction.

"This made me determined to make another trip and to take a larger number of canteens, so I would not have to make so many trips. The firing on the part of the Indians was very brisk at intervals. On our part we never expended a cartridge unless we were very sure that the body of an Indian was in sight.

"My next trip to the river was taken with more courage. But as on the former occasion, when I came to the bend in the ravine I halted and looked carefully around the corner. I was astonished at seeing a soldier sitting on a bank of earth facing the river, with his back towards me. I was curious to know who he was. I came up to him and saw that he had two camp kettles completely riddled with bullets. He had his gun in his hand and his eyes fixed on the grove of timber across the river, watching for the enemy. On looking him over,. I could see the reason for his sitting and watching as he did. I discovered a pool of blood a short distance from him which had come from a terrible wound in his leg. It was impossible for him to move further without assistance. I asked him how he received his wound. He told me he had gone to the river for water and when he was coming up from the bed of the river with his two kettles filled with water a volley had been fired at him, one of the bullets hitting him and breaking his leg below the knee, the others riddling his kettles. He had managed to make his way under cover of the ravine to the place where I found him. I then told him as it was my turn now I would proceed to business. He tried to dissuade me, but as I would not go back without water and it was useless for me to remain where I was, I laid down my canteens and grasped the camp kettle which I had left on my previous trip. I walked forward looking into the grove for signs of Indians, but not a sign of life could I see. Looking to see where the water was the deepest I made a few long leaps which landed me in the water with a loud splash. I knew it was useless for me to try to avoid being seen so I depended on my ability to escape the bullets of the Indians. A volley was fired, but I again escaped. Madden, the wounded man I had just left watched me with the greatest interest. When I returned to him I urged him to take a drink, but he refused to do so saying he was not in need of it. This caused me some surprise, as I knew he had lost a great deal of blood which is almost invariably followed by great thirst.

"I made haste to fill the canteens and started on my way to camp bidding Mike Madden to be of good cheer and he made a cheerful reply. When I reached the place of our defense I found that the firing was not so brisk. Only a few scattering shots now and then. But our men were still on the alert. There was no weak place unguarded, no ammunition was being wasted. Although we had 24 boxes of ammunition which amounted to thousands of rounds, the men only fired where they thought they were going to do execution.

"After leaving three canteens for the wounded at the hospital, I took the other two and gave them to my wounded comrades. After this, I began to feel very sick and looked around for a sheltered place to avoid the heat of the sun. This sickness was caused by the loss of blood and the pain in my hand, which at this time had swollen to a great size. I did not like to get under the canvas where the wounded were as that was already crowded, so I crawled under one of our horses which was standing in a group with the others. I could not but wonder what sort of a fix I would be in if the horse under which I was lying happened to get shot and fall down on me. But this soon passed out of mind, as there was always something going on which attracted my attention.

"I began to watch the actions of the men. A short distance from me was a man belonging to Company A. He was lying on his face so still that I thought he was dead. Two men came towards him dragging a piece of canvas with which they were going to construct a shelter for the steadily increasing numbers of wounded men. Toney, for that was the man's name, was lying in the place best suited for the shelter and the men called to him to get out of the way. But he never moved. One of the men began to kick him and yelled for him to get up. He struggled to his feet; his face bore tokens of great fear. He said he was sick. A more miserable looking wretch it would be difficult to find; the man was almost frightened to death. He walked a few steps and fell to the ground heedless of the heat of the sun or anything else going on around him.

"Another young man was going around in a most helpful manner. Here, there, and everywhere he thought he was needed. I noticed him quite frequently and it did my heart good to see in what a cheerful manner he performed his duty. He was a trumpeter, belonging to either Company I or L, and I am very sorry that I have fotgotten his name.

"With a few exceptions the soldiers performed their duty with great bravery and determination.

"The Indians had in their possession, three guns which, time and again our men tried to silence. These guns were in the hands of good marksmen. The position they occupied was behind some rocks in our rear. All we could see when they fired was a puff of white smoke, but the results were very disastrous to our horses and mules. The shot hardly ever missed its mark. The number of dead animals was growing very large. While leaning on my left hand and wondering what to do, the horse under which I was lying backed slightly and planted his hoof on my hand. I thought from the pain I felt that it was disabled, but after persuading the horse to raise his hoof so that I could release my hand, I found that I could still use it. This slight incident made me realize that I had no business to be loafing. So working my way from among the animals I tried to secure a gun, hoping that I might be able to use it in case the Indians succeeded in breaking through our lines.

"The left wing of the 7th Cavalry was thrown out as skirmishers facing the village. They had to take every opportunity the ground afforded to secure themselves against the fire of the enemy. In walking down the line, I noticed that Company D had made good use of their time during the previous night. They seemed to be better provided with rifle-pits than the rest of the companies.

"Here I saw an act of a member of Company D which showed the utter indifference in which some men hold their lives. His name was Pat Golden, a young man of striking appearance, dark hair and eyes, black mustache, tall, straight as an arrow, and nimble as a cat. It seemed that shooting from the shelter of a rifle pit was not suitable to him and to get a better view of the enemy he sprang out of the pit and commenced to fire at anything that appeared to him an Indian. He was urged by his comrades to come under cover as it was too dangerous to expose himself that way. Heedless of the danger he held his position amid a shower of lead, both a challenge and a target to the fire of the Indians. It was not long before he was hit by a ball, but he still kept his place. Again he was struck but he still kept his feet, firing when the opportunity presented itself apparently paying no attention to the entreaties of his comrades to come under shelter. He called out as another bullet struck him, 'Boys, that is number three, but I'm still here. Number four,' he shouted as another bullet struck him and he still kept his feet and loaded and fired his gun. Every man of his company admired his pluck, but could not help but see he was throwing his life away. Finally a ball went crashing through his brain, his lifeless body rolled back into the pit which became his grave.

"Finding I could not get a gun that was fit for use, I turned and made my way back towards the head of the defense and when I came to where the horses were huddled together, I heard a voice feebly calling my name. Looking up the direction of the sound, I saw a man by the name of Tanner, lying close to some sage brush. Some one had thrown the cape of an overcoat over him to protect him from the sun. Kneeling down by his side I asked him what I could do for him. He told me he was done for and asked me to get him a drink of water. I saw from the nature of the wound that his hours were numbered. I secured a blanket on which to place him. Having only one hand with which to do the work I found it hard work to move him. I then got an overcoat and made a pillow for his head, and used my overcoat to shelter him. I now made a hurried search for some more canteens and in making my way towards the head of the ravine, again my attention was called to the fact that Major Reno had at last come out of his hole. He held a pair of field glasses to his eyes looking in the direction of the village. Presently he dropped the glasses and looking around saw me. He motioned for me to stop, telling me, at the same time, that the Indians were concentrating for a united attack and ordered me to go back as it was dangerous for me to go down to the river. I had been aware of this for sometime. Evidence existed on every side which showed what they had been trying to do since daylight. As I stood looking at him I could not help wondering if he knew what his duty was. Here he was with about four hundred men surrounded by hordes of savages. If ever soldiers needed a good example it was here. Did he show such an example? Did he give cheer to his men? Did he show how a true soldier should act under difficulties, and die if needs be in defense of his country? No! Instead of this he kept himself in a hole where there was no danger of being struck and no doubt would have pulled the hole in after him if he could and if he even dreamed that by so doing he could have increased his security.

"Turning to the left I walked through the herd of horses until I got a sufficient distance from the Major not to be noticed by him and then made my way to the river. I found Madden had been removed and it made me feel a little lonesome on this trip. But I had become so indifferent to my surroundings that I did not care whether the Indians fired at me or not. So I walked slowly to the river, filled my camp kettles and as slowly returned to my task of filling my canteens. All this time the Indians did not fire at me. It occurred to me that the stillness was almost oppressive. After filling my canteens, I looked towards the timber. There were no signs of life there. When I reached the top of the bluff again, I saw Captain Benteen hard at work placing a few men here and a few there. He was as cool and collected as ever. I noticed that blood was making its way through the leg of his trousers and I concluded that he had received a flesh wound, but with the exception of a slight limp he gave no signs of pain. His presence was cheering and encouraging to the men. Wherever he went, their faces lighted up with hope.

"Lieutenant Wallace, a fine looking officer, over his duty. He had been in command of the Ree scouts up until the 25th, when all but three retreated to Tongue River where the wagon train was parked. Varnum was with Reno when the latter made the charge upon the upper end of the village. In the confusion of the retreat he had lost his hat and his head was now decorated with a white handkerchief.

"Lieutenant Wallace, a fine looking officer, over six feet in height, was also doing all he could to keep our position as secure as possible. What we needed more than anything else was artillery. If we had had but one piece, either a Napoleon or a Gatling gun the village could have been destroyed in a very short time. But we had neither.

"I thought I would go and see how Tanner was getting along. When I approached the place where I had left him I saw a man tugging away at the overcoat which I had placed under his head. Rushing forward I seized the man by the coat collar and sent him sprawling on the ground some distance. He sprang to his feet with a loud curse and with vengeance in his eye looked me over from head to foot. I said, 'Get out of here, and be quick about it.' We will call him Nelson although that was not his real name, but we will have reason to mention him again, so it is well to call him something. He was the most profane man I ever heard. After he had gone, I turned to Tanner and found that he was dead. He had died before his wish for a drink of water could be gratified. He was a man of excellent qualities. A bond of warmest friendship had bound us together which was only severed by death. I drew the cape over his face. It was the last thing I could do for him. I thought this was a hard way to die, and I did not know how soon my turn might come. I now picked up my canteens which I had dropped when I grasped Nelson I distributed the water among those who needed it but kept one canteen for Bennett. I told Mahoney, who was attending him that I would leave more water with him and that I might come around for a drink once in a while. I asked him if he thought Bennett would pull through. He shook his head sadly and said, 'I don't think so.' I knew Bennett would receive the best of attention so I made my way out of the basin in which the hospital was situated.

"I was too nervous to remain inactive and I was bound to see what was going on. I went to a point below, where the left wing was lying. The ground here was broken with the river a short distance away. I stood looking into the village to see how many Indians were in sight. I only saw one occasionally, making his way at full speed either to the upper or lower end of the village. A large herd of ponies were grazing near the village, guarded by a small number of Indian boys. I then looked into the timber where Reno had formed a skirmish line before retreating, but I could see no one there. I was in doubt as to where all the Indians had gone. There were none where I expected to see them. But I was suddenly made aware of their presence by a command given in a loud voice by one of their chiefs. This was followed by a heavy volley which continued for several moments. Our men did not flinch and very few replied to the Indian fire. A hissing sound near my head caused me to turn and I saw an arrow with its barb buried in the ground. I saw I had had a close shave. I picked up the arrow and on examination found it to be a regular hunting arrow. Whether it was poisoned or not, I could not tell. I knew that the one who had shot the arrow could not be a great distance from me.

"While thinking whether I should keep it as a souvenir or not, I heard a yell mingled with curses. Turning around I saw a man lying on the ground holding his leg in both hands. I went to see what was the matter with him. . I recognized him, Nelson of the overcoat incident. He stopped his swearing long enough to tell me he had been struck with a rock which had broken a bone in his leg. I did not know whether to believe him or not, until his limb was uncovered. The only thing visible was a red bruise on his shin bone, but his leg was broken. The one throwing the rock must have been very close to us. We had been standing on the edge of the broken ground, so it was possible that some of the Indians were closer to us than we were aware of. But we were unable to tell just where to look for them.

"As two men were taking Nelson away, a loud voice from behind the bluff calling me in good English, 'Come down here you white livered — — — —, and I will cut your heart out and drink your blood.' The loud bleat of a sheep was the only answer I gave him.

"The fire on the part of the Indians became continuous. If they had any hopes of driving us back from our position, they were disappointed. We were like rats in a hole; we could go no further. From about three o'clock in the afternoon until the day wore away the Indians' fire grew less; thus showing that they were getting disheartened at the prospect of getting our scalps or their ammunition was running low; the latter I think was the real cause for they had consumed a tremendous amount of it in their attacks on Custer's and Reno's commands.

"There was a large body of Indians engaged against us so they must have had plenty of ammunition.

"On my way down into the ravine I found the five other citizen packers. As packers they were a success, but as fighters they were failures. Before they had found the shelter of the ravine, the head packer had received a wound in the head by a spent ball; his bandaged head and blood stained face made him look 'tough.'

"A little farther down I found Sergeant Hanley, our quarter-master-sergeant, surrounded by enough food to last four companies instead of one. He no doubt thought that it was a good opportunity, while confusion reigned supreme to make provisions for the future. He had made a breastwork out of the cracker boxes. There he was, as far as we could see, a perfectly contented man.

"Seeing he had a new tin bucket, I could not resist the temptation of making another trip to the river. So borrowing it from him with the pledge to return it when I came back I started on my trip. The way to the river was easy enough, but on coming back I found I was very tired When nearing the head of the ravine and looking ahead, I saw two men separating from each other, one of them coming towards me. On coming up to the first one, he placed himself in my way demanding a drink. I told him he was strong enough and well enough to go after water for himself. I rushed past him and made my way as rapidly as possible towards where Sergeant Hanley was stationed. When the second man came up to me and made the same request as the previous one I told him that I was carrying water for disabled men and not for those who could help themselves. The man drew his revolver telling me he was going to have a drink or he would know the reason why. I lowered the bucket, placing it partly on my foot. Now I said, 'Fire away; in neither case will you get any water.' I saw Hanley make a sudden motion with his left hand. He held his gun in his right hand. When he saw he had attracted my attention, he motioned me to step aside, at the same time dropping on his knees and resting his gun on the upper cracker box and pointed his gun in our direction. The man still held his revolver in his hand and was not aware of the latter's intention. I knew Hanley was a dead shot, I also knew that when he fired it would be at this man. He kept shaking his head for me to get out of the way. I made a sudden grab for the bucket and jumped aside, with my eyes turned earnestly in Hanley's direction. This sudden movement of mine caused the man to turn around and what he saw caused him suddenly to vanish. After coming to Hanley, I asked him what he intended doing. He said he had been watching the men's actions and had either one of them made a bad break, he would have bored daylight through him.

I was very grateful to Hanley for the interest he had taken in me, but I determined to make no more trips to the river. I was becoming exceedingly tired. I quickly got rid of the water and returned the bucket to its owner. I then went to where some of my comrades were in possession of a rifle pit, and there spent the time in conversation and wondering as to the outcome of this unequal contest. From where we were stationed we could see a large portion of the village, and observe any movement the Indians might be making. As this long to be remembered day was drawing to a close we became conscious that the firing on the part of the Indians was gradually ceasing, and we began to move around with a little more freedom. About seven o'clock in the evening, we noticed that the Indians were massing their ponies close to the village. We also noticed that the tepees were being rapidly torn down and the women were packing their effects, and strapping them on their pack animals. As the evening grew dark, they began to move slowly away from the river, in the direction of the Big Horn mountains. We tried to estimate the numbers of their fighting men, but it was difficult to do owing to the fact that they had their families with them, and a large number of ponies. But a conservative estimate of the number of warriors was about 2800. A few of the Indians remained and kept up a scattering fire as if loath to give us up. As darkness closed around us, the last shots came whistling over our heads. Thus closed one of the shortest and bloodiest engagements between the government and Indians, which had taken place in recent years. With the exception of the sentries and the wounded, whose moaning could be heard at any hour of the night, our camp was wrapped in slumber. As for myself, I could have slept under almost any circumstances.

"On the morning of the 27th we discovered that three men, Lieutenant De Rudio, Private O'Neil and Frank Gerard, our interpreter, had come into camp during the night. On making inquiries of Gerard, I learned that during Reno's retreat, these three had become separated from their respective companies. De Rudio and O'Neil had lost their horses, but Gerard still retained his. On getting together, they decided to remain concealed, not knowing what else to do. I asked Gerard why he had not attempted to join Reno's command again, he simply shook his head. I had him attend to my wounded hand and as he unwound the bandage, he told me that he had seen two men, belonging to Company A, whose horses ran away with them, carrying them into a large body of Indians, where they disappeared, and undoubtedly were put to death. Sometime after this, Gerard told a strange story of General Custer and his brothers, Tom and Boston, his nephew, Anthony Reed, and Lieutenant Cook. He said that they came across a scaffold similar to others upon which Indians were buried. It was simply four poles standing in an upright position with cross poles fastened closely together on the top, with the dead on top of this. Then some cooking utensils, hunting outfit, usually consisting of a knife, bow and arrows, and if fortunate enough a gun and a little powder and food, which he could hunt with in the country through which he passed on his way to the Happy Hunting Grounds. Gerard went on to say that those five men despoiled that grave and took away such trophies as they fancied, and solemnly added that himself and Jackson were the only two left of the company that witnessed the affair. He intimated that it was the vengeance of God that had overtaken them for this deed. Yes, we know how Jackson left the field and never stopped until he reached the Tongue River some thirty miles away. We also know that Gerard never fired a shot at the enemy but lay secreted for over forty hours, until all danger was over.

"To us of the 7th Cavalry, it was a well known fact that Lieutenant De Rudio was closely associated with one important event of history, and I will here relate it.

"On the night of January 14, 1858, all Europe was startled by the news that an attempt had been made to assassinate Emperor Napoleon and Empress Eugenie, by the explosion of three bombs charged with fulurinating mercury, which had been placed under the wheels of their carriage, as they were driving home from the opera, in the Rue Lepelletier. Though the Emperor and Empress escaped uninjured, an unknown number of persons were killed or wounded. The London Times, in its issue of January 18, 1858, gives the following statement of facts:

" 'The assassins had provided themselves with hollow projectiles of the most deadly description, and contrived to fling them on the ground under the carriage, where they instantly exploded and spread destruction among the bystanders. One of the carriage horses was killed on the spot, the other wounded. The carriage itself was broken to pieces. General Rogwet who sat in front was slightly wounded it is said, and two footmen who stood behind were dangerously hurt. A fragment of the shell passed through the Emperor's hat, but did not touch him. The Empress was also unhurt. Several lancers of the escort were seriously wounded; two or three are said to have been killed. The number of persons hurt is probably not less than sixty. (Fourteen of them afterwards died.)

" 'Four of the chief conspirators are already in custody. They are Piere, Orsini, Soumes and another who calls himself Da Selva, but whose real name is De Rudio. All are Italians.

" 'Soumes was subsequently set at liberty; the other three were convicted and condemned to die by the guillotine. De Rudio had lived for sometime in the town of Nottingham, England, and had married there. His wife interested the socialistic elements of that city in his behalf, they were then called chartists, and also some of the newspapers. A petition was prepared and funds were raised to enable her to go to Paris and present it to the Empress and ask her to intercede for her husband's life. This was done and a commutation of sentence followed.

" 'At 5:30 last evening the warrant to execute the

sentence of the court of Assize, upon those convicted of the attempt in the Rue Lepelletier was received by the procurer General. As I previously announced to you, that warrant only included Orsini and Piere. The punishment of De Rudio is commuted into penal servitude for life. Since their condemnation it was deemed proper to employ the straight-waist-coat with the three convicts, as a precautionary measure against any possible act of violence, either on themselves or those placed in contact with them. The reprieve of De Rudio rendered that restraint no longer necessary, and the governor did not delay a moment in serving orders to free him from it. When the turnkeys who were charged with the duty entered De Rudio's cell they found him buried in sleep. They shook him once or twice before he awoke. When he opened his eyes and sat upon his pallet he stared fearfully at them, and for a moment seemed bewildered. He thought they came to announce that his last moments had arrived, and he recoiled from their touch. 'Don't be afraid,' they said, 'We are not going to hurt you, far from it. We bring you good news, you are to have a commutation of punishment, and we are going to take off your straight-waist-coat.'

"Piere and Orsini were the next day, Saturday, March 14, led to the scaffold. Both died with great bravery.

"I am just informed that De Rudio is to be sent to London to serve evidence against Bernard. Bernard or Dr. Bernard was a French chemist, living in London, who was arrested and tried at the demand of the French government for complicity in the plot. He was suspected of being the maker of the bombs. He was acquitted after a most exciting trial. De Rudio did not appear as a witness against him, yielding to representations that the entire Orsini plot had been hatched in London.

"Lord Palmerson introduced a bill into parliament to restrict the right of an asylum in England, but this raised such a storm of indignation that he was compelled to resign from office. This feeling, however, soon blew over, and next year he resumed power.

"De Rudio shortly afterward received a full pardon. He returned to Nottingham, and essayed to enter the lecture field, but the attempt signally failed. Notwithstanding what might be expected to be a natural curiosity to see a man who had passed through such peril; there were barely twenty-five persons in the hall with a seating capacity for a thousand. Two of these were reporters, the rest were scowling carbonaries, who sat in silence.

"Thinking that his life was in danger from his former associates De Rudio came to the United States.

"His military career is set forth as follows, in Hammerly's complete regular Army Register:

"De Rudio, Charles C., born in Italy. Appointed from New York, Private Company A. Seventy-ninth New York volunteers August 25th, 1864. Discharged October 17th, 1864. Mustered out January 5th, 1866. Second Lieutenant, Second Infantry August 21st, 1867. Appointment cancelled September 20th, 1867. Appointment renewed October 25th, 1867. Unassigned April 17th, 1869. Assigned to Seventh Cavalry July 14, 1869. First Lieutenant December 15th, 1875.

"The cancellation of De Rudio's commission in 1867, it is understood at the War Department arose out of the Orsini affair being called to the attention of the officers, who, after inquiry, ordered his re-appointment.

"It was about seven o'clock in the morning that a Crow scout came dashing into our midst with the news that a body of men were coming up the left bank of the river, but whether they were Indians or soldiers he could not tell. Major Reno then called for volunteers to go and ascertain whether they were friends or foes. The scout who had brought the report, Half Yellow Face or Two Bloody Hands by name, and one of the soldiers volunteered and away they went, full speed. I might state here that another Crow scout came to us with Half Yellow Face, early in the morning. He was badly wounded, being shot through the wrist and thigh, but he bore his suffering nobly. We were all in a great state of excitement at this time, wondering what the moving column could be. Were the Indians coming back to finish their deadly work? In about half an hour, the soldier returned, his horse covered with foam, with glad news that General Terry, with some of the 2nd Cavalry and Gibbons with his Infantry, were coming. We all gave a loud shout of joy, waving our hats in the air. Terry soon made his appearance and when he had looked around on the scene of desolation, he wept. He soon recovered himself, and ordered the 7th Cavalry to move across the Little Horn River, and camp with the troops which had just arrived and gone into camp on the site of the Indian village. It was about one mile from our camp to the new one, and it took us a long while to remove the wounded soldiers, as all had to be carried on rudely constructed stretchers. When we came to our new camping place, we saw the position Custer was in when he made his last fight. Dead men and horses were scattered all over the ground. It was an awful sight, not on account of the dead only, but because of the mutilated condition of their bodies. The only one which was not stripped of his clothing, and mutilated, was General Custer. He still had on his blue shirt, buckskin pants, with the legs pushed in the tops of his long legged boots. The rest of the officers and men were gashed with knives all over their bodies and their heads crushed in with stone mallets. The bodies were turning brown from the heat of the sun and were swollen to a great size. As they were not to be buried till the next morning, we turned our attention to the wounded. The tents which the infantry had brought with them were put up for the use of these suffering men, and everything was done which could possibly be for their comfort. General Terry had brought with him some artillery, and our strength made it impossible for any body of Indians to cope with us.

"The Indians no doubt had received information of Terry's coming, which was the cause of their rapid retreat. One company of soldiers was sent out to ascertain in what direction the Indians had gone. It was one of the companies of the 7th Cavalry. There was vengeance in every man's heart on account of the horrible way in which the Indians had treated our dead.

"Having a desire to get some trophy, as a memento of this affair, I commenced to search the site of the Indian village, but all I could find that was easy to carry was one of our Cavalry Snaps, belonging to a canteen. I saw quite a number of saddles, but all the leather had been cut away. I also saw a few muzzle loading Spencer carbines and gun shells of every kind. The Indians had left two tepees standing, with dead Indians inside. There were thousands of buffalo robes scattered around, a number of which were kept for the use of the wounded. The rest went up in flame and smoke, together with the tepees. Quite a number of stone mallets covered with hair and blood, which had undoubtedly been used by the squaws on the heads of the dead and wounded soldiers, were scattered around. The mallet is a rock made round by the action of the water in a running stream. It weighs about five or six pounds. A number of willows, of sufficient length to cover the stone and form a handle, are laid cross wise. The rock is laid in the center and the willows are gathered tightly around it. They are then bound from the rock to the end of the willow, thus forming a handle. While noting these things, I saw a couple of cavalry men running toward me, shouting 'Indians,' at the same time pointing to a body of men approaching our camp on a trot. I was inclined to run myself, but on taking a closer view, I discovered that it was the company which had been sent out on a scouting trip. Turning to the right, I was surprised to see such a number of ponies lying down disabled or dead. There must have been hundreds of them lying in the brush. While I was making my way to the river, I came across the body of one of the greatest scouts on the western plains, Mich Burey. He had become separated from Reno's command, and fallen into the hands of the savages. While looking at the body I heard a grunt behind me. Turning, I saw Half Yellow Face watching me. I was glad to see him as I was deeply interested in him. I asked him where he was when the fight took place. He pointed to a spot on the opposite side of the river. It was a small flat bordered by some underbrush. He told me that when the cowardly Ree scouts started for Tongue River, the Crows came to the determination to return and fight against their bitterest foes. Secreting themselves and their ponies on the right bank of the river, they kept up a continuous fire into the village, until they were discovered, then they had to retreat. In the meantime, his partner had been shot through the thigh, and a short time afterwards, while taking aim, a ball struck him in the wrist making him useless as a fighter. But the hardest work of all was for Half Yellow Face to lift his partner onto a pony, for he was a very heavy man. He succeeded, but none too soon, for some of their enemies had crossed the river and were trying to capture them. But with great determination he succeeded in keeping them at bay while they made their escape. He told this with a good deal of pride, that his partner had killed six while he, himself, had only killed five of the enemy. 'But,' said Half Yellow Face, 'Come, I show you him.' So we made our way slowly through the underbrush, to where his comrade was. He was a fine specimen of a warrior, but as I have stated before, badly wounded. He was cheerful and seemed glad to see us.

"An officer and a detachment of men had been left at our late place of defense with orders to destroy all food and government property that could not be removed, and to bury all the dead. The rifle pits came into use as graves. Early on the morning of the 28th what remained of the 7th Cavalry crossed the river to bury their dead. Some of the bodies of the officers were missing. Lieutenant Harrington's body could not be found. What had become of it, it is difficult to tell. It is supposed that the bodies of Lieutenants Porter, Sturgis and Assistant Surgeon Lord were also missing. If found, they could not be recognized, owing to the horrible manner in which they were mutilated. Major Reno says, concerning Harrington, 'I am strongly of the opinion that he is not only dead, but that he was burned at the stake, for while the great battle was going on, I, and some other officers, looking through field glasses, saw the Indians, miles away, engaged in a war dance about three captives. They were tied to the stake, and my impression was, that Harrington was one of them.' But I think Major Reno was mistaken. We never found any evidence that Harrington suffered such a death. But we all know that the Indians are capable of just such cruelties. Major Reno makes another mistake. He says that Custer bore down on the Indians, with his handful of men, for the purpose of gaining all the credit for himself. The attack which occasioned the massacre was unwarranted, because the Indians were the rightful possessors of the land and were entirely peaceable, and many a brave man fell in that fight, simply to gratify Custer's ambition. Major Reno forgets that General Custer was acting under orders. This expedition was undertaken for the express purpose of driving the Indians back to their respective reservations, which they had no business to leave for the purpose of committing lawless acts against settlers. Major Reno had ample opportunity to get some credit for himself on two occasions. First, when sent to attack the Indians on the right, giving Custer time to collect his forces and attack the enemy's flank, but he retreated and remained inactive for nearly three hours, even when urged to go to Custer's relief, by two messengers sent by Custer's command. One of the messengers was Sergeant Knipe of Company C. The command was to hurry up the ammunition and reinforcements, but the only effort made as far as the ammunition was concerned, was by Sergeant Hanley of Company C taking the pack mule, Barnum, and alone trying to comply with Custer's request. The next one to come, and the last, was trumpeter Martin, with orders to bring on reinforcements, and the pack train, undoubtedly meaning the ammunition mules, of which we had twelve, carrying twenty-four boxes of cartridges. It is useless for military men to say that it was impossible for Reno to do otherwise than he did. He had seven companies under his command, for Captain Benteen had joined Reno shortly after his retreat from the village, and so had Captain McDugal with pack train, making their united strength about four hundred men. I am aware of all the movements of Reno's command from the time he retreated from the village till we joined his command on the bluff: His conduct, to me seems cowardly in the extreme. His refusal to allow Captain Weir of Company D to go to Custer's relief when he begged permission, and his own inaction goes to show his incapability. Major Reno says, 'When we found the men dead on the battlefield they laid in such a position as to show that they fled after the first fire and the Indians pursued and shot them down, for in almost every instance they were shot in the back.'

"What a slander! Does he think that anyone will believe that the Cavalry dismounted for the purpose of running away from mounted savages? No one will believe it. They faced their foes like men and died like heroes, unlike their traducer who fled like a coward. Again Reno says,

" 'When I came to the body of Captain Tom Custer and saw his heart was cut out, I knew that Rain-In-The-Face had done it for Tom had him arrested for the larceny of some cloth.'

"But it was for murder that Custer had Rain-In-The-Face arrested and he should have been hung for it, but he had escaped from the guard house at Fort Lincoln. Tom Custer's body was mutilated and so were all the others with the exception of General Custer. He remained just as he had been shot, with two balls in his body. Again Major Reno says,

" 'General Custer lacked courage. I have known him to flourish his sword about his head and shout, 'Follow me, men, follow me!' and when the fight begen he would be found in the rear. During the rebellion I discovered him hiding behind a tree when the battle was raging.'

"This was the kind of talk Major Reno indulged in after the fight took place. A very unmanly act on his part. Early in the afternoon, when the bodies of officers and men had been covered by earth, orders were given to move camp five miles down the river slowly, for we had nearly fifty wounded men. The method of transporting the wounded was very simple. The only wheeled concerns we had, were the several pieces of artillery, brought up by Terry. Those who had been severely wounded were placed on a travelling travois. A travois is simply two long poles fastened to a horse, the same as the shafts of a cart, and two ends trailing on the ground, and cross pieces fastened at suitable distances behind the horse, to keep the poles from spreading. Rawhide is then stretched from pole to pole and fastened by rawhide thongs. Plenty of buffalo robes were placed on top of this. It made a fine bed and if the poles were long enough, so as to have plenty of spring, it was far superior to a wheeled vehicle. The two horse travois was built similarly to the single one. Only gentle horses were used for such purposes, and after what they had gone through, they were all gentle enough. For my part, I preferred to ride on horseback. I secured a horse that an earthquake could not excite. I experienced very curious sensations on this five mile ride. My head would spin round and I felt so sick, I feared I would fall off my horse. I placed my head on the horse's neck and grasped his mane with my sound hand, hanging on for dear life. An officer, seeing my condition, touched my arm and told me I had better get on a travois, but I only shook my head. I felt too bad to take any notice of anything that was going on around me, and glad indeed was I when we moved into camp. We remained there for twenty-four hours, until the cool of the evening of the twenty-ninth. Here I would state that the only surviving thing that came from the Custer battlefield, was a large buckskin colored horse belonging to Captain

Keogh. He was wounded in five different places and great doubts were expressed whether he would live or not. He did live for a great number of years afterwards. His name was Comanche. On the twenty-ninth we moved down the Little Horn five miles more. Such easy stages were very favorable to the wounded, and showed great consideration on the part of General Terry.

"Two messengers had been sent with dispatches to General Crook's headquarters, commanding him to join forces with Terry's command at what was called the supply camp, on the east side of the Yellowstone River, for the purpose of conducting a most vigorous campaign against the Indians. At this time, there were no railroads or telegraph lines in the country. All dispatches and news of importance had to be carried by couriers and a risky business it was, for the messenger generally had to travel by night, with the stars for his guide. All the men who volunteered to do this work as far as I have learned succeeded in opening communication with the various troops in the field. What was most needed in a courier was a cool head, plenty of courage and the best horse that could be found. They would sometimes make eighty miles or more in twelve hours.

"On the 30th we again moved slowly down the river bank and were told that the steamer 'Far West,' had succeeded in coming up the Big Horn River, to within a short distance of the north of the Little Horn. As darkness came on, bonfires were lighted to guide us to where the boat lay. It was nearly ten o'clock when we reached it. The wounded were carried on board while the cavalry and infantry camped a short distance away. Then we could see why Terry had been twenty-four hours too late in coming to our relief. The boat had to carry Gillon's command from the east side of the Yellowstone to the west. A cavalry horse is a hard animal to manage if he sees strange sights and hears strange sounds. On this account Terry lost one day in the operation. In traveling, infantry cannot make so many miles a day as cavalry, but on this occasion the infantry begged to be allowed to make a forced march, but their request was not granted them. The reason that Terry's and Custer's forces did not unite at the point agreed upon was that Custer gained a day by long forced marches from the time he left the Yellowstone on the 21st until he struck the Indians on the Little Horn on the 25th. Had the two forces united and then brought on an engagement with the Indians, the object of the expedition would have been accomplished. With the number of men and heavy guns Terry had with him, united with the 7th Cavalry they would have been able to subdue the Indians and make them return to their reservations. But on account of a blunder, 267 officers and men lost their lives, and the Indians were allowed to escape. It took years to remedy the mistake.

"The campaign of '76 cost over a million of dollars, and was an utter failure. Had the spirit of unity, instead of rivalry prevailed, which was so manifest in one of the officers in the field, the outcome would have been very different. Where was General Crook all this time? Could he be unaware of the existence of the Indians who had attacked him on the Rosebud on the 17th of June, only eight days before Custer had the fight with them? It would take a good deal of persuasion to convince the men that he was hunting the enemy.

"We laid over all day, the 30th of June, and placed on board the steamer all supplies not needed by the troops. It was only two days' march from where we were to the supply camps.

"The wounded horse, Comanche, and one of General Custer's horses were put on board the steamer.

"It was on the morning of the 1st of July, that the 'Far West,' moved out of the Big Horn, into the Yellowstone River, while the Cavalry, Infantry and Artillery moved down the west bank to a place opposite the supply camp. The steamboat was utilized to carry the troops across the river. But for the number of wounded on board, the crossing of the river would have been very pleasant. They all tried to be cheerful, but it was plain to be seen that some of them were not long for this world. It was late in the evening when we reached the camp. The wounded were transferred to hospital tents which were large and roomy, and were attended by doctors who gave them every attention. On July 2nd, the remainder of the command arrived on the west bank of the river. These were also transferred across the river in the steamer, first the horses, mules, guns and supplies arriving and lastly the men. We laid in camp all the next day, but on July 4th we commenced to steam down the Yellowstone River. Captain Marsh, of the steamer, endeared himself to all on board, by his fund of humor and his kind attentions to the wounded.

"The steamer was well protected in case of an attack by the Indians. The pilot house was covered with strong sheet iron. The first deck was piled around with cord wood.

"Our first stopping place was at the mouth of Tongue River, where we laid over for about two hours. This gave us time to hunt our blankets. Here a little incident occurred, which shows how unpopular a man may make himself. When the steamer touched the bank, a man named Billy Jackson, jumped on board and rushed up to the captain who was stationed on the upper deck. As he went past where the wounded were lying, a growl of savage rage greeted him, which made him quicken his pace. One of the men drew his revolver with the evident intention of shooting him, but Billy was too quick for him. The impression seemed to prevail amongst the men, that he was in part responsible for the disaster which had overtaken Custer. He led the five companies one mile below the proper fording place which was the one where Watson and I attempted to enter the village. How Jackson escaped from the boat without detection I do not know. I watched very closely for him after getting my blankets. I determined to speak to him if possible, but my plan failed. As we steamed down the river, I learned that when Jackson and the Ree scout returned with the information that the Indians were thirty miles away, and later with the news of Custer's defeat, the citizen teamsters demanded higher wages and guns with which to defend themselves. It was a difficult matter to settle, but was finally adjusted satisfactorily.

"Our next stopping place was Fort Beauford, where ice was taken on board, and one of the men named King, who had died, was buried. Fort Beauford is located on the Big Missouri River. The river was greatly swollen by the recent rains, so that when we started again, we went at great speed. Wood and bacon were fed to the hungry furnaces. As we were speeding along we saw a large herd of buffalo rush over the bank into the river, just ahead of the steamer. We went plowing through among them, but it did not check their course for the mass behind kept pressing those in front. No doubt numbers of them were drowned.

"Captain Marsh told us that they were undoubtedly stampeded by Indians, as he had seen the savages through his glasses.

"I will here relate an incident which has always remained a mystery to me. We had in our company a man by the name of St. John. Why they called him *Saint* I cannot tell. He appeared to me to be nearer related to fallen angels. He had been released from the guard house in order that he might serve with his company on the campaign. He was a good hunter, and while on the expedition, prior to the 12th of May, he was allowed to leave his command for the purpose of killing such game as he wished. He, of course, was not the only one who went on these hunting trips; but he is the one of whom I wish to speak. He did not possess a knife and it is almost as bad for a hunter to be without a knife as for a ship to sail without a compass. I overheard him speaking of his need, and feeling that I had no use for mine, gave him it. There was a name marked on the one side of the handle, and the initials of a name on the other. An oblong piece was broken from the end of the handle. I knew that St. John had the knife when he went into battle on the 25th of June. I walked back to the rear of the boat and took a seat near Bennett, who seemed glad to have me beside him.

"While looking around I saw an Indian leaning against the wheel-house. He had a bandage on one of his arms, which showed he had been wounded. I did not recognize him as one of our scouts, which made me take particular notice of him. He had two rifles in his possession and attached to the belt which he wore, was a knife scabbard in which I saw the knife I had given to St. John.

"To say I was astonished is putting it mildly. To make sure, I moved closer toward him, and the closer I got, the more certain I was that it was the same knife. The oblong piece broken from the end of the handle and the name marked in plain letters were visible. I wondered how he could have gotten possession of it. I began to study the face of the Indian but he soon noticed my attention and seemed to avoid my gaze. I determined to obtain possession of the knife if possible and I thought of the coming night when I might have a chance to get it while he was asleep. I forgot that we were nearing a small place called Fort Berthold. As we came in sight of the fort we saw an Indian woman by the water's edge washing some material. There was a little child a few feet above her putting out its hands to help her out of danger, as our steamer was hugging the bank very closely. We were wondering whether the wheel would strike the woman or not. I saw two rifles which had been thrown from the boat, fall on the bank of the river. Looking around to see who had thrown them, I saw the Indian I have already mentioned, make a leap from the boat and reach the bank in safety. I noticed the squaw still standing by the water's' edge unhurt and also saw the Indian scramble up the bank, take his guns, and go away. Was he a hostile or was he friendly? How did he get the knife, and why did he leap from the boat when it was going full speed? These are questions I cannot answer.

"Late on the evening of the 5th of July, we arrived at Bismarck, where we laid over till next morning, when we continued our journey to the landing at Fort Lincoln. We found that we were the first to bring the news of the disaster. When the news was broken to the widows of the dead officers and soldiers, it was a sight which brought tears to all eyes.

"The wounded were removed to the hospital and the dead were buried, in the grave yard on the hill.

"Poor Bennett died on the afternoon of the 5th of July with my hand clasping his. So died a man who always gave me good advice and always tried to follow the advice he gave."

"Peter Thompson"

THE INDIAN ACCOUNT OF THE BATTLE

What the Indians have to say about the battle may be interesting to the reader and we will add the statement published in North Dakota "Historical Collections" as given by Father Genin from his talk with Sitting Bull: "We knew the soldiers were coming upon us weeks before the fight, yet we did not want to fight if we could do otherwise. In our camp on the Little Big Horn were the tribes of the Tetons, etc. We did not go out there to fight. We took our women and children along and went to meet all the tribes of the region, to make laws and treaties and to visit each other, and to make our young men and maidens acquainted with each other, so they could marry, as our fathers have done for many generations. So, when we found the white soldiers were following us, we marched back into the hills a long way, still being pursued by the army in direct violation of the treaty of 1868, which first article pledges the honor of the United States to keep peace. We resolved to camp and wait the will of God, at the same time praying to God to save us from the hands of our enemies, now near, and coming without provocation to complete our extermination.

"For three days our scouts watched Custer marching toward our camp. I therefore sent all our women and children into places of safety through the low lands. We expected the soldiers would charge through the village, as they did at the battle of Washita in 1868, when Chief Black Kettle was killed, and the women and children trampled to death under the hoofs of their war horses. The Teton Indians are too brave and love their families too well to let them be butchered even by the soldiers of the United States, and not fight for them until death.

"So I sent my young men to light fires inside and outside the deserted tepees, placing conveniently at the door of each of the front tepees sticks dressed like men, and to put stakes in the front streets of the village, to which were tied pieces of blankets, so that when the fires were burning, and stirring the air, the pieces of cloth and old rags waved to and fro in the breeze and gave the appearance of a densely populated village. Then I marched behind the front row of hills with all my braves, and waited the opening of the soldiers' fire upon our camp. Everything worked as I had planned. True to their intentions, the United States soldiers killed my flag men whom I had sent to meet them and demand peace, and proceeding furiously forward, opened fire upon my empty camp of old tepees and rag manikins. I then fell upon them from the rear, with all my force, before they had time to recover from the shock of their furious charge and their surprise at finding the village deserted. My men destroyed the last of them in a very short time. Now they accuse me of slaying them. Yet what could I do? Nothing."

In referring to Reno's soldiers, Sitting Bull said, "These soldiers were not brave. When they saw our warriors, they ran away as fast as they could and hid in the hollows of the hills. I was not in that part of the battlefield. I sat on my horse on a hill and sent my young men to direct the movements of the head warriors. All my warriors were brave and knew no fear. The soldiers that were all killed were brave men, too, but they had no chance to fight or run away; they were surrounded too closely by our many warriors. As they stood there waiting to be killed, they were seen to look far away to the hills in all directions, and we knew they were looking for the hidden soldiers in the hollows of the hills to come and help them. But our soldiers first killed the soldiers who were holding the horses and rode them while charging close up and firing at the survivors. Let no man call this a massacre. It was a mere piece of warfare. We did not go out of our own country to kill them. They came to kill us and got killed themselves. God so ordered it."

In answer to a statement by Father Genin that it was reported that Sitting Bull killed General Custer he said excitedly: "It is a lie. I did not kill the Yellow Hair. He was a fool and rode to his death." He said further that he did not personally see General Custer during the battle; that his people searched for the body of the long haired white chief after the battle, but that no soldier with long hair was found.

On this point Father Genin himself says: "Our friend Colonel Keogh's body and that of another Catholic soldier were the only ones treated with respect by the Indians, who stripped the dead bodies of their clothing on the battlefield. Pagans though they may be, and used to savage practices, still they have learned to respect the cross wherever they find it, and finding on Colonel Keogh's neck a chain and cross, they did not cut up his body but covered up his face respectfully and left him his cross and went by. A scapular found on the body of another man was the cause of similar treatment."

Sitting Bull further said that when all of General Custer's men had been killed his warriors rushed to surround the soldiers on the hill with Reno, and that they would soon have killed them, too, but a false alarm was raised that some soldiers had escaped and were attacking the women and children, and the whole Indian army surged in that direction. That when the mistake was found out, and his command surged again to the hill where Reno's' men were concealed, he gave the order that there should be no more fighting. "We have killed enough" he said. "Let the rest go back and take care of the women and children, and tell the people how the Indians can fight." Whereat his warriors were sorrowful and wanted to kill Reno's men, and then to give battle to the "walking soldiers" (Terry's Infantry), when they should leave the steamboat, but they obeyed his orders, although greatly disappointed.

We will also set forth the story of the fight as given by Chief Gall, one of the main leaders in the battle. It was told on the battlefield during the occasion of the tenth anniversary of the fight and in the presence of Curly, the Crow scout upon whom Gall turned his back, with the statement that "He ran away too soon in the fight."

"We saw the soldiers early in the morning crossing the divide. When Reno and Custer separated, we watched them until they came down into the valley. A cry was raised that the white soldiers were coming, and orders were given for our village to move immediately. Reno swept down so rapidly on the upper end that the Indians were forced to fight. Sitting Bull and I were on the point where Reno attacked. Sitting Bull was a big medicine man. The women and children were hastily moved down stream where the Cheyennes were camped. The Sioux attacked Reno and the Cheyennes Custer, and then all became mixed up. The women and children caught the horses for the bucks to mount. Then the bucks mounted and charged back to Reno, checked him and drove him into the timber. The soldiers tied their horses to trees, came out and fought on foot. As soon as Reno was beaten and driven back across the river, the whole force turned on Custer and fought him until they destroyed him. Custer did not reach the river, but was about a half a mile up a ravine, now called Reno Creek. They fought the soldiers and drove them back step by step, until all were killed. The Indians ran out of ammunition and then used arrows. They fired from behind their horses. The soldiers got shells stuck in their guns and had to throw them away. They then fought with little guns (pistols). The Indians were in coulees behind and in front of Custer as he moved up the ridge to take position, and were just as many on the grass. The first two companies, Keogh's and Calhoun's, dismounted, and fought on foot. They never broke, but retired, step by step, until forced back to the ridge upon which all finally perished. They were shot down in the line where they stood. Keogh's company rallied by company and were all killed in a bunch. The warriors directed a special fire against the troopers who held the horses while the others fought. As soon as a holder was killed, by waving blankets and great shouting, the horses were stampeded, which made it impossible for the soldiers to escape afterward. The soldiers fought desperately and hard, and never surrendered. They fought standing. They fought in line along the ridge. As fast as the men fell the horses were herded and driven towards the squaws and old men, who gathered them up. When Reno attempted to find Custer by throwing out a skirmish line, Custer and all with him were dead. When the skirmishers reached a point overlooking Custer's field, the Indians were galloping around over the wounded, dying and dead, and popping bullets and arrows into them. When Reno made his attack at the upper end, he killed my two squaws and three children, which made my heart bad. I then fought with the hatchet (mutilating the soldiers). The soldiers ran out of ammunition early in the day. Their supplies of cartridges were in the saddle pockets of their stampeded horses. The Indians then ran up to the soldiers and butchered them with hatchets. A lot of horses ran away and jumped into the river and were caught by the squaws Eleven Indians were killed on Reno Creek, and several Indians fell over and died. Only forty-three Indians were killed altogether, but a great many wounded ones came across the river and died in the bushes. Some soldiers got away and ran down a ravine, crossed the river, came back again and were killed. We had Oglalas, Minneconjeaus, Brule, Teton, Uncpapa, Sioux, Arapahoes and Gros Ventres. When the big dust came in the air down the river (Terry and Gibbon) we struck our lodges and went up a creek toward the White Rain Mountains. The Big Horn ranges were covered with snow. We waited there four days, then went over to the Wyoming mountains."

THE BURIAL OF THE DEAD

The battle had occurred in the burning hot days of mid summer and the three days of exposure to the

Custer's Monument

intense rays of the sun, together with the mutilation of the bodies by the savages, presented a most trying task to the comrades to whom it fell the lot to bury the fallen soldiers. Heads had been smashed in with stone hammers, and in some cases hacked from the bodies, legs and arms cut off and strewn about and desolation reigned supreme over the field. The burial squads, with mouths and noses covered were able to work but a few minutes at a time, before the nauseating stench would compel their relief. A trench was dug or scraped beside each gruesome form, and then by the aid of sticks and poles, the festering and swollen mass was rolled over and into the ditch, and hastily covered with loose dirt. The dry earth was not of the same hardness in all spots and in those places where the ground proved to be quite hard, only shallow graves were dug. As a result, the coyotes soon feasted upon the dead so easily uncovered. At each burial plot, a tent stake was driven with a number on it and this number marked down in a record for future identification. It is said that Custer's stake number was seven. Several years later, the government sent a force out to the scene of the disaster to complete the work of interment, as many of the dead had been dug out by wolves. Each man was furnished with rubber gloves and thus the work was carried out. General Custer's remains were taken back to West Point military academy from which he had graduated and there they rest today. All of the other officers, except one, were likewise taken to other points. The one remaining was left there at the request of the father who felt that his son should rest among the boys who went down with him and in the soil consecrated with his blood.

THE SOLE SURVIVOR

The news column of the current issues of the daily press carries a story broadcasted from Billings, Montana, that "Curly, the Crow scout, sole survivor of the Custer massacre of 1876, died yesterday, at the Crow Agency and was buried there today. He was sixty-eight years old."

Every year or so, the "sole survivor" of the Custer massacre is honorably mentioned in this or that locality, and while it makes little difference to casual readers, there is one real, true survivor, that deserves the distinction, having been buried with military honors, and officially declared so. We have counted seven in the past decade and it may be considered that the wilds are "full of them."

The only authentic sole survivor of the tragic battle of the Little Horn, connected with Custer's company was "Comanche" an honored horse that was for ten years a guest of distinction at Fort Meade. No other living being was left by the contending forces on the bloody field. To detract from "Comanche's" distinction is unworthy and leaves a chapter in history that is misleading. "Comanche" fills a niche in the accounts of that disaster that should not be sealed. "Comanche" according to the military records, bore the gallant Captain Keogh to the fatal battlefield, where Custer made his last stand, and two days and nights after the battle was found standing in a creek, badly riddled by Indian bullets, patiently waiting and mutely pleading for relief. The condition of the poor creature seemed so helpless that the first impulse of his discoverers was to shoot him and end his terrible suffering, but upon second thought, the soldiers determined to save his life. He was taken to Fort Lincoln and after weeks of tender nursing and skillful treatment he recovered. In April, 1878, General Sturgis, commanding, issued the following humane order to headquarters of the Seventh United States Cavalry at Fort Lincoln:

"The horse known as 'Comanche' being the only living representative of the bloody tragedy of the Little Big Horn, June 25th, 1876, his kind treatment and comfort should be a matter of special pride and solicitude on the part of every member of the Seventh Cavalry, to the end that his life be preserved to the utmost limit. Wounded and scarred as he is, his very existence speaks in terms more eloquent than words of the desperate struggle against overwhelming numbers, of the hopeless conflict and the heroic manner in which all went down on that day. The commanding officer of Company I, will see that a special and comfortable stable is fitted up for him, and he will not be ridden by any person whomsoever, under any circumstances, nor will he be put to any kind of work. Hereafter, upon all occasions of ceremony at mounted regimental functions, 'Comanche,' saddled and bridled and draped in mourning, and led by a mounted trooper of the company will be paraded with the regiment." By command of Colonel Sturgis, E. A. Carlington, First Lieutenant and Adjutant, Seventh Cavalry.

In June, 1879, "Comanche" was taken to Fort Meade by the Seventh Regiment, where he was kept like a prince until 1888, when he was taken to Fort Riley, Kansas, where later he died and was buried with military honors. This is the authentic history of the sole survivor of the Custer massacre, as recorded by military authority. There may have been many who served in 1876 with honor, and with records unofficially attached to their passing away to the bugle call of eternity, but careful search of the records of that bloody catastrophy will bear out the statement that "Comanche" was the sole survivor of Custer's last battle.

NEWS OF THE CUSTER MASSACRE RECEIVED IN THE BLACK HILLS

The 20th day of July, 1876, was one that will long be remembered by the pioneers. It was on that day that news of the massacre by Indians of General Custer and his entire force on the Little Big Horn was received. The old Seventh was a popular regiment with the people of the west and many of the Hills had friends and acquaintances in its various troops, while the gallant commander was considered by all, the ideal cavalry officer. Early in the year an important military expedition against the Indians had been undertaken and a considerable force under Generals Crook and Terry had been for some time operating in the Yellowstone country. It was hoped and believed that the campaign by so large a force of soldiers would break the spirit of the Indians and give comparative safety to the Hills country. Tidings from the north were awaited with anxiety, all hoping for an announcement of a decided victory over Sitting Bull, Rain-In-The-Face and their forces recruited from the Cheyenne, Oglala and Brule branches of the Sioux nation. The news that reached the Hills of the various engagements preceding the Custer fight had been meager and unsatisfactory. Dispatches from the forces in the field had been carried generally by couriers to Fort Laramie by way of trails west of the Hills and reports were from Laramie brought back to Deadwood and other mining camps by wagon train.

The assembly of the Indian forces in the north evidently had drawn off many of the lower reservation Indians who had been harassing the settlers, and for a brief time comparatively few outrages had been committed about the foothills. Just at this time when a feeling of security had been general and the settlers had begun to move about with little fear of danger, came the news from the Little Big Horn that Custer with his entire command had been annihilated. The story seemed incredible, yet at last nearly a month after the battle, here were the details so minutely set forth that their correctness could not be doubted. The Pioneer issued an "extra" which was circulated in the various camps and eagerly read. In this account was given the name of every soldier killed, thus forcing conviction of the awful truth. In a short time Deadwood was filled with excited men who poured in from the surrounding gulches, all eagerly discussing the news. Experienced frontiersmen expressed the belief that the danger to the Hills people would be greatly increased by the Indian victory, and that even if the government should now push the war against the hostiles with greater vigor, as seemed probable, the Indians would scatter out in small bands, and while the Cheyennes might cross the land into the British possessions, the Brules and Oglalas, on their way south to their reservations, would certainly kill and destroy wherever they found it possible on their way. That there was ample grounds for such fears was made manifest. During the month of August and September stories of murder of exposed settlers or travellers, and thefts of horses and cattle were received each day. No small party could travel with safety. In one day six men were waylaid and murdered within ten miles of Deadwood. A day or two later four men were killed three miles from Rapid City, while lone travelers were ambushed on every road and trail. Raids were made on horse herds held in the valleys of the foothills, and much stock driven off. On one occasion, one hundred head of horses were stampeded from the Centennial Valley herd and a herder killed. Everybody went armed, and some of the more timid even feared an Indian attack on Deadwood and other gulch towns. The citizens offered a reward of two hundred and fifty dollars for every Indian scalp taken and advertisement to that effect was kept standing in the columns of the Pioneer. Parties frequently were sent out to raise the siege of beleaguered wagon trains held in corral by the Indians about the foothills.

Late in the fall, as the main body of the hostiles had found safety north of the British line, General Crook made a forced march from the Yellowstone to relieve the people of the Hills. H command was short of provisions and subsisted in part on the flesh of mules of the outfit. The march was a very trying one, the men reaching the foothills with many practically exhausted and their clothing in rags. On the way scouts of the command discovered a Sioux village in the Slim Buttes of the Hills. This was attacked and destroyed, a number of Indians killed and many prisoners, mostly women and children, taken. In the fight the well known scout "Pony" White lost his life. The story of the expedition was written by Bob Strahorn, a newspaper correspondent with Crook, for the columns of the Pioneer under the caption of "Crook's March from Yellowstone."

Crook and the officers of his staff visited Deadwood where they were met with an enthusiastic reception, in the Langrishe theatre. Speeches were made, and general good feeling prevailed, the belief being indulged that the worst of the Indian troubles were over. As winter came on, depredations became less frequent. The spring of '77 had only a few isolated cases of Indian troubles, and soon after the ratification of the cession treaty in April of that year they ceased altogether.

CROOK'S MARCH FROM THE YELLOWSTONE

"On the night of the 12th inst, our city was startled by the unexpected news that General Crook, with his entire army was only forty miles to the northward, enroute by forced marches to this vicinity. Further, that the troops were destitute of any food but horse meat, and had placed themselves in such trying

General G. A. Crook

circumstances in order to overtake the bands of hostile Sioux whose trail led in this direction. We have since had the pleasure of interviewing different members of the advance guard to the expedition, and gathered many interesting points concerning General Crook's recent unparalleled march in the northern wilds, his wonderful perseverance under a trying ordeal, and the late battle near Slim Buttes.

"Our readers already know how Crook stripped

his command of very ounce of superfluous equipage when he left the northwestern base of the Big Horn mountains six weeks ago; how, in compliance with a determined clamor of his country and superior officers, he joined Terry near Yellowstone; how Terry's lumbering and clumsy movements weighted down and retarded our quick-moving division from the south. And how both commanders soon agreed to what Crook had at all times maintained, that Sitting Bull could never be brought to a square fight by the two armies combined and never caught by such an unwieldly organization.

"On the 25th of August the heads of the two columns agreed to separate. They were then lying near the great Indian trail, not far from the mouth of Powder River. A small band of the hostiles had fired into one of Terry's boats on the Yellowstone the previous evening, and that General determined to take his entire command to the scene, leaving General Crook to follow the main trail of the savages. The trail led eastward toward the Little Missouri. Keeping it between his own and Terry's forces, Crook hastened forward, in hopes to strike the savages on the stream just named, if not sooner, on some of its western tributaries. Occasionally the trail split on one stream but was generally found to concentrate again at the next, or at least the smaller trail would keep the same general eastward course. Signs grew fresher daily. On September 2nd, scouts commenced picking up abandoned Indian ponies. That night the hostiles interviewed Crook's sentries, and got several well directed volleys for their pains, and the next day scouts far in advance had a little skirmish, in which one Indian pony was killed and the rider believed to be wounded.

"The question of rations now began to agitate those in authority. Terry had promised to have fifteen days' supply at the mouth of Glendive, on the Yellowstone, and although five days had elapsed since the date upon which he should have communicated, and General Crook had scouted the country in hopes of meeting his couriers, nothing satisfactory could be heard of the Yellowstone army's whereabouts. Not wishing to lose a moment of his pursuit, and realizing the uncertainty of a dependence upon the Yellowstone rendezvous for supplies, General Crook continued eastward, knowing that at the worst he could reach Fort Lincoln on the rations then at hand. The Little Missouri was reached on the 4th inst. Here everybody predicted that Sitting Bull would make a desperate fight, if anywhere. But the looked-for enemy only again divided his trail into dim and badly scattered bridle paths, most of them leading east or southeastward. Still pressing eastward one day, to be certain that no considerable body of the enemy had gone northward, the command halted on the evening of September 5th, on or near the head of Heart River. During the day Colonel Stanton and Major Randall, at the head of a dozen scouts suddenly came upon thirty savages, temporarily encamped. It was some fifteen miles from the column and a brisk fight ensued, the Indians finally scattering into the adjacent Badlands, leaving a dead warrior, and it is believed suffering the loss of several wounded. All trails now seemed to lead to the Black Hills, and some of the smaller ones were quite fresh. It did not take the brave and far-seeing commander long to come to the conclusion that the general southward move on the part of the enemy meant the devastation of our own beautiful frontier and the death of perhaps hundreds of our hard-working citizens. But what could we do? Fort Lincoln with her tons of supplies and sheltering barracks lay by an easy trail one hundred twenty miles eastward. The nearest settlement in the Black Hills, by an unknown route and over a strange country was two hundred miles distant. Scant three days' supplies remained on the pack mules, and a ten days' trip to Fort Lincoln would easily increase the rations to a fifteen days' supply. But hours were precious, and the ten days thus lost was in effect losing the result of the summer's hard work, for the quick-moving Sioux could over-run the entire Black Hills and be off in their wildest, safest haunts with so much time gained to them. To add to Crook's dilemma, he had an almost discouraged army. Fate seemed everywhere on the wrong side. Without an inch of canvas for shelter, with inadequate clothes or covering, with only the nauseating bacon and the chip-like hard tack to sustain overtaxed bodies, these brave two thousand had faced cold, pitiless rain day after day, had lain down in mud and water for many nights in succession, and were now the very picture of a hopeless, cheerless division. A fight to the death, or the certain prospect of one only would have thrilled them with a new life. But it was only march, march under descending storm and through a sea of mud and water. The four hundred weary infantry men especially, had cause to lose their patriotism, martial ardor and everything else inspiring, although we are informed they stuck to their work like heroes. Well, General Crook decided as everyone who knows the man would guess. Dispatches were sent in to Fort Lincoln, informing Sheridan of his position and his desperate resolve; also to the authorities at Forts Laramie and Fetterman to send not only his own train from old Fort Reno, but a train with twenty days' supplies from the nearest post—these to make all haste toward the eastern base of the Black Hills. 'Southward!' was now the watch-word. Twenty-five to thirty-five miles per day were accomplished over the wide prairies and occasional bad lands of western Dakota. Camps without wood—when bacon raw was the main article of diet—and sometimes waterless, were made, little matter where night found the weary column. Rain continued to fall daily. The descent from full to half rations, from half to quarter, and then resort to the inevitable horse meat, all came in rapid succession. Hunting was frequently permitted, but one-tenth of so large a command could not be supplied with game. Eye witnesses say that if a rabbit, squirrel or prairie dog happened to show himself near the column, there would be a general stampede, and that was about the only time an outburst of jollity would occur. There would be a perfect din of such yells, as 'nose bag him,' 'hobble him' 'lasso him,' etc., and if the animal was not trampled to death by the broken ranks, the scare usually finished him. Cavalry horses often dropped from sheer exhaustion, and their riders thereafter walked in the rear of the infantry battalion. It is estimated that no less than one hundred fifty horses were thus abandoned, while a few were driven along for the poor meat they could afford. Sick and sore footed to the number of about fifty were either mounted upon mules, or in extreme cases, carried quite comfortably upon mule litters. Of these it should be noted that not a man had been lost, a fact which speaks volumes for the organization of General Crook's medical corps. For such sufferers a few canned goods, jellies, beans, tea, etc., had been husbanded with great care, and proved a grand treat during those dark days.

"On the 7th inst, when the command had reached the south fork of Grand River, one hundred miles north of Deadwood, General Crook determined to send forward a detachment of one hundred fifty picked men and horses, under command of Colonel Mills of the Third Cavalry, to forage our settlement for provisions and return to the command as speedily as possible. Lieutenant J. W. Bubb, chief commissary of the column, accompanied to attend to the purchase and delivery, and Thomas Moore had charge of forty pack mules to transport the supplies. Frank Gruard, chief scout of the expedition, was entrusted with the difficult duty of guiding the detachment across the country—a region totally new to all.

"The detachment pushed away from the main body under cover of inky darkness, rode through the rain until after midnight, and halted for a few hours' rest. Up and off again without breakfast at daylight, the gallant riders floundered through rain and mud until nearly noon, when a brief halt was ordered for the purpose of making coffee and giving the animals an hour's graze. But moments were precious, and in an hour the little band was again facing the storm, determined to get the wherewithal to refresh their suffering comrades. About three in the afternoon Frank Gruard suddenly hastened back from his advance position and announced the discovery of an Indian village. He said it was quite small, and was located some three or four miles ahead in such a position that the troops could not possibly reach it by daylight without being discovered. Colonel Mills was under orders to attack any band of hostiles he might meet, providing he was satisfied he could thrash them thoroughly—no matter about supplies in such an event. There was only one thing to do to make a thorough job of it, and that was to secrete during the night, and advance before the break of day. A deep gash in the bluffs lay near at hand, and into this men and animals were huddled during the night. Promptly at two o'clock on the morning of the 9th the little column filed out, reaching the village of thirty-five tepees just before the break of day.

"The attack was quickly made, the inmates totally surprised, and the capture of nearly all the Indian ponies—some two hundred in number—effected. Many of the savages nearly naked rushed out into the uncertain light of early dawn perfectly thunderstricken, scattering into the neighboring ravines, or making good their escape over into the Badlands. Others took time to snatch their guns, and returned the fire of the troops with considerable spirit. But the brave soldiers stuck to their work, and soon the entire village was being destroyed, and its contents worth saving transferred to the pack mules. General Crook, sent for early in the morning, arrived in time to dislodge a nest of the secreted savages, and also to repel an attack made later in the day by an increased number of the enemy, who had evidently been occupying another village not far off.

"Before the ground was abandoned every inch of canvas, with every other atom of value to the Sioux, was destroyed, excepting, of course, such articles as could be utilized by the troops. Of the latter there were over five thousand pounds of dried meat, many sacks of dried and green berries, two thousand buffalo robes and other skins, arms, ammunition, cooking utensils, etc. There was an officer's fine overcoat, one of Custer's battle flags, a horse branded Co. D, 7th Cavalry, a pair of soldier's pantaloons containing a letter addressed to a private in Custer's regiment, several letters from Indian agents vouching for the good character of Indians engaged in the fight, and numerous other mementoes, proving exclusively that the owners were good agency Indians, and had also directly participated in the Custer massacre. A few more of the Indians were killed next morning, swelling their entire loss to some forty killed, forty wounded, and twenty prisoners. The latter were marched along ahead of the column, and are composed principally of squaws and get the same treatment as ordinary prisoners of war.

"Crook's loss was three killed, and fourteen wounded. The wounded are being brought along quite comfortably on travois, and all but one are in a fair way to be on duty soon.

"This is emphatically *the* event of the campaign so far as punishment for the Indians is concerned, and the participants under General Crook deserve the lasting thanks of our people, for without a doubt the den of redskins so thoroughly rooted out has furnished shelter for more than one of the plundering savages who have annoyed us recently.

"A detachment of fifty men, mounted on Indian ponies came forward immediately after the fight, and as stated at the beginning of this article, arrived early in the week. Lieutenant Bubb worked night and day in his efforts to purchase supplies adequate for the temporary needs of his command. We have had plenty and to spare, and thousands of pounds of Deadwood and Crook City flour, bacon, beef, beans, sugar, coffee, etc., are now being dealt out to the troops located some twenty miles below on the Belle Fourche. Our merchants dealt most liberally. In fact many of the supplies were bought at rates never before given in the Black Hills.

THE BATTLE OF SLIM BUTTE

"Commencing its forced march towards the Black Hills settlement on the 5th inst., the column inaugurated one of the most wonderful moves known in the history of military affairs on the frontier. The infantry battalion sadly weakened by the continued rain storms, insufficient and unwholesome food; the cavalry horses fatigued, the march of 160 miles on less than three days' actual rations was anything but a cheerful outlook. The weather had s. oiled much of the hard tack which accounts for the shortage in this amount noted in my last. The first day's course lay nearly due south. Rations with the exception of coffee were reduced one-half. At night no wood could be found. The troops could not even make coffee, and the weather grew severely cold. On the 9th, with nothing but raw bison and hardtack the columns moved 32 miles, and at night had rations reduced.

"In the afternoon General Crook determined upon sending forward to Deadwood or Crook City for supplies there to be forwarded to meet the command at the earliest possible moment. Quarter rations for three days remained, and it was hoped abundant supplies could thus be furnished the troops on the day this scanty allowance was exhausted. Major Anson Mills of Company M 3rd Cavalry, was placed in command of 150 men to make the arduous ride. Fifteen picked men and horses from each of the companies of the Third Cavalry were selected to comprise this force. The junior officers were Lieutenant Bubb, commissary of subsistence of the expedition; Lieutenants Crawford, Company G, Third Cavalry; Von Lutwitz, Company C, and Schwatka, same regiment. Thomas Moore had charge of twenty packers and forty mules to furnish necessary transportation. The little column filed out of camp under cover of darkness. It was assailed by a drenching rain, and finally halted for a few hours' rest at night, having ridden forty-five miles since morning. Frank Gruard, General Crook's scout, led the band and as usual, displayed wonderful skill. At 4 o'clock a. m. on the 8th, Colonel Mills again started forward in the face of a heavy rain. The detachment halted but an hour at noon to make coffee, and yet at 3 p. m. had only proceeded some twenty-five miles on account of the broken country and miserable footing. At the hour just named Frank Gruard suddenly motioned a halt from his position a few hundred yards in advance. Coming hastily backward he announced the discovery of an Indian village. He said it was four miles distant, that they were not discovered, and advised an immediate secretion of the troops in a gully adjacent. Having had instructions to attack any force he was confident of whipping, and being certain from appearances that this one was small Colonel Mills determined to strike the enemy. The troops were carefully led back half a mile and secreted in the bottom of a deep chasm formed by the Badlands. The rain still continued to fall, and the brave but tired and hungry men spent a most dreary night in mud and water, at places nearly a foot deep. At 2 o'clock this a. m. a start for the village was effected. An hour for the floundering through mud and water brought the column to the hill overlooking the hostile camp. The charge was gallantly made, the brave 25th making a complete surprise and sweeping nearly 200 ponies safely out of the reach of the thunderstricken owners. The gloom of a misty dawn rendered the firing on the part of the dismounted men rather uncertain even at a distance of 50 yards. Bucks, squaws, papooses got up from their beds yelling and making for the adjacent wooded ravines. As usual the warriors secured some guns and ammunition as they ran, in making their exit through holes in the tepees on all sides with their knives, not waiting to find the regular entrance. A hot fire was poured in on the cavalry, and the pack train was immediately brought up and couriers sent back to Crook, informing him of the state of affairs and asking for re-inforcements. The latter request was made in the belief that more villages might be near. The village was occupied at once, though not without some danger, as some of the savages lay secreted in a deep, thickly wooded gully adjoining the stream on which the village was located. There were thirty-five tepees, most of them very large, and of the nest construction. Piled in these were tons of dried and fresh meat, numerous sacks of green and dried wild grass, about 1500 buffalo robes and skins, agency blankets, small bolts of calico and other fabrics, corn, flour, cooking utensils of every nature, arms and ammunition, etc. As they approached a number of the most gallant charges were made at them by Lieutenant Crawford at the head of ten or twelve cavalry. Indeed his efficient conduct was marked by rare judgment, coolness, and bravery. In attempts to dislodge the Indians from the gully already noticed, several instances of wonderful daring upon the part of the soldiers were observed, and no less than two men lost their lives near the fatal spot. Not until after the arrival of General Crook who made a forced march at the head of fifty cavalry, at noon, was the nest of desperate savages thoroughly cleaned up. Sharpshooters made repeated attempts in vain to pick off the Indians, and finally a large squad of scouts and officers made a rush into the very pit itself. Squaws and papooses were pitched out like so many snakes, the former in one or two instances being found firing vigorously with revolvers. At the same time a steady fire was maintained on the warriors. The last two of these were ordered to surrender about the middle of the afternoon when they had only 24 cartridges left. Here Big Hat, the scout, settled an old time feud by giving the chief, American Horse, his death wound, leaping into the pit itself, in his determination to kill the savage, and here also Frank White, alias Buffalo Chips, met his doom in rashly attempting a similar act.

"The squaws acknowledged that another village was located about one day's march westward, and said their friends from there would attempt a rescue. Sure enough, about 4 o'clock bands of savages were seen riding down from the tops of the bluffs in that direction, and making a dash for the far out sentries, but instead of the paltry 150 men under Mills, they found Crook's force of 1800 on the ground, every man eager for the onslaught. The infantry battalion of ten companies was quickly pushed forward on the left of the force, Company B, and the Second Cavalry in the center, and the Third Cavalry on the right line of attack. The field could not have been more advantageous for foes as it speedily occupied rock-covered bluffs commanded aal approaches ;yet the one hour's fight that followed was little more than a beautiful and impressive skirmish drill for our troops, and a very ungraceful fight from all positions by the savages. Especially fine were the movements of the infantry. Each height was carried as though weariness and hunger were forgotten and each volley was delivered with enthusiastic hurrahs.

"Night is here, and 1000 camp fires light up a scene never to be forgotten. The soldiers last night, ragged, cold, weak, starved, and well nigh desperate, are feasting upon meat and fruits received from a savage enemy, or warmly clothed by the robes which last night wrapped the forms of renegades. Merry songs are sung, and everywhere the cry goes up 'Crook is right after all.' "

Colonel Mills and his handful of troops deserve much praise for the manner in which the blow was delivered.

THE TREATY

The disastrous results of the campaign of the Little Big Horn, and the hard fights with Indians through the summer, aroused much indignation among the people and accordingly Congress in earnest, took up the work of treating with the Indians. Finally, defeated, dismounted and practically disarmed, the Indians were prevailed upon to sign a treaty prepared for them beforehand by the government. The several tribes were approached in their reservations through their chiefs and leaders and thus the work was quickly completed. We will not relate all of the different sessions and the arguments had, but reprint here, an item from the Pioneer of September, 1876, which will illustrate how the Indians felt about the forced surrender of their ancestral lands:

"This evening the Commission consummated the treaty with the Sioux, Cheyennes, and Arapahoes at this agency. The Indians agreeing to the proposition made to them of the 7th inst, without the change of a single word, which propositions have already been published in full. The following named Indians were selected by their people to sign for the Ogalallas, after the treaty had been read and interpreted to them before signing: Red Cloud, Young-Man-Afraid-of-His-Horse, Red Dog, Little Wound, American Horse, Afraid-Of-The-Bear, Three Bears, Fire Hunter, Quick Bear, Red Leaf, Five Eyes, Man White Cow, Good Bull, Sorrel Horse, Weasel Bear, Two Lance, Bad Wound, High Bear, He Take the Evening Soldier, Slow Bull, High Wolf, and Big Foot. The Cheyennes and Arapahoes will not sign until tomorrow after which the Commissioners will start at once for Spotted Tail agency, to consummate the treaty there. To the surprise after they had affixed their signature to the treaty, the Indians held back and speeches were made by many of them before they would touch the pen, and make their marks. Red Cloud said, 'I am a friend of the President, and you men who have come here to see me are chief men and men of influence. You have come here with words from the Great Father, therefore because I am his friend, I have said 'Yes' to what he has said to me, and I suppose this makes you happy. I don't like it that we have a soldier here to give us food It makes our children's hearts go back and forth. I wish to have Major Howard for my agent, and I want you to send word to Washington so that he can come here very soon. If my young men come back and say that country is bad it will not be possible for me to go there. As for the Missouri river country, I think if my people should move there to live they would all be destroyed, as there is a great many bad men there and bad whiskey, therefore I don't want to go there. Great many of my white relations have no money, if they are employ-

"Chief" Red Cloud

Photo by Graves Studio Chadron, Nebr.

ed to go to Indian territory to look at the country, I hope they will be paid out of the money the Great Father sent with you. In addition to those I mentioned yesterday that I want to go with my young men, are Mr. Joot, Charlie Green, Mr. Raymond, Antione Ledeau and Sam Deon.' Young-Man-Afraid-Of-The-Horse said, 'This is the country where I was born. I never made any man's heart bad. I have thought that the Great Father intended that I should live here and raise my children here. I wished that the Great Father would take care of me, and that I should live here with my children. These white people who have married among us I give notice that it will take me a long time to learn to labor and I expect the President will feed me for hundreds of years, perhaps a great deal longer. The promises that have been made by the Great Father heretofore have not been carried out, therefore I have been unwilling to go and see him, although I have been often invited. Dr. Daniels will remember bringing me back from Washington, the word that here was where we was to raise our children. I have appointed to live here, therefore I have never travelled around to see other countries. You have never heard of me behaving badly.' With this he took the pen in hand and as he made his mark, said, 'That is to signify that the Great Father has to feed and clothe me hundreds of years and give me wagons and cattle.'

"Red Dog said, 'I want the Great Father to make haste and send me that man (pointing to Major Howard) for agent, and also Bisnet and Daniels to assist me.'

"Little Wound said, 'I told you before, I must have my annuities within two months, and provisions to last me until spring.'

"American Horse said, 'In regard to this arrangement about the Black Hills, it is to last as long as we live.'

"Man-Afraid-Of-The-Bear took hold of the pen

saying, 'The others have said enough,' signed and returned to his seat.

"Three Bears inquired how many years they would be furnished with cattle, and said that he thought it would be for five generations.

"Fire Thunder came up holding his blanket over his eyes and signed blindfolded and returned to his place in silence.

"Big Foot, who has been engaged in agriculture for several years, said, 'I am a farmer, I wanted a hundred wagons, but have never seen them yet. I am the man that is going down to see that country.'

"Crow-With-A-Good-Voice refused to sign the treaty and walked away with quite a show of indignation. But all others who had been selected and were present affixed their cross to the paper, a copy of which was given to them at their request."

Sioux Indians on Dress Parade

CHAPTER V.

HIGHWAYMEN AND ROBBERS

Not only did the pioneers have to meet the bullets hurled at them by some red marauder hidden along the way, but they also had to resist the murderous attack of their own race on the part of highwaymen and robbers who infested the trails leading to the land of golden dreams. So numerous were the various robberies and crimes of violence committed by the road agents, they would require a volume in themselves. Only a few of the most noted will be related in this chapter, as they are characteristic of the stern realities of wild life of the times.

THE PROGRAM OF A HOLDUP OF 1876

From the Sidney Telegraph of July, 1877, we well reproduce an account of how the ordinary holdup was conducted. It is a record of the time and no doubt was written by one who had had the experience. However it is true to life and will no doubt recall familiar scenes to the minds of any pioneer of that day who spent much time on the trails.

This is the way the road agents do it on the Cheyenne route to the Hills.

Captain of Gang: "Halt."

Stage Driver: "All right."

C. of G.: "How many passengers have you on board?"

S. D: "Four."

C. of G.: "You're a liar, you've but three for you dropped the banker at Crook City. Get down off the box and throw up your hands and stand with back to me. Passengers will alight on opposite side of the coach and throw up hands, and keep in line with the driver."

The captain then issues the following orders:

No. 1 Attend to the team and see it doesn't break away.

No. 2. Cover the passengers and shoot the first one who turns his back from you or lets his hands down.

No. 3. Search the passengers from hats to toe of boots.

These orders are carried into effect with mathematical precision, and almost invariable success, the captain of the freebooters having a general supervision of the raid, acting as sort of a double guard.

C of G.: "No. 3, have you searched that big brown bearded fellow's shirt? I saw him put away $300 in it at Deadwood yesterday.

No. 3.: "You told me so this morning, but I can't find it. The pocket is there but there's nothing in it."

No. 2.: (To impatient victim who attempts to turn his head) "Keep that nose to the front or I'll blow the top of your head off." Victim complies.

C. of G.: "Where the h--l are those fellows' watches? I saw a gold chronometer worth $250 on that little cub to the right at Rapid City this very morning, and he was more anxious to show it then than now. Look in his boots." Boots develop nothing.

C. of G.: "Search the stage, and pry off the treasure box, and don't lose any time. No. 2, see that your men are covered."

The treasure box is wrenched off, the mail rifled, passengers relieved of all they could not conceal, when the following order is given by the C. of G.: "Driver, take your seat on the box." Driver complies. The C. of G. delivers himself something as follows: "Passengers, these are hard times and it's every one for himself. You're here to make money and so are we. You've got valuable claims in the Hills and we've failed. Most of us have lost all we had, and there's a few of us who are professionals at the business. Worked stages in Montana, Idaho, California and even in Mexico. It's easy business and light work Only requires a little nerve and bluster. Now you fellows are all armed and have talked this subject of stage robbing over to the crowd, just how you would serve the d---d road agents, in case they molested you. Pointed out the exact spot where you would shoot and even contemplated scalping the robbing villains. And now here is the result of all that talk You stand there trembling in your boots, robbed, with hands above your head, while we road agents go through you for all that's out, and go back for fresh braves like you. When you get to Cheyenne tell an awful story of how you fought and shot and blustered and gave us a piece of your mind, when in fact you didn't have the spunk to draw a gun or open your mouths, and when you get home to the bosom of your families, tell them you're going to stay there, wouldn't scalp a road agent if you could and couldn't if you would. You will now take your places in the coach and proceed Hope you will sleep comfortable. Now let go the team."

And that's all there is to it. The robbers return to Deadwood, and the victims proceed on their meloncholy way. These are about the facts in the case of the usual stage robbery on the Cheyenne route, which occurs about twice a week in case it is a good week.

THE KILLING OF "STUTTERING BROWN"

Gilmer and Saulsbury started a stage line in the year 1875, known as the Black Hills and Cheyenne trail by stocking and equipping it with horses and coaches as far as Fort Laramie. They put on six good horse teams and fine Concord coaches and in 1876 they extended their line into the Black Hills. This company had years of experience in staging in the west and when the excitement created a stampede to the Black Hills, they started to run a daily line to the scene of the gold excitement. However, they had a great deal of trouble with horse thieves and Indians who would kill their stock tenders and make away with their horses. The company was determined to keep their line to the Black Hills and they established the following places after leaving Fort Laramie: Raw Hide Buttes, Running Water, Indian Creek, Cheyenne River, Red Canyon, Pleasant Valley, Custer City, Bull Dog Ranch and Deadwood.

The loss of their fine horses became so great that the company finally sent to Salt Lake for a man known as "Stuttering Brown," a well known western character to whom fear was unknown and who had had much experience on western stage lines. Brown took full charge of the trail into the Black Hills and made strenuous efforts to deal with the outlaws and Indians who continued to steal their stock from the different stations as fast as Brown could replace them. The government finally took a hand in the controversy and stationed some cavalry at Hat Creek, which made conditions better for a while, but even then the company would frequently lose a valuable team. Brown gradually worked his way toward Custer City in trying to keep the stage line open and had started back to see how the line was operating. He had left at the Hagers Ranch on the Cheyenne River, a very valuable pet team which was to be placed on the run north through Red Canyon. On this trip Brown was coming down with a four mule team and a driver, also an extra man to be stationed further down the line. On arriving at the Cheyenne river, Louis Hager informed him that the fine pet team had been stolen the night before. This news caused Brown to become furious and in a raging temper he went to the room where the Hagers camped, where a bunch of tough characters had assembled for that night. Among these Brown recognized a well known horse thief called Persimmons Bill, whose real name was William F. Chambers from South Carolina, who when he first came to the Black Hills was a peaceable and law abiding citizen but soon developed into a thief, robber and real outlaw. Brown, in his rage grabbed the gun belonging to Persimmons Bill as it stood in a corner and pointing it at Bill's head loudly cursed him and accused him of having stolen the stage horses, telling him that unless the horses were returned, he would blow his head off. Persimmons Bill protested that he knew nothing about the horses but Brown insisted that he did and the quarrel continued until Hagers interfered and succeeded in quieting Brown. Brown then angrily ordered Bill to leave the road or he would kill him. After his anger had subsided, Brown called everyone up to take a drink, but Persimmons

Bill refused to drink with Brown, saying that Brown had accused him of a crime which he was not guilty of and that under the circumstances, he would not drink with him. However, Brown put his rifle back in a corner where he had found it and then went into another room with his men and had supper. After the meal was over he found that Persimmons Bill had gone off in the same direction that Brown would have to take and was informed that he had sworn that he would be revenged. Hagers tried to persuade Brown to stay all night, but Brown was in a hurry and anxious to go down to Hat Creek station to see how the line was, and being without fear of anything, he ordered his men to hitch up the four mules to the wagon and with them he proceeded on his way.

When Stuttering Brown with his two men and mule teams had arrived at Alkali Springs between the Cheyenne River and Indian Creek, Brown took the reins from the driver's hands to give him a rest and a short time afterwards a shot was fired from the side of the road and Brown fell back into the bottom of the wagon badly wounded. The team being frightened, rushed madly away and Brown told the other men to save themselves as he was done for. The two men jumped out of the wagon, but Charlie Edwards, who after lighting on the ground was able to grasp the lines that were dragging alongside the wagon and hanging on to them, after being dragged a short distance, was able to stop the team. The men unhitched the teams and each of them took a mule and rode into Indian Creek, six or seven miles away, to give the alarm. Here they met a freight outfit under the command of Jim Bradley. Bradley took a strong force and started out for the scene of the shooting. About two miles from Indian Creek they found Brown lying on the prairie exhausted, one of the mules standing near him. Brown told them that after his men had left, he laid in the wagon a while and feeling somewhat better, he later concluded to make an attempt to reach Indian Creek and managed to get down and mount an old mule that was left near the wagon by his men that night, but as he had proceeded down the road he became exhausted and fell off, where he was found by Bradley and Rose.

Stuttering Brown was placed in a bed in the wagon and taken to Hat Creek Station, where a surgeon was sent for from Fort Laramie, but Brown had been shot through the stomach after the ball had crashed through his cartridge belt and smashed a shell. After a heroic struggle he died at Hat Creek. Mrs. Brown, his wife, came out from Utah and had the body returned to that place where it was buried.

THE KILLING OF JOHNNY SLAUGHTER

The first attempt to hold up the coach in the Black Hills occurred on the Cheyenne Trail March 25, 1877. The plan to rob the coach was figured out at the home of C. Lee which stood on the street in Deadwood which turns up to Ingleside and had been conceived by Charlie Barber. However, he was not able to take part in the actual commission of the crime for the reason that some time prior to that date he had been wounded by a shot from his revolver when the weapon fell from his belt and was discharged. This injury confined him to the Lee house but the other members of the gang proceeded with the plans as laid out. The men were Jim Berry, Joel Collins, Frank Towle, Sam Bass and another man named Reddy. It was decided to go up the gulch about a half mile above the mouth of Gold Run to stop the coach and rob it but to do no shooting unless it was absolutely necessary for self protection.

In the absence of Barber, Jim Berry became the leader and the gang proceeded on up the Whitewood Creek to the point already selected and with them they carried several bottles of whiskey which they continued to use until some of them were quite drunk. The coach was unusually late this day and the robbers were about to give up and had started back home when they heard the noise of the coming shay. Sam Ross said, "Here she comes, we will stop her right here," and the men accordingly arranged themselves in their

Stage Team Running Away

positions. The coach came rolling along until the shout "Halt" rang out. Johnny Slaughter, the driver, attempted to obey the command and bring his team to a stop. He had almost succeeded when the leaders became frightened at a man near their heads and sprang to one side. The man, Reddy, who was armed with a sawed-off shotgun fired and Slaughter tumbled off the stage coach dead and struck a big stump by the roadside. The same discharge from the shotgun slightly wounded Walter Iler who was a passenger and who was seated beside the driver. The team rushed madly away but they got so badly tangled in the harness that they were unable to proceed. Iler, however, succeeded in getting them under control again and drove them on into Deadwood. The robbers were thus unable to succeed in robbing anyone although there were several passengers and about $15,000.00 on the stage. Although it was 12 o'clock at night a posse immediately went out from Deadwood to the scene of the murder and they found the dead body of Slaughter near the stump and brought it to the city from where it was later taken to Cheyenne, Wyoming, in a special coach. The funeral that was held for him was the largest ever seen in Cheyenne. The whole city turned out to pay its last respects to a very fine and popular young man. The hearse was drawn by six of the finest dappled gray horses that were ever harnessed in the west.

The gang was quite angry at Reddy for having fired without command and were almost decided to kill him because of his hasty action resulting in the failure to rob the stage. However, they gave him a chance to leave the country which he did without delay. Later this man Reddy was captured in the state of Ohio and sent to the penitentiary there for a crime he had committed in that state.

The next day Sheriff Bullock who had recently been appointed to that office by the governor arrested Frank Towle on suspicion but as the evidence of his guilt was not sufficient he was released. Later he met his fate in the hands of Boone May who killed him while attempting to make another stage holdup and his head was cut off and delivered to Cheyenne, Wyoming, for a reward as is set forth in another part of this book. Joel Collins, Sam Bass and Jim Berry likewise continued on their work of outlawry until justice overtook them. Their last crime consisted of the robbery of the Union Pacific railroad in September, 1877. With them this time was also associated Jack Farrell who was not, however, a regular member of the gang.

ROBBERY OF UNION PACIFIC

An account of the robbery of the Union Pacific is taken from the Sidney Telegraph under date of September 22, 1877, and is as follows: "The first and boldest train robbery ever perpetrated on the Union Pacific road, took place at Big Springs, in this, Cheyenne county, at half past ten o'clock Tuesday evening, when Express Train No. 4, eastward bound, was boarded by fifteen masked men and passengers and express car robbed. At the time mentioned, the train which was on time, and which halts at Big Springs but three or four minutes, halted as usual, but the engineer, George W. Broman, noticed the presence of signal lights, and anticipating danger ahead, brought his train to an abrupt halt. He had no more than slacked his train when the engine was boarded by two masked men, who, presenting pistols, ordered all "hands up," and to which engineer and fireman promptly responded. Other parties then brought water and put out the fire in the engine. Meanwhile some of the robbers took possession of the telegraph office, tore out the instruments, cabbaged the operator and took possession of Express Agent Barnhart. The latter party they compelled to go to the express car and rap at the door, thus calling the attention of Messenger Miller. Miller opened the door, was siezed and pounded because he could not open the door to the safe. One of the Yale time locks manufacture which fifty Millers couldn't open under the best of circumstances, until the machine reached Omaha.

Other robbers seized Conductor Patterson as he alighted on the platform on his way for orders, and then the robbers had full sway. They went through the first class car, searched the passengers and secured $1,300 in money and four watches. The robbers in the express car gobbled $65,000 in gold and silver coin, and without doing any further injury to passengers or train men than mentioned, mounted their horses and rode rapidly north. It was not long ere the telegraph instruments were replaced, and the daring robbery made known to the railroad officials, who immediately made the following offer of reward:

"To All Agents: Ten thousand dollars reward will be paid for the capture of the parties who robbed the U. P. R. R. Express at Big Springs, Nebraska, on the 18th inst, and the return of the money which consists mostly of gold coin. Pro-rate of the above reward will be paid for any portion of the money so returned and for the capture of any of the robbers."

TRAIL AND CAPTURE OF ROBBERS

Among the various people who made an effort to effect the arrest of the robbers was a man named Leach who kept a small store at Oglalla, Nebraska, and at which place Berry, who was known to him, had purchased a pair of boots prior to the day of the robbery. The incident was expressly impressed upon the mind of Leach by reason of the fact that having known Berry in former years he had refused to let him have the boots without the cash, whereupon Berry went away and soon returned with a man named Collins who paid over the money to pay for the purchase of the boots which Berry then and there put on. At the same time the robbers had purchased from the store several pieces of calico. Immediately after the robbery Leach hurried to the scene and in examining the surrounding country, picked up a piece of the calico which he had sold and which had been used by the robbers as masks. This lead to their undoing as Leach was quite certain as to the identity of the men whom he had seen a few days before. An account of his work is taken from an article in the Mexico, Missouri, Leader after being reprinted in the Sidney Telegraph October 27, 1877: "During our interview Tuesday with Leach the detective who followed the Big Springs robbers through 200 miles of wilderness in Nebraska, until he obtained the information as to their destination, took occasion to say that one night, when he was taking a peep at the robbers, he heard Collins administer the oath to Berry and the rest of the gang, to the effect that no one of them should 'peach' on the other; and each one took a solemn oath that he would not be taken alive. The next night he slipped into the camp and the band were all asleep and did not think a human being was within a hundred miles of them, and stumbled upon the money ($60,000) sewed up in a blanket, fixed for strapping upon a mule. He tried to pull it out of camp but it was so heavy that he could not move it and while he was endeavoring to get into it and carry it off by piece meal, some one of the gang awoke and he (Leach) made himself scarce and only the darkness saved him. He says in his scouting he crawled miles after them, through grass on his hands and knees. He often saw them and knew Berry, Collins and some of the others. After the gang separated Leach followed after Berry and his 'pard,' to this place where Berry stopped. Berry's accomplice, however, taking the C. & A. train for the north Leach, at the time of Berry's capture, was in Callaway county, near Berry's house, endeavoring to effect his arrest."

The rendezvous of this gang was on the west side of the Black Hills from which point it was their habit of making expeditions to various parts of the country during their exercise of rustling cattle or horses or robbing stage coaches. At this time E. T. Peirce was serving as deputy sheriff of Custer county when he received the telegram stating that the robbery had been committed and offered a reward for the arrest of the thieves. He had noticed several men trailing a pack pony and proceeding after dark on the road toward Buffalo Gap which made him suspicious and he gave particular attention to the subsequent events The following account of the final chapter of the incident is taken from the pen of Doc Peirce. "One morning while travelling over the plains they saw cavalry coming and before the meeting the officers gave an order, and the troops rode on each side of the bandits. 'Halt,' was the next command given. 'You men are prisoners' 'Not much' rejoined the robbers, 'We have sworn not to be taken alive' and started to draw their guns. So the soldiers kindly killed them and found one-half of the stolen money and other property. I think the soldiers were from Fort Hays, Kansas. Jim Berry struck out for his home, which was close to Fulton, Calloway county, Missouri, where he had a wife and six children He stopped one night in Cameron, Missouri, and spent some money in carousing, telling that he had sold a gold mine up in the Black Hills and was paid in real money, as it was the only kind in circulation up there. When he rode into Mexico, the county seat of Audrain county, he thought best to go into Ringold's bank and exchange his coin for paper before going into the backwoods. He gave the cashier some stall about having sold a mine, when he seemed surprised at seeing so much gold, but they had the notice to look out for him and while the cashier was waiting on him a man slipped out of the back door and went for the sheriff, but Berry had gone before he came back. Glascock, the sheriff, knew his man so he took a shotgun and followed. When he first sighted Berry he was jogging along leading his pack horse, perhaps not mistrusting anything until the sheriff got close enough to be recognized. When he overtook Jim he called to him saying, 'Jim, I have a warrant for you.' 'No use, Glascock, I have taken an oath never to be taken alive' said Berry and started to draw his gun. But he was too late and fell from his horse with a charge of buckshot in his body. One more fourth of the money was obtained from the roll on his pack animal. That left one-fourth still unaccounted for. Some years afterward we were talking with a man who knew Jack Farrell well and he said he deemed the back trail the safest and so as soon as they had divided the loot he struck for the Big Horn Mountains and went up on the west side of the Black Hills on what was then known as the Minneconjo, made by Sitting Bull's tribe coming and going from the old Red Cloud agency on the Big White Clay river in northwestern Nebraska. Of course there have been other men who have lost their lives fooling with a piece of calico, but not with such a small piece."

THE KILLING OF FRANK TOWLE

Although Frank Towle escaped from the clutches of the law for his participation in the above crime because of the lack of evidence, in due course of time he paid the penalty for his wrong doing and went the way that most bad men of the west followed. The final chapter of his life is worded as follows: The robberies of the stage coaches became quite a common incident and while there were no regular guards and messengers provided for the protection of the stage coaches, it was the duty of the various shotgun messengers, after they had performed their duty in guarding the treasure coach to the end of the run, which had been assigned to them, and having turned over the coach to their successors along the line, to return back to their regular station and accompany passenger coaches that might be passing at that time. According to this rule, in the month of August, 1877, it became the duty of Boone May and John Zimmerman to return as guards for one of the passenger coaches on the trip to Hat Creek Station.

Along in the night time the old passenger coach went rumbling over its rocky highway toward the Hat Creek station with the two passengers or guards following at some distance behind and when the coach had reached the point known as Robbers' Roost, an ideal place for holding up stage coaches because of the location of the gulch or canyon to the road and the protecting timber and vegetation, the old familiar command of "Halt" rang out on the night air and in a few minutes the passengers were lined up and the robbers were proceeding to relieve them of their val-

Gang of Outlaws

SITTING BULL.

uables. The leader of the gang asked the stage driver whether or not there were any guards along with the coach and being informed that there were two of them coming along behind, the chief commanded, "Number one and two go back to the rear and kill those two '_____ _____' " and accordingly Frank Towle and his companion proceeded to sneak along under the cover of darkness toward the two messengers who had been approaching from the rear. But Boone May and his companions had heard the command "Halt" break the stillness of the night air and had immediately dismounted and were likewise creeping up within range of the holdup and as the two highwaymen came crouching along through the tall grass and brush and were within range, Boone May and his companion opened fire upon them. Zimmerman had a rifle and in the darkness missed his man but Boone May was armed with a shotgun and his opponent fell dead. The death of the robber and the sudden successful attack by the guards caused consternation among the other robbers who immediately hurried from the scene leaving the frightened and terror stricken passengers in the hands of the two guards who bundled them back into the stage and brought them successfully to the end of the run.

While talking over the incident in the station, Boone May was informed that there was a reward of several thousand dollars offered by the commission at Cheyenne, Wyoming, for the capture of Frank Towle, dead or alive, and accordingly the next day Boone May returned to the scene of the fight in order to get the head of his victim. He found that the body had been dragged up the gulch a short distance from the scene of the fight and secreted under some plum bushes. From the body of his victim, he took two gold nugget stick pins and then proceeded to cut off his head which he placed in a gunnysack and delivered to the commissioners at Cheyenne, Wyoming. However, his efforts were in vain for the commissioners claimed that the reward had recently been withdrawn and refused to give him anything for his work in ridding the country of one of the bad men at that time.

THE PASSING OF A MEXICAN ROBBERS' SPY

Some time after the incident of the killing and decapitating of Frank Towle in the fall of 1878, Boone May in company with another guard, Billy Sample, captured a Mexican named Joe Minuse. This Mexican while not actually taking part in the holding up and robbing of passengers and travelers, at the same time played his part in connection with these crimes in the roll of spy. He was engaged around Deadwood and informed the robbers out on the road of the going out of travelers who had in their possession money or other valuables and in this way the robbers would not get possession of the money and valuables.

The object that May and Sample had in capturing this Mexican was to make him reveal to them the whereabouts of the robbers to whom he was playing spy and they gave him an opportunity to produce this information but the Mexican absolutely refused. The two men then proceeded to put a rope around his neck and use a little persuasive force and drew him up to a limb several times until he finally revealed all he knew about the movements of his pals. During this procedure the guards wore masks so that the Mexican would not know them if he should meet them afterwards but just as they turned the Mexican loose, Sample's mask fell off and the Mexican recognized him. Unfortunately for the Mexican in his angered condition he said, "Sample, you damned Missouri s—— of a b——, I know you and will get even with you." Boone May said, "Mex, you have seen too much," and reached for his gun. Sample did the same, and that was the end of the Mexican's career.

THE WEB-MAY HOLDUP

In the month of August, 1877, a scheme was made up in Deadwood to capture and kill some of the stage robbers and in this way place a damper on the popularity of this sort of entertainment. Accordingly it was decided that Mike Goldman, Jim Lebby, two noted gamblers of Deadwood were to go out on the stage in company with Boone May who was one of the guards on this treasure coach and if a holdup was staged there would be some chance of killing the robbers. Boone May consented to this scheme with the understanding that there should be no one else on the coach but themselves. However, at the last minute a lady and her little girl were taken on as passengers much to the objection of Boone, who finally gave his consent.

When the stage reached Robbers' Roost east of Hat Creek, three men brought it to a halt and demanded that the passengers shell out. Boone May tried to get out and make a fight but Lebby and Goldman hopelessly terror stricken held him back and the woman begged him not to fire lest her little girl might be killed. May became so disgusted over the acts of the two men that he threw his gun out of the window and told the robbers to help themselves. When they found that they had captured a celebrated bandit hunter, Boone May, they proposed to kill him at once but for some reason changed their minds and after taking everything of value that they could find, let him and the rest of them go.

Some time after this the same robbers appeared in Deadwood and were recognized by May and Lebby. May was exceedingly anxious to have them arrested but for some reason Sheriff Bullock refused to make arrest. One of the men, named Prescot Web, was armed with two revolvers. The other two men had no fire-arms but one had an old hunting knife in his belt. They had left their guns in their camp upon Sherman street. May started to follow them on Lee street and as he turned the corner into Sherman street, Web turned like a flash and fired at Boone hitting him in the wrist of his left arm and making a very painful wound. Web then ran across the street where a man dismounted and tied his horse to go into the postoffice. Web cut the horse loose just as May fired, hitting him under the right shoulder and nearly killing him. Two more shots from May's revolver struck the horse as Web mounted but May's gun balked and he was only able to make the cylinder revolve by using his broken arm. Web in return fired several more shots at May and rode up the street firing right and left.

Sheriff Bullock, Deputy John Cockran and Captain Willard had just gone to the jail for supper when the sounds of the battle reached them. Cockran was mounted and Bullock ordered him to ride down Sherman street and Willard to run across the flat near the old grave yard so as to cut off escape in that direction, while the sheriff himself went into a little draw to the west. Cockran reached Web, who was galloping up Sherman street and commanded him to halt, but Web fired upon him and then turned up the hill. Before he had gone half the way the horse fell dead penetrated by two bullets. Just as Web came over the hill, Willard arrived on the scene and with drawn revolver ordered him to surrender. Web cried out, "Don't shoot, I am killed anyway." He was bleeding from the mouth and staggering. Willard ran up to catch him before he fell, returning his gun to the bolster, but like a flash the wounded man pulled out his own gun and drove it into the pit of Willard's stomach and pulled the trigger. The hammer came down with a snap but the cartridge failed to explode and Willard catching his wrist, tore the gun from his hand and was about to strike him when Bullock came up and restrained him. Mike Whalen, the night deputy, now arrived on the scene and was ordered to take Web to the jail. The prisoner was covered with blood from head to foot and the blood spurted all over those near him. Bullock and Willard then hurried after the other two men who were soon under arrest and in jail.

Dr. Babcock was called at once and found Web in a bad condition and expecting to die He called for a priest and gave the men his mother's address in Texas but he finally got well and was taken to Cheyenne for trial with the other men where they were acquitted.

Years afterwards when Willard was sheriff of Custer county, Web, who had turned over a new leaf and became a good, clean, law-abiding citizen with a wife and two children and had become a county official, often spoke with regret to Willard of his cowardly act of snapping his gun after he had been arrested. Harry Wisdom, the other member of the gang, obtained work afterwards in the freighting outfit between Cheyenne and the Hills and Connors, the third member of the holdup men became a trusted employe of the Gilmer-Saulsbury Stage Company and helped to run down the robbers along that line.. After their acquittal they admitted that they had robbed the coach but claimed that it was the only time they had done such work.

THE KILLING OF BOB CASTELLO

In September, 1877, a party of men were leaving the Black Hills for Cheyenne, Wyoming, and when near a point fifteen miles southwest of Custer City they camped for dinner. Three strangers came riding down the road on horseback and stopped at the wagons, and one rider casually dismounted from his horse, between the men and their rifles. He quickly picked up a shot gun and yelled "Throw up your hands," a command instantly obeyed by almost everyone in the party, except a man who fell over backwards in a draw and sneaked away, and a boy named "Kid Meyers," who noticed what was going on and sneaked around to where his father had his gold dust hidden in a sack, to the value of sixteen thousand dollars The "kid" had his shot gun ready and at the command "Throw up your hands," fired upon Castello, who fell dead. The other robbers broke and ran, while the boy picked up his rifle and fired at the fleeing bandits, wounding one of them in the foot, but leaving their horses they made their escape in the hills.

The alarm was given to E. T. Peirce, deputy sheriff at Custer, who had some difficulty in understanding from the excited messenger, just what happened. He finally gathered together George Hart, August Haage, and Pony Sharp and proceeded to the scene of the holdup. An examination of the dead man disclosed the fact that he was Bob Castello, a border outlaw, and that there was a ten dollar bill on his person, which those who had robbed the body, had failed to find. After the inquest they took the shirt off his body, placed it over his face, dug a little hole for him, piled the dirt over him and tramped it in.

The expedition then went to the Eighteen Mile ranch to wait for another train to strengthen their expedition When the second party came up later, as they passed the scene of the holdup, they found that wolves had dug up the body of the outlaw and that his bones were scattered over the valley.

It seems that Castello was out on bonds for having shot his own father, in Bismarck. His name had been tattooed on his arm, and this identification and his final disposition saved his bondsmen the trouble of producing him in court.

WALL AND BLACKBURN HOLDUP

The Deadwood-Cheyenne trail of 1877 was the scene of a good many holdups and robberies, and one of the most successful gangs that operated on this line was Wall, Blackburn, Lame Bradley, Lame Johnny, Webster and Hartwell. In the summer of 1877 they held up the stage and at that time one of the members of the passengers was Ed Cook, the superintendent of the line, who was on his way down the road to pay off the men. Before his departure, Cook, realizing the danger of travelling across the country in those days, had purchased an old out of date, large bore shotgun and down the barrel of this he had stuffed his money. In due time the stage rolled in and the old command of "Halt, hands up" rang out and the passengers were lined up and duly searched. Lame Bradley had a grudge against Cook and took a shot at him, shooting off a part of his ear and making a very painful wound. However, before Bradley could fire again he was stopped by Blackburn who remembered that once upon a time in the past Cook had befriended him. One of the gang had also taken Cook's watch from him, which was a very fine gold timekeeper, but Blackburn likewise compelled him to return it to Cook This almost caused a fight among the robbers. When the men searched Cook they found very little money on him and looking at his old, practically worthless shotgun, and berating any man who would be fool enough to venture forth upon the road with such a disreputable weapon, with an oath hurled it into the bushes. Afterwards when the robbers left Cook was only too glad to make his way back to the scene and recover his out of date gun which contained three or four hundred dollar's worth of paper. Bradley called himself "The King of the Road" but for once was out-witted and threw money away which he actually had in his hands. This same Bradley had killed a man named Powell on the Cheyenne river just before this robbery. These two men were members of the same gang but got into a fight; Bradley, however, proved to be too quick and shot Powell before he could draw his gun This gang of robbers made their headquarters at Crook City and came into town at night whenever they wished. Donahue, the deputy sheriff there never attempted to arrest the pair but once; that time he went out one day looking for Jim Wall and found him, but Wall arrested Donahue, took away his weapons and everything he had and sent him home afoot. About the time of the holdup, Charlie Francis was living on a ranch near Crook City and learned of their whereabouts. He made arrangements with Sheriff Bullock to watch the movements of the gang and notify Bullock when these two men were in town. Accordingly on a certain summer night of 1877, Francis peeping through a window of one of the most notorious dance halls, saw these two men on the floor dancing with much abandon and apparently without fear of any danger on the part of the officers of the law. Francis quietly mounted his horse, rode into Deadwood and reported to Mr. Bullock who was there alone, what he had discovered. He suggested to Mr. Bullock that the men would leave town about three o'clock in the morning for their camp and that by going to a certain place, Mr. Bullock and a deputy would be able to either capture the men or kill them. Accordingly, Bullock and Francis proceeded to the spot in order to carry out the plan as made. As they were going along they heard someone riding up through the brush, whereupon they promptly moved to one side to wait the coming of the rider. As he approached near them, he proved to be Johnny Cochran who was a deputy sheriff under Bullock and this greatly surprised Francis who did not know that Bullock had arranged for anyone else to be with him. Cochran was a brave and efficient officer and it was arranged that Bullock should have the first station, Francis the next and Cochran the third. Accordingly, soon after this two men came into view, walking single file along the trail and talking in low voices, but before they had arrived opposite to Bullock, he fired and the two men made a hurried leap into the brush and disappeared. Bullock afterwards explained the escape of these noted outlaws by saying that his gun was dischargel accidentally.

The Wall-Blackburn band of highway men were so aggressive and troublesome that a special United States marshal was appointed in an effort to capture or kill the men. His name was Charles Hayes of Cheyenne, Wyoming Territory, and he soon located the men near the Coffee and Cuney ranch near Fort Laramie. He called upon Mr Cuney who was a deputy sheriff, to assist him and they accordingly surprised and captured Wall and Blackburn and Webster, a young fellow known as "Kid Webster." The criminals were taken to Coffee's ranch and Hayes left Cuney to guard Wall and Blackburn while he went to search the vicinity. The officers paid no attention to "Kid Webster" who was allowed to go outside but as soon as Hayes was out of sight, the "Kid" secured a rifle, re-entered the building from a side door and fired upon Cuney, killing him almost instantly. Blackburn and Wall now being released, secured arms and went out to settle the matter with Hayes. A running fight took place and the marshal was obliged to flee and save himself, so the gang escaped this time.

THE ROBBERS' ROOST HOLDUP

In the fall of 1878 a gang of robbers held up and tried to rob the stage coach at a place on the Cheyenne trail called "Robbers' Roost." Scott Davis and Johnny Denny were on the coach that day besides three soldiers who were acting as guards. When the coach was stopped the soldiers all jumped out of the coach and took to the brush leaving Davis and Denny to fight alone. After a few shots were fired Denny lost his head and followed the example of the soldiers, thereby leaving Scott to fight single handed. Scott stood by his post and shot until the Henry rifle that he had, jammed and refused to eject the shells. While trying to extract the shell in various ways Scott was struck down by a bullet in the hip and left lying there. The robbers then went back to the brush, captured the soldiers and disarmed them but did not get any treasure or money in the deal, as they were very much afraid themselves and took to the timber as rapidly as they could, leaving the soldier's gun and Denny's gun at a tree up the gulch at which spot the men sent out by Davis the next day got them. Alec Benham, superintendent of the stage line, was on the coach that night but did not take any part in the fight, merely holding on to the lead horses to keep them from running away.

Two of the robbers engaged in this holdup were known by the names of Dunk Blackburn and John Wall. Later on they ran off a lot of horses owned by the stage company near Lance Creek and were the same men who had been engaged in the killing of Marshal Cuney, an account of which we have heretofore given. Accordingly when Scott Davis who was the chief of the guards of the Treasure Coach had recovered from his wounds received in his fight with these robbers, he concluded to put a stop to them. In the month of December, 1878, he took up the trail of the outlaw band from Lance Creek and followed it like a blood hound day and night, through snow and cold. For a time he had with him a squad of soldiers but the weather was so cold and travel so difficult that they turned back and Davis continued on the trail. He followed them across the Sweet Water and on up to the South Pass where he sold his horse and took the stage to Green River. There he found he had passed the robbers' trail somewhere. From here he got a stage driver named Charlie Atkins and returned back to Alakli Springs where he located Wall and Blackburn. A red hot fight ensued in which Wall was shot three times but Blackburn escaped in his bare feet. He took his underwear and tearing them to pieces wrapped his feet with the torn clothing and walked thirty-five miles into Green River. Davis after making secure the arrest of Wall proceeded immediately after Blackburn and located him in Green River eating a meal. His feet were very swollen and black and blue caused by the frost and bruises. However, Scott Davis put him under arrest and took him and Wall back to Cheyenne where they were convicted and sentenced to the penitentiary for eight and ten years. The intrepid treasure guard had not only captured the notorious robbers but had also recovered fifteen head of very valuable horses. In carrying out this remarkable exploit he had followed the band for three hundred miles sometimes on foot and nearly starved, suffering from the drifting snow and intense cold, but with unlimited nerve and endurance he continued on in the struggle and brought his efforts to a successful climax. After a rest he again took up his work as guard on the Treasure Coach.

THE CANYON SPRINGS STAGE ROBBERY

In the early days of the stage coach lines in the Black Hills, that is, in the years 1877 and 1878, the holding up of passenger coaches and the robbing of passengers of all the valuables they had, sometimes including wearing apparel, became so common that it did not provoke very much comment or create very much interest among the people in the Hills. But once in awhile the monotony of the ordinary holdup was varied by an attack upon the Treasure Coach, which was used to carry the gold bullion from the different mines operated throughout the Hills, for delivery to the Union Pacific railroad at Cheyenne, Wyoming.

The frequent holding up of the passenger coaches caused the passengers who were going out from the Hills, to entrust their gold dust, their watches and valuable jewelry to the Express Companies for shipment upon these Treasure coaches, and sometimes the aggregate value of the treasure contained in these coaches would run up as high as $140,000.00, and an attack upon one of these coaches was a matter of passing interest. The Treasure coach was a steel lined affair, considered to be bullet proof, and so arranged that the guards from the inside could shoot out through the port holes and stand off an ordinary crew of highwaymen.

On the 28th day of September, 1878, occurred one of the most inhuman and bloodthirsty robberies in the history of stage coaching in the Black Hills, and has come to be known as the "Canyon Springs stage robbery." Canyon Springs was one of the stations for the change of teams in the rapid moving of the Treasure coach

About two o'clock in the afternoon of that day, two men appeared at the barn and asked John Miner, the stock tender, and another man that happened to be there, who were quietly sitting on a bench on the outside of the barn, for a drink of water. The visitors appeared to be ranchmen without any visible weapons, but after quenching their thirst they turned quickly and pointed two six shooters at the unsuspecting stock tender and his companion, with the order to "Throw up your hands." The two men were then taken back to the grain room and locked in. The robbers proceeded to knock the chinking off between the logs to make port holes and be ready for the stage as it would come rumbling up the road.

As the stage driver would come to these change

stations he would give a yell, or in some manner give a warning of his approach in order to have the stock tender ready with his next team. Warning in this case was given as usual, and in due time the coach came up to the door with Gene Barnett as driver, and by his side Gail Hill, a slim, thin faced lad from Missouri, to whom the word "fear" was absolutely unknown. But there was no station tender to meet them, and there was not a sound of any kind. Hill jumped down from the box and turned towards his team, his back towards the barn, when a volley was fired by the robbers, striking him in the back and coming out through his right lung. Gail quickly turned, facing the barn, and received another bullet in his left arm while he was raising his gun to shoot.

It was against the rules for passengers to ride on the treasure coach, but in this case an exception had been made in favor of Hugh Campbell because of the fact that he was a telegraph operator at Custer and was needed there. One of the bullets from the same volley that had pierced Hill, struck Campbell in the forehead, but he crawled out from the coach and fell down a few feet in the rear of it, calling loudly for water. His pleas for water were answered with an oath and more bullets from the holdup men.

Bill Smith, who was one of the messengers on the coach, was struck by a splinter from the top part of the coach, and was so frightened that he believed he was shot, and fell down in the bottom of the coach and remained there until the fight was over. But Scott Davis, the captain of the messengers, realizing that unless some heroic effort was made to save the treasure, the whole party and treasure were doomed, jumped out of the coach on the opposite side from the robbers, and ran for a pine tree a short distance away, and from this point he motioned to Barnett, the driver, who was still in his seat, to drive on with the coach. Barnett began to obey, when the outlaws seemed to realize what his action meant, and ordered one of the members to get in front of the team and hold the leaders. This compelled the robber to get out

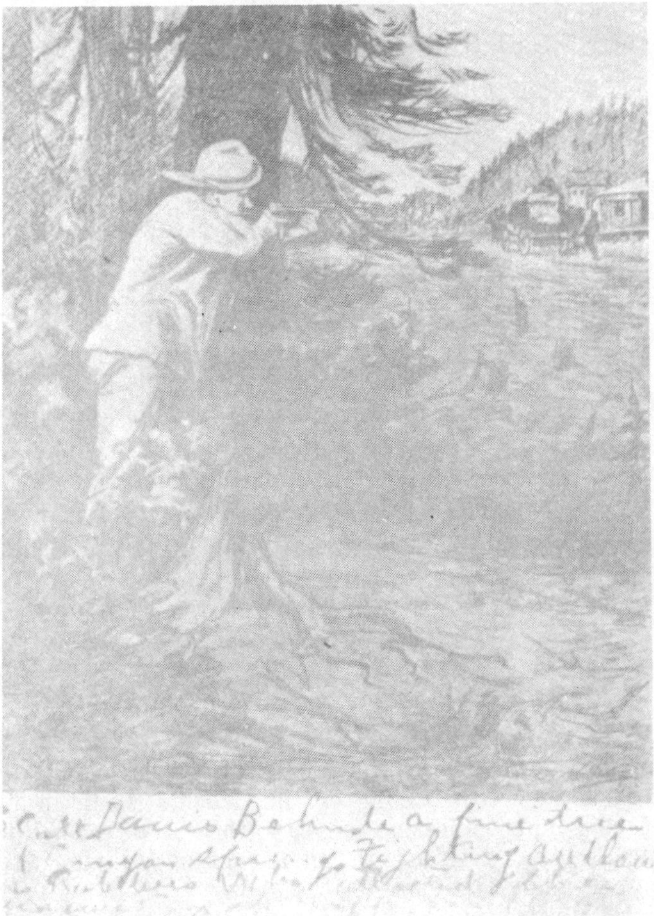

in front and Davis opened fire upon him, bringing him down with a bullet through his bowels.

Another one of the robbers then proceeded to go back of the barn so as to get a line of cross fire on Davis and drive him from his protecting tree. In the meantime Gail Hill, who had been one of the first to

Gail Hill

be shot, had staggered along back of the barn and was lying down in the edge of the brush, when in his half conscious condition he saw the man crouching along and endeavoring to get a shot at Davis. Hill promptly shot him dead on the spot

Barnett, who had not yet driven off with the coach, was ordered to come to the barn door, and Jim Carey, the leader of the gang, using him as a shield, ordered him to march towards the tree where Scott Davis was putting up his fight. Barnett yelled to Davis not to shoot, and Davis, seeing the condition of things, and not wishing to endanger the life of

Barnett made a leap for the brush close by and disappeared

From Jenney Stockade, in the southwest part of the Hills, to Deadwood, a distance of sixty miles, was a day-light run in both directions, and a holdup had never occurred in board day light, so there was no one on scout duty between these two points. However, for some reason, Boone May, John Brown, William Taylor and Jesse Brown, feeling that something might be wrong, mounted their horses and started up the line to meet the treasure coach. After a few miles they met Scott Davis, and were informed that the coach had been robbed and they were too late.

Davis, May and Jesse Brown pushed on to the scene of the holdup, and the other men went back for more ammunition, but when the men arrived at the coach the safe had been broken open and the contents, consisting of gold bullion, gold dust and jewelry, gold watches and other valuables, had been taken away. This safe had been guaranteed to withstand the roughest treatment that could be made upon it for twenty-four hours, and the guards had hoped to get there before the robbers could open it The names of the men who had robbed this stage coach were Jim Carey, the leader, Frank McBride, Doug Goodale, Al Speer and Big Nose George.

When the news of the robbery reached Deadwood, posses were organized, and they started to scour the country in every direction. William Ward, the superintendent of the stage line, and Uri Gillette, a ranch man, were the first two to strike the trail that the robbers had taken. They followed on until they found where the men had bought a team and harness and spring wagon and then taken the wounded man, Frank McBride, with them. They also found where the man that Hill had shot was buried. The trail led out into the open prairie around Rapid City. Another posse from Rapid City was formed and took up the trail towards Pierre. The freight line between Rapid City and Pierre was lined with teams. From some of these freighters it was learned that the robbers had passed on for some distance towards the east. At dark the robbers had not been overtaken, and it was concluded that they must have pulled off the main road and went into camp.

After proceeding farther on the road, the posse decided to double back, and some distance to the north, or to one side of the road, they heard the neighing of a horse, and it was decided to surround the camp where the horse was heard neighing, and watch for the men and catch them as they would be ready to move out in the morning. But when morning came and a charge at the break of day was made on the robbers' camp, they had nothing but the old spring wagon to reward their efforts.

Further efforts were made to pick up the trail again, but after scouring the country in all directions, and no trace being found, and the horses being tired, the posse turned towards home.

However, William Ward, the superintendent, rode on to Ft. Pierre, where he learned of a young man crossing the river with a horse and a pack on his saddle. Ward continued on the trail of the young man and traced him to Atlantic, Iowa, where he remained for a day or so. One morning as he was walking along the street he saw two gold bricks in a bank window, which he at once recognized as being part of the loot taken by the robbers.

He learned that a man by the name of Goodale was president of the bank, and that his son, Doug Goodale, had just returned from the Black Hills, where he had sold a gold mine, and on account of the scarcity of gold coins had been compelled to take gold bricks in payment, and that the bricks on exhibit were a part of his reward.

Ward went to the sheriff and sought to have young Goodale arrested, but the sheriff demanded that Ward should be identified and after some telegraphing to bankers in Deadwood, the sheriff was satisfied that Ward was right, and although the father and grandfather of young Goodale were the wealthiest men in the country and men of good reputation, Ward got legal possession of the bullion and had the young robber arrested and surrendered to his possession.

Together they set out on their return trip to the Hills, but the young man had with him his father and an attorney, and a merry good time was had all along the line until they reached the station of Lone Tree, Nebraska, where the father and the attorney left the train. After the train had proceeded along a short distance the prisoner asked permission to go to the back of the car. Ward, after waiting a short time, went to look for his companion and found him gone. The alarm was given, the train reversed and backed down to the station. Ward jumped off and the train proceeded on its way. An immediate search was begun in the country in all directions, but no trace of Goodale was ever found.

This was the story that Ward put up when he returned to Cheyenne, but the stage company relieved Ward from any further services with them.

SIDNEY, NEBRASKA, THE SCENE OF A THREE HUNDRED THOUSAND DOLLAR THEFT

From 1875 to 1880, I suppose, Sidney, Nebraska, had the reputation of being one of the roughest, toughest towns along the Union Pacific line. The haunt of the surething gamblers, and the birth place of the bogus gold brick. In 1875 came the forerunnings of the Black Hills excitement and in '76 the pack of gold hunters was in full cry. Sidney jumped to the front as the great outfitting point for the Hills. Miners' Delight, Fort Robinson, Fort Meade and many large ranches that had been established at Greenwood, Pumpkin Creek, Platte River, Snake Creek, and White River, gave more or less protection to the great rush of gold seekers. Sidney supported fifty-three saloons, and numerous dance houses of the knock down, drag out type, added to the gayety of the wildest town in America.

In 1879, Gilmer and Saulsberry inaugurated a stage line from Sidney to Deadwood, having changed the Cheyenne route to this one as it was shorter and a better road. And as gold was flowing from the Hills in larger quantities, "Old Iron Sides" as it was called, was guarded by eight picked men, armed with rifles, Colts, six shooters, and sawed off shot guns, with Scott Davis as captain. The names of the men were Ross Davis, Boone May, Gail Hill, William May, Billy Sample, John Cochran, and Jesse Brown. The treasure coach carried no passengers on the outward trip, but coming into the Hills it did. The treasure coach did not appear to be much of an inducement to the road agents along this line, as it was not molested after the guards were increased from four to eight. Two of the guards mounted on good swift horses, rode in advance of the coach, keeping a lookout for any sign of danger. If a bridge had been tampered with, or any indication of robbers, the coach could be halted and placed on guard. Two of the guards rode behind the coach on horse back and four inside. The orders were no sleeping after night, but of course there were little naps taken occasionally

The stage stock were as good for the purpose as could be found in the west, but the eastern horse could not stand up to the hardships as well as the western. There were regular stations established with stock tenders at every station. The only robbery that occurred on this line was at Sidney after we had turned over the shipment of $300,000 to the express agent of the U. P. R. R. at that point and had the receipts for it. And that brings us to the famous Sidney express robbery of 1882 which we will let Scott Davis tell about.

"We arrived at Sidney behind our schedule time on March 7th, delayed by bad roads, but still in time for the agent, Chet Allen, to receive the shipment and get it aboard the express car. The train pulled in just as we wheeled up to the express office. It had to stop twenty-five minutes for supper and as there was a standing order to give thirty minutes leeway when necessary, this would have given fifty-five minutes to make the transfer, which could have been completed in half the time. As all the packages were wrapped and directed to destination, all the agent had to do was check them. "You are too late" he replied, "You'll have to hold it over until tomorrow." "Hold nothing," says I; then noticing Sheriff McCarthy standing there I appealed to him on the matter of time. He said it was no concern of his. Allen was stubborn so we drove back to the stage office, unloaded the treasure and put three of our men to guard it. Allen said he would receive it next morning at 11:30 and we delivered it and got his receipt for $299,500. There was one thousand in currency, and two small bricks valued at $550.00 each, the rest was in a larger sized bricks. We wheeled all this into a room adjoining the office. 'Why don't you put it in your safe?' I asked him. 'No,' he says, 'it is only an hour until train time and it will be perfectly safe on the truck.'

"At 12:40 I came out of the hotel and saw an immense crowd of people gathered about the express office. I heard a man say that the express office was robbed. I went across into the office and Allen was sitting in a chair, his face hid in his hands. 'They got it all,' he moaned. A square hole in the floor showed how the robbers had gained ingress, and how the gold had been taken out, through the coal bins underneath. Sheriff McCarthy proposed getting a team and he and I made a circle for tracks of the robbers. There was a slight snow on the ground and as a wagon would have been required to carry the gold, and as there was no tracks leaving the building I refused to go with him. But Boone May and Billy Sample did of their own accord procure saddle horses and circled the town but found no tracks leading either to or from the town. In the meantime, I and two of my men without making any noise broke into the coal cellar. The sides were protected by lattice work and the snow had drifted over the coal and footprints were plain to be seen leading to the coal pile. We found shovels and dug into the coal pile where the tracks ended. In a short time we struck something heavier than coal. It proved to be one of the Homestake gold bricks, then another and kept on until we had the whole shipment except the currency and the two small bricks spoken of before. We figured up and found $297,400 leaving $2100 short, which could have been carried away in pockets, etc. I examined a hole in the floor, it showed that it had been bored through with an auger leaving enough of the wood between the holes to support the square surrounded. Off on one side there was a jack screw which had been adjusted under this square to hold it up in case anything heavy should fall on the spot, we also found the part of the floor which fitted into the hole. I sent for Joe Caliburn, a Union Pacific mechanic, and he identified the jack screw as one that had been stolen from the shops about a month before, and he examined the hole in the floor and thought it might have been bored for sometime. It was obvious that the robbers had laid the trap and waited for a rich haul.

"Allen had left the office at 11:30 to go to dinner, where McCarthy spent the dinner hour could not be learned. Allen returned at 12:30 and upon trying to open the door found the keyhole plugged on the inside. He had Joe Caliburn to come and remove the plug from the keyhole and entering the office discovered the robbery. McCarthy appeared on the scene while Caliburn and Allen were fussing around the room. During this time Robert Oberfelder telegraphed S. H. Clark at Omaha, general manager of the Union Pacific railroad, and he came on a special with several sleuths to Sidney. I stated above that McCarthy appeared on the scene and as Allen was on the verge of a nervous breakdown, McCarthy led him away from the office. We locked the door, and when we dug up the treasure from the coal bins, we put it up through the hole into the room adjoining the office, and then I crawled up and was sitting there guarding it when Allen and McCarthy returned. The two stared at me as if greatly surprised. I says, 'There is your gold, Allen, all except two small bars and the currency. Do you know where they are?' facing McCarthy. He did not answer just stared at me, and says, 'Where did you find this?' pointing to the bullion.

I told him in the coal cellar. 'Better put it in the safe, Allen.' And he did. The sweat was pouring from his face, but he seemed to be relieved of the nervous strain. We kept guard over the treasure until General Clark arrived and took charge. Allen was discharged and placed under arrest, was tried by a jury and acquitted, the evidence not being sufficient to warrant a

Billy Sample

verdict of guilty. He went to Pueblo, Colorado, and secured a position there and died there a few years afterward. McCarthy had been elected sheriff by the tough element, and his association of law breakers, and shortly after the expiration of his term he was run out of Sidney, in a general clean up of the town.

Clark left a couple of his sleuths in Sidney to try and unravel the threads of the robbery. One of them, James L. Smith, got into an altercation in the Capitol saloon with Patsy Walters, a gambler, both pulled guns and fired. Walters was fatally wounded and

Smith was shot through the arm. He ran to my room for protection from Walters' friends. A couple of officers came to arrest Smith without a warrant and my brother, Ross, and I disarmed them and told them that we would deliver Smith at the jail next morning, which we did He was tried in justice court and acquitted as the evidence showed self defense. Smith killed another man after that and was acquitted but was recalled by Clark.

Several years later I met Billy Feen in Chicago, one of the suspected robbers. I asked him how much McCarthy realized on the two small gold bricks. Feen said that McCarthy had given him and a man named Dempsy the bricks to dispose of and they went to Denver, and after sawing and remelting they sold the gold for eleven hundred dollars and divided the money between themselves. McCarthy got the one thousand in currency. He engineered the job from start to finish."

DEATH OF CURLY GRIMES, 1879

In the fall of the year 1879, the United States Secret Service sent W. H. Lewllyn from Washington, D. C., to search for members of the gang who had robbed a postoffice on the Sidney stage line near Nebraska. Lewllyn was a young officer, ambitious and anxious to make a name for himself and like a great many other men who are given authority was not any too scrupulous as to how he might gain a reputation. In this work he employed Boone May as his assistant and they finally located a man known as Curly Grimes whom they suspected as being associated with the gang who made the robbery. As a matter of fact, it is very doubtful whether there was any evidence at all against the man or whether he was one of the party who had committed the crime. However, the secret service officer started on his return trip to Deadwood and in the evening they arrived at a ranch below Sturgis known as the Bull Dog ranch where they had supper and then proceeded on their way toward Fort Meade.

THE BLACK HILLS TRAILS 275

It was in the dead of winter. The weather was cold and the snow was drifting and blowing and after proceeding on their way for a distance, the prisoner is reported to have complained that the irons on his wrists were freezing his hands and requested that Lewllyn remove them, which he did, warning him not to made any attempt to escape. They reported that all went well until they arrived at a point on the military reservation. Here there were trees and bushes quite near the road. The prisoner made a wild dash for the bushes and upon his failure to observe the command "Halt" the officer opened fire upon him and he fell riddled with bullets. The officers proceeded on their way to Fort Meade and reported the incident. After the storm had subsided a party went out and recover the body of the dead man where it lay frozen and stiff beneath the snow and buried it.

As the act occurred on the military reservation it came within the jurisdiction of the United States court. As there was considerable excitement caused by the killing of this man and great doubt existed both as to the guilt of the deceased and the truthfulness of the story of his attempt to escape, the matter was finally taken up. When the United States court convened, an indictment of murder against the officers was returned and a trial had, but the men were promptly acquitted as there was no evidence to contradict their story. However, Lewllyn left the country and carried on work in secret service and later became quite prominent but it is reported that he tried to carry out the same kind of unlawful act in the case of an outlaw known by the name of Doc. Middleton. He had planned after he had gotten hold of and succeeded in arresting the man to have his assistant fire from the roadside upon him and Middleton as he passed by and murder the defendant. However, when the time to fire came, the man who had been engaged to do the work had too much honor left within his breast and refused to pull the trigger, for which act he was subsequently roundly upbraided by his superior. It would appear that Lewllyn figured that if a man was accused of crime it was a waste of time to give him a court trial and the best way to do was to promptly destroy him.

HOLD UP OF HOMESTAKE PAY TRAIN

With the coming of the railroads into the Hills, the occupation of the road agents was gone, and it was prophesied by many that "the gentlemen of the road" would turn their attention to trains, but this had not been the case.

The holdup of the treasure coach at Canyon Springs was the last one for the coach, and the first and only holdup of a railroad train was the holding up of the pay train of the Homestake Mining Company on the Black Hills & Fort Pierre railroad in Reno Gulch on Friday, October 1, 1888.

When one considers the almost criminal carelessness with which money has been packed about the country, it seems strange that similar attempts have not been made, and it certainly speaks well for the law abiding spirit of the citizens of the Black Hills.

The Black Hills & Fort Pierre railroad, built in 1881 from Lead City to Woodville, was extended in 1883 to Brownsville on Elk Creek, and its main business was the hauling of the wood and timbers necessary for the operations of the Belt mines.

Pay day for the wood and timber choppers and haulers was always upon the twelfth of each month, when what was known as the Brick Store, now the Hearst Mercantile Co., would take out sufficient money to cash checks and pay the men employed in the various wood and timber camps. Alexander McKenzie was manager of the Brick store from 1886 to 1904, and the custom was for him to pack the money from Lead City to Brownsville, carrying it in an ordinary hand valise.

This had been done for a number of years without any guard, and as a result, prior to 1888 there had been more or less talk among a gang of rounders who infested Brownsville and Deadwood as to the chances of holding up McKenzie, making a cleanup and getting out of the country. These rounders were nearly all tin horn gamblers and all were frequenters of the notorious Gem Theatre in Deadwood, and it is a fact that the scheme was often discussed there.

In the end, only four of them took an active part in the final holdup, but the others contributed in the way of advice, outside help, and later on, in helping Jack Doherty get out of the country. The first attempt was made upon August 12, 1888, at the big trestle where the railroad crossed Bear Butte Creek. It was planned at a dance hall in Sturgis and at Telford's ranch on Alkali creek. It is not known positively just who composed the gang that day, but the outside party who was to furnish the guns failed to show up and nothing was done.

The next attempt was on September 12th, one month later, at Woodville, or the Lake station as it was more generally known. Woodville is on a flat divide between Whitewood and Bear Butte creeks. The railroad coming from Lead makes a Y there, swings around a low ridge and then on down Bear Butte creek. The train consisting of one engine and a string of empty flat cars, usually with freight on the last one would leave Lead at 7:00 a. m. and McKenzie with the money in a yellow valise and sawed off shot gun for protection would sit on the last car so as to get as far away as possible from the smoke and cinders from the engine. At Woodville the empties would be set in on a side track on the Lead side of the Y, the engine would then cut loose and go down Bear Butte for a train load of wood and timbers, so with the engine crew gone, it would have been an easy job to hold him up, together with the few passengers who were on this morning train on pay days. The gang consisting of Wilson, Doherty, Murphy and possibly one other had arrived at Woodville the night before, picketed their horses on this low ridge, cut the telephone wires on both sides of the station and at daylight secreted themselves in some bushes along the side track and about thirty feet from where the last empty was usually left and waited the coming of the train from

Lead, and the money. But this morning the machinists and mechanics of the Homestake company had a picnic at Horse Shoe grove, making the train from Lead over an hour late. As a result the train crew working between Brownsville and Woodville had time to make an extra trip and when the pay train reached Woodville all it had to do was to cut loose its empties carrying McKenzie and the money, which were at once picked up by the Brownsville engine and pulled out down Bear Butte creek. Among all the plans discussed by the gang as to the easiest way to hold up the train and get the money, this was the best one and would have succeeded if it hadn't been for the picnic.

As it was, they were so angry at losing out on what apparently was a cinch, that they broke from their cover, ran across the low bridge where their horses were and tried to intercept the train of empties with the money on its way down Bear Butte creek, but they were too late and lost out.

After this second failure to get the money, the gang separated, but later on got together at the ranch of John Telford on Alkali creek east of Sturgis, and there made up another plan to get the money. Among those composing it were John Telford, a gambler, and saloon man, originally from Rapid City, and while he took no part in the actual holdup he provided the necessary horses and guns and together with a woman he was living with named May Brown, furnished a lot of help.

Another member was John Wilson who had drifted into the country as a cowboy, a reckless and desperate character and wanted at the time by the sheriff of Lawrence county on a bench warrant, and when a posse went after him from Sturgis he stood the whole outfit off with a Winchester.

Another one was Jack or Doc Doherty who had been brought into the Hills by John D. Hale, his full name being Napoleon Bonaparte Doherty. He was a very decent sort when he first came to the Hills but got into bad company, gambling and all that went with it, though he was a brave and nervy man.

The fourth member of the gang was Alfred G. Nickerson who was going under the sporting name of "Spud Murphy," a foot racer and tin horn gambler, who had had some trouble in Rapid City shortly before this and was wanted by the authorities there.

In the afternoon of October 11th, Telford left his ranch in a buggy, taking a Winchester, shot gun. wrench, axe, bar and lantern with him, and that night about 10 o'clock met the gang at the old Lawrenson ice house above Thompson's toll gate, or what is now Pluma on the C. B. & Q. road. Wilson, Doherty and Murphy, with revolvers, left shortly afterwards on horseback in the direction of Bear Butte Creek, crossed over on to Spring creek, through Whitewood and Crook City and reached Deadwood about 10 o'clock that night and on up to the Lawrenson ice house. Telford was already there with the guns, etc., which he turned over to them and they went on up to Reno gulch. At daylight Wilson and Doherty removed the fish plates or splices from the rails, spreading one rail out about four inches and spiking it down, cut some bushes and stood them up for about sixty feet from the track, and then all sat down around a small fire they had built and waited for the pay train.

Although the picketing of the horses and the cutting of the telephone wires at Woodville the month before had been reported to the Homestake office, and there was but one conclusion to be drawn—that it was an attempted holdup—still nothing was done about it and no extra precautions taken to guard the money. Upon October 12th, Mr. McKenzie was laid up with rheumatism and unable to take the money to Brownsville as usual, so for the first time it was placed in charge of Wm. A. Remer, paymaster of the Homestake Mining Company.

The train left Lead City on time with a crew of John B. Commiskey, engineer; Reese Morgan, fireman; Charles H. Crist, conductor and Charles Laviere brakeman.

Richard Blackstone, superintendent of the railroad, and H. P. Anderson were seated on some freight on the first flat car back and H. P. Swindler, section boss, and some section men were on the last flat car. The money, consisting of about $12,000 in currency and silver in the old yellow valise as usual, was in the tool box on the tender and Remer was in the engine cab on the fireman's seat. He had an old double barreled sawed off shot gun loaded with buck shot and three extra shells, and there was an empty gun in the cab which was being taken out to the Brownsville store. Reno gulch is about five miles from Lead. Approaching it there is about fifteen hundred feet of straight track, the longest stretch on the road, with a sharp down grade to a trestle forty feet high, crossing the gulch and just as the track approaches the curve leading to this trestle was where the robbers had spread the rails and stationed themselves in the brush near the track. The train usually would go down this piece of straight track at full speed so as to make the grade on the other side of the trestle. If that had been done that morning there is no question but that the engine, cars and crew would have been piled up in the ditch and the getting of the money would have been an easy job. But this morning, when the train reached the head of the straight track it almost stopped to let off the section crew and was not under full headway when it reached the spot where the rails were spread. The manner in which the money for pay days had been carried about the country was almost like hanging up a purse for robbers to pull down if they could and the wonder is that it had not been grabbed before, and about all that ever did save it was "Homestake luck," for just as it was saved the pay day before by a picnic, it was saved this day by letting off the section crew.

The spreading of the rails was so slight that the engine was almost over it before the engineer discovered it, but when Remer saw Commiskey jump and reverse the engine he realized the ball was open, sprang to his feet and he, Commiskey and Morgan were standing close together in the gangway of the engine when the shooting began. As it was, the engine ran its length and that of a flat car on the ties before it stopped. The moment it did so the robbers raised up from behind their brush cover and yelling "Hands up, throw up your hands you -----" began shooting, and this was the first sight the crew had of the robbers.

The engine had run past them about fifty feet, so they were about one hundred feet away and to the rear, Wilson and Doherty together behind the bushes they had set up, Wilson had a Winchester and Doherty had a double barreled shot gun, and Murphy was about fifteen feet nearer with only a revolver. The shot from Wilson's rifle passed between Morgan and Remer, struck the boiler head and splashed, tearing out the glass in the fireman's window. At the command of "Hands up," Morgan stepped off the engine on the side towards the robbers and with one hand up walked coolly around the front of the engine and across the trestle. Commiskey and Remer had dropped down in the gangway and Remer, raising up to see what the situation was, discovered Wilson and Doherty ready to shoot again, so taking deliberate aim, resting across the tool box where the money was he fired one shot at them and dropped back behind the wings of the tender. Doherty's first shot was at Blackstone and Anderson on the first flat car back, but the shot was too low as the marks of the shot were found later on the car wheels. Blackstone had a Sharps rifle, but in the barrel was a wiping rod and when he and Anderson jumped off on the lower side of the train he stumbled and drove the rod firmly into the barrel and it was some time before he could get it out. In the meantime, Remer had loaded the extra gun and given it to Commiskey, knowing he could be depended upon, and told him that he thought he got one of the robbers, but was not sure, that they were being given no show for their lives and must make a fight for it, that the money would be safe anyway, for Blackstone in the bush with his Sharps rifle could stand them off until help came, not knowing that Blackstone was out of it temporarily with a spiked gun.

John B. Commiskey was a veteran of the Civil War, quiet, gentle mannered and as brave a man as ever lived, and he never has been given the credit due him for his courage and cool headedness in this affair, for if he had lost his nerve that day and not reversed his engine, several might have been killed in the wreck and it is a cinch that the gang would have gotten away with the money. Soon after firing the first shot Remer discovered a man sneaking through the brush, evidently trying to get opposite the engine and rake through the gangway at Commiskey and him, so they left the engine, taking a position on its lower side. About this time Blackstone who had climbed up to the track on the opposite side of the gulch called out that he had discovered their horses just above the trestle. Remer told him to kill them so as to set the gang afoot and prevent them getting away, but while this was being discussed, Murphy, the man who had been sneaking through the brush, slipped into the saddle of his horse and rode rapidly up the gulch and out of sight.

While Commiskey and Remer were on the lower side of the engine the water in the boiler was getting dangerously low, so Morgan went back into the cab and started the pump. It was suggested to blow the whistle for help from the other engine which had been heard whistling at Woodville, so Remer crawled back into the cab and lying on his back in the gangway stuck the brush of the engine broom into the handle of the whistle, jiggling out a series of whistles which were far from being any known signals. They were heard, however, by the crew of the other engine who now realized that something was wrong and came at once to the rescue. Commiskey and Remer then left the engine and got behind a log in the bottom of the gulch from where they could cover the engine tool box where the money was.

The other engine soon came and with it several men and guns and search was at once made for the robbers. A black cambric mask with a bullet hole under the right eye and covered with blood was found behind the bushes where the robbers had stood and two trails leading up the hillside. W. W. Sweeney, the fireman on the Woodville engine followed one of them and soon came upon a man lying on the ground face down. It proved to be Wilson. One buck shot had struck him under the left eye and another had hit him in the side, passing through the spleen, causing him to break down. He was carried down to the track and was evidently suffering intense pain and begged that they kill him and put him out of his misery. He was told that unless he told the truth as to his companions, etc., that they would kill him, and yet there he sat on the track, shaking like a leaf with pain, and lied like a horse thief, told them his companions were named Jones and Clark and a lot of other lies. He did say that Clark (Murphy) had made his getaway on horseback and that Jones (Doherty) was shot in the face and had passed him going up the hillside. Later the bloody finger prints of Doherty were found on some quaking asps where he had pulled himself up over the quartzite rim of the gulch. The section men who had been let off heard the shooting and one of them, E. J. Zeljadt, not waiting for results, ran all the way to Lead City and gave the alarm. He reported that Commiskey and Remer had been killed and the money taken. This report with many exaggerations was spread at once along the Belt and to Deadwood, causing considerable excitement. Superintendent Grier at once organized a posse and soon the woods at Reno gulch were full of men on horseback, all in plain sight of Doherty who had made his way to the top of Sugar Loaf Mountain, laid in the brush there that day and got out of the country that night with the help of his friends.

Commiskey soon had his engine back on the track and returned to Lead City with Wilson in charge of a deputy sherif, and Remer took the money and went on to Brownsville to pay off. Reaching there the engine was met by about two hundred wood choppers, all looking as if they had lost their last and best friend. With them was O. W. Hurlbut in charge of the Brownsville store who remarked to Remer that he was glad that nobody was killed as first reported, but that it was a bad piece of business losing the money. At the same time Remer was taking the old yellow valise out of the tool box, and when the crowd saw him carefully hand it down to Hurlbut, they knew it wasn't empty and put up a yell which could have been heard on Dead Man's Hill, Bill Sweeney joining in with, "You bet your sweet life they didn't take the money away from Buck Shot Bill, and Remer is known by that name today among the old timers in the wood camp. Murphy tried to get out of the country but got lost on upper Spearfish creek, came back to Deadwood that afternoon and that night was driven to Rapid City by one George Young and he and Telford were arrested there next day. A vigorous hunt was made for Doherty, as all kinds of reports of him having been seen were floating around. One came into Lead "that a man shot in the face" had been seen at the Salt Wells in Wyoming, near where Cambria now is, so Sheriff Knight, with a posse composed of N. W. Gregory, Remer, Sam Blackstone, Billy Fawcett and others left for there, they did not find Doherty but they did round up Buck Handon and Von Rippen, a couple of notorious horse thieves. On December 5th, Murphy was tried and Telford on the 13th, Wilson testifying for the State. Both were convicted and sentenced to the penitentiary for fifteen years.

    The Homestake company had offered a reward of $1,000 for Doherty, dead or alive, and about February 6, 1889, he was arrested at Douglas by John T. Williams, the sheriff of Converse county, Wyoming. Sam Blackstone left the same day to identify him and an attempt was made at Chadron by Doherty's friends to take the prisoner away from Williams and Blackstone, but they stood them off and delivered their man to Sheriff Knight in Deadwood and the

$1,000 was paid to Williams. The story is that Williams split the reward with a gambler in Douglas who had given Doherty away to him, invested his $500 in sheep and it was the starter of the fortune he afterwards made in sheep and cattle. Wilson broke jail on the night of February 15th, but was captured three days later in Boulder Canyon by Deputy Sheriff Wilbur Smith. Doherty was arraigned for trial upon March 11th, with A. J. Plowman as his attorney. It was expected he would go into court the next day and plead guilty, but he didn't. The night of the 12th he and Wilson and a prisoner named Stewart broke jail, stole two horses from the sheriff and one from S. V. Noble and made their getaway. It developed later that for several nights they had been drilling out the rivets in the lattice bars of the steel cage, using the handle of a slop bucket and a broken file as a brace and bit, then using one of the heavy iron doors of the cage as a battering ram they smashed a hole through. Later it was learned that Wilson and Doherty made their way to Canada, disposed of the horses and saddles this side of the line, believing that if they did not take stolen property across they could not be extradited

Doherty finally wound up in Rossland, B. C., changed his name and went straight and is a respected citizen today. Later on when Remer was sheriff the mounted police there sent him a report on him and he sent back word to Doherty that as long as he stayed out of the United States he had nothing to fear. About the same time he was advised by the sheriff of Whitman county, Washington, that Wilson had been killed there while resisting arrest.

Telford and Murphy remained in the penitentiary until February of 1891, when they were released on a writ of habeas corpus brought by a lawyer named Allen of Sheldon, Iowa. The contention was that there was no crime unless there was a statutory penalty therefor. The statute provided that robbery by two or more persons should be punished by imprisonment for life and a crime frustrated or intercepted by one-half of the maximum penalty, consequently in the case of these men the court was called upon to decide what was one-half of the remainder of their lives, clearly an impossibility. No answer was put in by the authorities of Lawrence county and the men were released.

Telford was in Salt Lake City a few years ago and is reported to have made money as a contractor. Murphy resumed his right name and is now a respected citizen of Nebraska, is married and has several children and is superintendent of the Sunday school.

Harney Peak Above the Clouds

CHAPTER VI.

NECK TIE PARTIES, FORMAL AND INFORMAL

The problems of life that confronted the pioneers of the last century in the Black Hills demanded men of quick action, firm purpose and unflinching courage. It was a time when the elemental law of the survival of the fittest was in full sway. Home, loved ones, life itself were thrown into the balance and often lost. The game was fast and furious. Great was the wager made and heavy was the loss to many. From out the seething caldron of human passions, law finally emerged and order succeeded chaos. The cruel and crushing force of justice as it tread through the tangled mazes of the formative years to its rightful throne is seen from the following stories of tragedies where young and old, high and low, ignorant and educated paid the supreme sacrifice.

SWIFT JUSTICE

Down on the south side crossing of the Platte river in Nebraska on the Sidney and Red Cloud road, in 1875, there was a most cruel murder committed by a man who claimed his name was Patterson, but went under the name of One Eyed Ed. He was one of the best pistol shots in the West, and he was in constant practice when opportunity presented. Pratt and Ferris' big bull train was encamped on the south side loaded for the agency with Indian goods. The next day a large herd of Texas long horn cattle arrived at the river, on their way up for delivery to the Indian department. The herd was under the charge of Robert R. Porter. There were many calves in the herd and as they did not count in the delivery, Mr. Porter came over to the bull train and inquired of the boys how they were fixed for fresh meat. "We are living on sow belly straight," was the answer. "Well, boys, I can help you out, you may shoot all of those young calves you want, but don't shoot anything that will count on the delivery." One Eyed Ed stole out of camp, thinking that would be good practice for him, but instead of taking calves, he shot a couple of two year olds. When Porter was told that the bull whackers had been killing the cattle, Porter rode over to remonstrate. He was riding a splendid black horse and he stopped at the lower end of the corral, and asked why they had killed cattle instead of calves. "Now you have made me short two on count, and I will have to account for those to the owners." One Eyed Ed standing back from the wagon, raised his pistol and fired and Porter fell from his horse, and was dead by the time the boys reached him, having been shot through the head. There was a commotion in camp, not only for the killing of Porter, but they felt sure that the cowboys would soon swoop down on them to get revenge. The horse would not leave his rider but pranced around him whinnying and pawing up the dirt as if he sensed what had happened. Skinny Bill ran down and caught the horse and tied him to a wagon wheel, then rubbed the foam from the horse's sides, as he was lathered with sweat. That night Skinny and the negro cook stood guard over the body, but they sent word to the cowboys and they soon circled the plains and had Ed in custody. They waited for the coroner to come from Sidney, before they could do anything in camp. When the body was viewed by the coroner's jury next morning, the verdict was murder in the first degree, so the cowboys tied Ed on a horse and went back with the body to Sidney. Just north of Sidney where the coulies divide, the boys in charge of the prisoner swung down into the middle coulie, and as they neared the mouth of it there came a group of cowboys under Jim Reddington. They surrounded the escorting party, when one of the vigilantes took down his rope and riding around Ed several times swinging his lariat, finally dropped it and the loop found its mark around Ed's neck. During this performance Ed never showed one particle of fear, not one word escaped his lips, but died like the dog he was. Heroic treatment some will say, but reader, what would you have done under the same circumstances? In conclusion, let me say that the kid spoken of as Skinny Bill, is now William Francis Hooker, editor of the Erie Magazine, New York City. Those days he was considered a boy lunger, and was a bovine agitator. Recovering his health, he went back to the east, and took up the newspaper work, working on the old Inter Ocean of Chicago, and led a useful and busy life since deserting his first love.

THE FIRST HANGING IN THE BLACK HILLS

There were four of us sitting together around a cheerful pine fire upon the site of a grassy knoll among the foot hills about forty miles from Custer. One of the party was a mountaineer, the rest were members of a large well armed train of Black Hillers, then toiling and working its way through a wilderness of sage brush, endeavoring to reach the trail our party had discovered a few hours before. We had selected a spot for rest where wind or sun or perhaps both had melted away the snow from a huge pine knot almost petrified by age. The grass, too, was luxuriant and offered an inducement for us to halt and rest until the train came up. The fire lit the north in a blaze, we brought forth our pipes to smoke and watch the misty curtain raise. 'Twas a glorious scene on that crisp, frosty morning and the man who died there that day should have felt proud of his magnificient death chamber. Nature seemed to have lavished unlimited wonders and beauties upon the Black Hills and fate seems to have lead Dick Burnett to a most beautiful spot in the Black Hills in which to die. While we were calmly smoking around the fire watching the canopy rise like a feathery veil from the valley beneath us; while we silently admired the magnificient back ground of glistening snow and bright green pines which in the morning sun appeared more beautiful than ever before; while we were just quietly admiring the beautiful blood red iron tinctured valley below us now plainly visible beneath the slowly rising curtain of mist, admiring the winding creek in its center which with its beautiful fringe of orange kinnikinic willow appeared like a huge yellow snake in a basin of blood, a man rode suddenly upon us. He sprang to his feet, rifle in hand. The stranger turnd his horse away in alarm and rode quickly away. He was a white man and we could not and had no reason to halt him. He rode out to the side of the road and dismounted. Then he proceeded to arrange and write upon some paper which he placed in his bosom and after some hesitation lead his horse to our surprised party and halted about thirty paces distant, rifle and pistol in hand. "Hello there." "Hello there yourself!" "Is this the Custer road?" "Don't know, have been lost all night." "Who are you?" "Pilgrims from Sidney. Been lost on the trail two days." Then the lonely stranger rode up and stood restlessly awaiting interrogation. He said he had left Custer two days before, that he was drunk when he left and did not know what he had done or how he had got lost. He received lots of letters from our party and soon after bade us adieu. He said he was going to the States and we bade him look out for his scalp and said good bye.

Poor fellow, unfortunate drunk, it cost him his life. It was late in the afternoon when we met him again. We were in a dry camp, a camp in which snow must be melted for water for man and beast. The boys were just at work shoveling snow into camp kettles and melting it for the horses. Supper was over and the guards were out. A shot awoke reverberating echoes of the hills and in a minute afterwards every man of fifty-five people was prepared for duty. A party of vigilantes rode into the camp. They had come upon the guards suddenly and had been fired upon. They were rough looking men but all quite civil. They inquired for a lawyer, we had one so he came forward. They asked for a judge, we had none so they elected one. They asked for a preacher but found none. A clerk was found in a reporter. They had brought back the strange man of the morning. He was a prisoner and seemed to realize his position. He called the reporter and handed him back mail matter and requested him to write a few short letters for him. This was done and he signed them while court was being held. The judge seated upon the pile of harness, the jury upon a wagon tongue. "Dick Burnett" shouted one of those strange, cruel men. Dick Burnett turned to the reporter and handed him his papers and said in a trembling, shaking voice, "It is all over with me I reckon, they all know me and there is no use squealing." He walked over to the wagon while two of the party went to a barkless old cottonwood tree where a lariat was thrown over a projecting limb. "Dick Burnett," said old Colonel Lyon, "you have been caught in the act of stealing a horse from the people of these Hills. You have also been found guilty of shooting and wounding with intent to kill Peter S. Lambert, and with stealing his horse. This here party of true and good men have this fact and say you must hang. What have you to say against it?" Dick, while old Lyon was speaking manifested little or no feeling. He looked in the vicinity of us and seemed to expect some interference from the members of our party. He said, "I shot Peter Lambert but he wanted to get the drop on me. I took his horse and I may have taken a few others but what I done I done when I was drunk. If I have got to swing I will do it like a man, only give me time to fix up matters before I go." Then the poor fellow sat down and with tears in his eyes wrote a letter to his father at Stubbenville, Ohio, and one to his brother at Saint Louis, and still another to a lady in Coshocton, Ohio. Then he arose and dashing the tears from his bloodshot eyes said he was ready. He gave his rifle and horse to Colonel Lyon to be sent back to the owner, Peter Lambert, and folding his arms walked to the horse. For a moment he hesitated, life was sweet to him, he was not thirty years of age, but he was seized, pushed forward to the tree and mounting the horse without hesitation, the tears gushing from his eyes while his arms were belted down to his side. The rope was passed over his neck and drawn taut. Suddenly in another moment the horse received a blow that sent him dashing away and Dick Burnett was struggling between heaven and earth. It was soon over, the rope was untied and he fell to the earth and was left to the pilgrims to bury. We rolled him up in a saddle blanket and buried him in the blood red soil of Red Canyon with a pine board at his head "Richard Burnett of Stubbenville, Ohio, died February 26th, 1876." (Deadwood Pioneer 1876.)

THE RAPID CITY NECKTIE PARTY

Among some of the outlaws and bad actors of 1877 that infested the Hills were a couple of fellows known as Louis Curry and A. J. Allen. The final chapter in the history of the lives of these two men was concluded during the month of June, 1877. Another man of ill repute whose life was snuffed out also at the same time was a fellow known as "Kid" Hall or James Hall. He had become so disreputable and his presence in the community so objectionable that he was ordered out of Deadwood and Crook City and started on his journey south on foot. While travelling along the trail he was overtaken between Crook City and Rapid City by Louis Curry and A. J. Allen or better known as "Red" Curry and "Doc" Allen, who had with them six horses. In those days the western people did not insist upon the formality of introduction nor did they inquire as to one's pedigree and when the two outlaws came upon "Kid" Hall tramping through the dust they invited him to mount one of their horses and ride with them. This offer to the "Kid" was gladly accepted and he proceeded on the way with his two new companions.

When Rapid City was being built the people resorted to the nearby hills to chop the logs of which the huts were constructed. On the afternoon of June 20, 1877, a small party of house builders consisting of Charles Hunt, his father and David Markel were out in the hills north of Rapid City preparing building logs. Late in the afternoon Dave Markel, on horse back, had gone in search of more logs. In his travels it took him over the top of the hill north of Rapid City. When in the distance he saw several head of horses about some bushes in the shade of which several men were seen lying, he immediately decided that they were Indians and rushed pell mell toward his companions calling out to them that there was a party of Indians over the hill and then hurried on to Rapid City where he reported to the little band of settlers and Sheriff Frank Moulton that there were Indians north of town. The men who were gathering logs piled them on their wagons and hurried to Rapid City. In the meantime Sheriff Moulton and a posse of men who promptly assembled at the alarm of Indians rode out to the place where the horses and men were and surrounded them. The men on the ground were easily captured for they were asleep and when aroused surrendered without trouble. Off in the distance a man who had been placed on guard and afterward proved to be Powell was seen galloping away down through the draw and out of sight. The fellow later met his death at the hands of the outlaw, Lame Bradley, in a row. The men captured under the bush proved to me "Red" Curry and "Doc" Allen and "Kid" Hall and in their possession were the six stolen horses. They and the horses were taken in charge by the sheriff and the men were placed under guard in a log cabin belonging to the stage company.

About this time Ed Cook, in charge of the Northwestern Stage and Transportation Company, arrived from Deadwood and Crook City with the stage and coming to the place where the horses were held immediately recognized four of them as his own property that had been stolen from the stage barn at Crook City. The other two horses proved to be those that had been taken from a freighter at Crook City. Ed Cook in conversation with McIntyre said, "What are we going to do with those fellows? How are we going to stop this stealing of horses and stock in this country?" McIntyre replied, "The only thing that I can see is to give a jug of whiskey to the boys and do away with them." The three horse thieves had been placed in the little red log cabin belonging to the stage company and several armed men were placed there to guard them preparatory to giving them a preliminary hearing. While in the granary "Kid" Hall the youngest of the fellows, a fellow about twenty-two or twenty-three years of age and weighing some one hundred and sixty pounds, put his head out of the window and said to the bystanders, "You s-----b-----, you would not have gotten us if we had not been asleep." That evening the preliminary hearing was given to the three men and they were bound over by Bob Burleigh, justice of the peace. In the hearing "Doc" Allen and "Red" Curry admitted their crime but said that "Kid" Hall had absolutely nothing to do with the theft of the horses and that they had overtaken him on the way to Rapid City and finding him on foot invited him to ride with them. However, the justice of the peace bound all three over to appear before the circuit court for further investigation, the fellow known as "Kid" Hall having a bad reputation and being a worthless rounder.

About twelve o'clock that night a band of masked men assembled around the little log house and demanded that the guards surrender to them the prisoners which of course the guards were compelled to do. The guards were also obliged not only to surrender the prisoners but to accompany the visiting committee. As they proceeded to march away with the three prisoners the midnight jury took the men to the hill just west of Rapid City where there stood a lone pine tree and where they placed about the necks of the two older men a piece of clothes line rope, and making them to stand on rocks, tied the rope to an overhanging limb and kicked the rocks from beneath them. The question then was what was to be done with "Kid" Hall and the leader of the committee said, "Dead men tell no tales, up with him" and in a few minutes "Kid" Hall was kicking and struggling in the air with his other pals.

The next morning the party of log seekers who had made the hurried trip from the hills to their

Historic Hangman's Hill

camps along the creek upon looking out over the hills saw over the horizon the three bodies hanging to the limbs of the pine tree. They hurried up to the tree but by the time they arrived there they found that Justice Bob Burleigh had preceded them there and was holding a coroner's inquest. Hanging beneath the tree were the three bodies with blackened faces, protruding tongues, and their toes touching the ground. The men had not been hanged but strangled to death. For years afterwards the people of Rapid City were known as the "Stranglers." After the inquest was concluded several of the bystanders cut the rope and removed the bodies to a level place on the west side of the hill, where they were buried.

Afterwards the father of Curry came to Rapid City and was quietly investigating the hanging of his son and endeavoring to find out the names of the parties involved. When his presence and purpose became known he was interviewed by a committee of men who after warning him that they were aware of his purpose kindly advised him if he wished to return all together he had better leave town immediately, which counsel apparently was followed to the letter for no more was heard of him. The hangng of these three unprincipled characters had a very wholesome effect on the unruly element and placed a very effective damper on cattle rustling and horse stealing.

TWO BUTCHERS WHO BECAME PROSPEROUS

The following article is written by J. S. McClintock of Deadwood, a pioneer who has been quite accurate in his statement of pioneer incidents and illustrates the swift justice that often was meted out to thieves in those days:

One of the main industries of Deadwood during the summer of 1876 was the traffic in horses. Many animals changed hands in a brief period of time. The better class sold here had been driven in by immigrants and freighters from Iowa and Missouri. An inferior grade were brought in as saddle and pack horses. from the surrounding country. Many of this class were picked up by "rustlers" on the range around the outskirts of the Hills, where they had been turned out to graze by their owners.

One of several parties who were known to be engaged in this precarious business, and with whom I had some acquaintance having purchased a horse from him in December of that year, was known as "Bean Davis." Most of the time he stayed out in the valleys, but was seen frequently on the streets here, and at Central City where he had a partner named George Keating who was at that time owner of, or an interested party in a butcher shop business.

The butchers in these Hills towns would go out on the range and purchase cattle and drive them in to slaughter pens to prepare them for market. No one suspected that Keating was procuring his supply of meat in a different manner, but it was developed in the summer of 1877 that he, in connection with Davis, who had shifted from horse stealing to the more profitable business of cattle rustling, were picking up their supply on the range without permission or paying therefore. These animals were driven, in small lots, into the timber where they were prepared for the meat market.

While the owners of these stolen critters were missing their cattle they were unable to determine whether they were being rustled or had strayed. However, their suspicions were aroused and the following interesting incident resulted:

Keating and his partner, Davis, having more beef than they needed for their own shop, sold part of a load to another butcher. Just after payment was made by the purchaser, a stranger stepped in the front door. Keating, or Davis glanced at him and made hasty exit through the back door. This occasioned surprise among those who witnessed it and aroused suspicion. It inspired the editor of the Central City Enterprise (Bartholomew was his name, I think), to report the affair under the heading "The wicked fleeth when no man pursueth." It is presumed that the stranger was recognized as one of the ranchers whose cattle had been rustled.

From that time on the Vigilantes of Spearfish valley, under the leadership of "Who was Who," were engaged in finding the rendezvous of these two enterprising young business men. It was located and one night the Vigilantes descended upon them while at their cache, which was located at a spring at the foot of Lookout Mountain, about two miles east of Spearfish. They were aroused from slumber, taken under pine trees and swung from earth. The bodies were left swinging to be found next day, cut down and buried.

It was only one of the many deadly dramas of those stirring days. The suffering of these two young men who paid the penalty of frontier justice was of short duration. But who can tell of the grief of the mothers "back home" over their erring boys.

LAME JOHNNY

One day about the middle of the last century a little boy was riding his brother's horse, bareback, down the cobble stone paved streets of the city of Philadelphia. The horse stumbled over the uneven pavement and threw the boy to the ground with such force that he became a cripple. And ever afterwards he moved about with a limp. This boy was Cornelius Donahue. However, the boy continued on his career, graduated from the Stephen Girard College of Philadelphia and wandered on west into Texas. Down in the Texas country they were troubled with the stealing of horses by the Indians and finally Donahue reciprocated and became an expert horse thief himself and succeeded in stealing a great many horses from the Indians. After a time he wandered into the Black Hills and became one of the pioneers of the early '70's where he was known as John A. Hurley and because of his crippled walk was commonly known as "Lame Johnny." In the year 1878 he was a deputy sheriff of Custer county and proved to be a very efficient officer of the law. For a time he served as a bookkeeper in the Homestake Mining Company office. One day while working in the office an acquaintance who knew him down in Texas came into the building and recognizing Johnny addressed him as a horse thief from Texas. This caused Lame Johnny to become very furious and soon after that he quit his job in the Homestake and was not seen for sometime in the Hills.

After awhile there was a rumor that he was back at his old trade of running off Indian horses and it was also rumored that he sometimes included the horses belonging to white men. He went from bad to worse and in the fall of 1878 he and his gang, one of which was Lame Bradley, engaged in the holdup of a coach on the Gilmer and Saulsbury stage line on the Lame Johnny Creek in Custer county about which we have heretofore written. Ed Cook the superintendent of the division was one of the victims and recognized Johnny but did not tell him so. However, he cautioned the messengers on the line to be on the lookout for the men.

From there Johnny went down to the Pine Ridge looking for an opportunity to run off a bunch of Indian ponies. Captain Smith, a stock detective from Cheyenne, was in Pine Ridge when he heard that Johnny was around and he succeeded in capturing him under a warrant charging him with horse stealling done previous to this time. He brought him up to Red Cloud, a stage station, and here he learned that he was wanted for robbing the coach. As Johnny had taken the registered mail pouch at the time of the holdup Smith decided to bring him to Deadwood to be tried on the charge of robbing the U. S. mail. Jesse Brown, one of the guards of the Old Iron Sides stage coach, a man of unquestionable bravery and absolutely trusted by his employers, was in charge of the coach that reached Red Cloud from Sidney on the day which Captain Smith brought Johnny to that station under arrest, shackled and handcuffed. Passage on the coach for Rapid City was secured and the marshal proceeded on the way with his prisoner. Jesse Brown describes the trip and the following incident in his own words:

"The last holdup had been committed in Pennington county, and Rapid City was the county seat. So Lame Johnny was placed inside the coach in my care, and the marshal rode on the driver's seat. Everything went along all right up to Buffalo Gap, when looking out towards the foothills to the west, we could see a horseman riding parallel with us at a swift gallop. Johnny became restless and nervous, saying that he did not like the appearance of the stranger. I asked him what he observed about this horseman to make him feel suspicious. His answer was, 'I think I recognize this rider as Boone May,' and it was Boone May, one of the guards. As yet, I did not have the least suspicion that there was any kind of job under way to do violence to any person. Teams were changed at Buffalo Gap, and there I had to take my saddle horse to Battle Creek, so as to have him there on the next trip down. We had reached a small creek, that now perpetuates the name of "Lame Johnny," when sure enough, the old, familiar command of 'Halt' was heard. I dismounted quickly, tied the reins to a sage brush and left the road to the right, intending to creep up concealed by the brush, and see what was going on. Up to this time I did not know whether it was some of Johnny's friends attempting to release him, or a holdup to rob the passengers and mail. Just as I was reaching the brush a voice from within said, 'Go back. Don't come any farther.' And at the moment I heard my wife and girls running back on the road, thinking that I was still behind. So I called to them and went to them. They were frightened almost into hysterics. I succeeded in in getting them quieted somewhat, and then there was some shooting on the creek where the coach stood. Pretty soon, Smith, the deputy marshal, came back where we were standing in the road, and asked if I would let him take my saddle horse, as he wanted to reconnoitre a little. I granted his request, and with my family got aboard the coach. But there was no prisoner there and I do not know up to this time just what happened. For it was very evident to me that whoever it was that had ordered me not to come any farther, knew that I was riding behind the coach and was watching for me. Or it might have been that they (the mob) expected me to protect Johnny, which would have been my duty. The marshal left my horse at the station and I have not seen him since. I cannot understand how anyone could have known that Lame Johnny was on the coach on this particular day, unless the marshal communicated with some of his friends before leaving Pine Ridge agency. Johnny was hanged to a limb of an elm tree, just where he had robbed the coach, and one of his gang, Lame Bradley, shot at Ed Cook, the bullet penetrating his left ear. Cook was superintendent of the stage line."

The next morning Pete Oslund, in charge of his bull freight train came by the place and there he found Lame Johnny hanging to the limb of an elm tree. Oslund and his men dug a grave at the foot of the tree and buried Johnny there. Years later his body was dug up and probably carried away for there was a highheeled boot that once belonged to him held by a man in the Hills years afterwards and the shackles that were on his body are now to be seen in the State Museum in Pierre. Lame Johnny had a very large mouth and John B. Furey, a United States Postoffice Inspector, in passing by the grave a few days later nailed to the tree above it a board on which he wrote the following epitaph: "To Lame Johnny: Stranger pass gently o'er this sod, if he opens his mouth, you're gone by God."

THE CAPTURE OF TOM PRICE AND HIS BAND OF ROAD AGENTS

This gang was made up of Tom Price, captain, Archie McLaughlin, Billy Mansfield and Jack Smith. Everyone who came into the Hills over the stage line knows or heard more or less about Road Agents along in 1877-78. There was scarcely a coach got through without some experience with them. This particular gang referred to here had been operating along the line between Jenney's Stockade and the Cheyenne River. They held up several passenger coaches at different times and we were on the lookout for them. (Jesse Brown, narrator.)

One Sunday morning in Deadwood, in Wes Travis' livery stable, very unexpectedly Archie McLaughlin came walking into the back part of the barn. One of the messengers happened to catch sight of him as he entered the door. He called to his aid one of the bystanders and placed Archie under arrest, took him to the jail and turned him over to Johnnie Manning, sheriff.

I met them as they were coming back. Bill May was the messenger, and they told me what he had done and that Archie had told him that Mansfield was in town. So Bill and myself went on a search for him and found him up on Sherman street in a house belonging to an actor in Jack Langrish's theatre troupe, I have forgotten the name. We got to the door before he saw us. He was standing at a table drinking a glass of milk. He set the glass down quickly and reached for his gun, but he was covered before he got it. He threw up his hands as commanded and we put him in a separate cell from Archie. In the afternoon we went up to the jail and had an interview with each one separately. They both told about the same story in regard to their companions, Smith and Tom Price, and where their camp was.

The next morning we got saddle horses for Bill and Jim May, Wes Travis, Archie and myself, and went to the place where the camp was supposed to be. There was some smoked dry bread and a small piece of bacon and a few magpies sitting around, nothing more. Archie then told us that this camp was only temporary and the main camp was 10 miles from there, southwest from Lead City. Nothing daunted, we struck out for camp. After we had traveled about seven miles we were on a ridge. Open timber, not much underbrush, but to the west of us there was a small valley covered with a very dense growth of quakenasp, spruce and willows.

Archie and I were riding together behind the others when he pointed down to this thicket and said, "Down there is where our saddles are cached." I called the attention of the others to this and we halted for a minute and concluded to go down and see if the saddles were still there. So Archie pointed out the exact spot as near as he could. We thought that it would not be best to take Archie into the brush and I was delegated to guard him while the two Mays and Travis went to search for the saddles.

It was only a minute until the whole scene was changed from comedy to tragedy. Sure enough, not only a camp was found, but it was occupied, and by desperate men. The first thing I heard was to "throw up your hands," but the command was not obeyed— two guns went up instead. We might say five, because the five of them fired at about the same time. I made Archie sit down on the ground and place his arms around a tree and I handcuffed his hands on the opposite side of the tree. Then I ran down to where the battle was going on. I met the three men coming out of the brush and asked if any of them were hurt and they said no, but there was one man in the brush that was pretty badly hurt so far as they could tell and one had got away.

We surrounded the brush patch as well as we could, watching in every direction, but saw no Smith. Then we went into the brush and searched back and forth but never got a glimpse of him, neither then nor since.

After it was all over the Mays and Travis went to Teeters' ranch where Englewood is now, and got a team to take Tom Price to town. He was shot through the stomach, the ball coming out close to the spine. After they got back with the team and fixed Price in the wagon on some hay, we let Teeters drive back to his place and we went to the main camp about three miles farther south expecting that Smith might attempt to reach it and get some things that he had there before leaving, but he was not there.

They were well supplied with provisions, blankets, ammunition and everything that went to make up an outlaws' outfit.

Tom Price got well. He was attended by Doctor Babcock of Deadwood. There were 21 days that everything that he ate passed through the bullet hole in him. He was taken to Cheyenne, tried and convicted, and sent to Lincoln, Nebraska, to serve five years in the penitentiary.

McLaughlin and Mansfield were also taken to Cheyenne for trial, but when we reached there court was over for the term and they would have to be held there in jail for about six months, so the conclusion was to take them back to Deadwood and keep them there and perhaps to try them on a charge of grand larceny. They stole some cattle in Lawrence county some time before this.

We started back on the coach, stopped at Fort Laramie for supper and started out again at about eight o'clock. I rode inside with the prisoners. Jim May was out with the driver. We had just entered the timber approaching the Platte river about a mile from the Fort, when that ominous cry was heard. "Halt." The driver pulled up his team quickly but had scarcely stopped when I struck the ground. I jumped right into the arms of a great big fellow who caught my gun and yanked it from me. I looked ahead and there was May standing disarmed and I was ordered to stand along with May. Then one of these men went to the coach door and ordered McLaughlin and Mansfield to come out, and when they did so one man took them and left the road. The other fellow told May and myself to follow up. I protested and asked them what they wanted us to follow up for. He says, "Damn you, do as you are told." They only went a little ways when they halted and one of them picked up a rope. It commenced to dawn on me that there was going to be some dastardly work done, and it was done quickly. The rope was placed around Mansfield's neck first and he was drawn up. Archie was next and while they were fixing the rope on him he wanted to say something to me, I presume about his folks down in Missouri, but he was told to shut up. The rope went up and he was hoisted between heaven and earth and left there.

When it was all over these men went about twenty feet away, left our guns and disappeared in the woods. Just prior to this they had warned us that if we were wise we would keep our mouths shut. I could not make out what manner of men they were as their faces were masked except their eyes.

THE HANGING OF FLY-SPECKED BILLY

When Abe Barnes, the foreman of a freight outfit was on his way to Custer City, Dakota, in the month of February, 1881, he overtook a sore-footed and almost starved traveler who introduced himself as Jim Fowler. Barnes took pity on Fowler and invited him to join his outfit and gave him food and assistance. After they had arrived at Custer City, Fowler, who was commonly known as "Fly-Specked Billy" borrowed Barnes' six shooter and soon after proceeded to shoot up the town making things very unpleasant for people on the street. Finally he came to a saloon where Barnes was playing billiards and asked him to take a drink with him but Barnes politely refused, whereupon "Fly-Specked Billy" in his drunken fury, blazed away, and killed Barnes almost instantly. The murderer made a rush for the door but was struck down by a man called Red. John T. Coad, the sheriff, arrived upon the scene and arrested "Fly-Specked Billy" but before he could be placed in the jail a crowd gathered, took the prisoner away from the sheriff and rushed him over to the south side of the creek where he was strung up to a convenient tree limb, and thus ended the career of "Fly-Specked Billy."

THE STONEVILLE BATTLE

A few years ago, there was published a so-called

account of this fight in the "Literary Digest," by a man named George Bartlett. He says that he was in the battle and led the posse of officers. He was not in the fight at all, and did not arrive on the ground until forty-eight hours after the battle. His story is so unfair that A. M. Willard was persuaded to write the facts for the first time, not for the purpose of injuring anyone; but to have the plain history of this battle published, which story follows:

A short time before this event, warrants for the arrest of George Axelbee, Campbell, Alex Grady, Charlie Brown, (Broncho Charlie), Jesse Pruden, and others, all known as "The Axelbee Gang of Outlaws," were placed in the hands of Al Raymond, deputy United States marshal for the territory of Dakota. One of the gang, Jesse Pruden, was arrested at Miles City, Montana, by Jack Johnson, sheriff of Custer county, Montana. He wired Raymond at once and Joe Ryan, a special deputy marshal of Spearfish, Dakota Territory, was sent after the prisoner. My brother, Fred A. Willard, and myself were deputies, and had been trying to locate this gang of outlaws after Joe Ryan had left Miles City with his prisoner. Fred Willard, who lived at Spearfish, found out that Axelbee and his gang were at Box Elder, Montana, about eighty miles north of the Black Hills, and they were there for the purpose of holding up Joe Ryan and releasing the prisoner, Jesse Pruden.

Fred called me on the 'phone and wanted me to go out with him and meet Ryan; but I did not think that there was any danger and did not go at the time; but Fred and Jack O'Hara, another deputy, started at once.

That afternoon, Raymond received a dispatch from Sheriff Johnson at Miles City, saying that the Axelbee gang would be at Box Elder, Montana, and would make the attempt to kill Ryan and release the prisoner.

I then prepared to go out and overtake Fred and Jack, if possible, but my horse was at Spearfish, fifteen miles away. So Raymond sent two deputies,

John Duffy and Frank Jackson, to take me to Spearfish. We made a quick trip to Spearfish. My horse was gone! I took a team out of my brother's stable, and found a man, named McNarboe, who offered to go with me; he was a "cow puncher," formerly in the employ of the "Hash Knife Cattle Company," and he was posted on all the trails in the Little Missouri river country.

We left Spearfish that night to overtake Fred and Jack, if possible; it was very cold and the snow was deep, making it very slow travelling. We drove all night although it was twenty-five degrees below zero. We reached Wisner's ranch on Hay Creek, Wyoming, about four o'clock in the morning of February 14, 1884. We rested the team about one hour and started out again. Duffy and his man had kept up with me so far; but their team was nearly exhausted. I gave Duffy strict orders to keep up if he possibly could. I knew he would as he was a fine officer and I had seen him tried out on several occasions.

We arrived in sight of Stoneville, about noon. McNarboe wanted to drive over to the saloon; but I did not like the looks of things around there, as I had noticed some pack horses there, also I noticed several horses saddled and there were rifles on the saddles. I knew then that the outlaws were there; how many I could not tell, as no one was in sight; it would be well at this time to give a description and a brief history of Stoneville.

Stoneville had been a trading post, in the days when large herds of buffalo ranged between the Black Hills and the Yellowstone River, Montana, and was headquarters for the hunters and trappers in that part of the country. There was a hotel and post office and a house owned and occupied by Lew Stone, an old hunter and trapper. The principal place of business was the saloon, where all the different elements of the country, cow boys, hunters and outlaws of all kinds, congregated, and was out of reach of the officers of the law. The place was about seventy-five miles north of the Black Hills and about one hundred twenty miles south of Miles City, Montana. This place was a favorite place for the oultaws, George Axelbee and his gang; it was impossible for the officers to obtain any information of the outlaws from anyone in that part of the country.

I told Mac to drive over to old Lew Stone's place. This house was about two hundred and fifty yards in a northeasterly direction from the saloon. A barn stood about one hundred feet south of Stone's house and nearly east from the saloon. We had just unhitched the team when Axelbee and several of his gang came out of the saloon. As soon as Axelbee saw us, he yelled at us, asking who we were; as they did not know us at first. I told McNarboe to go to the house and I would cover him, and see that no one would trouble him.

About this time Axelbee knew me and commenced to call me names. After Mac had reached the house, I started after him. Axelbee raised his rifle, but changed his mind and did not fire. I reached the house and went in and was surprised to find Fred and Jack there. Up to this time, I did not know where the boys were; they were very glad to see me for once in their lives, at any rate. They had been there for several hours, at a loss as to what to do, as there were six outlaws. Besides, there were several of the outlaws' friends there.

"Boys, you have come a long way, looking for a fight and I reckon you will find one before we leave here!" said I.

All this time the gang was calling us vile names and daring us to come out and fight. We held a council and decided to make the attempt to capture the gang.

It was not long before they commenced to prepare to leave. The bridge across the Little Missouri river was the point where they would be obliged to cross the river; it was nearer to our position than it was to theirs. This bridge was about four hundred yards from where we would be lined up. We had planned to wait until the gang had started for the bridge and then we would make a quick move and take up a position so as to cut them off from the bridge. There was a large crowd of cowboys and most of them were drunk and firing their six shooters around promiscuously, so that we did not know what to expect from them. It was not long before the outlaws mounted and yelling at us to come out and fight they started for the bridge.

I had told Fred to call on them to surrender and be ready to shoot at the same time, as I had no idea that they would comply with the order at all. We knew we would be out in the open as there was no place that we could get under cover. We ran out around Stone's house and took up our position; Fred Willard on the left of the line, Jack O'Hara in the middle and a little to the rear of me, just as we had planned it; this only took a short time. We were about one hundred yards from Stone's house. Fred called out to them to surrender. Campbell and Fred fired at the same time. Campbell fell off his horse and then fell over the bank of the river, out of sight. The firing was very hot for awhile. Axelbee fell from his horse, badly wounded. He went over the river bank and his horse followed him over the bank, out of sight. Tuthill fell from his mule with a badly shattered arm. In the mix up, four horses were killed.

Just then Jack groaned and said, "Cap, I'm done for" and fell near me. I spoke to Fred and said, "Jack is gone; do not spare one of that crowd."

Fred turned to look at Jack. He was in the act of putting in a cartridge, a ball struck him between the shoulders, making a very painful but not a dangerous wound. Just then a ball struck through my coat and I turned as another ball grazed my left ear. I saw that those shots came from a group of cowboys near the saloon. I told Fred that the "punchers" were firing on us. We faced the other way; the cowboys fell back behind the saloon, there was none of the outlaws in sight, so Fred and I went back to Stone's house. I stopped at the corner of the house so that I could watch the river bank where Axelbee had fallen. A shot rang out and a ball struck in the logs of the house, about a foot above my head. I knew that shot was from Axelbee's gun, but he was not in sight. Just then two shots rang out across the river from the saloon and Jack Harris and Billy Cunningham, two cowboys, fell. We could not understand that move then. I then discovered that O'Hara was still alive, and called old Stone and Billy Thacher and had him carried up to the house. He lived only a few minutes after he reached the house.

Up to this time, we had supposed that the cowboys had fired on us. McKenzie, the proprietor of the saloon, came out and raised a white flag. I went over and had a talk with him. I was very much surprised to learn that the shots fired from that direction were fired by one of the outlaws, Billy McCarthy, (Billy, the Kid). He had taken a position in among the cow punchers, and he was the one who had done most of the damage. Axelbee, after firing on the cowboys, although badly wounded, mounted his horse with Grady and Brown, both badly wounded, and rode up the river, keeping under the banks of the river, out of sight, getting away at the time. They stopped at a house up the river and got bandages, medicines and grub. Then they made a circle and after dark, struck down the river. I soon found out that Campbell was not killed. Although wounded in the head, he had wandered down the river, out of sight. I also learned that Axelbee had a score to settle with Harris and Cunningham (the two cowboys whom Axelbee had shot in such a cowardly manner). These boys were working for Driskill, up the Little Missouri River, and Cunningham had told Axelbee to keep away from the ranch as it was giving the ranch a bad name, their coming there, and they did not want men of his kind around. Axelbee was very angry and swore that he would "get even," so when he (Axelbee) found that he was wounded and would be obliged to get out at once, he stepped behind a tree and deliberately shot these two boys down in cold blood. They were shot in the back. He killed Cunningham instantly and wounded Harris, who died of his wounds later. I made up my mind that Campbell would go to a certain ranch four or five miles down the river. I kept watch that evening and saw a young man come up the river. I kept close watch and saw him hand a note to Hood, the foreman of the "Hash Knife Company." Hood gave me the note. In the note was a request from Campbell for Hood to send down a horse so that he could escape. I held up the young man who had brought the note and kept him until after dark. We then took a posse and went down to this ranch where Campbell had gone. We also took the young man. We tied a horse near the house where Campbell could see it. I instructed this young man to go in and tell Campbell that there was a horse for him and that he had better go at once. Campbell was all ready and went out at once, and he was armed with a Marlin rifle and revolver. He was called upon to surrender; but he refused and commenced firing. He fell, riddled with balls. That ended the Battle of Stoneville. The next day Fred Willard concluded to start for Spearfish with O'Hara's body, but was delayed. I commenced to organize a posse of "cow punchers" to follow two outlaws who had escaped. I was kept over another day. That night, more than forty-eight hours after the fight, Al Raymond, W. O. Frost, Doctor Babcock, George Bartlett, Doctor Louthan, John Bell and others arrived at Stoneville.

Fred went back with the body of O'Hara. I took my posse and struck out after the outlaws that had escaped. I met Joe Ryan and his prisoner on Box Elder Creek, twenty miles north of Stoneville, sent a man with him and went on. The weather was very cold, but we scoured the country, but did not capture any of the gang at that time. After a long, cold ride, we returned to Stoneville, found Tuthill, the wounded outlaw, in a very bad shape. I had him sent into Spearfish and I followed him the same day and had him placed in the hospital at Spearfish, and returned to my home at Deadwood, where I was very much surprised that the news of this fight had caused considerable excitement. They were printing "extras" every day, also at Fort Meade a troop of the Seventh United States Cavalry, were ordered out; but my coming in stopped the expedition. Some time after this—two weeks, I should judge, Tuthill was taken out of the hospital and hung, making six men that lost their lives at Stoneville. The names of the outlaws engaged in this battle were George Axelbee, Campbell, Axel Grady, Charlie Brown (Broncho Charlie), Harry Tuthill, and Billy McCarthy, (Billy, the Kid), six outlaws. The names of the officers were Fred A. Willard, Jack O'Hara and A. M. Willard, Duffy and Jackson did not arrive on the ground until after the fight, their team played out much to their disappointment. Duffy rendered some valuable services in various ways. Duffy and John Bell buried the dead, and did other things that helped me very much. Bartlett, in one of his articles, says that he killed Campbell and took the six shooter off of Campbell's body, and kept it as a relic of that battle. Campbell was killed and buried forty-eight hours before Bartlett arrived at Stoneville. Bartlett never saw Campbell, dead or alive. Broncho Charlie died of his wounds afterwards. Axelbee and one of his men were killed about four months afterwards.

TUTHILL

The short span of the life of Harry Tuthill presents a picture of tragic interest. His father was a most efficient and brave officer of the United States during the civil war and the duty of examining all ships entering the port of New Orleans devolved upon him. At last he fell a victim to the yellow fever and with him went his wife also, leaving Harry Tuthill, the baby boy to be buffed about by the hands of fate. His family belonged to wealthy and prominent people of New York who took him there and held him for several years, but they found that the boy was too high spirited to grow up in a large city and sought a home for him on some western farm.

After careful investigation and search the home of a most honorable family on a farm in Iowa was selected and the youth of aristocratic lineage and proud family was sent to the west for training.

The good people of the western home came to love and admire the honorable, upright and generous orphan and sought to adopt him as their own, but the boy was an heir to a great fortune from ancestors in England and his relatives would not consent to this move. However, the child grew up strong and healthy, developed a keen intellect and became the big brother to the little boy of his foster parents. He was the champion and protector of his little playmate and was ever his guardian. Then there came the time when Tuthill answered the call of the wanderlust, left the kindly people and his only chum, and went forth to battle the world alone.

At his majority he voyaged to England, claimed and received $20,000.00 of his inheritance, but on the return trip fell in with gamblers and landed in New York penniless. A wealthy aunt came to his rescue, furnished him money and started him out in the drug business in a town in Minnesota. He had with him a partner, and again unkind fate sent the wheel of fortune spinning against him and the partner soon had him seeking for a place to sleep and a means for livelihood. Tuthill, being an expert horseman and shot, went west and made a living for awhile shooting buffalo. His love for horses soon called him into the business of buying, selling and trading horses out in the west.

In his work of dealing in horses, he no doubt met Axelbee's gang and did business with them. But there seems to be no evidence of his ever having taken any part in stealing horses from the settlers. However, it is known that he was intimately acquainted with the police officers and that in talking with one of them he was apprised of the fact that the officers were to proceed from Deadwood and prevent the Axelbee gang from interfering with the delivery of the arrested man, **Pruden. Accordingly he left the** city of Deadwood, ahead of the officers, and arrived in Stoneville shortly before the coming of Willard and his men. Being loyal to his friends, and knowing the danger that was menacing the Axelbee gang, he no doubt sought to avert the probable blood shed. Be that as it may, he was in the saloon on that fatal day with many other men, and when he came out of the building and started to ride away on his mule, a bullet from the officers went crashing through his elbow smashing the arm which flopped about as his mule, startled with the smell of blood, went bucking and snorting down the creek. However, Tuthill could not be unseated and although wounded, conquered the frightened animal and sought aid from a farmer who took him into his cabin, and bound a fresh deer skin thong above the jagged wound. This was so tight as to almost stop circulation and the upper arm became swollen to such an extent that the wounded man could not endure the torture and insisted upon the thong being cut. Another man then washed a silk neck scarf and drew it back and forth through the mangled arm to clean it, the pain caused by this treatment being almost unendurable.

Later, men came out from Spearfish and brought the wounded man to the hospital for treatment. In the quiet hours of the night, six men, among whom were some of the officers of the law, dressed in buffalo overcoats, came to the room of the man. Angered by the loss of their companion, and forgetting the law, they tore the half dead sufferer from his bed, clad only in the single short shirt, dragged the tortured man through the biting and stinging snow to a tree on the edge of town and placing a rope about his neck pulled his body up to a branch. In the morning the people of the town beheld the frozen form blackened and distorted in the agony of strangulation, swaying beneath the tree in the cold blasts of the wintry wind.

The body was removed and buried in the town grave yard. Above the grave was placed a pine tree trunk, painted a bright red, the sign of the outlaw.

Many succeeding winters came and went and summer followed summer until the grave of Harry Tuthill became overgrown with the wild grass of the prairies and the red paint of the wooden shaft had almost faded away. Then one day, when the people had gathered in May time to place upon the graves of loved ones the young flowers of spring, they were astonished to see a man at the foot of the weather worn shaft of red, tearing away the wild grass and weeds above the neglected grave of the so-called outlaw. It was the playmate of his childhood, the boy whom long years before he had shielded from the blows of his fellows. He was a minister now, obedient to the divine precept, "Inasmuch as ye have done it unto the least of these ye have done it unto me."

FIDDLER

The people of the Black Hills during the period of the 70's and 80's were very stern and firm in their ideas of justice and preservation of order. Throughout all of the Hills towns and mining camps any serious infraction of the law received immediate attention from the common people as well as the sworn officers. They did not stand long upon the theory of the law or the letter but were very practical and we find that duels took place, all kinds of shooting scrapes and fights ensued, often resulting in very serious injuries to those engaged.

The people of Sturgis in those days were not in the least backward in their efforts to enforce respect and protection for property. The first record we have of a lynching taking place in Sturgis was one that grew out of the robbery of an immigrant, the substance of which is taken from the Sturgis Record of June 13th, 1884, as follows:

A month ago Theodore Schraum, a German of pretty good circumstances as the world goes, started from Minnesota for the Black Hills to take up a farm and settle down. He had with him a team and some little money and when near the Dakota and Minnesota lines he bought a mule to add to his outfit and started overland. He finally arrived at Fort Meade and was dumbfounded when his recent purchase, the mule, was taken possession of by the authorities at the Post who claimed it had been stolen, and was a government mule. Schraum had no recourse and tried to buy another mule and in so doing disclosed the fact that he had the money with which to do it. He was unsuccessful, however, and as he was unable to travel further the authorities at the Post hitched a government team to his outfit and hauled it off the military reserve, leaving him just over the line near Downer's brewery. He was about paralized at the turn things had taken. This occurred on Monday and Tuesday.

Wednesday evening three men, two in soldier's clothes and one in citizen's clothing, approached him and one of the men suddenly bounced upon him with a big revolver and striking him over the head several times rendered him nearly insensible. While he was in this condition the three footpads went through him and relieved him of about $335.00, all the money that he possessed in the world and then they made their escape. Mr. Schraum says that he hardly thinks he could identify any of the parties but while his assailants were battering him on the head the revolver went off over the fellow's shoulder but he did not know where the shot went. Upon investigation it was learned that a soldier had been shot at Fort Meade but when search was made for him he was not to be found. Later about twelve o'clock at night he was discovered and suspicion immediately attached to him because he was found in an old cabin about three quarters of a mile from the Fort and was absent from his quarters without leave. An examination of the wound disclosed the fact that the bullet went through his arm and into his side. After several hours of grilling he confessed and told that a fellow, Alex Fiddler, a dissolute character about town, was the man who had been the leader in the crime. He said that Fiddler pounded the victim with a gun and still more got all the money and that the other soldier was named Brown. Judge Jewett, the local justice of the peace, immediately proceeded to have Fiddler arrested and accompanied by Cole and Roy carrying shot guns and Scollard and Green with self cocking six shooters made the rounds and found Fiddler in a house of easy virtue. When ordered to throw up his hands the tough complied with alacrity and was escorted to Jewett's office and arrangements made to have a preliminary hearing given to him on Friday. In the mean time he was confined in the city jail. That night about two o'clock in the morning a body of masked men filed into the room where Fiddler was under guard with Dan McMillan as special deputy.

At the solicitation of several guns McMillan weakened and the visitors promptly blindfolded him and Fiddler. The procession then started west to grow up with the trees. When nearly opposite the Catholic church they met a man whom they made sit down in the grass in company with one of them. He said he was so frightened he was afraid to breathe and almost unwilling to wink for fear his eye lid would squeak and that gun would go off. McMillan was faced about and ordered to go home and home he went.

When Sheriff Souter went out to hunt for his late prisoner he found that personage about two feet above the ground, a brown rope was around his neck and the other end around a branch of the tree, which stands just around the bend in the road on the way to Bullis' ranch on the other side of the Catholic church. Souter came back, procured a wagon and went back after the body but life had flown. Fiddler was taken down, the rope disentangled and the body brought to town where it was laid in the office of Judge Jewett and covered with a Sturgis Record and a Police Gazette. As before stated no explanation has been offered for his demise. Some claim that he feared the disgrace that would follow his arrest and it was suicide, others think that he was robbing birds nests and falling became entangled in the rope, others think that his guard tied him too short."

Fiddler was a rough and tough. He had murdered a man in Pierre and blood and hair were found on his revolver. In spite of this he escaped the penalty. All of the witnesses were spirited away so when the trial came on no one appeared to give testimony. An uncle in Colorado gave $6000.00 to clear him and the attorney a retainer's fee of $2500.00. W. J. Gidley saw Fiddler lying in the judge's office stretched out on the long table and said he had known the man for five years between here and Pierre and that he never saw him look so well as he did that day. At the same time, while the coroner's inquest was proceeding, Fay Cowden and a tinhorn gambler, who were on opposite sides of the corpse got into a fight and proceeded to pelt one another across the dead body of the robber which rolled back and forth between them. This violation of official etiquette, an open contempt of court, was speedily stopped by Judge Jewett ordering the gambler put in irons, a pair of bracelets for which purpose was furnished by W. W. Sabin.

It appears that the man Fiddler had been ordered out of Sturgis last winter but had refused to go. After the news of the lynching had been noised about and the soldier, Brown, heard of the disastrous end of his friend, Fiddler, he sent for Souter and offered to give him his money. Souter accordingly took him down to his quarters at the Fort and took $100.00 out from behind a looking glass and handed it over, $75.00 was also recovered from Fiddler's solid girl. Hughes refused to yield up his share of the game.

ASSASSINATION OF DOCTOR H. P. LYNCH

One of the events in the early days of Sturgis that caused an unusual amount of excitement at the time and later led up to the outrage committed by the Twenty-fifth Regiment of the U. S. Cavalry, the same regiment that years afterwards repeated a similar crime in Brownsville, Texas, and called forth the just wrath of President Roosevelt, was the assassination of Doctor H. P. Lynch, during the month of August, 1885.

The following account in the main is taken from the Sturgis Record, August 28th, 1885:

Saturday night last, about eleven o'clock, Doctor H. P. Lynch was sitting in his drug store reading a paper. His right side was toward the door and he was leaning against the counter. He was shot down from the front of the building through a window. The ball entered the right side, passed through the spinal column, lodging on the left side and a little above the heart. He did not struggle and appeared to suffer very little although he groaned and it is thought called for help once or twice in an agonized voice but when help arrived he was dead. The crack of the pistol sounded like a 22 but in reality it was a 44. To get the full facts of this dastardly deed it is necessary to go back a little.

The murderer's name was Ross Hallow but he enlisted in the army under the name of Hallon and became a corporal of Company A, Twenty-fifth Infantry. Sometime ago he had a quarrel with his paramour, one Mamie Lewis, a colored woman of the town. He struck and abused her and finally kicked in two of her ribs. Doctor Sanderson attended to her and afterwards Doctor Lynch, who is said to have advised the girl to have Hallon arrested for the beating. She must have told him about it for it seems at different times he made threats against the Doctor for his counsel in the matter. On Friday night preceding the murder Hallon asked Price Rann for a revolver. Rann was going on guard at the time and did nothing about it but the next morning was again approached by Hallon to whom he gave the key to D. I. Green's box where the gun was. Hallon took the key, got the gun and returned the key to Rann and went on about his business.

That evening Corporal Hallon and Private John Bufford came up town together. About ten thirty o'clock Hallon asked Bufford out back of Abe Hill's dance hall and gave him a drink of brandy out of the bottle which he carried. Bufford took a small drink and Hallon a large one. Subsequently Hallon asked his companion to take another which he refused to do but the owner of the bottle took another long pull at it. This put enough courage in him and he proceeded to carry out his plans as formed. He asked Bufford if he did not want to change blouses for awhile but the private refused, Hallon insisted. Then it appears that Bufford was a little afraid of him and consented. The change was made in the alley between the dance hall and the building lately occupied as a tailor shop on the corner. Hallon then told Bufford to go down and wait for him in front of Ingall's house on the Fort Meade road and he would soon be along. Hallon said he would give Bufford ten minutes to get there in. He had a dog which he wanted Bufford to take with him and even stoned him to induce him to leave him. Bufford went down the street. It seems that he said he was afraid something was going to happen and he did not even know but what he had been marked out as a victim.

When below the Pierson house he met Frank Martinus, a soldier called "Mexican Frank," and asked him for a revolver but Frank refused to let him take one and he passed on down the street. When near the bridge at Ingall's he stopped as per agreement and soon heard a shot fired. At that moment Louis C. Raymond, corporal of the Seventh Cavalry, came along from town and Bufford asked him who fired the shot. Raymond said he did not know, then went on down toward the post. In a few minutes Hallon appeared at the lower corner of Ingall's fence where they changed coats, Bufford taking his private's blouse and Hallon his with corporal chevrons on the sleeves. They walked up toward town and when about opposite Campbell's Forest Saloon, Bufford asked his companion for the pistol which he had taken from his blouse and was examining. Hallon very readily gave it up. When the two men got up as far as the bank corner they could see the group of men in front of the drug store. Bufford wanted to go over but Hallon kept on up the street. Bufford knew that there had been trouble and that Hallon has caused it and he recalled that he had the weapon with which the deed, if any, had been done and his only thought was how he could get rid of it.

He met "Big" Anderson, a soldier, and offered him the gun telling him of his suspicion. Anderson refused to take it and told Bufford he had better make a clean breast of the whole affair. However, Bufford hid the gun under the sidewalk near Hill's from where it was taken by Hallon.

Through the efforts of Deputy Sheriff Souter, Bufford and Hallon were soon placed under arrest and from the testimony of the witnesses held before the coroner's jury it was clearly evident that Hallon had become angered over the fact that Doctor Lynch had counseled the negro woman to have Hallon prosecuted for the cruel beating he had administered to her and that the negro soldier had murdered Doctor Lynch for revenge and Bufford accordingly was released and Hallon was placed in the city jail on Monday morning to await a preliminary hearing. The coroner's examination, although private, had been so held that the evidence became known and the verdict to the effect that the deceased came to his death from a pistol shot at the hands of Corporal Hallon was published abroad and it was feared that an effort might be made to effect his rescue. Consequently two guards, Norman McAulay and John P. McDonald, were armed and placed inside the jail as guards. About nine thirty o'clock the guards were aroused by a knock on the outside of the jail door and in reply to the inquiry as to who was there the answer came that it was Souter. The hook on the inside was lifted up and McAulay opened the door about six inches. A rush from the outside followed, McAulay was siezed and blindfolded and snaked outside. McDonald saw several double barrel guns with muzzles as big as the top of a barrel pointing at him and under the circumstances surrendered. The prisoner, Hallon, was thereupon siezed by his rescuers and all were rushed west of town to a large tree near where the Northwestern viaduct is now located. Hallon was a strong and powerful man and walking a short distance must have escaped from his rescuers by a sudden plunge and fled away in the darkness. When he was next seen he was hanging to the tree where Alex Fiddler met his fate. However, before he was swung to the tree Hallon confessed to the crime and told how he had changed blouses, drank vast amounts of brandy to nerve him up, fired the shot, ran away down the alley and after the shooting, the shock of the crime drove every fume of liquor from his head and, now that his end was near, did not have anything to conceal. Just then his feet failed to connect with the ground and his rescuers knew he had escaped them. They thereupon separated and have never been seen since.

As soon as the guards were released by the posse of men who had proceeded up the street a short ways they were told to go home and further, not to turn back or look around or they would be filled full of holes like a sieve. McAulay had a family and McDonald hoped to have one, naturally neither one of them looked back. They came down town and informed Sheriff Souter of what had occurred and that officer collected a crowd of men for the purpose of capturing the escaped prisoner. They searched the country but without avail. Meanwhile a detachment from the Seventh Cavalry with Lieutenants Scott, Baldwin and Wilcox were searching for the prisoner. They passed right by the tree where shortly afterward Hallon was found hanging but saw him not. Upon their return later, within fifteen minutes, they discovered the lifeless body of the murderer. Hallon was hanging about two feet from the ground and Lieutenant Scott seized him around the legs and immediately lifted him up so as to release the strain on his windpipe, a soldier climbed up and released the rope but when let down the body of Hallon was minus a soul. The remains were brought to town and deposited in Judge Jewett's office where an examination was held on Tuesday, the next day. The rope was also brought that had been broken. A number of witnesses were examined but a very lamentable ignorance was apparent on all sides. A rigid inquiry was made as to who had sold the rope that afternoon or evening but it was discovered that the rope that had supported the man was an old one and had a snap on the end like those used by the government, in fact it was claimed that it was a quartermaster's rope. The coroner's jury, consisting of Messrs. Witcher, McMillan, and Cole returned a verdict to the effect that the deceased came to his death by strangulation or some other climatic disease at the hands of parties unknown. It was said that on the evening the corporal failed to touch the ground that a large number of men from Troop Twenty-fifth Infantry started for Sturgis with arms but were overhauled by the detail from the Seventh Cavalry and turned back. It is not known what their intentions were but it was surmised they intended to liberate the prisoner Hallon. Many threats had been heard from irresponsible colored soldiers and a few white ones. The coroner's jury in particular was threatened but it was supposed that such talk was merely buncombe and the statement was made at the time in the columns of the Record: "But as sure as daylight and dark come each in its turn if anyone is detected in any way or act or at any attempt to carry out the threats made he or they will swing to the 'Fiddler's Tree' inside of fifteen minutes."

How futile was this boast and how serious the conditions the affair had created in the frontier town will be realized by recital of the event that occurred the very next month in the shooting up of the Abe Hill's dance hall by a mob of colored soldiers, an account of which is taken from the Sturgis Record of September 25th, 1885, as follows:

NEGRO INFANTRY RUNS AMUCK

Last Sunday morning at about two o'clock a crowd of colored soldiers from Fort Meade, members of Company H Twenty-fifth Infantry, marched up the main street of Sturgis in files of four with their arms, the property of the United States and under command of one of their members fired up fifty shots into various buildings. They killed one man, an inoffensive cowboy who at that time was looking out of Abe Hill's club room.

This crowd of murderous men had escaped the sentry guard and patrol which is supposed to keep them inside the garrison and taking their guns from their barracks with which to commit this crime. They marched up the street with military precision and at the word of command given by John Taylor, who was apparently the commander of the squad, came to a halt in front of Hill's place. Some one in the back called out and asked if there was any soldiers in the house and said that they had better get out as the place was to be fired on. Again Taylor gave the word to make ready and to fire, whereupon a terrible crash ensued from the army rifles and the place was riddled with bullets. A general scatter ensued. All the balance in the place at the time ran out the back door knowing that they stood little show behind a thin wall while five hundred grains of lead were crashing through. After these defenders of our country fired several more volleys and at random, Judge Ash experienced a narrow escape as he was looking out the window of his home. Whenever and wherever a citizen showed himself these men fired and were it not for the poor marksmanship of the mob there would have been more than one death to account for. From there the mob went back down the street and shot at various buildings on that side of the street and stopped at Dolan's where their leader called a halt. A systematic assault was made on that place, the soldiers shooting at the lamps and furniture and at the retreating forms of parties who were in the house. After satisfying in part their brutal desire for a fancied revenge, they called in braggadocio style for Souter and Cole, making threats against them and then went up the street again opposite the place of the first assault where the body of their victim lay on the floor of the dance hall and then dispatched down the side street. While they were in the town everything was at their mercy and they knew it. The raid, and such it was, was so unexpected that it took the authorities as well as everyone else by surprise. However, had the peace officers desired they could not have arrested one of the crowd. One man or two men would have been powerless with such brutes armed with heavy guns and just crazy enough to shoot at everything in sight. They were crazy and cursed wildly and went on shooting. Between every volley they would shout against Sturgis and assert they were getting revenge. As soon as word was received at the Post that the mob was up here a company was dispatched up but of course all was quiet when it arrived. A patrol was left on the street.

Monday morning an inquest was held on the body of the victim and a verdict was returned to the effect that death resulted from the effects of a gun shot in the hands of one of the mob and identified Evans, Watson, Greer and Taylor of Company H as four of the crowd. The dead man was Robert S. Bell, a young man who had just only arrived in town and had been employed by Clark Tinley in the 7 D outfit. The bullet passed through one of the four-inch awning posts, through the wall of the building and through the body of the victim just having sufficient force to perforate the body and drop down inside his clothes. The ball had entered the body between the ninth and tenth rib and passing up through his body had injured his heart before it passed through into the lower part of the sternum. He clasped his hands over his breast and cried out, "My God I am killed" and crawled across the room and fell outside through the back door where after about twenty minutes he died.

Immediately after the inquest Coroner Wright filed a criminal complaint against the four men who were at the time in the jail at the Post, they having been arrested by the military officers with a dozen or so other ones none of whom, however, had been identified. When brought before Judge Jewett they waived examination and were bound over without bail for an appearance at the next grand jury. They were never tried as the evidence was not sufficient to convict.

THE FIRST LEGAL HANGING

The instances hereinbefore described when men paid the penalty with their lives through the medium of the twisted rope, were when the regular procedure of the courts of justice had not yet been firmly established. However, in due course of time the strong arm of the law held sway and was first displayed in all its grim reality as the closing chapter in the life of James Gilmore and as the results of the following incident:

James Layton Gilmore was the son of a wealthy and prominent southern family. He was drawn to the west along with many other fortune and adventure hunters and had been engaged in the cattle business in Montana besides working for a time as a muleskinner or freighter. He was a handsome young man and very popular wherever he was acquainted. He came to the Hills from Montana with his partner, William Thomas, known as "Smoky Tom." He and "Smoky Tom" were on the Pierre Trail with a freight outfit in June, 1879, and with them was a Mexican by the name of Bicente Ortez. When about fifty miles west of Fort Pierre, Gilmore quarreled with the Mexican and became insanely angry. The great fault with Gilmore was his quick, violent and unreasoning temper. He walked away from the Mexican who was sitting on a yoke. "Smoky Tom," knowing that Gilmore was going to get his revolver, admonished the Mexican not to sit there and be shot like a dog, but his counsel was not heeded. Gilmore went to the bunk where he and "Smoky" slept, and not finding his gun, took that of his pal and returning to the Mexican ordered him to stand up and then shot him. The Mexican, defenseless, threw his hat at Gilmore who then shot him dead with two bullets more. After supper that evening, Gilmore started away from the freight train, but when about three hundred yards away, accidentally shot a finger off his hand and returned. "Smoky Tom" found that the finger was hanging by a small piece of skin and accordingly cut it off and wrapped up the injured hand for his friend, who under the cover of darkness and with a purse of $17.00 given him by the boys in the freight train, again took up his flight and wandered down to the Niobrara country.

In the Niobrara country he started and ran a low dive or dance hall for a couple of years. The trouble that arose there caused an army lieutenant to proceed to the place with a detail of soldiers to arrest Gilmore in 1881, as this was on the reservation. Lieutenant Burdow did not know that the dive keeper was the murderer of the Mexican, and did not expect much trouble. He had ordered the place closed up, but the moment that he and a private entered the room, Gilmore opened fire upon them with a shot gun and killed both men. Gilmore and a companion, who was a desperate character, skipped out and in disguise reached Ft. Pierre. The companion of Gilmore had a hand shot in the mixup and he sought a druggist for treatment. The clerk became suspicious and called the marshal over the phone, but when he arrived the two men had escaped. They were traced to Six Mile Timber by the soldiers and Indian police who caught them asleep and with drawn guns captured them without further bloodshed.

Gilmore was brought to Deadwood and tried by the United States court for the murder of the Mexican Ortez, upon the government domain. Despite the able work of A. J. Plowman, his attorney, he was found guilty, "Smoky Tom" proving to be a very valuable witness for the government. When Judge Moody sentenced the man to hang in accordance with the verdict, the fellow received the words of death with a brazen smile. Judge Moody noticed the sneer and remarked, "Young man you must have a hard heart to meet your death sentence with a smile." The condemned man replied with a curse upon the judge.

After several reprieves had through the influence of powerful friends the day for final action came. The prisoner was young and magnetic and made many friends, especially among the women, so when the time for springing the trap came, the executioner was heavily disguised. Gilmore went to his death stolid and unrelenting on Friday, December 15, 1882, at 2:44 p. m. The first fall broke his neck. The rope was preserved in Deadwood for many years afterwards.

THE HANGING OF J. HICKS

In the year 1893, there lived in the eastern part of Meade county an old man aged about sixty years, named John Meyer. He was more or less of a hermit and lived alone by himself. He was supposed to be fairly well supplied with money and this reputation was the cause of his horrible death in the month of December, 1893. One of his neighbors in going to the cabin home found his body lying upon the bed with the bed clothing and other material in the room piled on him and nearby a pile of fire wood which had been charred. Over the bed clothing and body a can of kerosene had been emptied but the fire that had been started in the pile of wood had simply burned through the wooden floor to the earth and then went out. Investigation disclosed the fact that a number of young toughs in the neighborhood had been to the home of the old hermit and that the old man had shipped a car load of steers. It was supposed that he had returned from town with the money upon his person. He had remarked that the numerous bank failures going on throughout the country made it very unsafe to leave his money in care of the bank.

J. Hicks, Bob Hicks and William Walker were arrested and placed in confinement. Under the plan of Thomas Harvey, the county attorney, William Walker was placed in the Custer county jail. This plan of separating the men resulted in Walker confessing the whole deal and his story sent Bob Hicks to the penitentiary for life, himself to the penitentiary for ten years and J. Hicks to the gallows. According to the confession made, the men had supposed that the old man had lots of money with him but they found only $30.00 for their trouble. The check for $1000.00 arrived a day or two after the old man's death. During the time the men were being held in the prison they escaped and a great deal of excitement was aroused in the effort to recapture them. They were promptly apprehended and compelled to suffer for their wrong doing. This was the first legal hanging that occurred in Meade county.

CHIEF TWO STICKS PAID THE PENALTY

It will be recalled that in a former chapter we mentioned the murder of several cowboys at the camp of Humphrey below Rapid City, during the time of the excitement of the Messiah craze and Wounded Knee troubles. In this story we will set forth more of the details of that sad incident and the resulting events, as given by W. A. Remer, sheriff of Lawrence county at the time.

In the year 1893, Stenger and Humphrey of Rapid City had a beef camp on Battle Creek and near the Pine Ridge Agency. This was not far from the Nebraska line, and on the night of February 3, 1893, two boys, aged thirteen and sixteen years, Charles Bacon and William Kelly, had come up from the neighboring state to hunt strayed horses, and stopped at the Humphrey cabin where there were two cowboys, R. Royce and John Bennett. Not far from this cabin, Chief Cha-Nopa-Uhah, or Two Sticks, a Brule Sioux, and a warrior from the Custer fight, was camped on Battle Creek with several hundred of his followers. This Indian chief, although over seventy years of age, and his braves had been indulging in the pastime of ghost dancing and war dancing and in accordance with his confession made soon after the murder of the boys, stated that the Great Spirit had told them to kill the cowboys because the white men had killed off the buffalo and took their land from them.

Accordingly, after putting on their paint and donning their war bonnets they danced the war dance until after dark. Then Chief Two Sticks, with five of the band, consisting of his two sons, Fights With and First Eagle, his nephew, Kills the Two, and White Faced Horse, rode to the camp of the cowboys. It was a very cold night and the Indians went into the cabin which was part dug out, and joined the white men there. The cowboys were seated by the stove and the two young boys from Nebraska were on a bench. The Indians joined in with the smoking of cigarettes and according to their plan, each one selected his victim. Then upon Two Sticks coughing and thus giving the signal as agreed upon, the Indians fired upon the unsuspecting men, three of whom never knew what struck them. However, the boy, Bacon, was not killed at the first shot, and tried to crawl under the bed but one of the sons of Two Sticks shot him with a revolver at such short range as to set his clothes on fire. The murderers ransacked the cabin, taking the camp utensils, bedding and horses and went to No Water's camp nearby. The young braves boasted of their deed and laughed about it among their fellows, and the next day Eagle Louse went to the cabin where he saw the bodies of the dead, frozen stiff, lying in the icy pools of blood that held them solid to the floor, in the zero weather.

The ones guilty of the treacherous crime did not make any effort to conceal their identity and Sergeant Joe Bush with a detail of Indian police went to the camp of No Water to arrest Two Sticks and his party, but their friends urged them to resist and they opened fire upon the police, who returned it with effect, First Eagle being killed and White Faced Horse and Two Sticks being shot. White Faced Horse escaped, but Two Sticks was shot through the shoulder and lung. He was very near death and confessed how he had planned the cowardly deed. The other members of No Water's band were inclined to join in the fight and provoke a general battle, but the courageous interference of Young-Man-Afraid-Of-His-Horse and his band prevented further bloodshed.

Fights With and Kills the Two were brought to Deadwood the following week where they pleaded guilty to manslaughter and were sentenced to serve a term of five years in the penitentiary at Sioux Falls, South Dakota, where one or both died. Two Sticks recovered from his wounds sufficiently to be brought to Deadwood October 11, 1894, and went to trial October 24th, with William McLaughlin appearing as his attorney. However, there were many witnesses against the old warrior to prove him as the instigator of the crime and when the father of the young boy, Bacon, wept on the witness stand as he told how he found the child lying in his frozen blood, with body distorted in the agony of death, the jury did not long hesitate in returning a verdict of guilty of murder. Hon. E. S. Dundy of the United States Court, sentenced the defendant to be hanged on Friday, the 28th day of December, 1894.

The gallows was erected on the south side of the Deadwood jail, between it and the stable, while on the west side was a high shed, and the east side a sixteen foot fence, completed the enclosure of about forty by sixty feet, to hold the witnesses to the execution. The gallows was sixteen feet high, the scaffold eight and one-half feet from the ground and the trap three feet square. In the jail at this time there was another man charged with murder, Cussola, who had killed a man in a restaurant fight in Lead. While the jail fence was being built and the gallows erected, the inmates of the jail told the chief that the thing was being built to hang Cussola, and that the Great Father at Washington would not hang a great Indian chief like Two Sticks. On the morning of the execution, Sheriff W. A. Remer learned of this state of affairs and immediately had another Indian, a half breed named Walker who could speak English well, inform the chief that this was his last day on earth and that the gallows out in the yard was built for him. The only sign of emotion on the part of the chief was the setting of his jaw and a solitary grunt or "Ugh," meaning "Yes." Soon after breakfast, Father Digman, his spiritual adviser and Mr. McLaughlin, his attorney, were admitted to the jail and conversed with him for some time. He was told that the Great Father had refused to interfere with his sentence and that he must hang that day. This did not startle or unnerve him, though he became more serious and thoughtful.

At 9:30 in the morning U. S. Marshal Otto Peemiller, entered the jail accompanied by Deputies Bieglemeir and Bray, Frank Young, interpreter, Sheriff Eikenburg of Nebraska, Sheriff Blakely of Hot Springs, and several representatives. Two Sticks was seated, but arose and shook hands with all, after which the death warrant was read and interpreted to him. Upon being asked if he had any reason why the sentence should not be carried out, he showed that he had been waiting for the chance to make a statement and in a clear, resonant voice, spoke as follows:

"My heart is not bad. I did not kill the cowboys, the Indian boys (meaning White Faced Horse, Fights With, Kills the Two and First Eagle) killed them. I have killed many Indians but never a white man. I never pulled a gun on a white man. The Great Father and the men under him should talk to me and I would show them I was innocent. The white men are going to kill me for something I haven't done. I am a great chief myself. I have always been a friend of the white man. The white men will find out sometime that I am innocent and they will be sorry they killed me. The Great Father will be sorry too. My heart is straight and I like everybody. God made all hearts the same. My heart is the same as white man's. If I had not been innocent, I would not have come up here so good when they wanted me. They know I am innocent or they would not let me go around here. My heart knows I am not guilty and I am happy. I am not afraid to die. I was taught that if I raised my hands to God and told a lie that God would kill me that day. I never told a lie in my life."

The condemned man then raised his hands and sang his death song. It was not very musical but fervent and impressive. It was a weird chant to those not familiar with the language and customs of the Indians, and held that his heart was good towards God and everybody and that God must take him when he died. He was permitted to sing for several minutes but he became more and more excited until it was necessary for Father Digman to quiet him. He then grasped the hand of the priest and said he was a good man, and then took the hands of the marshal and attorney and said that they had been good to him and had done all they could for him.

It was not possible to strap his hands behind his back owing to the wound in his shoulder that left his arm stiff and compelled him to stand bent over to one side. A rope had to be procured and Deputy Beiglemeir left the jail corridor for that purpose. Lying on the chair near the chief, were the straps ordinarily used in that work and among them some that had been used by Sheriff Remer in assisting at the hanging of Jay Hicks at Sturgis a short time before. The marshal's attention had been diverted for a few moments, whereupon, Two Sticks grabbed up the strap, put the end through the buckle and quickly passing it over his neck gave it several violent jerks to tighten it, but this not proving successful, he thrust the end of the strap through the cell bars to Eagle Louse. The action was noticed at once and the strap taken away from Eagle Louse, but Two Sticks still persisted in pulling the straps in an effort to strangle himself. The strap was taken away from him and Father Digman told him that he had done wrong, that God would not like him, that he should be resigned to his fate and have a good heart. Two Sticks replied that if he had to die he wanted to be hanged by his own people and not by white men, that his heart got bad just for a minute, but he was now sorry.

His hands were finally fastened behind him and the death march to the gallows began. The chief became very excited and rushed through the jail to the gallows at a rate that made it difficult for the guards to keep near him. In the meantime he shrieked out repeatedly, "Wasta, you bet, wasta, you bet." meaning, "Good, you bet." He was placed on the trap and while the straps were being adjusted, Father Digman read a prayer for him, which he listened to with bowed head and approving understanding. Then he lifted his head and in a loud, clear voice once more sang his death song. The noose was adjusted about his neck while he stood steady and with no indication of emotion except a slight flushing of the face when the rope was drawn up. The black cap was pulled over his head, a pause, a grating sound as the bolt was withdrawn. The drop of seven feet had dislocated his neck and death was instantaneous, although there were several muscular contractions that drew up his legs and shook his shoulders. The body was allowed to hang for fifteen minutes, when Drs. Wedelstaedt, Freeman, Howe and Rogers, pronounced him dead, at 10:30, when the trap fell. The remains were removed to the undertaking rooms of S. R. Smith and at 2:30 the funeral services were had and interment made in the Catholic cemetery at Deadwood, where they still rest.

HANGING OF NEGRO CHARLES BROWN

In the year 1897, Mrs. Emma Frances Stone was conducting the popular Syndicate restaurant and rooming house in Deadwood. She and her husband, Col. L. P. Stone, were highly respected and widely acquainted people of the city. On the morning of May 14th, 1897, one of the waitresses in the restaurant in passing the room of Mrs. Stone, happened to notice the door was partly open and in looking into the room, she was horrified to see blood stained sheets on the bed, and the room in general disorder. Upon the bed lay the dead body of Mrs. Stone, with a wound made by a cleaver that split the face and head open from the right ear clear to the outer edge of the left eye. A little pet dog also lay dead near the bed, and everything in the room had been ransacked. The report of the terrible deed spread like wild fire and soon the whole town was aroused to the highest pitch of excitement, as the woman was a much admired and kindly person.

The officers got on the trail at once and caught the negro, Charles Brown, in Whitewood and had him back in Deadwood by noon. However, they kept their counsel and the thousands of people who were on hand as they passed into town were not sure of their ground and also found that the fellow and his companion were guarded with a score of deputies with drawn revolvers. John R. Wilson was state's attorney and he was assisted by J. P. Laffey. Through careful investigation, and the aid of the companion of Brown, who was found to know nothing about the crime until after its commission, they succeeded in having a full confession of the crime, in which it was shown that the negro had spent the fore part of the night in gambling, losing his money, and that he then conceived the plan of robbing the woman. He claimed that he broke into her room about three o'clock and the little dog awoke and he killed it but struck the woman accidentally. He then took a gold watch and other valuables and went to his hut in Whitewood, where he hid the articles.

A trial was had on the 10th of June, with Tom Harvey and W. L. McLaughlin, appearing for him, but putting in no defense. The jury soon returned a verdict of guilty, and thereafter Judge A. J. Plowman passed sentence, that he be hanged on July 14, 1897. Before the day for execution the negro professed religion and great sorrow for his crime. Finally the fatal day arrived, and promply at a few minutes after 10 o'clock in the forenoon, the condemned man, after a few moments in prayer, was marched under charge of Sheriff Plunkett, to the scaffold. There he saw two hundred spectators gathered within the fence built around the spot and the houses and hillsides thronged with thousands of people who came to witness the passing of the wretch. After acknowledging his guilt and asking pardon from the people and the husband of the dead woman, who stood on the platform facing him, the black cap was put over his head, his arms and legs strapped down tight by Sheriff Plunkett, assisted by Jesse Brown and Deputy Harris. Then Plunkett struck the lever and the negro went hurling downwards with a drop of eight feet. A mighty cheer arose from thousands of people as they saw the murderer pay the penalty for his dastardly deed. The fall did not break the neck of the man, and it was over twenty-three minutes before death by strangulation was pronounced by the attending physicians, Drs. Paddock, Marshall, Spaulding, Howell, Wade and Naulteus. The body was taken to the morgue where many visitors viewed it. The Chinese wife of the fellow was much prostrated as she looked upon the remains. This was the first hanging in Lawrence county under the supervision of the county authorities.

BRUTAL DOUBLE MURDER

In the year of 1902, a couple of young men from Sioux City, Iowa, located on a homestead in eastern Meade county, South Dakota, and there they had built a cabin, fenced their claims and were making great efforts to establish for themselves a home out on the broad prairie. They were fine, industrious and honorable young fellows and at odd times worked among the ranchmen in the neighborhood in order to make the money for their several needed improvements.

In the early days of the west the latch string was hung out and everybody that came to the home of the man on the prairie was welcome whether the hour of coming be day or night.

On the 4th day of June, 1902, William Horlocker came riding into Sturgis upon a foaming horse and reported to the sheriff, John Smith, that the day before upon going to the cabin occupied by the men, George Puck and Henry Ostrander, he noticed that the door was ajar and in walking in he found before his startled eyes the evidence of a foul murder and in going to the bed in the room he found it occupied by two forms who were strangely still beneath the covers. He turned the covering down and beheld their faces smeared with blood and crushed in a horrible manner. As investigation by the authorities failed to disclose any immediate clue but on the 6th day of June, 1902, a young half breed Indian had attended a picnic at Whitewood and had passed to one of the merchants in that little town a check for

Hanging of Ernest Loveswar at Sturgis

$25.00 drawn upon a Rapid City bank, made payable to Ernest Loveswar and purporting to have been signed by George Puck. The next day the check was returned to Whitewood by the Rapid City bank on the grounds that it was an absolute forgery. The cashier of the Whitewood bank thereupon called up Henry Perkins, cashier of the Meade County Bank at Sturgis, who immediately reported this information to Jesse Brown, acting deputy sheriff. Brown at the time was alone in town as both the sheriff and deputy were absent on other duties and he immediately proceeded to ascertain the whereabouts of the Indian, Loveswar, as he realized the check was an important clue pointing to the Indian as being implicated in the murder. Before he had proceeded very far he was met by Mr. Smith, the sheriff, who was returning from the inquest and who upon learning of the news from Brown decided to rest his horses and proceed out into the country in search of the Indian. Accordingly Smith and Brown, after a change of teams went to the Smith ranch on the Belle Fourche river, made another change of teams, and then after a night of travelling arrived at the place where they expected to find the man, Loveswar. Here, hiding their team behind some bushes just about sunup they quietly proceeded to the house, each one to take a separate door to prevent the escape of the Indian if any attempt should be made. There happened to be but one door leading into the kitchen and as they came quietly without warning they greatly frightened the lady who was preparing breakfast. Paying no attention to her screams, Brown quickly moved to an adjoining room where he soon had Mr. Loveswar under arrest as he had left his guns in the kitchen. A close search of the Indian failed to reveal anything that would connect him with the crime. However, the Indian was taken along with the two men and a stop was made for a time at the Jewett's road house where Sheriff Smith, who had not been asleep for two days and nights rested for awhile. While he was resting Mr. Brown did not ask the Indian any direct questions as to his knowledge of the crime but volunteered the information that the party, whoever it was, that had committed the deed made a mistake. The Indian thereupon became interested and asked in what way and Brown replied, "In not burning the cabin." This had the effect of causing the Indian to appear to be very much occupied in deep study and convinced Brown that he had the right man.

The next day the prisoner was taken to the sheriff's office in Sturgis and very closely examined and questioned but he denied any knowledge of the crime whatever. He was finally asked where he was on the night of the murder and he replied, "At the Pete Culbertson ranch and that no one had seen him because it was late and he had slept in the barn." The officers told him that two cowboys slept in the barn that same night and that no one else slept there, and in this way several other excuses volunteered by the Indian were rebbutted until finally he weakened, broke down and cried and admitted killing the two men. In his confession he told that he went to the home of the boys and asked them to permit him to stay all night. They told him to come in and gave him a cot to sleep on and he waited until they were in a deep sleep then he quietly took Puck's gun from the wall, placed it to Puck's head and his own gun to Ostrander's head and then pulled the triggers of both guns at the same time. Then he procured an axe and crushed the skull of Ostrander but spared the head of Puck. After covering the faces of the dead men with the blankets he carried Puck's gun away, but on the road near a Cottonwood tree he threw it away. The gun was later picked up by Frank Smith and Doctor McSloy. In due course of time a charge of murder was placed against the Indian to which he entered a plea of guilty but Judge Rice refused to accept the plea and ordered that a regular trial be held. States Attorney McClung introduced the evidence on the part of the State and Michael McMahon appeared for the defendant. The evidence on the part of the State of course was mostly circumstantial and the defendant on the other hand had no witnesses except himself. He took the witness stand and denied everything and claimed that the confession had been obtaind by duress and that he had been annoyed and bothered so that he did not remember what he had confessed to but the fact that he had told where the gun he had taken from Puck might be found and that the gun later was found just where he said it would be, and despite the fact that he explained the possession of the check as being the difference paid to him in a horse trade made with Puck whom he claimed wrote it out in the field, explaining the difference of the check signature and the original signature on file at the bank, the jury after retiring brought in a verdict of "Guilty" and placed the penalty at death. Thereafter on the 6th day of August he was sentenced to be hanged on the 19th day of September, 1902. The sentence was duly carried out on that day before a number of invited officials and within an enclosure erected at the side of the court house. This was the last legal hanging in Meade county.

The Indian made out and delivered to Jesse Brown the following written confession: "I am going to write just what I have done in this matter, just the truth so that you all may know. Well, I had a quarrel with Ostrander. I come pretty near having a fight with him. It was about a girl but I will not tell who the girl was but he said he would take her away from me. I waited to get him alone but they were always together so I had to kill both of them. I had nothing against Puck. Well, I went to that house about dark. They said, 'Stake out your horse and come in.' I did just that and went to bed. When they were asleep I get up and take Puck's gun off the wall, held guns in each hand, placed one to Puck's head and one to Ostrander's head and pulled both triggers. The thing was done. I ain't got time to look things around the house. I looked for money but found none, I get blank checks and gun. Now this is all."

(Signed) "Ernest Loveswar."

CHAPTER VII.

LAW AND ORDER ESTABLISHED

With the great rush of gold seekers to the Hills from all parts of the continent and into a country beyond the protection of the law, there necessarily followed a most chaotic condition of society. It became imperative that the peace loving and property owning residents should band together for mutual protection and we find that ideas of trial by jury went with the crowds wherever they camped.

In February, 1877, after the signing of the peace treaty between the United States and the Sioux tribes, three counties were organized in the Black Hills and the officers appointed by the governor until election. In Lawrence county Seth Bullock was appointed sheriff, F. T. Evans, John Wolzmuth and Capt. Lavender, county commissioners; A. J. Flanner, prosecuting attorney and Granville G. Bennett, district judge. The first term of court was held early in August in the summer of 1877, and ten convictions had, which created a very wholesome effect throughout the Hills.

But the struggle up from the crude and rough days of the pioneer settlement, through the later times to the present century may prove of interest to the reader and we herewith submit accounts of several controversies wherein the scales of justice were more or less crudely balanced, although not perhaps so very different from many in our present so-called high state of jurisprudence.

FIRST EFFORTS TO ESTABLISH LAW AND ORDER

A mass convention of the people living near Custer and the southern Hills was held in March, 1876, in the town of Custer, and a provisional government was established, with Tom Hooper as Supreme Judge, Dr. Bemis, mayor and E. P. Keiffer, justice of the peace, and also twelve members of a city council. In November, 1876, another election was held in which a new set of officers was chosen, among them George V. Ayers, as mayor.

Thomas Hooper alike with Thomas Harvey enjoyed the distinction of having been retained in the first civil controversy tried before a peace officer in the Black Hills, for in February, 1876, these two lawyers argued the questions of law and fact arising over a dispute between William Coad and one Swartout, relative to the ownership of a town lot in Custer. According to the excellent work of Mrs. Annie D. Tallent, "The Black Hills, or Last Hunting Grounds of the Dakotahs" the first criminal trial took place before Justice Keiffer, in March, 1876, in Custer. A desperado named C. C. Clayton had murdered a half breed Indian, known as Boueyer, and was brought to trial before the newly elected officer and a jury. The verdict of guilty and sentence of hanging was decided upon, but Tom Harvey appeared for the murderer and maintained that the court had no legal authority to pronounce sentence. In the meantime, a large number of friends of the criminal gathered in the court room and by their attitude and presence, influenced the justice to release the defendant, who was quickly escorted to the edge of town and advised to decamp, a decree that he was not slow in obeying.

THE DUEL OF TOM MOORE AND SHANNON

Crook City was one of the first towns to be established in the northern hills and like all of the early frontier camps, it had its quota of saloons, dance halls and bad men. Among the most noted of the bad actors were two men known as Tom Moore and Shannon, who had a reputation of being gamblers. With two such characters in a mining camp, it was only a question of time when they would come to a clash.

The pioneers of Crook City in the year 1876, decided to celebrate the Fourth of July and a big program was arranged; the principal event of which was a horse race, upon which a great amount of gold dust was wagered. Shannon was backing one of his own horses in the race and asked Moore to loan him some money on a mere promise to pay, but Moore refused and Shannon took this refusal as an insult and the two men quarreled. Finally Shannon challenged Moore to meet him with rifles and the challenge was promptly accepted. It was agreed that they were to shoot on sight in the old western style and they were to arm themselves and shoot as soon as they met. Shannon went away but was careless and came on the street unarmed. However, Moore noticing this fact, refused to take advantage of Shannon, although under the western code Moore would have been justified in shooting Shannon down at once. He politely informed Shannon of his mistake and offered to wait until Shannon had gone to his cabin and armed himself. Shannon soon returned with his rifle, a Sharps Old Reliable, while Moore had his old favorite, a large bore Needle Gun. When Shannon stepped into Main street, both men fired at once. Shannon fell dead with a bullet through the heart, but Moore was unhurt. He gave himself up to the citizens at once and asked for a trial by jury, which was done and Joe Cook was chosen as foreman. Dr. R. D. Jennings, afterwards of Hot Springs, presided over the trial as judge, and when all the evidence was in, ordered the jury to consider their verdict. Cook, as foreman of the jury made a motion, "That as the evidence showed it was a fair fight, the defendant, Tom Moore, be and is hereby discharged." The other jurors agreed to this and Moore was released from arrest. This disposition of the matter proved satisfactory to the crowd and they proceeded with the celebration. Thus ended the first criminal jury trial in the northern Black Hills.

The funeral of Shannon was not allowed to mar the festivities of the holiday and was postponed until the next day. A grave had been dug for the remains some distance out of the town, but the people were so afraid of Indians, that they refused to proceed that distance from the protection of the camp and accordingly a new grave between Crook City and the present town of Whitewood was dug and the remains buried there. However, when the city grave yard was later started, the friends of the deceased objected to the party lying in the same location with the gambler and accordingly a regular grave yard was laid out on the other side of the creek.

THE HINCH MURDER

In the town of Gayville on the night of July 9, 1876, a party of gamblers among whom were John R. Carty, Jerry McCarthy and a man named Traynor were engaged in a game of chance in a saloon. Jack Hinch, who was a friend of Traynor, was standing by watching the progress of the game and concluded that his friend was being robbed by the other two men and persuaded him to abandon the game. This caused a row between the men. However, it was quieted down at the time and Hinch later retired to his quarters in another saloon. Some time later in the night, Carty and McCarthy came into the room, aroused him from his sleep and asked him to get up and drink with them. Hinch, believing that this was an offer of peace started to get up when McCarthy fired two shots at him. Carty likewise joined in the firing. He was armed with a large sheath knife with which he inflicted several wounds on Hinch before he could get upon his feet. So severely had the man been wounded that he died at 10 o'clock on the following morning. Upon the death of their victim the two gamblers immediately prepared to get out of the country and disposed of their rich mining claim to several friends. They made their escape and although a large posse of Hinch's friends followed them, they did not overtake them. The subsequent events were set forth by R. B. Hughes, who was a reporter at the time, as follows:

"On the ninth of the preceding month, in an altercation arising over a game of cards two men named Carty and McCarthy, partners in a rich hill claim overlooking the camp of Gayville, killed a Nevada gambler named Jack Hinch. Both Carty and McCarthy fled, but the former was apprehended in the neighborhood of Fort Laramie and brought back to the Hills. Carty was a giant in statue, a man of sinister appearance, which was not lessened by the fact that he had but one eye. The man who captured him was a deputy marshal named Jack Davis. He was about five feet six inches in height, and weighed not more than 130 or 135 pounds.

"When it was known that Carty had been brought back, a miners' meeting was called. The response was so general that no building in the gulch was large enough to accommodate the crowd, and the court was organized and held on the main street, as stated. Both Carty and Hinch had many friends in the crowd, one faction apparently being determined to hang the prisoner without a trial, while the other was as firm in the demand that he be given every proper chance for acquittal. Cries of 'hang him' were frequently heard from the partisans of the dead man, and these were responded to by Carty's friends with shouts of defiance. As fully four out of five men in the crowd were armed, had a fight been precipitated it must have resulted in heavy fatalities. Collisions between individuals did occur, and more than once revolvers were drawn, but so dense was the crowd and so effective the efforts of those determined on order, that none were discharged. For fifteen minutes after Carty was led into the street, it seemed improbable that he could escape with his life. Finally Davis, who had the prisoner in charge, mounted a barrel and catching the attention of the crowd, thus harrangued it: 'Boys, I have brought this man from Fort Laramie through a country swarming with hostile Indians, in order that you might try him for his life. When I took him I gave him his choice, to be taken to Yankton and tried by the regular courts or to come back to the Hills to be tried by the miners. He chose to come back here, and when he did I promised him that he should have a fair trial and by —— that he shall have. Try him, and if you find him guilty hang him and I will pull the rope, but until he has had a fair trial the man who touches a hair of his head will first walk over my dead body.'

"As may well be imagined this speech struck a responsive chord, and was cheered to the echo. From that moment until a verdict should be reached Carty's life was safe, though as an extra precaution ten men with rifles were selected to act as guards during the trial. The wagon boss of a bull train just in from Pierre suggested that a man named O. H. Simonton, who had once been a justice of the peace in the stockyards district of Chicago, would be a fit man for judge, and he was elected without dissent. Forty names were suggested by the crowd and from these a jury of twelve were drawn. The twelve jurors were, E. B. Parker, Curley, Ed Dunham, John Balf, John Kane, G. Schugart, George Mimrich, A. O. Lobdell, D. W. Schurle, John W. Gill, S. M. Moon and George Atcheson. A. B. Chapline, a young attorney, afterwards a member of the law firm of Young and Chapline, was appointed to prosecute and Carty secured Miller and Hollis to defend him. All day long and well into the night the trial lasted. Until its close the notes from which the above is written were taken by this historian. Seated beside him for the same purpose on a pile of house logs, was Rev. Smith, the minister who was killed by the Indians a few days later between Deadwood and Crook City. The jury finally rendered a verdict of assault and battery, the tendency of the evidence being to show that while Carty had held Hinch during the affray which resulted in the latter's death, McCarthy had inflicted the death wound. Evident dissatisfaction with the verdict on the part of Hinch's friends moved the court to appoint a guard of ten men to escort Carty out of the country, and under protection of this posse Carty stayed not upon the order of his going.

"In closing this account it may not be inappropriate to state that Simonton, who acted as judge, became an itinerant preacher, visiting and holding services in the smaller camps, but finally became mentally unbalanced and died. McCarthy, like the slayer of Wild Bill, was apprehended, taken to Yankton, tried, convicted and hanged. Jack Davis died three or four years later on an incoming Sidney coach. His body was brought into Rapid City and prepared for burial. Looking down upon the face quiet in death, a pioneer remarked, 'There lies as sandy a little man as ever lived,' to which this writer mentally assented."

A DUEL IN DEADWOOD

Shortly after this event, Deadwood celebrated its first duel on Main street. In this fight two gamblers, Charles Stormes and John Varnes, had a little trouble over financial matters and agreed to settle it in a man to man fight with revolvers. They separated and soon afterwards met again on Main street, promptly opening fire at each other. Both revolvers were emptied without either men having been hit or injured and being well satisfied with their maneuvers, they declared the fight off. However, as it often happens in cases of this kind, a bystander, Joe Ludwig, was badly wounded and his friends were inclined to take a part in the fight but finally dropped the matter.

THE KILLING OF ED SHAUNESSY BY DICK BROWN

In November, 1876, Captain Willard made a trip out to Fort Laramie, Wyoming. On the stage coach the return trip he had a fellow passenger, a man named Ed Shaunessy who was a big man, about thirty years old and at this time quite drunk. As he had no blankets and the weather was very cold, Willard shared his blanket with him and took care of him until he became sober. Shaunessy became friendly and told him of his troubles. He related that he had become infatuated with a woman named Fanny Garettson, formerly a singer at the McDaniels theatre in Cheyenne, Wyoming territory. He imparted the information that he was going to the Black Hills to look for her and try to persuade her to return to him again.

The woman whom he sought had arrived in Deadwood in the summer of 1876, and had an engagement at the Belle Union theatre at Deadwood. Here later she met and married a man named "Banjo Dick Brown" a performer in the theatre. The marriage took place on the stage of the theatre and the ceremony attracted a large crowd as it had been widely advertised by the theatre and it was a subject of conversation of all classes of people for many days afterwards.

Captain Willard informed Shaunessy of this event and advised him to keep away from the actors, but his advice was not heeded and the man expressed himself as determined to see the woman at any cost. The next night after the arrival of Willard and his companion in Deadwood, Willard entered the theatre in search of a friend, when Shaunessy apparently sober and very quiet, walked into the theatre and noticing Willard there came over to him and shook hands with him, thanking him for the kindness shown him on the trip from Fort Laramie. While the two men were there talking, their position being near the stage, the curtain went up for the evening performance and revealed Dick Brown and Fanny Garettson among the performers on the stage. Shaunessy shouted out something and threw an article on the stage which appeared like a bundle of letters and then moved toward the performers. Brown ran back into the wings of the stage and seizing a gun, fired upon Shaunessy, who fell to the floor mortally wounded. The crowd in the theatre was in an up-roar and for a moment a bloody fight was threatened. However, the excitement subsided and Shaunessy was picked up from the floor and carried to his room where he died that night. Shaunessy was unarmed and had never been in the habit of carrying fire-arms.

After the treaty was made with the Sioux Indians all such cases of this sort were taken up and investigated by the courts and Dick Brown was accordingly arrested and given a trial. He brought in several witnesses to prove threats made by Shaunessy and also brought into court an axe which he swore Shaunessy had thrown at him, and as the matter had taken place so suddenly and Brown had so many of his friends as witnesses, he succeeded in being acquitted and the matter ended.

EXPERIENCE OF A PIONEER LAWYER

"I'll tell you one of my early day experiences in Deadwood, when the camp and the country were new, before the Indian title to the Hills was extinguished, and such whites as had made their way in were here under the ban of the government as outlaws." The speaker was Tom Harvey, a well known lawyer of Lead City, and the place where the story was told was on a Gilmer and Saulsbury stage coach enroute to the Union Pacific railroad at Sidney, Nebraska. In conversation with the lawyer one of the several tourists on the coach learned that he was a pioneer of the Hills, and urged him to tell some of his early day experiences.

"You probably realize that in the hurly-burly and rush of '76 there was more work for a man of most any other calling than mine. Such courts as we had were not held in very high esteem, that in Deadwood operating under a provisional government established by the people who had located the camp and were building a town with Mayor Farnum acting as justice, ex-officio, besides those who became involved in difficulties of a character that in a more settled community would have given employment to a lawyer, had a way of settling them outside of court in a manner more likely to call for the services of an undertaker. Thus the fees that an attorney picked up were few and far between. I lived in Custer, where I barely pretended to keep an office open and spent a considerable part of my time prospecting, hunting and visiting the various districts of the Hills where discoveries of mineral were reported. On one of my trips to the northern Hills it was my good fortune to be called upon to do some legal work for a bank about to be opened in Deadwood. In payment for my services I was given the sum of sixty dollars all in bright new ten dollar bills. To a fellow who hadn't handled anything more nearly resembling real money than

French or Spring Creek dust for months, and mighty little of that, you may believe those nice new crisp bills looked pretty good, and I shoved them down into my jeans, comfortable in the knowledge that my transportation home and grub for some time in the future were secure. Deadwood then consisted of a single street, occupied chiefly by saloons, everyone of which was also a gambling house. As a good many claims had been opened up in Deadwood, Gold Run, Bob Tail and Black Tail gulches and were turning out large quantities of dust, everything was on the boom. Claim owners were paying seven dollars a day for shovelers, who received their wages at the end of every shift, and a great part of their earnings found its way into the gambling resorts. I knocked about town until about ten o'clock at night and then went to the I X L hotel, that had just been opened by McHugh and Van Daniker and went to bed. The hotel was a three story building put up hurriedly of rough, green timber and so urgent was the demand for sleeping accommodations that it had been opened to the public before the bedrooms had been provided with doors. In one of such rooms on the second floor, I retired, and as I had had a long, active day, soon fell asleep from which I did not awake until the sun was looking down into the gulch from over the White Rocks. When I was aroused and looked about me I saw my clothes, which for want of a wardrobe I had placed upon the bed, were scattered about the floor. On searching my trousers pockets I found that my precious six ten dollar bills were gone. Clearly I had been robbed while I slept. You possibly may be able to imagine my feelings as I saw in prospect a sixty mile walk to Custer, and bade farewell to the flour, bacon, canned salmon, the coffee, beans and sugar with which my imagination had already stocked my larder. I say it is possible you may imagine my feelings, but by no stretch of imagination can you do justice to the language I used to express them. I cursed the man who had robbed me, I cursed the trap of a room in which I had spent the night, but most of all I cursed my own stupidity in allowing myself to be robbed. Surely anyone but a fool would have taken more precaution in such a place against such a disaster. To complain to the proprietors would be worse than useless, it would but show me up to them for the imbecile I admitted myself to be. I could have a row with Jim Van Daniker, anyone could do that on a very little provocation, but that would avail nothing toward the recovery of my money. In no enviable frame of mind I dressed and went out on the street, where after a while I was fortunate enough to strike an old acquaintance for enough money to pay my fare to Custer. This arranged I was passing the time in watching the crowd up on the street until the stage would leave, when I was accosted by C. Stapleton, the city marshal with, 'Tom here's a fellow I was taking to the lockup, but he says he knows you and wants to see you.' The prisoner he had in tow pressed forward eagerly, saying, 'You remember me don't you, Tom?' 'No, I don not remember that I ever saw you before, and the way I am feeling now I don't care if I never see you again.' 'Sure you know me, I am Jack Rhodes. Don't you remember that you defended me in Cheyenne last fall?' And then I did remember that I had defended him on a burglary charge in Cheyenne the year previous. 'What do you want to see me for now?' I asked. 'I've got into a little trouble here, and I want you to help me out.' 'Not on your life,' I said, 'I've paid my fare to Custer and I want to get out of the d---d camp just as soon as the Lord will let me.' 'No, no, Tom you must stay and help me' urged the prisoner. I asked permission of the marshal to step a little to one side, and inquired what he was charged with, what he had done. He said that he was accused of robbing a man down at the I X L hotel last night. The thought flashed through my mind that I was not the only victim of this so-called hotel. 'Well,' I says to him, 'If I stay here and defend you it will cost you one hundred dollars.' 'All right,' he says, 'here is the money,' and he pulled out a roll of bills large enough to choke a cow and commenced peeling off the bills and counting out my fee. And the first six that he handed me were my own bright, new ten dollar bills. I stuffed them into my pocket saying, 'You blankety, blanked, blank, you stole these out of my pants pocket down at the I X L last night. Now go ahead and count out the one hundred more of the other fellow's money.' To this he did not demur in the least. Without batting an eye he counted out and handed me one hundred additional. Then I went with him to Judge Farnum's office and cleared him of a charge of robbery preferred by another guest of the I. X L and didn't even miss that day's stage for Custer."

THE KILLING OF BRODOVITCH BY SAM MAY
(TURKEY SAM) AND BLAIR (DARBY)

During the month of April of this year (1876) some Slavonians who had just come into the Hills located a claim up on the hill near the old grave yard (now within the city limits of Deadwood.) A gang led by Sam May, known as "Turkey Sam" and Blair, alias "Darby," undertook to jump this ground. Brodovitch was killed and another one of his friends was wounded. The sheriff promptly arrested the parties engaged in this affair. May and Blair were convicted and sent to the pen. Chapman was acquitted. This was the first case tried in the courts after the county was organized. John Burns, a young lawyer from Chicago, acted as prosecuting attorney, as Mr. Flanner, the regular appointee, had not arrived in the Hills yet. He was from the south.

This was a good and wholesome lesson to the toughs and it gave them to understand that law and order would be enforced.

BLACK HILLS ORGANIZED

(Correspondence to the Sidney Telegraph June 2, 1877)

The Dakota portion of the Black Hills was during the last session of the Dakota legislature organized into three counties. The northern portion was designated Lawrence county, a strip of twenty miles in the central portion with the 44th meridian bisecting it was designated Pennington county and the southern part Custer county. Instead of allowing the several counties to elect their own county commissioners, Governor Pennington induced the Dakota legislature to authorize him to nominate them. The governor made his nominations over a month ago, but they did not seem to have given much satisfaction to the people of the Black Hills. One of the commissioners for each county was sent from Yankton, the other two the governor nominated from amongst the residents of their respective counties, one from each of the two most important towns in the counties. The first duty devolving upon the county commissioners was the location of the county seat. As every one of the resident commissioners thought themselves duty bound to vote only for the town they represented, the decision rested virtually in each county, with the commissioners imported from Yankton—his vote given with either of the resident commissioners deciding the matter. Rumors were floating about in Custer City, as well as in this town that the biggest purse would secure the location. In the case of Custer county it was long doubted whether Custer or Hayward City would carry off the honors. Custer City had no cash but town lots that would be worth a great deal some day. Hayward City was supposed to be "well healed" with the yaller stuff. The honors were finally carried off by Hayward City.

In Lawrence county the commissioners decided that Crook City would be the most desirable county seat; they were induced to review their decision, and it finally appeared to their vision that Deadwood City would, after all, be the most desirable location.

A few days ago posters containing the following were one morning seen posted up over the town:

"NOTICE

"County Seats Located, Removed and For Sale
"Apply to Black Hills County Commissioners"
Thinking a county seat might be a good invest-

ment, your correspondent inquired if there were any left, but found that all had been sold already.

There is another question agitating the public mind of the politician and that of the expectant of favors from the public in shape of bread and butter. That question is, the formation of a new territory to include the entire Black Hills region with a large tract of fertile agricultural land. At the present time the boundary line between Dakota and Wyoming Territories goes through the center of the Black Hills, but nobody knows yet exactly where the line intersects. Some vague calculations have been made, and it is estimated that Custer and Deadwood Cities, as well as all the important mining camps so far located are east of the 104th degree of longitude, and consequently in Dakota Territory. A travelling correspondent of that truly veracious (?) sheet, the Cheyenne "Leader," invented in his brain, (bran-box) a story that Deadwood and Custer Cities were situated west of the Meridian—consequently in Wyoming. The "Leader" ever since has been harping on the subject, giving gratuitous advice to the people of the Black Hills as to what steps to take to get themselves annexed to Wwoming and become good and obedient children to the Mother Shy Anne. A few of the local residents who came here from Cheyenne and whose interests are bound up in that town also maintain the same theory—the wish in their case giving birth to their theory.

Not many residents of the Hills bear any warm love to Governor Pennington nor to Yankton, but they bear a little love to Cheyenne. What they want is the formation of a new Territory; they had sooner be annexed to Nebraska than Cheyenne.

A convention was called last April to discuss matters which appointed a chairman, a secretary and some committees and then adjourned subject to call by the chairman, Mr. Brearly, a barrister formerly of Washington, D. C., but now one of the leading members of the local bar. The convention was recalled and held a session yesterday. As I understand that your correspondent, L. F. W., has already given you an account of the proceedings of this convention, it is unnecessary for me to do so; suffice it is to say that Dr. Myers and Captain Walker were elected by a large majority of the convention to present to congress the wishes of the people of this country to be formed into a new Territory to be called "Lincoln."

The new territory is to comprise an area of 70,000 to 80,000 square miles and it is to have the following boundary: The southeast corner will be latitude 43 degrees, and longitude 102 degrees—then to go along the 43 Meridian west to longitude 107 degrees, then north to the Yellowstone River and along its banks to the 47th degree north latitude; then east along that Meridian to longitude 104 degrees, thence south to latitude 40 degrees, then again east to longitude 102 degrees and south to the point of starting.

The oppositions were not much pleased with the result; if they don't pray and sing psalms, they do something else, and vow at the same time that Messrs. Myers and Walker will never be able to represent the county of Washington. Time will show which is which "Lohar," (Sidney Telegraph, May, 1876.)

COURT BUSINESS ON THE FRONTIER

Her maiden name was Jenkins. I had not time to examine her pedigree, but I strongly suspect that she is a descendent of the old Jenkins about whose, ear, once on a time, men made such a fuss and which eventually plunged two of Europe's nations into war. She is as lovely as a turtle dove, and as graceful as an angel (albeit one fallen from grace). She kept a dance house and when Drake, one of Hayward City's gallants, beheld the fair Annie he was a goner. Her well matured charms so fascinated his heart that life seemed to him a blank without her; he accordingly wooed and won his ducky love. On, or about the 12th day of May, 1877, (such avers the petition in re: Johnson vs. Drake) 'Squire Vos Burgh was called into requisition to put a stop to this game of ducks and drakes—which he did by making the twain into a brace of Drakes. What would a wedding be without a wedding supper? So supper was the word. Now the gallant Drake's financial credit did not stand very high, but that of his ducky love was unimpeachable. So Mrs. Annie Drake, nee Jenkins, calls on her next door neighbor, Johnson, a sturdy Norseman, and orders the supper which Johnson agreed to supply at 75 cents per head. I may not say how many guests partook of the wedding supper as the court ruled that question out.

The bride's wedded bliss was of short duration, for Drake, the loving swain, deserted his little duck before the honeymoon had waned, and Johnson, the caterer, sued the gentle Annie for $75, as the price of the wedding supper. The case was called up to the justice's court, but the canny Norseman thought it would be too complicated for the judge and demanded a jury of his peers. The sheriff arrested every man he met in the streets and the judge's court was soon as thickly packed with human bodies as the famous "Black Hole" of which we read in Marchman's History of India. On motion of the learned counsel, panting for aid, the court adjourned to a bar room close by. Being hard up for paper on which to write this, I am unable to give a report of this most important of trials. I will only observe that it was better than a first class show and the audience had a great treat in listening to the trial.

It was held in the bar room. On one side stood the bar; in another a faro game was in progress and the court modestly took up in another corner. The trial proceeded in due form whilst the rattling of poker dice on the bar was kept up and the gamblers of King Faro would "God bless" (?) everything. Occasionally the judge, jurymen and learned council would adjourn to the bar to partake of a drop of tiger's milk, and then everything "went merry as a marriage bell" till the court would order the sheriff to bring the jury back into their places. One of the jurymen took out a railroad prospectus whilst the learned counsel for the plaintiff was tackling the case and perused it most attentively; but he was no doubt taking in the lawyer's valuable argument at the same time. The trial was great fun, better even than seeing John Dillon. (Sidney Telegraph, 1877).

CHINATOWN IN 1877

On an evening in the month of October considerable excitement and mystery was created from "Chinatown," of Deadwood, South Dakota, for even in the pioneer days the slant eyed men from China were drawn to brave the hardships of pioneer life in their anxious search for gold. Being among strange people and in a new country they banded together with their fellows in considerable numbers so that it became known as "Chinatown." One day from one of the houses in which a Chinese woman had lived a bunch of Chinamen were seen to run out and down the street and hide among their neighbors. An examination of the house soon showed that they had killed a young Chinese woman, and she was literally chopped to pieces with an axe. The young woman had upon her person very valuable jewelry but nothing was taken. Several of the Chinamen nearby were arrested but it was absolutely impossible to gain any information or find out any cause for the murder of the young woman. All efforts to solve the mystery failed and the death of the young Chinese woman remained one of the early days' unsolved problems.

THE KILLING OF KITTY LEROY

Among the great mob of people from every walk of life that came to the Hills in 1877, was a beautiful, tall and graceful girl known as Kitty LeRoy. She was a professional dancer and immediately accepted a place at the Gem Theatre. Her grace and beauty soon won a swarm of admirers but there was one whom she seemed to favor more than the others. He was a gambler, a desperate character and known by the name of Sam Curley and he seemed to be very fond of the graceful girl. In due course of time a ceremony of marriage was performed by Charles Barker, justice of the peace, and this was a great event among the class of people to whom the participants belonged. But in a short time trouble arose and Sam was very jealous of his good looking bride. They had a very violent quarrel over another gambler and finally Sam Curley left Deadwood and proceeded to Cheyenne, Wyoming. But along in the fall of 1877 he quietly returned to Deadwood, left the stage coach above the city and warned the stage driver not to let anyone know he had returned. Under cover of darkness he came into town and tried to locate the man whom he blamed for his domestic trouble but his search was fruitless. He then proceeded to the "Lone Star House" where Kitty LeRoy roomed and shortly afterwards the neighborhood was aroused by several pistol shots. When they rushed up the stairs and pushed open the door they found Kitty breathing her last and Curley dead lying near her. The young woman had just finished dressing herself in a very attractive manner and there she lay in all her young beauty while near her was her husband with his brains blown out. Thus ended another tragedy of the early pioneer days of the Black Hills.

A FATAL QUARREL

There are no doubt a number of people yet living in this section who remember the gun battle which took place in Central City in the summer of 1877, between John Bryant and William Adams, in which they were both shot to death. The trouble between these men arose from the act of Adams in posting notice of claim to a millsite on Placer Claim No. 13 (I think it was) above Discovery on Deadwood gulch, upon which a portion of Central City is located, and which was owned at the time by John Bryant.

The right of Adams to make this location was disputed by Bryant. Whether these parties had had any quarrel over the matter at the time the notice was posted is not known. However, on the following morning, Adams, who at the time was in partnership with Gus Oberg in the restaurant business, remarked after eating his breakfast, that he was going down to take possession of his millsite. He was advised by his partner and other friends to be careful and not get into trouble. He persisted and walked down past the Bryant cabin with his belt strapped around him and with his revolver in plain sight.

Bryant, also with belt on and six shooter in plain view, was standing near his cabin. A conversation was started and hot words ensued. According to two witnesses, each man was keeping an eye on the gun of his adversary as though he was expecting a quick movement. Instead of drawing the gun from his belt, Adams, who had evidently planned a ruse, whipped out another pistol which it is thought he held in hand from the first, and shot Bryant through the body. He then turned instantly and ran, but had made only a rod or two when he was overtaken by a bullet from Bryant's pistol, which caught him in the hip and felled him as he was crossing a small stream of water. In falling he turned his face to Bryant, who was following, threw up his hands and his head back just as Bryant fired the second bullet which entered his mouth and up through his head killing him instantly. Bryant then walked back into his cabin where he lingered in great pain for a day or two and died.

Thus suddenly passed two young men of promise, who, had they both been disposed to be guided by reason might have lived to become useful citizens in their communities. Bryant was a native of Illinois and was a brother of the late Frank Bryant the well known and highly respected mining man. Adams was employed for a time in a grocery store in Deadwood and was I think, considered to be honest and reliable. I never knew where he hailed from but presumed that he came from Salt Lake. (J. S. McClintock.)

AURORA MINE 1877

Henry Keets who was the owner of the mine known as the "Keets Mine" sold his interest out to a mining company that in order to develop the mine had obtained permission from the Aurora Mine to run a tunnel through part of the mining grounds owned by the neighboring mine company. The tunnel ran through part of the ore streak of the Aurora Mine and it was not long before the men of the Keets Mine were accused of stealing ore of a high grade from the walls of the tunnel owned by the Keets mine. This stirred up a real fight and the Keets manager hired a bunch of fighting men who built a barricade near the tunnel. The Aurora men ordered the Keets men out of the works and Tuttle, one of the managers gave them a certain time in which to move out as he intended to blow up the tunnel. He accordingly prepared a blast and lowered it into the shaft of the tunnel and when the time was up fired off the charge. The ensuing blast had the desired effect but when Tuttle went down on the dump he was immediately shot and died that night. Johnson, another owner in the Aurora mine, was in a shack just above the dump and witnessed the shooting. He joined in the fray and made it so hot for the men they abandoned the barricade and ran for a log cabin nearby, in which Johnson continued to make them fight for their lives. Johnson escaped without injury although his shack was riddled with bullets. Sheriff Bullock and Captain Willard arrested the men who had fired upon and killed Tuttle but after a long sensational trial the men were acquitted.

The Keets mine was also connected with another serious difficulty that occurred in the fall of 1877. A man named Connelly, had a large contract in this mine but failed to pay his laborers. The miners took possession of the occasion, laid in a big supply of guns, ammunition and prepared for a siege. Warrants were placed in the hands of Sheriff Bullock but the men refused to surrender to him and stood him and his deputies off. Attempts were made to starve them out and smoke them out but they failed and the sheriff called upon the U. S. army at Fort Meade to come to his assistance. A detachment from the U. S. 7th Cavalry under the command of Lieutenant Edgerly and Lieutenant Sickles responded and a line of guards was placed around the mine Some of the men were called to the shaft for a parley and were informed by Lieutenant Edgerly that they must come out and surrender. After considerable argument the miners surrendered but they felt very bitter toward Sheriff Bullock for calling in the soldiers. The miners were placed under a light bond but later the matter was dropped. However, the men never received their pay as Connelly had gambled away all their hard earned money. Harry Goddard, who later became the editor of the Edgemont Express, was among the unfortunate miners.

FIRST POLITICAL CAMPAIGN IN LAWRENCE COUNTY

In these days of modern political manipulating, it might not be without interest to read how the pioneers of 1877 played the game and we herewith submit several accounts written by L. F. Whitbeck, for the "Sidney Telegraph:"

"This is a funny country—is the Black Hills territory—if an outsider can wander through the many camps and closely note the many peculiarities presented without his visibilities being effected, he will prove an anomaly among tenderfeet. Such a condition of things is after all not to be wondered at considering that our population is made up of all classes, races and conditions of men—is in fact the most cosmopolitan probably, upon the continent. One of the principal peculiarities of Hillers, is their uniform good nature. No matter what their embarrassment may be, nor how great their sorrow, it does not affect the pleasant smile, word and salutation. A chivalrous disposition towards an enemy; honest love for a friend and a kindly feeling for everybody are the principal ingredients of the average citizen. This trait of character was never more clearly manifested than is now presented in the political arena. 'Politics in the Hills?' Lord bless you, yes. Strange as it may appear, this country, which only eight months ago, was held and largely occupied by Reds is now the scene of a hot campaign, waged upon one side by straight out-and-out democrats, and upon the other by an amalgamated array of all sorts under the title of 'People's Party.' Doc Meyer is the great Maukhiar Pasha of the first named, while the latter 'fights mit' Bullock, our present sheriff. It will be remembered that the Penningtonian appointments made at the organization of the three counties of Lawrence, Pennington and Custer, were all republicans, commissioned until 1878. The democrats, and other outs anxious to get in office, considered the extension of such tenure unconstitutional, and called a convention, at which a full ticket was placed in the field. Subsequently a per-emptory mandamus was secured compelling the county commissioners to call a general election this fall. This aroused the republicans to a sense of their danger and the necessity of doing something awful wise, and of doing it at once. They realized their minority, and therefore conceived the idea of getting up a 'people's movement,' being encouraged therein by many democrats opposed to individuals upon party tickets. The democratic convention was held and resulted in the nomination of John Manning, proprietor of the 'Senate' for sheriff; Charles H. McKinnis, local wholesale liquor dealer, for register of deeds—the two principal offices. The people held their grand conclave yesterday, and for a neutral movement (or, in fact, any other) was a gratifying success. There were several wires—one pulled by the old Yankton ring to secure nomination; another in favor of Frank Raborg against A. P. Carter, proprietor of a large saloon, for register of deeds —a very lucrative office.

"Seth Bullock and Mr. Carter were unanimously nominated, while the Yanktonians 'got left.' As a result of the last 'disaster,' many sore heads are running around today, loudly talking of organizing a straight republican party, and of putting a third ticket in the field. In the event of a three cornered fight, the democracy will carry the day, but so evenly balanced are the powers as now disposed, that—well I wouldn't advise you to gamble on the result.

"The 'Times' is the 'organ' of the people; the 'Pioneer' is on the fence; the 'Herald' is democratic, $150 worth, while the 'Miner' removed from Crook City to this city, is issued daily as a red hot campaign 'Muldoon'—(Times' phrase for the democrats) sheet—the first number appearing today.

"Politics being all the rage I have had little opportunity to glean very much other matter of news. The bar of this county is being scandalized to a rather immoderate extent and interesting developments are anticipated. Your readers will remember that one Cephas Tuttle was killed during a disturbance created at the Keets Aurora mines, and that eight men were arrested for the murder, or as accessories. The present grand jury failed to indict, and so reported to the court, whereupon District Attorney Flanner, and his associate Col. Parker, made specific charges of bribery and corruption against the jurors and certain members of the bar. Great consternation was thereby created, and Judge Bennett, in the most solemn and intensely earnest manner charged the grand jury to exclude suspected members, and at once institute a thorough investigation, and to report in writing, promising that guilty ones should be severely punished, and that accusing counsel must make their charges good or suffer the court's displeasure. On yesterday the jury reported there were 'no grounds for accusation,' and everybody is on tiptoe of expectancy over tomorrow's events. Col. Parker will probably be disbarred.

"Mining matters are, as ever, very encouraging. The Golden Terra has just been sold for $90,000—yes I said ninety thousand dollars, and I know whereof I write—to a California company of experts who pronounce the Hills the richest quartz country in the world. They will put up expensive works at once.

"For real genuine fun of the Donnybrook fair order (whenever you see a head hit it) commend your friends to the Black Hills during the prevalence of a political campaign. One has just closed, and greater excitement never raged, even in national politics when the welfare of the entire country was at stake. There were no issues other than personal ones between the contending parties, but you can bet your boots that those were made the most of in the way of discussion. Talk about mud throwing, why putridity would smell sweet compared with the rakings from the various editorial sanctums. 'You lie' was a tame expression, and even to accuse a candidate of being an escaped convict scarcely rose to the dignity of slander. Porter Warner of the 'Times' (people's organ) did succeed in arousing his opponents (the muldoons) to an appreciation of his words by throwing out the defiant charge that a couple of democratic candidates were escaped penitentiary birds. He gave no names, and the entire ticket took it upon themselves to resent what they considered a personal assault. They accordingly mustered under the guidance of 'Doc' Meyers, in the Senate saloon, toddled across the street, tumbled upstairs, and burst into the 'Times' editorial room, twenty-five strong armed cap a pie. The way they bulldozed Warner and his trembling local, was fearful to behold and is best told by saying that within an incredible short space of time an 'extra' appeared on the streets saying that the published accusation war—all true, and giving names in full. Rome howled; that is the muldoons did, and will never get over it. The funniest part of the whole thing is that the ex-convict (who has never contradicted the charge) was elected by 'a large majority.' Excitement is on the decrease now, and attention is turned to more legitimate pursuits."

In the election, Bullock had arranged to have a large number of soldiers from Ft. Meade to dress in citizen clothing and become repeaters at the polls in Sturgis. However, the supporters of Manning discovered the scheme, and outbidding the healers for Bullock, won oer the fraudulent soldier vote before Bullock's agents could get in shape to meet the unexpected turn of events. Bullock would no doubt have won the election, if his plan had not been revealed by some incautious helper or traitor and he was quite confident of his success. But when the returns came in and the little town of Sturgis rolled up a great vote, he saw with chagrin that he had been beaten at his own game and refused to surrender his office, well knowing that illegal voting had been done. For a time there were two sheriffs in Lawrence county, but after the sting of defeat had lessened its pain and wiser counsel prevailed, he finally movd out and Manning took over the office.

THE CASE OF MARTIN COUCK

A woman named Mrs. Callison was known as the first school teacher in the Black Hills. In the month of August, 1878, her lifeless body was found in her home where she had been brutally murdered by someone who had beaten her head to a pulp by the use of a blunt instrument. The horrible manner of her death created great excitement and the prosecuting officer made a special attempt to bring the guilty party to trial. It was found that a man known as Martin Couck was a lover of hers and it finally developed that a quarrel had ensued over another woman and in the row he had murdered Mrs. Callison. A long and sensational trial took place and the verdict of "guilty" was returned by the jury and a sentence of death given by Judge G. C. Moody. This sentence was later changed to life imprisonment and Couck took up his residence at the state penientiary. But Couck had many faithful friends and as a consequence, it was not very long before he was successful in securing his pardon and was released from the penitentiary. He came back to the Black Hills and hunted up Captain Willard, who was deputy sheriff and very earnestly requested him to assist him in bringing to trial the real murderer in the case and asserted that he was absolutely innocent. An effort was made to assist the man in this work and considerable time spent, but to no avail and one day Couck came to Willard very much discouraged and informed him that he was going to leave the Black Hills, but if there was anything that might come up to prove his innocence, he would return and try once more.

Years afterwards there appeared in the "Denver Republican," an account about a fellow who was hanged for the murder of a man in New Mexico. His name was given as Martin Couck and on the scafford he confessed to the murder of Mrs. Callison in Deadwood. All these years he had spent time and money in an effort to convince people that he was innocent, while as a matter of fact, he was absolutely guilty and on the last day was brought to confess his wrong doings."

"THE PAGAN" JURY

The years of 1878 and '79 were noted for some sensational trials in the courts of the Black Hills district; the most noted one perhaps was a murder trial which was very much in evidence while it lasted. It was a case that created a great deal of excitement. A young man living at Lead City was the owner of some mining ground that the Homestake Mining Company wanted for the purpose of building a large mill on it. The owner asked what the Homestake Company thought was an exhorbitant price for the ground and the Homestake representatives tried to intimidate the owner. Some Homestake gunmen were stationed near by and after some threats they shot him down in a cold blooded manner; it was looked upon as a very brutal, cold blooded murder and there was considerable excitement over it. John Manning was sheriff at this time. The gun men were promptly arrested and lodged in jail. I was in the employ of the State, Express and Transportation Company at this time as treasure guard, running to the Missouri River, but I also had an appointment as deputy sheriff in order to be able to act in the interest of my company; also to assist the sheriff when possible to do so. I had arrived in Deadwood the night the gunmen were arrested and lodged in jail. I had a day to lay over in before starting out on my run so the next morning I went down and offered my services to the sheriff. While talking with the sheriff a call came from the jail asking Sheriff Manning to come up there at once. I went up with the sheriff. We found the jailer (Black Jack Manning, a relative of the sheriff's) walking the floor very much excited. When I asked him what the trouble was he told a very strange story. It seems that a notorious character by the name of John Flaherty had come to the jail in the middle of the night and, according to Black Jack's story, Flaherty offered Jack a large roll of bills said to contain five thousand dollars if he would open the jail door and let the gunmen go. I said, "Well, Jack did you take the money?" He was very indignant to think that I would ask such a question. I said, "Jack you have lost a very fine chance" and he replied, "Would you have taken that money and let those murderers get away?" I said, "Not but if you had taken that money and locked Flaherty up you could turn in the money to the court and thereby made a fine case against this gang and besides you would have made a very fine name for yourself." Jack never thought of that. He was a good, square boy but was not up to all the tricks going on around at that time. The sheriff had been a very interested listener all during this conversation and said that he believed he did not know all that was going on inside of his office but would look into things a little closer from now on and asked me to co-operate with him.

The gun men were held for murder and later placed on trial in the district court held in Deadwood, Dakota Territory, Judge G. C. Moody presiding. After a long and very sensational trial the case was submitted to the jury who finally brought in a verdict of "not guilty." Everybody was, to say the least, astonished, none more so than Judge Moody. He scored the jury unmercifully, telling them very plainly that the verdict rendered by them was not in accordance with the evidence presented and also told them that no doubt this jury had been bought by the

Homestake Company money. He also said, "I would sooner have a jury of Pagan Indians try cases in this court than men of your kind, you can always secure money now from the Homestake Company as they have bought you outright." The judge said more along the same line, then turned to the sheriff and said, "Mr. Sheriff, if you ever bring any of these men into my court again to serve as jurors I will commit you for contempt of court. They are a disgrace to the country." There was no response from the jurors. The bailiff having charge of his jury was arrested charged with being implicated, also he was said to have handled the money that reached the jury but nothing could be proven although it was a well known fact that several of the jurors had plenty of money after the trial was over. This jury was afterwards known as the "Pagan Jury." (A. M. Willard).

CROW DOG AND SPOTTED TAIL

Spotted Tail was the head of the Brule Sioux Indians and one of the most influential Indians in the Sioux Nation. In the month of August, 1881, he had been summoned to Washington and before departing on this trip he called together a large number of his people to counsel with them as to the purpose of his visit. After the meeting had adjourned, Spotted Tail at the head of the party of his braves proceeded on his way toward the camp, when he met Crow Dog or "Kangi Sunka" with his wife, coming toward them in a wagon. As Spotted Tail approached Crow Dog, who had gotten out of the wagon and was stooping down, Crow Dog was seen to suddenly arise and shoot toward the chief, who immediately fell from his horse. Spotted Tail arose from the ground, took three or four steps toward Crow Dog while endeavoring to draw his pistol, then reeled and fell backward dead.

Intense excitement was created among the Brules, but no outbreak ensued. Crow Dog put up the excuse that Spotted Tail had insulted Crow Dog's wife and besides, Spotted Tail had many people in his own tribe that were unfriendly toward him and these people were not at all displeased at his murder. Under the treaty of 1868, Crow Dog was amenable to the law for his crime and accordingly was placed under arrest by the Indian police and sent to Fort Niobrara for safe keeping until his act could be inquired into by the United States government. Investigation disclosed the fact that jealousy over women was not the cause of the shooting but that Crow Dog wished to become the head chief and that Spotted Tail was not a hereditary chief but had gained his place in leadership by his prowess in war and superior intellectual power. It seems that Black Crow and Crazy Dog had entered into a conspiracy with Crow Dog to force Spotted Tail to resign as chief but failing in that move, had determined on other means; either fair or foul, to rid themselves of the influence of the diplomatic and powerful chief, Spotted Tail, and if necessary, they would kill him.

In due course of time the charge of murder was filed against Kangi Sunka and he was brought to trial before the United States district court at Deadwood at the March term, 1882, Judge G. C. Moody presiding. The friends of Crow Dog had employed a young attorney, A. J. Plowman, to defend them, who, at the time of the trial presented a novel defense and one that was not without merit. The basis of the defense put up by Mr. Plowman was the fact that during the time that the United States government was investigating the killing of Sinta Gleska, the Brules in accordance with the tribal customs and laws had arrested Crow Dog and given him a hearing and found that he had wrongfully killed Spotted Tail and as a penalty for his misdemeanors, imposed a sentence requiring Crow Dog to deliver to the relatives of the dead chief, a certain number of ponies, robes and blankets. This was done and according to the tribal laws and customs of the Sioux Nation, Crow Dog was free from any further penalty and the crime had been expiated. Therefore, it was the contention of the attorney, Plowman, that the United States had no jurisdiction over the crime since the government had always considered the Sioux Indians as a separate and distinct nation by making a treaty with them and in other ways acting toward the Sioux Indian tribe as a distinct and foreign nation. However, his objections were overruled and the case proceeded to trial and the jury brought in a verdict of "guilty of murder" and Crow Dog was sentenced to be hanged. Plowman secured a stay of proceedings and put up such a vigorous fight that the case dragged along for many months. During this time, Crow Dog was kept in jail and there became acquainted with James Leighton and they became very warm friends. James Leighton or James Leighton Gilmore, had likewise been tried and found guilty of the crime of murder, his victim being a Mexican named Ortez, whom he killed on the Indian reservation. He belonged to a very prominent southern family and through their influence, reprieves were granted and the execution delayed several times. The time for execution finally arrived and the Indian chief received permission to see his friend Leighton for the last time. They had a long and earnest conversation in the Sioux language and when the time came to go they looked each other square in the eye and after a firm hand-clasp, Crow Dog turned abruptly and walked away. Leighton walked calmly between the marshal and sheriff, took his place on the scaffold and in a few minutes was dead.

After the execution of his close friend, Gilmore, it was very hard to keep Crow Dog in jail and Marshal Raymond decided to allow him the liberty of the jail yard during the day time. Crow Dog had been chief of police at the agency and had a very fine army uniform with shoulder straps denoting the rank of major of artillery, and it was his custom from time to time to array himself in his military trappings and strut around the yard. He finally got to visiting the houses near the jail and soon had a large circle of friends among the children in the neighborhood. One night when the jailer was preparing to close up, Crow

Dog could not be found. He had struck out for the reservation where it was found he had joined his family. Crow Dog was the chief in an organization among the Indians, known as the Pape Maza Ospaye "Iron Hand Band" who were considered to be the most warlike and famous as fighters in the Sioux Nation. Marshal Raymond sent a special deputy known as Billy Wilson to the reservation with orders to bring Crow Dog back at once. Wilson was a little fellow and without a great deal of tact. When he went to the reservation he very nearly started a war by ordering Crow Dog to return with him at once and attempting to place him under arrest. Crow Dog absolutely refused to leave the reservation and ordered Wilson to get out as he had no intention of going to the Black Hills again. The influence of the Iron Hand Band was very much in evidence and Wilson finally took up the matter with the agent who talked with the chief and tried to persuade Crow Dog to return to Deadwood with the deputy, but to no avail. The agent then appealed to the chief saying that the soldiers would come and a bloody war would follow and many warriors would be killed, but for a long time the Indians remained obstinate and declared that they would fight the soldiers as long as there was a man left in the Pape Maza Ospaye. At last Crow Dog was told that if he would return to Deadwood and surrender to Deputy Marshal Raymond, his friends would try to secure a pardon from the Great Father at Washington. Crow Dog consented to go to the Black Hills but refused to go with Wilson as he considered it an insult to have a big chief arrested by so small a white man. He said, "Tell that little man to go home and in two suns, I, Kanga Sunka, will start for the Black Hills. Wilson started for home at once but on the way became dead drunk and Crow Dog arrived in Deadwood ahead of him. The chief reported to Attorney Plowman, whom the Indians called Wi-Cas-A-Ci-Qua-La-Ho-Tonka "Little Man With A Big Voice." Crow Dog was again given the same liberty as before, after he had promised not to go away until "Little Man With A Big Voice" gave him permission to go and he kept his word.

One day a message arrived from Washington and the court ordered the chief brought into court. Deputy Sheriff Willard went to the jail and informed the man that he was wanted in court. The chief made the sign of hanging a man, but Willard informed him that he did not know what was going to be done. However, the Indian was impressed with the idea that he was to be sentenced to be hanged and dressed himself carefully in his major's uniform and placed on his bosom his various medals. When he arrived in the court room, he appeared to be much surprised to find so many people there but he walked with a very dignified manner. The judge made a very long talk with the aid of an interpreter and informed the Indian that the Great Father at Washington had sent a pardon for the great chief, Kangi Sunka, and that he was now a free man and could return to his people at any time he wished. It was some time before the chief could realize that he was now a free man but when he did so, he caught Plowman up in his arms and said, "Wi-Cas-A-Ci-Qua-Lo-Ho-Tonka, (Little Man With A Big Voice) heap damn good man." He hugged the little lawyer like a bear, almost breaking his ribs. He then went to the judge, and seized his hand, almost crushing it, saying, "You heap damn good man too!" This nearly broke up the court and they finally managed to lead the Indian away.

The chief was thereupon released, but before leaving for his home he bade his friends good-bye and hunted up the little children and bade them farewell. He remained on the reservation until the Sitting Bull war, which he joined and was one of the most fearless leaders.

THE STRUGGLE BETWEEN FATHER DESMET AND HOMESTAKE MINES

The period of time covered in this history saw some of the most important controversies tried out before the courts of law that have arisen in this nation and we are indebted to W. H. Bonham of the Deadwood Pioneer-Times for an account of some of the interesting legal struggles that took place before the bar of Lawrence County.

"That which made the deepest and most lasting impression upon my memory, and as illustrating the greatness and spirit of Deadwood and her people, were the courts and attorneys, especially those of the days of litigation involving titles to mining properties and water rights and determining ownership. Coming from an Illinois farm where my only knowledge of the law or lawyers was gained from pettifoggers and bullyraggers in a justice of the peace court, my admiration for the Deadwood bar knew no bounds. I believed they were among the truly great of the earth, and I have never been disillusioned, if illusion it was, but I don't believe it. The Deadwood bar was made up of the best legal talent from the mining states and territories of the west and was surpassed by none. The great Homestake and Father De Smet corporations had grappled in a life and death struggle for the possession of what each believed to be the richest gold prospect in the world. A great array of legal talent assembled on each side. The contest was waged for weeks, and the bar of Deadwood became known throughout the country. The dignified and able Gideon C. Moody presided, and rendered the now famous water-right decision which was approved by the federal courts, that is read and quoted everywhere today as the best law on riparian rights. And all of those lawyers have distinguished themselves here or elsewhere. The Deadwood bar claims a United States senator, a congressman, supreme, district and circuit judges, United States attorney, numerous lawmakers, state and county officials, promoters of all classes of industry, mine superintendents, active participants in political and civic affairs and all things pertaining to the public welfare It was with the Deadwood bar that the idea of forming two states from the territory and their admission to the union originated and was consummated under the leadership of Hon. G. C. Moody. Of the many attorneys of those early days who stamped the impress of their character and spirit upon the people, but few remain. Those were the days that tried out the stuff that was in men, and that same spirit and character is with the bar and the people today. The space I have already taken precludes a much desired personal mention of the members of the Deadwood bar.

"Among the many incidents of the Lawrence county court, humorous, pathetic and otherwise, I can only mention one, of interest because of its barbaric character and the spectacular setting of the trial. This was the case of Crow Dog, charged with killing Chief Spotted Tail. The day for the display of forensic eloquence arrived. The arguments to the jury were to begin, the morning papers had announced and assured the people that probably there would never be another such trial witnessed in any court of law. The elite and eliteses of the city were present, arrayed in their best and brightest apparel, and the Indian was there too, appareled in all the gorgeous colors of his tribe, warriors and squaws, displaying all the colors and paints, beadwork, plaited through the hair, war bonnets of eagle feathers sweeping the floor, buckskin suits showing the best bead and needle work that the cunning brain could devise or hand could execute, and blankets of every hue and all as solemn as the most important council meeting. Arguments to the jury began and continued to the end under this most inspiring audience. It was a scene never to be forgotten. The arguments concluded, the jury instructed by the court, retired to deliberate, returned a verdict of 'Guilty of murder,' and in due time Crow Dog was sentenced to be hung. Crow Dog was confined to the county jail awaiting the result of an appeal to the supreme court of the United States, which finally reversed the verdict on the ground that the trial court had no jurisdiction to try a case where Indians alone were involved. While waiting in the county jail, Crow Dog was allowed to wander over the hills alone during the day and report at night, with sentence of death by hanging over him, the most disgraceful death for an Indian. One evening he was missing and a search of the city and hills made for him. An officer was sent to the agency and there found him seated before his tepee holding on his knee a pair of twins that were born to him while in jail. The officer made known his mission to which the Indian replied that he wished to see his children before he died and as they were too poor to come to him he had gone to them. He assured the officer that his object was accomplished, he would return as he came and not fail. His word was accepted, and although the officer returned by stage and rail, Crow Dog arrived in Deadwood about the same time.

"The most amusing incident of early Deadwood life is known as the "Water Election." Water in the early days was more valuable than at present because of the more uses for mining and other purposes, not for drinking. The Homestake and Father DeSmet Mining companies were each acquiring title to all the loose water in reach, and each wanted the contract to furnish the city of Deadwood with water for fire and domestic purposes. The Homestake mines and mills were located at Lead City at the head of Gold Run gulch, emptying into Whitewood Creek. The Father DeSmet was located on Deadwood Creek above Central City, their properties being separated by the Deadwood and Golden Terra at Terraville, all of which, including the Father DeSmet is now the property of the Homestake.

"The fight for water was the beginning of the struggle between the companies which resulted in the absorption of the weaker by the stronger. Deadwood was the metropolis and mining center of the Black Hills and every Black Hiller claimed Deadwood as his home and the right to vote there on any question. An election to determine which company should supply the city was authorized by the county commissioners. The DeSmet was the most popular, with the people and the officials thought they had an easy victory. Each company was constructing ditches and flumes to convey water to Deadwood, and it was announced that the first to reach the city with water would be the favorite. Interest in the race grew and spread to every camp in the Hills. Opposing forces were organized, large sums of money were placed in the hands of the more 'influential' citizen, voters were paid their own price. On election day from ten to fifteen thousand voters had assembled to share in the glory and profits of determining which company should furnish Deadwood with water. Voters were housed and corraled in 'blocks' of hundreds while the spokesmen or leaders negotiated the sale of their franchise. One block of about 300 were housed on Sherman street awaiting a deal. Soon it was announced that the deal had been made, and then the other company got in its work. Instead of raising the ante it hired the firemen to turn a stream of water into the building. As one of the nozzlemen I expected to be mobbed but they came out like wet rats from a hole, each one considering the joke was on the other and not on him. Along in the middle of the afternoon the hired men of the company concluded they had a majority of votes in the ballot box and ordered the polls to be packed to prevent more voting. This was done and hundreds of voters could not get within fifty feet of the polls.

HE CARRIES NINE BUCK SHOTS

Sturgis in the early years of its existence was known to all of the pioneers and people throughout the Hills as Scooptown. This very appropriate name for the existence of that village at that time was well earned and well deserved because it was the resting place of many of the toughs, gamblers and outlaws as they came over the prairie into the Hills. There was a constant occurrence of robberies, holdups, shooting scrapes and the freighters and travelers of those days that were acquainted with the bad character of the rough element of Sturgis made it a point to camp either outside of Sturgis or move on to some other more satisfactory camp site. It was a constant struggle between the officers who tried to preserve law and protect property and the lawless elements. Sometime those who showed their disrespect for the law paid the penalty with their lives. An instance of this kind is recorded in the columns of the Record of June 6th, 1884, which in substance is as follows:

"For several weeks there had been three or four hard looking citizens loitering around Sturgis. Not much attention was paid to them at first as they appeared to be cowboys or bull whackers, but their stay at last aroused suspicion without, it appears, doing any good. The first occurrence that reminded people of the gentry was the sudden disappearance of two saddles, worth $50.00 each, from the Crowdin and France's livery stables. Monday it was reported that the tollgate had been robbed by two men and a short time after two men came in from above town stating that several of their horses had been stolen. Cowdin and France immediately upon discovery of the theft from their premises started the officers in pursuit and went out themselves to scour the country. Matters progressed quietly enough until about two o'clock Tuesday morning when two shots from the bluffs from Sages' corral told the story.

"The saddles were stolen Sunday night. Monday morning a fellow named Brigham, a well known character on the Pierre road, was arrested but subsequently turned loose. William Lindsey, otherwise known as 'Red' was also suspected but he was not to be found and it was ascertained he had gone down the road toward Rapid City. Monday night another phase of the case developed. A deserter from Fort Meade named Miller was collared by Souter and said he wanted to confess as he was badly scared at the way things were going and probably thought the the safest way out of the difficulty was to peach on the crowd.

"He stated that Brigham and Lindsey stole the saddles and had them cached in the brush north of town, that all three had intended to saddle up some horses that were picketed near town and leave that night for the Little Missouri, but on account of the arrest of Brigham and the absence of Red they had agreed to defer the trip until the next night. The plan was for Lindsey to get a horse from Rapid City, to come back to Sturgis, get Brigham, go out to where the saddles were cached, saddle two other horses near by and then the trio were to strike out for the Little Missouri. As this plan had been interfered with by the arrest of Brigham and the deserter, Miller, who had government carbine and cartridges. On promise of immunity he agreed to take the officers to the cache and show them where Red was when he came back. Dick France and Bill Ray, who worked for Scollard, were thereupon deputized by Souter to accompany the deserter to where the saddles were hidden and then to wait for Lindsey. Souter gave strict orders that if anyone came that they were to draw on him, call upon him to throw up his hands and if he failed to do so to take no chances but to turn loose. The men were warned by the guide to be careful as Lindsey had frequently said that he would never be taken alive and was a very dangerous character. About three o'clock Tuesday morning the watchers heard someone coming and Miller gave the signal. Then he flattened out on the ground and tremulously told France and Roy again to be careful. The coward was evidently afraid that Red would kill him if he escaped. As Lindsey came up the hill he was ordered to throw up his hands. Instead of complying he reached for his revolver. Two charges from shot guns, each with thirteen buck shots in front started for him and William Lindsey alias 'Red' went home. It was not yet daylight and at close range they did not know which one did the work. The body was taken to the undertaking rooms and the saddles to the stable. Tuesday Coroner Smith came down and an inquest was held. The jury returned the verdict to the effect that the deceased came to his death from the effects of a gun shot wound from the hands of

France and Roy and that it was justified homicide under instructions from an officer.

"The soldier deserted about a year ago and went to Brownsville where he was known as 'Big Miller.' A short time ago he went down again and enlisted, deserting Sunday or Monday. He will have the pleasure of working and earning his living at Fort Leavenworth for the crime of desertion. He later took the officers to the place where a lot of tools were concealed. He said a scheme was on foot to blow up the safes in the banks and capture the currency. This 'soldier' must have been a fine partner to have either in crime or anything else.

"Lindsey was about thirty years of age with red hair, a mustache and a six weeks' growth of red stubbles on his chin. He worked at Rapid City and was later in the employ of Mr. Elsner here. It is thought his premature transit from this world to the next will break up a rather hard gang that has been gathering here from Pierre and other points."

BUFFALO GAP

The year 1886, saw the town of Buffalo Gap the terminal of the F. E. and M. V. railroad. The town soon became a typical western town, but of the toughest elements that could be got together. Sure thing men, desperadoes, gamblers, dance hall rounders, and in fact more bad men than decent men comprised the bulk of the population. There were continual rounds of holdups, robberies and shooting scrapes until finally the business men held a secret meeting to decide on how to handle this situation. They concluded to employ a nervy city marshal and for this purpose chose a young cowboy, who by his quiet manners and orderly behavior when he came into town with other boys, had marked him as a law abiding citizen. After considerable persuasion, the business men secured the services of this man whose name was Archie Riordan. The tough element accepted the challenge and decided to put the marshal out of business immediately. They chose a desperado by the

name of Charlie Fugit and the plan was to shoot up
the dance hall and in a general disturbance, kill the
marshal without giving him a show, the minute he
would come into the room. However, Riordan was informed
of what was going on and when the fighting
commenced, walked in and as Fugit made a draw for
his gun, he fell dead from a well placed bullet from

Archie Riordan

the marshal. The gang of robbers realized that the
officers meant business and the decent people were in
the fight for a finish. They soon decamped for other
pastures and Buffalo Gap became a place where people
could go about their business without fear.

Riordan afterwards was appointed deputy sheriff
of Custer county and proved to be a very efficient
officer. He later took up his residence in Hot Springs,
South Dakota, of which city he has been mayor for
several terms.

BROKE JAIL AND DIED

Roy Sewell is dead and the next county court will have one less case to contend with.

On the 15th of June, Sewell was arrested for alleged cattle stealing. The charge was made that he had been selling calves to local butchers. He was held to the next term of court and being unable to furnish bonds was placed in charge of the sheriff. He has been a quiet and tractable prisoner until yesterday.

About half past six, Jailor Kelly let Sewell out in the jail yard for a few moments, as has been customary. When the prisoner returned instead of turning into his cell he ran out through the office and down the street. Somebody gave the alarm and the trouble commenced. Kelly got his shot gun and started after the fugitive. Sewell ran down the alley and entered the market where F. A. Willard holds forth. He knew there was a Winchester rifle hanging on the wall, and coming from the rear had the gun before anyone was aware of it. There were two customers in the market at the time. He "threw her down" on the trio and said he would kill anybody who interfered. As Sewell passed out the front door he met Marshal Beaver who had heard of his escape, and saw the man running. Beaver had run through the vacant lot east of Spark's. When Sewell ran against the marshal, he pointed the gun towards the officer and backed off into the street. Having no weapons Beaver let him go. Sewell went to Martin and Bunting's stable, where he ordered a horse saddled and then seeing Kelly coming around with a shot gun, walked quickly down to what is known as the Starr and Bullock corner. There he took a stand and threatened to shoot Kelly if he even dared to move the gun that he carried.

In the meantime Willard began to fret about his rifle. It was a good gun and shot pretty close. He needed it in his business, it was an old friend and cost money. So he went over to Anderson's hardware store, picked out a rifle, got a few cartridges and went up the street. Sewell was still on the corner "holding up" the deputy sheriff when Willard reached Blatt's corner. The men were not 50 feet apart. Willard said, "Roy, put down that gun." Roy was crazy with excitement. He had threatened three men in the shop, the marshal, the deputy shcriff and Martin in the stable, and was even then saying that he would kill all he could and die before going to jail again, so he wheeled around, pulled a bead on Willard and fired. The two rifles were fired simultaneously. Sewell's jugular vein was severed and he died in ten minutes. The shot from his rifle missed Willard's head by about two or three inches. It cut the mid-rib of Blatt's window, and passed through the outer sash into the main casing.

Sewell's body was removed to Voorhee's undertaking rooms where an inquest was held. The jury consisting of Messrs. Jones, Sevey and Cary, returned a verdict to the effect that the deceased came to his death from a gun shot by Willard, the latter being in discharge of his duty and the killing entirely justificable.

Yesterday a telegram was sent to the boy's relatives in Pierre and a reply immediately received ordering the body placed in charge of the undertaker until the relatives can arrive, which will be tomorrow or maybe today.

Nobody can regret the occurrence more than Mr. Willard, who was suddenly confronted with the fact that he must defend himself against a man who was no doubt temporarily demented.

Roy came of an excellent family and was very bright, but wanted to be a little tough. He said to Deputy Kelly, after he was shot, "I'm glad it's over." He had the night before, cut out a hole in the ceiling of the jail and also cut at the door with a knife. (Record, August, 1896)

STOLE BORGER'S TEAM

When Jim Merryman went around Wednesday morning to feed the team on the Borger dray line, he found that "Bismarck" and "Maud," the old familiar bay and sorrel, were gone. The harness was also gone as well as the pole straps, and then strange wagon tracks were seen. Half a minute's investigation showed that Jim O'Neill's buckboard had been drawn by hand up to the barn, the horses harnessed and hitched to it, and then driven back by the same track. After going as far as where the buckboard should have been and not finding it, Merryman forgot to follow up the track and see which way it went, and by the time the others thought of it, of course there was no use.

Three parties were immediately made up and started out. F. A. Willard, and W. E. Cathay went north, headed toward the Bismarck trail; Charley Stewart and Billy Mance also went north but hit a trail further west; Deputy Smith and Borger went down the road intending to watch the eastern end of the country.

Up to last night nothing had been heard from the absentees. M. M. Baird says that when coming in to town Wednesday morning he saw a buggy track on the road west of the Butte, that didn't keep in the road at all—sometimes on one side and then on the other. This dray team wasn't used to the country. Mr. Henderson who lives about two miles beyond Lynch on Nine Mile, reports that about four o'clock that morning a team with two or three men passed his place and the rattle woke him up. That would be about the time the men should reach there if they took that road. No other clue whatever has been received.

The fellows, whoever they were, showed poor judgment in the selection of a team for a long trip. This was a dray team, seal fat, and couldn't stretch out ten hours at one time if they were killed for it.

Stewart and Mance came in last night about six o'clock and had seen nothing of the gang. Sam Moses came in also this afternoon and stated that Willard and Cathay had stayed at his ranch on the Moreau-

80-Miles- night before last. They were watching that trail.

OUR HORSE THIEVES RETURN. ONE OF THEM HAS A FEW WOUNDS IN A TENDER PLACE, BUT THE OTHER FEELS FINE

The two young gentlemen who attempted to get away with Borger's dray team and O'Neill's buckboard Tuesday night of last week are now enjoying the hospitality of Sheriff Smith. Fred Willard brought in one of them Tuesday afternoon, suffering from a gun shot wound in the inner part of his leg, and Wednesday morning the other one appeared with Fred Harvey in a buggy.

The Record last week published a full account of the disappearance of the property, of the three different parties being out on the search, the return of two—but like the dime novel, left it all to be continued.

The two men, who will be called Hansen and Murrill, for want of better names, as they gave those names when questioned, struck out north past Jim Hoover's place and all that North Moreau country. They drove that old gray team between 125 and 150 miles in two days, showing that they knew how to take care of horses and work them right.

Willard and Cathay were at Sam Moses' ranch, but took a circle west. They went past the Flying V Ranch out to the line camp, and there ran upon the trail still going north. They rode all that afternoon and all night, and finally came upon the two horse thieves at Ed Hanks' ranch on Grand River at daylight Friday morning. The boys (for such they were —22 or 23) were in bed and their heads covered by blankets. After being aroused the fellow, Hansen, asked if breakfast was ready. The other one, Murrill, he calls himself, had evidently been in similar places, or had heard of them, for he wanted awfully to get hold of a gun that they had stolen the day before at the ranch, and which was standing by the side of the wagon full of cartridges. By the way, the two thieves had stopped at a ranch house on the way up, taken coffee, sugar, canned goods, tent, camp outfit and a rifle with ammunition.

After breakfast the two officers started back for home, it being the intention to drive as far as the Flying V ranch, leave Borger's team there, and then come on. Willard was ahead with the tired out team and Hansen, Cathay followed with the buggy and team, his companion being Murrill, who made no resistance. Both teams were jogging along, but being further apart, when Cathay stopped to fix a holdback strap. He left everything—gun and all, in the buggy. His prisoner hit the team a sudden blow, the buggy knocked Cathay down, and once more the fellow was free. There was nothing to do but the three pile in one rig and start towards the Hanks ranch, which was reached as soon as possible.

Murrill next turned up at the ranch of a Swede named Sanwick, right at the forks of Grand River. He got there with his thoroughly jaded team about nine o'clock and as he himself says, intended to get a fresh horse from the stable as soon as the folks had gone to bed. But the woman of the house had seen him in the moonlight crossing the yard to the corncrib and reported it to her husband and another man. They went to the building, looked through the cracks and saw Murrill with his head down as if asleep—he had been on the go for three days. The gun that he had run away with stood beside him. Sanwick opened the door, grabbed the young fellow, after which to use his own words, "Sometimes one was on top and sometimes the other." The Swede finally won and Murrill was a prisoner once more. Cathay had gone down after the runaway, having procured a fine team at Hanks' and come upon the scene Friday in time to start back to Hanks' ranch. Night overtook them at a road ranch and Cathay was in charge of the prisoner, whose legs had been fastened with chain and padlock. Cathay went to sleep, being sick anyway and fagged out, and when he awoke his prisoner had disappeared. Murrill had wriggled his way out of bed, swung his shackled legs out the window, drawn himself through, hopped down to the creek, and pounded off his legirons on the rocks thereabouts. He now had the north pole as a final resort and started for it. Willard and Hanks had started down the trail towards the forks, and appeared on the scene again. Sunday morning Cathay and a stock inspector named Fleming, took one branch of the creek while Willard and Hanks took another, and once more the search was instituted for any track that might lead to the discovery of the slippery gentleman. A shoe track was noticed in the road leading towards the North Dakota line. It was a pointed shoe and as none of the stockmen out that way were addicted to the toothpick shoe habit, the trail was immediately taken and followed. It kept in the road so was easily followed and about five o'clock Sunday afternoon Willard saw some small, dark object disappear over the top of the hill at one side of the road. It might have been a hawk or a coyote, but he got out of the buggy and climbed the hill, because the shoe tracks were now very fresh, and he ran right onto the gentleman, half concealed by a rock and a hole in the ground. Murrill immediately started to shoot. He had a six shooter that he had stolen from some of the ranches he had passed or had been given to him. Willard was not fifty feet away and he took one shot that struck the fugitive in the fleshy part of one leg, going through it into the other and incidentally doing a painful piece of work between times. The unfortunate man made a remark or two about knowing when he had had enough and the incident was closed. He was helped into the buggy and all started toward the ranch which was reached in due time and Monday morning the journey home set in.

Charley Stewart and Fred Harvey had started out again Friday night as soon as they had heard of the whereabouts of the two men so that they were at the ranch when the crowd came in. Ice was procured and Willard and Stewart came in with Murrill, getting here Tuesday afternoon. Fred Harvey arrived Wednesday morning with Hansen and Cathay brought in the tired dray team yesterday.

Drs. Smith and Sexton say there is no particular danger in the wound unless blood poisoning sets in which is not likely.

Murrill won't talk much. He claims to be 18 years old, but is 23 if a day. He had a note book in his pocket containing a pass to allow one Charles Wilcox to cross the Cheyenne Indian reservation, dated last April; also various dates and names—two being names of Deadwood girls. He also claims to have been on the northern ranges and rode roundups, so that he is familiar with the names of the various ranches down this way. The other one, Hansen, claims to have worked at Blackhawk four years ago, after which he went to Chicago and then to Lead, where he met Murrill, both of them working for some weeks as porters in Fannie Hill's house of ill shape; that times got dull and they were discharged; came to Sturgis and that night Murrill sent him down to the fair grounds to wait until the team was properly stolen. This latter must be a lie because the Chinaman says he saw two men hitching up the team.

Too much praise cannot be given all who started out so quickly after the horse thieves when notified last week and stayed with it so long. Willard rode down twenty-two horses on the trip, counting those under the saddle and in harness. Ed Hanks, whose ranch is 125 or 150 miles from here, hitched up a pair of standard bred stallions and pretty nearly killed one of them. His ranch was headquarters all the time and nothing was too good. Bob Packer and Gene Allen, at the Flying V ranch rushed around after fresh horses as if the whole Sioux nation was after the country. Everybody out that way tried to do more than the other and each was afraid the two culprits would escape.

Wednesday morning a purse of about $150.00 was raised here to help defray the expenses of those who had gone out so quickly and willingly to help capture the thieves.

Preliminary examination will probably occur today—at least of one of the prisoners. State's Attorney McClung says he don't know whether it is worth while to bind them over to circuit court, as there is no sure thing they will be convicted. The average Meade county jury is an uncertain quantity.

ATTEMPTED JAIL DELIVERY

There came pretty near being one less on earth and one more somewhere else, last Friday night.

Some few minutes after ten o'clock there was a concerted action among the prisoners at the county jail to escape. Deputy Sheriff Frank Smith went down stairs to lock them up in their cells, when Hansen, one of the horse thieves and a boy who was supposed to be rather innocent of any real guilt in the abduction of Borger's horses, and a very nice young fellow, threw a spitoon at Smith's head. Then Murrill grappled him and a pleasant rough and tumble fight ensued between the three. Finally Smith got away and drew a little six shooter which he had in his pocket. With this he shot Murrill about the pit of the stomach and the gentleman immediately quit. The shooting frightened Hansen who ran for his cell. But another prisoner turned out the lights.

Smith stood at a place where he could cover both exits with his six shooter, and sent for help. Phil Smoot came down on a double quick march and told what had happened. In less than no time there were dozens of people hurrying to the court house, but there was no need for an alarm, as the rest of the prisoners were as peaceable as could be imagined.

Dr. McSloy was sent for but he did not dare probe for the ball in Murrill's interior department, so he dressed the wound to allay inflammation and yesterday afternoon the patient hardly knew he had been shot. His wound that Willard gave him on the occasion of his arrest had hardly healed and now he has another, but he said to the physician, something to the effect that he wanted a good job made as he would try the same thing again.

Much credit is given Deputy Smith for the way he "held the fort" and the only regret is that he didn't shoot a little lower. (Sturgis Record, Sept. 7, 1900.)

CIRCUIT COURT—EVERYBODY PLEADS GUILTY OR GETS IT IN THE NECK

Yesterday morning circuit court convened in order to give the prisoners who had been in jail a show for freedom or something else.

Edward Murrill and Harry F. Hansen, the two young men who stole Borger's team, were brought up for trial. They waived time, plead guilty and were sentenced to two years each in the Sioux Falls penitentiary. Murrill's true name came out as Edward Ditmon. (Sturgis Record, Sept. 21, 1900.)

In the Black Hills

CHAPTER VIII.

FOUR FAMOUS PIONEER NAMES

In all ages and in every clime, the story of the development and lives of a people reveal certain outstanding characters and individuals who by the good or evil that they have done, have stamped their names upon the times. The tale of the Hills is no exception to this rule of social science and out from the thousands of men and women who gathered in the shadows of the mountains, lured thither by the longings of the human heart, we find four names that stand forth, distinct and pre-eminent, the result of the paths they marked on the fleeting sands of their day.

History tells us that in the discovery of the New World, both by the sturdy Norsemen and the persevering Columbus, the cross led the way. So likewise, in the early history of the West we find that the devout missionaries braved the hardships and dangers of the wilderness to bring the story of the Redeemer to the heathens. It is especially true that in the long years yet to come, future generations shall come to honor above all others, the memories of two pioneer soldiers of the cross in the early history of the Hills, who came here not for the fading glory of gold, but for the noble and ever resplendent task of leading their fellows in the footsteps of their Redeemer, Father DeSmet and Rev. Smith.

FATHER DESMET

First in order of time, first in duration of the task, and first in magnitude of his work, we will consider Peter John DeSmet, S. J. He was born in Belgium on the 31st day of January, 1801, and came to America in his early youth. After completing his education, he joined the Jesuit Society and was sent as a missionary to the tribes along the Missouri River. He established the first church in western Iowa at Council Bluffs in 1838, and from this point as headquarters spent the most of his life preaching among the Indian tribes of the Northwest. He was in Green

River, Wyoming, on July 5th, 1840, and there he celebrated the first Mass ever heard in that territory, his congregation being a motley crowd of Indians, traders and trappers, the altar being made from materials at hand and decorated with wild flowers of the prairie. He is said to have been the first white man to discover gold in Wyoming.

From time to time, he reported to his superiors in the east and from his letters we have a glimpse of the life he led and the scenes that he saw in the days of the later forties. We quote from Father Rosen's "Black Hills," wherein a report of a trip in 1848, across the prairies to the Black Hills is made. "We met not a single Indian, and no vestige of human habitation greeted the eye. But ever and anon we distinguished small artificial mounds erected by the hand of man; irregular heaps of stones and tombs containing the mortal remains of Indians, carefully wrapped up in buffalo robes. At times a solitary post marked the spot where some brave had fallen in the field of battle—where reposed some ancient Nestor of the desert. These monuments, though with no epitaph to attest lofty deeds or transmit names to posterity, are a tribute of a feeling heart, a mute testimony of the respect the Indian bears to the memory of a father or of a friend, and of the value he attaches to the glory of the ancestors. Some herds of bison and dense flocks of deer, of several species, that fled at our approach, alone beguiled the tedium of the march.

"In so long a march, through regions so singularly various, two great inconveniences are sometimes experienced—want of water and of wood. More than once we had no other fuel than dried buffalo-dung, and three times at our camping ground, water failed us. This is a hard trial for men and horses, especially after travelling all day under the burning sun of the month of August.

"Another kind of torment, still less supportable when the heat is intense, is the appearance of fantastical rivers and lakes on the verge of the horizon, seeming to invite the weary traveler to advance and refresh his wasted strength upon their banks. Fatigue and thirst picture in the distant verdure, shade and coolness awaiting him. The illusion increases the desire to quench your burning thirst. You hasten onward to reach the goal. Hour succeeds hour; the delightful mirage heightens in brilliancy, and the panting, exhausted traveler presses on without a suspicion that the phantom flies before him. In an open, elevated region, where the atmosphere is in continual agitation, this effect may be easily produced by the reverberation of the sun's rays from the surface of these vast prairies, throwing the various tints of the verdure upon the deep blue of the firmament."

Father DeSmet was a close observer of nature in his travels and after describing the annoyance caused by gadflys, gnats, mosquitoes, and swarming winged ants on the hot August days, he mentions the prairie dogs of the plains as follows:

"They pile up the earth around their dwellings about two feet above the surface of the soil, thus protecting themselves against the inundations which, in the rainy seasons or at the melting of the snows, would ingulf them and their little homes. Guided by instinctive foresight they carefully gather all the straws which are scattered over the plain, and carry them into their subterraneous asylums, to protect them against the rigors of the winter. At the approach of a horseman, alarm is rapidly communicated to all the citizens of the singular republic. All quit their habitations, and with head erect, the ears pricked up with anxiety, and a troubled stare, remain standing at the entrance of their abodes, or at the openings of their conical hills. After a momentary silence, they break forth into one loud and repeated chorus of shrill barking. For some minutes life, motion, and restless agitation reign throughout the extensive field they occupy; but at the first gun shot, all is tranquil, every animal disappearing like a flash."

He recounts his experiences in the Badlands and how he had to use the water therein although thick with the white mud so fine as to defy separation from the water. He pictures the country in these words: "The actions of the rains, snows and winds upon the argillaceous soil is scarcely credible; and the combined influence of these elements renders it the theatre of most singular scenery. Viewed at a distance, these lands exhibit the appearance of extensive villages and ancient castles, but under forms so extraordinary, and so capricious a style of architecture, that we might

Badlands

consider them as appertaining to some new world, or ages far remote. Here a majestic tower, surrounded with turrets, rises in noble grandeur, and there enormous and lofty columns seem reared to support the vault of heaven. Further on, you may decry a fort beaten by the tempest, and surrounded by mantellated walls; its hoary parapets appear to have endured, during many successive ages, the assault of tempest, earthquake and thunder. Cupolas of colossal proportions, and pyramids which recall the gigantic labors of Egypt, rise around."

He made note of flowers and grasses of the prairies and mountains as he travelled over them and found many un-named specimens, but his opinion of the Indians of his time may prove of most interest to the reader and we quote as follows from his report of 1848:

"I have several times observed that the Indians inhabiting the valley of the Upper Missouri, are generally more cruel than those sojourning west of the Rocky Mountains. Probably this arises from their almost incessant wars, which inflame them with a love of plunder and a thirst for vengeance.

"At the epoch of my visit to the Sioux, a troop of these barbarians were returning from a war against the Mahas, with thirty-two human scalps torn from defenseless old men, and from women and children whose husbands and fathers were off hunting. When they re-enter their villages, after the combat it is their custom to attach these horrible trophies of their shameful victory to the points of their lances or to the bits of their horses. At the sight of these spoils the whole tribe shouts with joy, and every one considers it the highest gratification to assist at the scalp dance and feast, which is celebrated amid the most discordant yells and fearful gestures.

"They plant a post daubed with vermillion in the midst of the camp; the warriors surround it, flourishing in their hands the bloody scalps which they brought back from the battle, each one howls his war song to the lugubrious tone of a large drum; then giving in turn his stroke to the tomahawk on the post, he proclaims the victims that his hatchet has immolated, and exhibits ostentatiously the scars of the wounds which he has received.

"Such is, even at the present day, the degraded condition of the unfortunate Indian. They never take the field without endeavoring to draw down the favor of the Great Spirit, either by diabolical rites or by rigorous fasts, macrations, and other corporal austerities. They even go so far as to cut off joints of their fingers and toes. Add to the thick shade of heathen darkness a shocking depravity of manners and you will have a faint idea of the lamentable position of these wretched tribes. Yet these same men welcomed me with open arms, as a messenger of the Great Spirit. A vivid emotion depicted on every countenance, accompanied their respectful attention to my discourse, while I instructed them in the great truths of religion."

Father DeSmet has made several trips into the Hills and spent many years among the tribes near the Hills and knew of the mineral contained in the mountains. His knowledge of geology enabled him to realize that the territory would some day be the mecca for thousands of adventurers and that their coming would bring disaster to the Indians. He therefore kept his discovery to himself and while admitting that there was gold within the gulches, he refused to give any details or accounts to arouse the cupidity of the would be trespassers.

His work, however, was not that of an explorer, but he labored as a missionary. For many years he travelled from tribe to tribe throughout the Northwest, enduring all kinds of privations and dangers among the red men, in his great task of telling the story of Christ to the savages. In his untiring efforts, he made twenty-four voyages across the sea, collected some two hundred thousand dollars for missionary work, and travelled 260,929 miles, thus gaining for himself the name of "The Great Missionary," and "The Apostle of the Rockies." That his work was not in vain is evidenced by the fact that when treaties were later made with the several tribes, one of the demands made by the chiefs, was that "blackrobes" be sent among them that they might have the helping influence of their teachings.

As old age came upon the intrepid, pioneer missionary, the rigors and privations of his ardous labors, compelled him to cease his efforts among the Indians, and he became a professor in St. Louis University, where he spent the closing years of his life. There on the 23rd day of May, 1873, death drew the curtain of eternity over his spirit. His remains were placed at rest in Florissant, Missouri, among his brethren, where a simple grave marker gave forth his name and age.

PREACHER SMITH

While the work of Father DeSmet among the Indians of the West came to a close a few years before the gold rush to the Hills and he passed on to other fields, we find the story of the Nazarene was not to be forgotten and that with the pioneers of seventy-six there came a soldier of the Master whose life blood was destined to flow upon the pine clad hills and whose life was to be snuffed out by a hidden foe, Rev. Henry Weston Smith.

In the diary of George V. Ayres of Deadwood, under date of Sunday, May 7th, we find this entry: "Weather cold and stormy. Went to the first church held in Custer City this morning. The Rev. Smith of the Methodist persuasion preached. He took his text from Psalm 34:7 and preached a very interesting sermon. The congregation consisted of about thirty gentlemen and five ladies who all paid strict attention to the sermon except when there was a dog fight outside."

This is the first record that we find of the Rev. Smith of the Methodist church. He was known among the pioneers as Preacher Smith and this first sermon was delivered in a log house with sawdust floor. On the 16th day of May, 1876, Captain C. V. Gardner, in charge of a freight train hauling some eighty-two thousand pounds of merchandise to the Hills arrived in Custer. After inspecting the new town, he decided to proceed to Deadwood with a part of his load, and loading up some two thousand pounds upon a light wagon, hitched to mules, he started for the new camp. Just as he was leaving the town, a man came to him and asked him for permission to go with him. Gardner informed him that if he would walk he would haul his baggage and the proposition was accepted.

The train and travelers proceeded on the way until they went into camp near Hill City. By the time that the team was unhitched and the men prepared for their meal, they were agreeably surprised to find that their new companion had a fire started and water ready for the cook with which to prepare their supper. However, when supper was ready, Gardner found his passenger absent, and in searching for him discovered him sitting on a log a few rods away intently reading and upon going up to him was more than surprised to find the book he was so deeply interested in was a Bible. The man then informed Captain Gardner that he was a Methodist minister to which information it was volunteered that he was up against a rather hard proposition. "Possibly so but I will do the best I can," was the reply. The outfit was more than three days reaching Deadwood and at the end of the trip he offered to pay Captain Gardner $5.00 but this was refused.

Here in Deadwood among the hurly, burly, noisy and boisterous crowds of those days the work of Rev. Smith began in earnest. It is said that while he would be preaching in one part of the street and the throng would be gathered about him, above the voice of the minister could be heard the shouts of the gamblers and sports crying their trade and caling upon the crowds to come to them and spend their time and money on their games and not to waste it on the minister. However, Rev. Smith did not enter the saloons and gambling houses and point out to them another and better way of life but contented himself in calling the people's attention to their God in the streets of Deadwood in front of the store buildings. He was never without an audience for in those days the streets were crowded with an ever changing throng of people from all parts of the continent.

Smith made his living at manual labor and worked at various occupations in the Hills, such as cutting timber, chopping wood, and doing carpenter work. He was a quiet and earnest man and labored consistently in his efforts to lead his fellows to a higher and nobler life. He decided to extend his field of labor and on Sunday, August 20, 1876, after preaching on the main street of Deadwood he informed his friends that he was going to go to Crook City as he had done for several times, in the afternoon.

These were the days when the Indians were exceptionally vicious and warlike and the roving bands on their way south from their successful slaughter of Custer and his men, waylayed and murdered the small parties of men that they might meet around the foothills. The friends of Preacher Smith warned him of the great danger but the minister showing a Bible replied, "This is my protection." However, the landlord with whom he had roomed replied, "I would rather have a cap and ball revolver for protection against the Indians." But Smith replied, "It has never failed me yet and I am not afraid to put my trust in it." And the landlord with the parting injunction said, "It is very good in its place but it don't shoot quick enough in an argument with Indians." He proceeded on his way alone and on foot and when about five miles out from Deadwood, at a point known as "The Rest" he was fired upon and killed by Indians. Charles Pfrunder, who had a milk ranch nearby was on his way to Crook City when he saw the body near the road and gave the report. A party of men went out from the city, among whom were Richard Clark and Louis Wolfe, and arrived at the scene of the murder at the time that Joe Armstrong came up with a partly loaded hay wagon. The body of the minister was placed on the hay and hauled to Deadwood, where it was given into the hands of friends for interment. C. E. Hawley conducted the funeral services.

This was the day of the great Montana horse herd stampede and one of the most eventful days of north Hills history as heretofore noted. On this day Charles Mason, who had been out in the valley was shot by an Indian and his friends brought his body in for burial. A double grave was made and the remains of the minister and Mason were interred side by side in the same grave, in a place now occupied by residences in the fourth ward of Deadwood. And this fact, together with the fact that two other victims of Indian bullets of that day, Holland and Brown, were later buried in the same row, enabled the identification of the minister's remains, when they were removed and re-interred in Mt. Moriah cemetery, and a statue placed over it by the pioneers and friends.

On this same day, J. S. McClintock, who has a distinct memory of the incident in essential details, states that a man rode into Deadwood with an Indian head tied by the hair to his saddle. And after announcing that he had killed the fellow, let it be put up at auction to the highest bidder. It was auctioned off for twenty-five dollars and fell to the lot of Dan Dority, a keeper of a low order of play house. It was kept in a saloon for a time until its condition became repulsive and then found a resting place under the floor, from where it was taken several years later and cleaned up by Louis Schoenfield who finally sent it to a friend in Kentucky.

As the years rolled away and men took time to look back over the stirring events of the frontier days,

Rev. H. W. Smith's Monument

they began to realize the greatness of the quiet and noble follower of the lowly Nazarene, as he labored at manual toil during the week and spent his entire Sunday in trying to call his fellowmen to the path of righteousness. Then they erected to the memory of the murdered minister, a dignified and simple monument, that stands on an eminence above the lonely gulch where his labors ended, and looking out over the panorama of hills and valleys from whence countless thousands shall come to do homage to his memory.

No one seems to have known much about the past life of the man and in those days it was not well for one to be too inquisitive about his fellow, but we have found a poem written by Rev. Smith that was dated June 1, 1876, and from it one may get a glimpse of the high ideals and the aspirations of the first man to preach to the gold seekers of '76.

THE GOLD HUNTER'S REVERIE

I am sitting by the camp fire now
    On wild Dakota's Hills,
And memories of long ago
    Steal o'er me like the rills,
Adown yon canyon deep and dark
    Steal through the leafy glades;
A glimpse, a murmur here and there,
    Then vanish in the shades.

This evening is the first of June,
    And the snow is falling fast.
The tall pines sigh, howl, and moan,
    Responsive to the blast;
The shades of night are gathering round.
    The fire is burning low,
I sit and watch the dying coals,
    And think of long ago.

I see a black eyed, dark haired boy.
    (That was forty years ago)
He draws a hand sled to the woods
    Amid the falling snow.

I see him slip, and toil and tug,
    With steps that often tire,
He brings a load of wood to feed
    A widowed mother's fire.

They tell him at the village school
    That he has talents rare,
And, if he does not play the fool
    He may fill a statesman's chair.
I am a toil worn laborer now.
    My hands are hard and dry,
And looking at that bright faced boy,
    I wonder—was it I?

I see a throng of worshippers
    Within a shady grove;
They listen to the of't told tale
    Of Jesus and his love.
And he who spoke the word that day
    Had surely felt his power,
And many a suppliant knelt to pray
    And blessed the gracious hour.

Says one, "He seems to have the power,"
    Another says, "No doubt
He'd make his mark upon the world
    But for one gracious fault."
I tread the forest paths alone;
    Alone I raise my cry
To Him who notes the sparrows fall
    And wonder—was it I?

I see a lovely cottage home,
    With humble comfort blest,
I see at eve' the workman come
    In loving arms to rest.
I am a lonely wanderer now,
    No friends or kindred nigh,
And gazing on yon love-lit home,
    I wonder—was it I?

And when I sit on Zion's hill,
　No more in need of gold,
And sing with those who love me still
　The songs that ne'er grow old,
Perhaps I'll look on this sad eve,
　Beneath this stormy sky,
And think that this was long ago.
　And wonder—was it I?
　　　　　　　　—Henry Weston Smith.

Deadwood City, D. T. June 1, 1876

As the names of Father DeSmet and Rev. Smith stand out prominently in the fight for righteousness among the pioneers of the border, we have on the other hand, directly contrasted to these great and noble characters, the names of two others whose deeds and lives were spent and whose reputation and names go down in history in an entirely different color and phase of human character. First of these, we will treat of the noted gun man, scout and gambler of the West whose name likewise stands far above all competitors in his field and that is "Wild Bill" or James B. Hickock. A sketch of his life with the closing scenes in the Black Hills is set forth as follows:

"WILD BILL"

One of the characters of the early pioneer days whose name is more widely known and about whose reputation there has been woven many wild tales of romance was a fellow known as "Wild Bill" whose name was James Butler Hickock. This name is forever linked with the pioneer days of the Black Hills and especially with the city of Deadwood. James Butler Hickock was born in 1837, near Mahomet, Champaign county, Illinois, and spent his early days working on a farm. From there he went to Springfield, Missouri, where he remained until the latter part of the war. During the Civil War he became a very daring scout. While living at Springfield he became engaged in a quarrel with a gambler whom he killed as a result of the fight. After the war Bill came to

Kansas where he settled on a homestead in Montecello township of that county where he was appointed constable. Later he hired out to a company hauling freight over the Santa Fe trail but took no part in the territorial troubles. While engaged in this work he was attacked by a bear in the Rocky Mountains and was sent to the Rock Creek station on the Oregon trail to recuperate from his wounds. This station was located in what is now Jefferson county, Nebraska, near the present town of Fairbury. D. C. McCanles had been in charge of this station but had become more or less of an outlaw and a leader of a wild gang of horse thieves. He had with him a young woman known as Kate Shell whom he had induced to follow him from North Carolina. While located here the young girl had become enamored of Wild Bill and had deserted her former companion, McCanles. As a result of this relation McCanles and his gang came to the Rock Creek station on July 11th, 1861, a place seven miles southeast of the present city of Fairbury, Nebraska. McCanles was met at the door by Wild Bill who handed him a drink of water but both realized there would be a fight to the finish. After Bill stepped back from giving McCanles a drink McCanles reached for his revolver but immediately fell dead with a bullet from Bill's gun that pierced his heart. The fall of the leader demoralized the rest of the gang who immediately fled but Bill succeeded in bringing down two of them mortally wounded. The others escaped on their mounts. The woman, Kate Shell, who was present in the house at the time, seized a grub hoe and with it killed the wounded robber named Woods. There was also with Wild Bill at the time in the house a friend of the McCanles gang who when he beheld the sudden turn of fortune proclaimed his loyalty to Wild Bill who thereupon put him to the test and ordered him to shoot the other wounded man. Accordingly the fellow took a shot gun and killed the other wounded man by the name of Gordon. The remains of the leader, McCanles, were buried near the spot where he was killed but in 1879 the body was removed to the cemetery in Fairbury and the man who was killed with him was buried there also. The third man, Gordon, lies buried on a knoll a short way from where the shooting took place. The three parties were charged with manslaughter and the trial was held at Beatrice, Nebraska, but all were released be-

James Butler Hickock
(Wild Bill)

cause there was not sufficient evidence to substantiate the charge of manslaughter against them. The woman in the case, Kate Shell, who was known to be a very beautiful girl, was placed on the first stage going west and disappeared. After this fight and release of Hickock whose action met with the approval of the community, he went to Julesburg, Colorado, where it is reported he killed a man over cards. From there he drifted back to Abilene, Kansas, a city at the time that was infested with all kinds of toughs and outlaws. The better element of the city hired Wild Bill to accept the job of city marshal at a salary of

$1000.00 a month. In a short time he had killed a number of desperate characters and so terrorized the other scoundrels that they moved for newer and safer stamping grounds. From Kansas Wild Bill wandered through various western towns and we find him in Cheyenne, Wyoming, in June, 1876, where he joined a party of gold seekers on their way to Dakota.

He was a tall, well built man with steel blue eyes, long dark brown hair and long flowing mustache, a lighter brown in color than his hair. Despite the rough and harsh character which has been ascribed to him we find that after all he had his pleasant side and that he had staunch friends who knew him and loved him well. A few years before his death he became acquainted with Agnes Lake, who was an equestrienne in a circus in Wyoming. To this woman he was married and from a letter to her we get a glimpse of the nobler side of his character. The last letter he wrote to his wife has this statement in it, according to his old friend, Captain Jack Crawford: "Agnes darling, if it should be that we never meet again, while firing my last shot I will gently pronounce the name of my wife, my Agnes, and with a kind word even for my enemies I will make the plunge and try to swim for the other shore."

He was not wild and boisterous but quiet mannered and always in control of himself. He was not quarrelsome but was absolutely fearless and known as one of the quickest and most accurate pistol shots that ever pulled a trigger. He killed many men in his time, but always in such manner as to be within the law and justified, usually being a fraction of a second too quick for the other fellow. He seldom became intoxicated, but was a man of quick temper and one whom the miners and gamblers knew it was not wise to arouse. He occupied his time when not engaged as a scout or officer of the law, in gambling.

Wild Bill came to his end in Deadwood, and very many misleading and false accounts of his death have been published, but the following account is from the lips of an eye witness, A. C. Tippie, who states that on the second day of August, 1876, he had come into the saloon on lower Main street in Deadwood, known as Number 10. Here he saw Captain Massie, Wild Bill, Jack McCall and several others playing poker. A pot was made up with Wild Bill and Jack McCall in it. McCall made a bet and threw in his sack of gold dust. Wild Bill called him and won the pot and when McCall's cash was paid in it was found to be $3.00 short. In those days gold dust was the medium of exchange and was measured out by small balance scales. Wild Bill said to McCall somewhat angrily, "Don't you ever do that to me again" and then ordered the bartender to weigh out $3.00 to McCall saying, "This will buy you your supper and do you for the next forenoon." After the game Captain Massie said to Tippie, "I will not play in that game any more for I am afraid of Wild Bill" but in the afternoon Massie and Bill with several others were again playing poker in the same place. After awhile McCall crossed into the room very leisurely and proceeded to the back part of the house, where he took up a position behind Wild Bill. Shortly afterwards a harsh voice spoke out loudly and was followed by a piercing and loud report, and McCall came rushing out with his six shooter in his hand and snapping it several times cried out to the crowd, "Get out of my way." He ran to his pony standing in front of the saloon and tried to mount it but his saddle turned under him and he left the horse and ran up the street, where later he was arrested.

Over at the table where the game had been going on, Wild Bill was lying dead on the floor with a bullet wound in his head, the missile having entered the back of his head and coming out the right cheek. The ball whizzing through the head of is victim, crossed the table and hit Massie on the wrist. Terror stricken, he rushed out of the saloon yelling "Wild Bill has shot me." After the excitement had passed, friends of the dead scout and gambler, among them "Colorado Charley" carried the body over to Bill's camp across the creek at a clump of trees near where the Burlington depot now stands, and there E. T. Peirce prepared the remains for burial.

This event took place soon after the establishing of the Deadwood camp and no legally constituted officers had as yet been named. But the people did not allow such a deed to pass unheeded and much attention was given to the matter of investigating. The account of the proceedings was published in the Pioneer of August 5, 1876, and we herewith reproduce it as published.

The first account of the murder of Wild Bill was that which appeared in the Deadwood Pioneer under date of August 5, 1876, as follows:

"Assassination of Wild Bill. He was shot through the head by John McCall while unaware of danger. Arrest, trial and discharge of the assassin who claims to have avenged a brother's death in killing Wild Bill.

"On Wednesday about three o'clock the report was started that J. B. Hickock, 'Wild Bill,' was killed. On repairing to the hall of Nuttall and Mann, it was ascertained that the report was too true. We found the remains of Wild Bill lying on the floor. The murderer, Jack McCall, was captured after a lively chase by many of the citizens, and taken to a building at the lower end of the city, and a guard placed over him. As soon as this was accomplished, a coroner's jury was summoned, with C. M. Sheldon as foreman, who, after hearing all the evidence, which was to the effect that, while Wild Bill and others were sitting at a table playing cards, Jack McCall walked in and around directly back of his victim within three feet of him, raised his revolver exclaiming, 'Damn you, take that,' and fired, the ball entered the back of his head and came out the center of his right cheek, causing instant death, rendered a verdict in accordance with the above facts.

"Preparations were then made by calling a meeting of the citizens at the theatre building. Immediately after the theatre was over, the meeting was called to order by W. Y. Kuykendall, presiding. After a statement of the object of the meeting, the gentlemen, numbering one hundred, elected Judge Kuykendall to preside at the meeting as judge of the trial of McCall. Isaac Brown was elected sheriff, and one deputy and twelve guards were appointed. It was then decided to adjourn to meet at nine o'clock, Thursday, August 3, in order that the gentlemen might have time to announce the meeting and its object to the miners of Whitewood and Deadwood mining districts.

"At nine o'clock Thursday, the meeting was called pursuant to adjournment, when the action of the previous meeting was presented for adoption or rejection, and after some remarks, was adopted. Colonel May was chosen prosecuting attorney and then A. B. Chapline was selected by the prisoner, but owing to sickness, Mr. Chapline was unable to attend, and Judge Miller was chosen in his place. A committee of three was appointed by the chairman, one from each district, whose duty it was to select the names of thirty-three residents from each of their respective districts, and from the persons so chosen, the jury was afterwards obtained. Mr. Reed of Gayville, James Harrington of this city and Mr. Coin of Montana City, were elected for this purpose. At this time the meeting adjourned.

"At two o'clock the trial was commenced and lasted until six that evening. The evidence in the case was the same as that before the coroner's jury, so far as the prosecution was concerned. The defense was that the deceased, at some place in Kansas, killed the prisoner's brother, for which he killed the deceased. The jury, after being out for one hour and thirty minutes, returned the following verdict: 'Deadwood City, August 3rd, 1876. We, the jury, find Mr. John McCall not guilty.' Signed, Charles Whitehead, foreman, J. J. Bump, J. H. Thompson, J. F. Cooper, K F. Towle, L. A. Judd, L. D. Bookaw, S. S. Hopkins, Alexander Thayre, J E. Thompson, Ed Burke and John Mann.

"Thus ended the scenes of the day that settled the matter of life and death with one living whose life was in the hands of twelve men, whose duty it was to decide the guilt or innocence of the accused charged with the murder of Wild Bill, who while the trial was in progress, was being laid in the cold, cold ground in the valley of the Whitewood by kind hands who were ever ready to do his wishes while living and ready to perform the painful duty of laying him in his last resting place."

After the verdict of the miners' jury was returned, Jack McCall was released, but he was such a disreputable sort of fellow, and Wild Bill had had several staunch friends, who gave little credence to the story put up by McCall, that he was not long in deciding that Deadwood gulch was not the most desirable place in which to establish a residence. He soon disappeared and was next heard of in Cheyenne, where he posed as the man who had killed Wild Bill. He became more bold as the days went by and once, while drunk, he stated that his story about Wild Bill shooting his brother in Kansas was without foundation. This confession was reported to the Federal officers and when the federal courts were established in the former Indian reservation, the United States marshal placed McCall under arrest and took him to Yankton, to stand trial before the United States District Court.

When Jack McCall was arrested and brought back to Yankton his defense to the charge of murder when he was first interviewed by the officers was quite different from that which he set out before the Miners' jury in Deadwood. In his cowardly nature he attempted to turn state's evidence and thus avoid the consequences of his dastardly deed. He claimed that he had been hired by John Varnes to kill Wild Bill and set forth as the reason why Varnes desired the death of Bill, that Varnes and another party had been engaged in a poker game when they got into a dispute and in the middle of the fierce quarrel, Wild Bill intervened as peace maker and compelled Varnes to back down at the point of a pistol. No shooting occurred in the fight because friends had interfered and prevented further trouble but Varnes had never forgiven Wild Bill for the manner in which he settled the dispute. However, investigators of the story were unable to find Varnes and as McCall had given so many conflicting statements, the trial proceeded against him and he was accordingly convicted and duly hanged.

At the time of the firing of the fatal shot from the gun of the assassin, it is said that Wild Bill held a hand of aces and eight spots and henceforth among the gamblers of the Hills, such a combination of cards was known as the "Deadman's hand." The undertaking work on the part of "Doc" Peirce over in the wagon canvas tent among the pines, was rudely interrupted that evening when the Mexican came yelling up the street swinging the gory Indian head by its long black hair as hereinbefore mentioned.

The remains of the famous winner of so many duels, were at first buried on the hill where Ingleside is now located, and as indicated in the photo, taken some time later. Over the grave his friend "Colorado Charley" placed a board with the inscription: "Wild Bill, J. B. Hickock, killed by the assassin Jack McCall, Deadwood, Black Hills, August 2nd, 1876. Pard we will meet again in the happy hunting ground to part no more. Good bye. Colorado Charlie, C. H. Utter." In the summer of 1878, Utter and other friends had the remains of their companion disinterred and buried in Mount Moriah cemetery where it now rests overlooking the city of Deadwood. In this work J. S. McClintock of Deadwood assisted and when the body was exhumed it was found to be in a remarkable state of preservation, even the folds of the pleated shirt that he wore being plainly visible. The body, although firm, was not petrified or turned to stone as has so often been claimed. His rifle that was buried with him was quite rusty though intact.

Over his grave there have been several stone monuments, but curiosity seekers had so mutilated the stones that they had to be replaced and finally a high fence was placed about the lot to prevent the desecration of the grave itself. And to this spot high on the mountain, thousands of visitors from all parts of the continent have toiled up the steep and rugged path, to view with emotions ranging from mere idle curiosity

Wild Bill's Grave

to admiration and sorrow, the grassy turf whose rootlets pierce the mould of the famous scout of the Hills and West. Many detractors there may be, many false stories are told, many faults he may have had, but the fact remains that Wild Bill was always found on the side of law and order and that those who fell at his hands were of the class that had to pass before the coming of a better day.

CALAMITY JANE

The fourth name that we have chosen as one of the most widely known characters of the pioneer days and whose reputation and personality was known on

all the Black Hills trails far and near, is that of
"Calamity Jane." Around this name like that of
"Wild Bill" have been woven some of the most fantastic yarns and most varied accounts of a woman's
life. We will, however, set forth a few of the real
facts as to her life and picture her in her true light.

Martha Jane Canary was born near Burlington,
Iowa, about the year 1851. It is said that her father
was a Baptist minister and that Jane in her younger
days was well cared for and trained, but self willed
and full of the joy of life. We first find her running
away from home as the mistress of an army lieutenant on one of the expeditions to Wyoming. She later
gave birth to a young son, at Sidney, whom the officer
took and sent back east to his parents to raise as a
foundling orphan from the plains. The boy was given
a good education and no doubt never knew the truth
as to his parentage.

We again find her in company with her mother
and her step-father, named Hart, a retired regular
army soldier, crossing the plains to Salt Lake, Utah,
where they lived for a time. From Salt Lake, Jane
ran away to Rawlins, Wyoming. Her step-father followed her to this place and found that she was at a
hotel there, but was informed that she was attending
school regularly. This appeared strange to him as he
was unable to get her to attend school in Utah. However, being assured that the girl was going straight,
he returned to his home. Soon after this, Jane skipped out to Ft. Steele and became an inmate of a bawdy
house and quite a pal with soldiers and teamsters.
She became expert in tying the diamond hitch and
handling teams, and when an expedition was made
out to the north, she donned men's attire and with the
aid of her fellow packers, obtained a position as a
packer with the government pack train. In this work
she prospered for several months, but when at Hat
Creek station, she and her fellows took an over dose
of whiskey and went on a wild spree. As a result,
the pack train master discovered her sex and promptly discharged her and signified his intentions of dis-

charging any of the men who were responsible for getting her into the train, but they all kept their secret.

For a time she was an inmate of a resort in Green River, Wyoming, from which place her brother ran her off at the point of a gun, taking several shots at her by way of good measure. The brother later passed out of notice when the gold rush to the Hills took place. Her mother wandered from Salt Lake to Blackfoot, Montana, where she presided over a notorious dive known as "Madame Canary's." Jane was married a number of times, her first husband being named Hunt and her second White. White sold out his property and became quite wealthy. He decided to quit the wilderness and rigged his wife out in the finest clothing to be had and repaired to Denver. A few days of the fancy apparel and classy hotels was enough for the wild, untamed spirit of Martha Jane, and she made her escape. Her husband made search for her and waited some days for her return, but knowing the spirit of the woman, gave up the search and went his way alone.

From then on, Calamity Jane became a free lance, roving from town to town and dive to dive, with soldiers, packers, muleskinners and freighters, as the occasion offered, and making her headquarters at Cheyenne, Wyoming. Whenever there was to be a trip across the plains, an expedition against the Indians, or anything to vary the monotony of the small town life of the west, Jane was on hand and usually contrived to get away, by dressing in male attire and being smuggled away by her pals. On the occasion of General Crook's expedition, she was many miles away from the starting point but upon hearing of the trip, she hired a team and buggy from W. Ward, a livery man of Cheyenne, for a ride, and then, when out of sight, drove rapidly away, smuggled herself in among the soldiers, and decamped, leaving the liveryman, Ward, to recover his outfit sometime later upon finding that she had placed it in care of a man in Ft. Laramie from whence the expedition had set forth. At another time she had joined a military expedition and was having the time of her life, but when the command had halted along the banks of a stream and the members were enjoying the delights of a cool dip in the waters of the creek, an officer passing by spied the form of Jane splashing about with her fellow troopers, and the remainder of the journey found her under guard.

Calamity Jane's first introduction to the Black Hills was in the year 1875, for there we find her dressed as a soldier in the military expedition under General Crook, who in August, 1875, ordered the miners to leave the Hills until treaties could be made with the Indians. Again she came to the Hills in 1876, with the band in which Wild Bill and Charlie Utter were members. However, she was not the consort of "Wild Bill" as has been claimed, for he was not the kind of a man that was attracted to a woman of Jane's class. "Colorado Charley" was perhaps her champion for it is said that he furnished her with a splendid suit of men's buckskin clothing, in which she often appeared.

No doubt by this time the reader will have concluded that Jane was nothing more than a common prostitute, drunken, disorderly and wholly devoid of any element or conception of morality. And the question will arise as to how it comes that out of the hundreds, yes, thousands of her fellow women of the underworld, who threw youth, beauty and life itself into the fiery altar of the Moloch of passion and immorality, the name of Calamity Jane alone should endure in the annals of time. The answer will be had from the other view of her double sided life.

In 1878, there came a terrible scourge of small pox among the miners and people of Deadwood. Hundreds were prostrated upon their rude beds and most people were afraid to go near them. Women were few to be had and they too were in terror of their lives. In the hour of terror and death, there came to the front, a willing volunteer, the mule-skinning, bull-whacking, and rough, roving woman from the depths, Calamity Jane. Day and night she went among the sick and dying, and for week after week ministered to their wants or smoothed the pillow for the dying youth whose mother or sweetheart perhaps, was watching and waiting for the one never to return. It made no difference to her, that she knew them not, or that no gold would there be to repay her for the labor, the sacrifice, the danger. They were fellow beings in distress and needed help.

Another time, while waiting table in Pierre, she heard of a family in destitute circumstances, and sick with black diphtheria. Neighbors would not go to their aid. Jane had saved up twenty dollars in gold and proceeding to a grocery store, she purchased fifteen dollars' worth of food and medicines and nursed the family until the sickness was over. In 1878, the young sister of C. H. Robinson, now sexton of Mt. Moriah cemetery, was sick with typhoid fever. Calamity Jane had known the family for years in Kansas and promptly came to their aid and for two weeks nursed the child until death claimed her as his own.

Calamity Jane never hesitated to spend her last dollar to aid an unfortunate and never hesitated to ask for money from others to help some one in need. Her idea of helping others caused her arrest in Deadwood in the early days. It seems that a fellow had had what was then known as a "hell of a time" in one of the resorts of the town in which Jane was an inmate. When he awoke from his drunken slumbers the next day, he found that he was minus some thirty dollars, and at once made complaint to the justice of the peace that he had been "rolled," that is, his pockets rifled and his money taken. Recalling that Jane was there, he charged her with being the culprit and she was brought to the bar of the court. When informed of the charge, she stated tha she found the fool drunk under one of the tables and searching his pockets found the money therein, and knowing that if she did not do it, the other girls would, she took the money. The judge then asked her what she had done with the money and she replied that she had given it to the hospital to pay the hospital charges for a young girl who was lying sick there without funds, or friends. The justice, Hall, promptly turned her free and scored the sporty gentleman who was so unwise as to carry money with him to a dive and expect to take it away with him.

Many other tales of how she had helped the needy and unfortunate might be added here, but we will pass to another phase of the life of this unusual woman. Calamity Jane was an expert packer, an able teamster and a crack rifle shot. She loved the great outdoors and the excitement of the trail. She was the pal of the men of the fighting line. It is said by E. H. Warren of Spearfish, that once while speaking to a pioneer, a woman came up to the pair, looked them over and finally demanded a dollar from the man, who without question, handed it over to her, and she walked away. After she was gone, the pioneer said: "That was Calamity Jane and as long as I have two dollars in my pocket, she can have one, for she saved my life once. We were on a trip, when the Indians opened fire upon us and shot my horse from under me. Jane stopped her horse, grabbed me by the arm and swung me on behind her and we escaped." Another time, she and "Antelope Frank" were out riding as scouts for a party, when the Indians appeared and opened fire upon them. They turned their horses and fled in the direction of the party, but the scout's horse fell in a hole and broke its neck, leaving him afoot. "Antelope Frank" also known as "Buckskin" told her to ride on into safety and that he would take care of himself, but she said: "Damned if I will, Buck I will stay right with you and we will see how many of those red ——— we can drop." And she did, the pair getting into a buffalo wallow and opening fire upon the band with their rifles, sent them away in retreat, with the loss of five of their number, Jane having done her share of the execution.

As time went by and the wild days of the frontier gave way to the more sedate times of later development, Jane wandered about from town to town making a living by selling books, photos and receiving charity from the pioneers. She had a daughter whom she placed for a time when she was fourteen years of age in the Sisters' convent school at Sturgis, South Dakota. Once, a kind hearted woman of wealth sought to lift her out of the slough and took her back to Buffalo, New York, but the lure of the Hills was too strong and Jane soon bade farewell to the stiff and conventional life of the east, and hastened back to the big hearted westerners.

In physical appearance, Calamity Jane was a medium sized woman with dark brown hair and eyes. In her youth she was of splendid form, clear complexion and uncommonly good looking. In older age, the rough life of the plains and trails coarsened her appearance. She could swear like a trooper, drink like a sailor and rough it with the roughest. Yet when sober, she could do the part of a real lady, and at all times was very fond of children in whose presence she was watchful of her conduct. She was seen in every town, camp and fort in the west and had wandered over all the trails. So variant were her moods so many the different incidents of her life, that accordingly there are numerous impressions and ideas of her character. She was a strange mixture of the wild, untamed character of the plains and mountain trails, and generous, kindly hearted womanhood. But under the rough exterior there beat a heart so big and friendly as to be without measure. Brave, energetic, unfettered, kind, always on the line of action, with helping hand ever turned to the poor and unfortunate, the personality of Calamity Jane became indelibly stamped upon the minds of the pioneers.

The close of the last century found the rover near to the end of the trail and in the summer of 1903, she came back to her haunts among the Hills and told her friends that she was sick and going to soon "cash in." One day she came to a hotel in Terry and being sick asked for lodging, but the manager turned her away, thinking her a mere drunk. Upon soon after learning her identity, he took her in, but dissipation had done its work and pneumonia made her an easy victim on August 2, 1903.

The friends of the deceased took her to the undertaking rooms of C. H. Robinson at Deadwood. There while lying on the cooling board, numbers of curious women came to look upon her, and many clipped locks of hair from her head, to the extent of defacing the remains. "Smoky Tom" one of her early consorts, upon coming to the room and noticing the work of the vandal hands of women, who would have scorned the deceased on the street, protested against the mutilation and a wire screen was placed over the head.

The pioneers gathered for the funeral and Rev. C. B. Clark of the Methodist church conducted the funeral services, assisted by other prominent people of the city. Interment was made in Mt. Moriah cemetery across the aisle from Wild Bill. And fate decreed that C. H. Robinson, whose little sister, Calamity Jane had so long ago faithfully watched over in the futile struggle with death, should now lay her form in the couch of dreamless sleep.

CHAPTER IX.

FRONTIER SKETCHES

The foregoing chapters of this book have been devoted in the main to that phase in the story of the pioneers wherein life and liberty were the pawns in the great game of winning the West, and consequently tragedy has stalked throughout the pages in all its grim and soul stirring power. In the present chapter, we turn to present another view of the life of the early days that the picture may be the more complete. The stories that we shall here offer are from pioneers and are set forth, not as accounts of deeds of great moment, but tales of the smaller things that have their place in the fashioning of the life of a people.

LIFE IN DEADWOOD IN '76 AND '77

As stated in a previous chapter, the year of '76 witnessed the great stampede to the Northern Hills. Deadwood Gulch had become a name familiar throughout the entire country, and all pilgrims turned their steps in that direction. The town of Deadwood grew rapidly, and before the beginning of summer the main street presented a scene of great activity. Sunday was the busiest day of the week, and as the miners and prospectors from the tributary gulches and the outlying districts usually visited the town on that day to procure supplies and in hopes of getting mail from the states, every Sabbath saw Main street crowded with men. Among them could be found representatives of every prominent mining district of the west, as well as "tenderfeet" from every state of the Union. In the throng the buckskin clad hunter jostled the dandified gambler and the pilgrim from New England. On every side was heard the sound of the hammer and saw, in the construction of new buildings which could not be erected fast enough to house the incoming multitude. On one hand could be heard the impassioned call of an itinerant minister of the

Deadwood in the Early Days

Gospel for the people to pause from their labors or pleasures and consider matters of their spiritual welfare. In close proximity would be a loud-voiced gambler crying his game.

As the placers of Deadwood, Whitewood, Gold Run, Blacktail and Bobtail gulches began to yield heavily, gold dust became the well nigh universal medium of exchange, and gold scales were an indispensible part of the outfit of everyone who had anything to sell. Provisions, which during the spring and early summer had been very high in price, became more plentiful with the coming of large freight outfits, and by the early fall many stores had been established and carried large stocks of everything necessary at prices that could not be deemed unreasonable when the distance from sources of supply was considered.

With the coming of a freight train chief interest centered about the place where the mail was unloaded, for the trains gathered up all mail for the Hills, at such terminal points as Fort Laramie, Sidney, Fort Pierre or Bismarck, and brought it through. Often this mail, sometimes tons in weight, would be many weeks on the road, on several occasions even held up by Indians for days at a time. But to the prospector who forsook his cabin in some distant gulch to visit the town it meant news from home, and even though belated, it was joyfully received, even at the established price of fifty cents per letter and half the amount for a newspaper, in gold dust weighed in at the place of distribution. Upon the arrival of the mail, usually unloaded at the store to which the freight was consigned, it would be alphabetically arranged, and a man would stand on a box on the street and call off the names of those to whom it was addressed, while his assistants would be busy weighing the gold received for it. In the meantime lists of names in alphabetical order would be prepared and tacked up on the outside of the building where they could be examined at leisure. This method was followed until late in August of '76, when a pony express line was established by Dick Seymour and Charley Utter between Deadwood and Fort Laramie. While the risk of the express riders was great in traveling a country infested by the hostile Sioux, the mails thenceforth arrived frequently and with reasonable regularity. Of course, with the ratification of the treaty with the Sioux ceding the Hills to the government, and the establishment of regular government mail routes, the pony express was discontinued.

The Deadwood Pioneer issued its first number on June 8th of 1876, and copies were in great demand each week at twenty-five cents per copy. Frequently Al Merrick, one of the proprietors, would spend the day of publication and half the night weighing in the dust as the papers were handed out to customers.

A casual visitor from a staid community of the east would perhaps have been shocked by the prevalence of drinking and gambling, and certainly both were prevalent. They were, however, conducted so openly and were made so conspicuous that the false impression might be made that they were the chief pursuits. The truth is that the population comprised people not only from all quarters but also of every kind. There certainly was a large percentage of the undesirable class, who invariably rush to a place of excitement, but there were as well many men of fine character, some of them having brought their families with them, and many more being joined by their families later. As the more boisterous and undersirable individuals were most conspicuous, they gave to Deadwood a bad reputation not wholly deserved. If it was heralded abroad that a minister had held services in a noted gambling resort, such was imagined by some people to be the usual custom, while in fact it occurred but once, and while no doubt in attendance were many who "came to scoff," this writer, who was present on the occasion, believes that at least a number "remained to pray." The minister was a man named Rumney, who had been colonel of a Georgia regiment during the war, tall and of military erectness. He arrived in Deadwood in April of '77, and was tendered the use of "The Melodeon," a notorious gambling house, in which to hold a service. Whether this offer was made in good faith by Billy Nuttall, the proprietor, or whether it was a "bluff," it was accepted by the minister, who, after praying for a time, delivered a very acceptable sermon. During the service no irreverence was manifested. To provide an auditorium the chairs, tables and other gambling paraphernalia had been pushed back to the walls and the audience behaved with perfect decorum. With the close of the service, after a collection had been taken and presented to the minister, the activities of gambling were resumed, the stentorian voice of "Nutshell Bill," a well known gambler, calling out: "Come on! Come on! The old gentleman has been telling you how to save your souls now I'm going to show you how to win some money."

As stated above, this was the only instance of the holding of a religious service in a Deadwood gambling house, though the story of the occurrence was greatly magnified in its circulation throughout the country. Rumney, the minister who conducted the service described, died in Rochford district a year or so later, and his remains are interred in the little cemetery in the deserted camp known one time as Myersville.

In September of '76 a provisional government for Deadwood was established by the election of E. B. Farnum as mayor and ex-officio justice of the peace, and A. P. Carter, Keller Kurtz, Sol Star and H. C. Philbrooke as councilmen. Con. Stapleton, a well known Montanian, was made marshal, and John Swift clerk and treasurer. Under this government the community remained until the ratification of the cession treaty and the holding of a regularly authorized election. It is interesting to note that in the election for a provisional government 1139 votes were polled.

CELEBRATION OF JULY 4TH IN THE CENTENNIAL YEAR

Though the pioneers did not have the sanction or consent of the government in their occupation of the Hills, and though they felt much dissatisfaction over delay in extinguishing the Indian title and putting an end to the Indian atrocities, they still considered themselves patriotic sons and daughters of Uncle Sam. Therefore they decided they could not allow the centennial anniversary of the nation's birth to pass without proper observance and celebration. Moreover, this seemed a fitting occasion to call the attention of congress and the nation to their claims for recognition. In Deadwood and Whitewood gulches three more or less distinct celebrations occurred, one in Deadwood, another in Elizabethtown and a third in Montana City, then a busy mining camp on Whitewood Creek, a mile below the mouth of Deadwood. All were participated in by goodly numbers, and all were eminently successful. At Deadwood Judge Kuykendall, formerly of Wyoming, presided as chairman, with Judge Miller as orator of the day. General A. R. Z. Dawson read the immortal declaration, and followed this by reading a memorial to congress, which is here reproduced:

"To the Honorable Senate and House of Representatives in Congress Assembled: Your memorialists, citizens of that portion of the Territory of Dakota known as the Black Hills, most respectfully petition your honorable body for speedy and prompt action in extinguishing the Indian title to and the opening for settlement the country we are now occupying, developing and improving. We have now in the Hills a population of at least seven thousand honest and loyal citizens who have come here with the expectation of remaining and making this their homes. Our country is rich, not alone in mineral resources, but is abundantly supplied with timber and with a soil rich enough to produce all that will be necessary to sustain a large population. Your memoralists would therefore, earnestly request that we be not deprived of the fruits of our labor and driven from the country we now occupy, but that the government for which we have offered our lives at once extend a protecting arm and take us under its care. And as in duty bound your memorialists will ever pray."

As may well be imagined, the above memorial met the hearty approval of all, and steps were taken at once to send a special envoy to Washington to present it in person to congress. That this petition, together with the energetic work of the ambassador and the co-operation of western members of congress generally, had much influence in hastening the work of securing the relinquishment of the title by the Indians there can be no doubt. A commission was appointed consisting of senate and house members to visit the various Sioux agencies and secure the necessary signatures to the session agreement. So rapidly was this matter pushed, that the winter of '76 saw the necessary signatures secured, and the following April the treaty was ratified by the United States Senate.

But to return to the story of the celebration of the Fourth of July:

At Elizabethtown Dr. McKinney presided, Dr. Overman read the declaration and A. B. Chapline delivered the oration. At Montana City, Judge H. N. Maguire, one of the most gifted orators of the west, spoke to the assemblage. While the Hills has since had many men of fine ability as public speakers, it may be doubted if an oration delivered in this section since that memorial fourth in the Centennial year has had the power to thrill its hearers as Judge Maguire's audience was thrilled on that occasion.

It is narrated in American history that once during the revolution in order to supply a national flag to a frontier fort a patriotic woman sacrificed a portion of her wearing apparel. This occurrence actually was repeated in the celebration in Whitewood Gulch. National flags were not to be had ready made. Such as were displayed were, with one or two ex-

ceptions, hastily improvised from such materials as were at hand, and in order to supply the necessary colors in one instance a patriotic lady made a contribution of a part of her wardrobe, described by the poet as:
 "A garment of a mystical sublimity,
 No matter whether russet, silk or dimity."

Many years have passed since the centennial, but anyone who participated in the celebration of the Fourth of July of that year in the Northern Hills will remember it above all others of his experience.

HOW PACTOLA WAS GIVEN THAT NAME

The forest service is collecting data concerning the Black Hills and more particularly the National Forest. The following narrative of how Pactola received its name was related by J. C. Sherman of Pactola, S. D., one of the first white men who ever saw the present location of the town, and who was present when the place was named. When General Crook was returning from his Yellowstone expedition in 1876 he camped for a short time where the town of Pactola now stands. From this camp ground the local miners came to call the place Camp Crook, and it was so called up to '78. All mail was addressed to Camp Crook, S. D., and was brought in by pony express riders and various ways from Sidney, Cheyenne and Bismarck. At last the miners decided that they wanted a postoffice, and accordingly petitioned the postoffice department for one, proposing the name of Camp Crook. At this time, however, the town of Crook City, below Deadwood was a thriving burg, and the postal authorities refused the name of Camp Crook as it was too near Crook City. The miners then called a mass meeting to decide on a name for the town. About two hundred men were present from the various camps along the creek. There were many different names suggested for the town, but for reasons given, none appeared to be satisfactory. At last a local celebrity by the name of Judge Maguire, suggested Pactola. He was formerly a newspaper man and lawyer who had given up the more peaceful professions of editor and the law to try his luck with the pick and gold pan. When he mentioned Pactola it meant nothing to that crowd of miners, except the first syllable of the word sounded strangely familiar to them and was not altogether agreeable, after they had packed everything they owned two hundred to three hundred miles. They did not want a name that even remotely suggested pack. Maguire managed to hold their attention long enough to tell of the Greek myth of King Midas and the golden touch and how it was in the Pactolus river that the old king was supposed to have bathed in order to rid himself of the gift of the fairy. When he explained that the literal translation of Pactola is the river of golden sands every miner present seemed to want to be the first to vote for the name regardless of the fact that the name suggested something that was distasteful to them. Judge Maguire was the same man who gave the eloquent Fourth of July oration at Montana City.

THE ILLICIT STILL IN EARLY DAYS

The conversation about the camp fires had turned upon the high prices paid for grub of all kinds and other supplies, for this was before the railroads had penetrated into the Hills and all freight was hauled by bull or mule teams three or four hundred miles. Among articles specially mentioned as high in price was the whiskey and beer dispensed in the camps, various ranches and road houses. For a drink of this beverage two bits or a quarter pennyweight in gold dust was the price exacted. "And why shouldn't it be high in price," asked Dan Hanley, a prospector on his way to the southern Hills, "when the machinery for making it and all the ingredients, except water have to be carried so far?" "You don't mean to say do you, that there is whiskey made here in the Hills," queried one of the stage passengers. The place was the Ten Mile Ranch, that is ten miles south of Deadwood, first station out of Deadwood on the Cheyenne route, where a crowd of men comprising a coach load of travelers from the east, and a number of hunters and prospectors had taken refuge from a winter's storm. "I don't know where or how the whiskey is made but I do know that whiskey has been made here that never salted a gauger, and as we probably will have some time to spend here I will tell you about it. In the fall of '76 I was prospecting with Dan Sullivan over on the west side of Green Mountain. We are just beginning to understand that the ores in those flat formations over there may carry good values without showing up anything in the pan. At that time, however, we were green in the district, and didn't know this, neither did any of the other fellows. If our samples crushed in a mortar and panned, didn't show color, we simply considered them no good and started another hole. When a fellow named Clark came nosing around talking about the difference between silicious and free milling ores, we dubbed him 'Professor' and gave him the laugh. I've begun to think that maybe we did not exactly have correct ideas as to who the laugh was on. We had become pretty well discouraged and were thinking of striking out for the Queen Bee district, where it was reported that Cap Griffin and Billy Hall had struck some rich rock. While sitting by our camp fire one evening, discussing the question of whether to stick a little longer or pull out, a stranger with a pack burro came up and accosted us saying that he would like to spread his blankets in our shack for the night. Of course we made him welcome, and my partner and I put some bacon and coffee on the fire for his supper. He ate like a man who had earned an appetite by a stiff tramp, as indeed he had for he had come from Deadwood, and some of you know that the trail up over old Baldy and to the west side of Green Mountain is enough to make a fellow wish for some more of the flap jacks and bacon he had for breakfast. Our guest was a little sawed off Irishman, who after having inquired and learned our names, gave his own as Kelly. He had little to say, lying back on his blankets after he had finished his supper and taking evident enjoyment in his pipe. The pack which he had taken from his burro contained, besides his blanket, a pick much heavier than that generally carried by prospectors. A square or railroad shovel instead of the spring point in general use in the mines, and, strangest of all a stone mason's hammer instead of the light striking hammer or poll pick usually seen. The gold pan which is considered indispensable in a prospector's outfit was conspicuous by its absence. Such an outfit naturally aroused our curiosity but we put him down for a tenderfoot, upon whose innocence 'Cheap John' or some dealer in second hand goods had imposed. In the morning after breakfast, Kelly evidently was satisfied with our names, at least they sounded about right, and who was pleased to note in our speech a trace of brogue that has persisted through many generations of Sullivans and Hanleys in America. He thanked us for our hospitality and suggested that if it would not inconvenience us he would like to camp with us for a while. We willingly consented and leaving his burro and the greater part of his pack, and taking a lunch with him he shouldered his tools and struck into the brush. At nightfall he returned minus his tools, tired and hungry and showed evidence of having been hard at work. This continued for sometime, our departure for the southern hills having been delayed on one account and another. Every morning Kelly would leave camp with his lunch, every night he would come in tired and hungry. He became more talkative on longer acquaintance, but never spoke of his work, or prospects and noticing the care with which he avoided this subject we never questioned him on them. When finally we determined to break camp and pull out, Kelly expressed much regret, asking us to postpone our departure for a few days beyond the time we had fixed to leave. He refused to give a reason for his request, but urged it so strongly that we consented. On the evening of the third day on coming into camp he carried a small leather hand bag, from which he produced a veritable surprise package, no less than a full quart of good whiskey. We joined him in drinking a toast which he proposed, 'Here's luck to all travelers,' to which he added, 'I don't know how long I'll be on the road myself.' Where he had obtained the liquor was a mystery to us for as far as we knew he had not been to town. Now that we were about to part from him he took us into his confidence. While we naturally supposed him to be working on some mineral claim, he had in reality been engaged in installing a still in a place difficult of access, in or near Annie Gulch not far from where it joins Spearfish Creek. The bottle he had wished to share with us contained a sample of his first run. How or when the still head and worm had been transported there or who furnished him with the supplies necessary to make the stuff we never knew, further than that a certain dispensary in Deadwood handled his product. We never saw Kelly again after we bade him good-bye the next morning, but for six months ensuing when we visited Deadwood once each month, for supplies we never failed to find at a designated place a package containing a quart of 'Oh be Joyful,' and enclosed with it a piece of paper on which was scrawled in pencil 'From Kelly to his friends, the two Dans.' " As the prospector ceased speaking one of the stage passengers asked, 'Do you know what became of Kelly?' 'I don't know for certain, I presume he pulled his freight. I can only tell you that with the last package we received from him there was added to the usually brief message 'Luck to all travelers, I don't know where I am going, but I'm on my way.' Hanley added, "When one of these companies that are opening mines on the west side of Terry's Peak some day comes across an old excavation and unearths a buried still head and worm, with the scent of something or other than roses still clinging to them, you will know that this story of Kelly is not all fiction."

R. B. Hughes.

BLACK HILLS SALT SPRINGS

The fact that the western portion of the Black Hills contained deposits of salt was first ascertained by a party made up of Bart Henderson, G. D. Stillman, Charles Calderbaugh and J. A. D. Graves on the 8th day of July, 1877. They were prospecting through the western hills, and found a small tributary of Beaver Creek which put into the main creek below Jenny's stockade, which was quite salt to the taste. Following the stream up they found a narrow point between the two streams, about half an acre covered with salt springs. These springs proved to be about seventy in number, and according to an analysis made afterwards would yield three fourths of a pound to the gallon. of water. The party soon made a rough estimate by boiling some of the water in a camp kettle, and the result was so encouraging that they moved their camp there in September following. Mr. Henderson was something of a veteran in the mountains and had with others discovered salt springs in Idaho in 1861, knew that they were valuable, and under his counsel and directions the party during the following year erected two furnaces for the evaporation of the water. These furnaces were supplied with two pans each four by ten feet and had a capacity of one thousand pounds. These salt works were quite crude and were put up cheaply and simply for the purpose of prospecting the discovery, and to ascertain if a salt industry would pay in the Hills country. The product of the first large test was taken to Deadwood and introduced in the market and among the people that its quality might be tested by the consumers. The excellent quality of this home made article was found to be above criticism, therefore arrangements were made to supply the market of the Hills. In fact they were called to furnish salt for a much larger field. In order to do this their facilities were greatly enlarged, and they produced a coarser preparation for stockmen. Then the silver mines at Galena called for salt, and teams were put on the road that gave constant employment for a long time. For some reason the making of salt has ceased.

A CARGO OF CATS

By way of changing needles and omitting the tragedy stuff, let us consider the true story of how Phatty Thompson, the Cheyenne freighter, made a stake in a shipment of cats. Phatty was a large, whole-souled man, good natured, like the most of large people are. He was running a shot gun freight outfit between Cheyenne and Deadwood in the year of 1876. A shot gun freighter was one who purchased his own freight, which generally consisted of butter, eggs, sluice forks or anything that was needed in a mining camp where the supply was short. We have seen one of these men offered and receive twenty dollars for a common sluice fork, which is used to throw rocks out of a sluice box.

On one of his trips that summer Phatty was importuned to bring in some cats for pets. The dance house girls told him they would pay almost any price to have a pet, so as Phatty drove back to the railroad that idea worked in his brain pan and by the time he reached his destination he was ready to load his wagon with a consignment of felines. He passed the word around to the Cheyenne kids that he would pay twenty-five cents each for cats, irrespective of pedigree, color or education, and that his headquarters would be at the Elephant corral, Cheyenne.

Did the kids rustle the cats? Listen. They arrived in singles, doubles and finally by the sack, until the crib where he stored them was filled. One kid crawled into a brewer's kitchen and stole an exceptionally large maltese Thomas cat, which he sold to Phatty for two bits and which came near causing a tragedy. The woman who missed her pet went in search of it and was told to look in the corral, so she sent her husband, who was a large German brewer and had some original ideas of property rights.

Phatty was loading his wagon when the German arrived and discovered his Maltese. Then there was blood on the moon. Both the men were large and had voices that would have served for fog horns. They were holding an animated conversation, Phatty on his side saying that he had bought the cat from a boy and the German accusing him of stealing it. Outsiders interfered and a compromise was made whereby the German got his wife's pet and Phatty was out the purchase price.

Phatty had a long crate built in which he loaded his live freight and started for the Black Hills, everything passing off smoothly until he reached Lightning Hill, where you go down into first water on Spring Creek, this side of Hill City. There his wagon upset and distributed his load in the gulch. Phatty called them to feed and after repairing the crate succeeded in getting them all except one that ran up a tree and refused to return to quarters.

When some prospectors came along Phatty was throwing stones at the cat and using strange and fearful language. The miners, true to their traditions, threw their packs and went to the relief of a brother in distress, soon having the kitten tucked in its crib. When Phatty reached Deadwood he stopped at the lower end of Main street. You may have sometime noticed a fish peddler in the spring when the shad made their first run. Well, that would be a dead calm to Phatty's experience. Nothing sold at less than ten dollars and fine Maltese brought twenty-five each. Some industry, we would tell a man, and some originality.

There was a story on the street that day that Phatty had a sextette of Tom cats that yodeled, some actor having explained to Phatty how he could train them if he gave them nothing to eat but Swiss cheese with plenty of holes in it. We have always thought that yarn originated in the brain of one George W. Stokes, a former newspaper man of Denver, who was then living in Deadwood. Outside of this allegation, this is a true story. Re qui es scat!

E. T. Peirce.

A BEAR STORY

"Bears are as different in disposition as people," remarked an old market hunter as he sat by the campfire taking his after supper smoke. "I've known them to run like a whipped hound when hurt, I've known others to attack whatever came into their way, either man or beast without the least provocation whatever. I've thought sometimes that it all depended maybe on the humor that the bear happened to be in, at the time. Maybe if he was hungry or got up in the morning with a headache, he would be more dangerous than at other times. Maybe if the world looked pleasant to him and he had no trouble on his mind he would rather avoid a row than look for one, just like some men. As I said at the beginning whether they will run or fight is uncertain." That the hunter had some incidents in mind tending to fortify his opinion was apparent, and the others about the campfire insisting that he tell something of the bears he had known, he willingly complied.

Well, you know some of those fellows who claim to know all about wild animals say no bear will jump on a man unless provoked. They're clearly wrong about that as many people in this district remember how Fritz Wolfkin was killed up near Green Mountain. Well now Fritz was the biggest and strongest man in the Homestake wood camp. A perfect giant in size and strength. When out hunting one day, with two others they came across a bear track of unusual size and followed it. Fritz was ahead of the others a little ways carrying his gun in his right hand and his body in a stooping position when the bear which evidently had discovered that it was followed and had doubled back on his track, jumped on him from the side. Wolfkin's gun was knocked from his hand as the bear struck him. Even thus, bare handed the man proved no mean antagonist and his giant strength enabled him to throw the bear, but the brute outwinded him and finally fastened his teeth on Fritz's lower jaw and crushed every vestige of it, and tore it away.

The other two men finally killed the bear, but too late to save Fritz because in the scuffle there was no opportunity to shoot for fear of hitting him. The bear was a silver tip and weighed 700 pounds when taken to Deadwood.

In the summer of '77 three Austrians were making hay on middle Box Elder two miles west of Mountain Meadow ranch. They were camping in a log shack, in which an opening had been cut for a door but no door had been hung. One day one of them had killed an elk. A portion of the meat had been hung up on a pole, and the remainder had been salted in a barrel inside. That night they were awakened by a noise outside, and discovered that three bears were devouring the meat, which they had torn down from the pole. Gus, one of the three got his gun and fired point blank at the largest bear at a distance not greater than a few yards. The bears made a rush for the brush and escaped. Gus thought he had dealt one of them a mortal wound. In that he was certainly mistaken, for the next night they awakened to find the three inside. They had upset the barrel and were having a feast. This time Gus determined to make sure and quietly taking his gun and laying the muzzle close to the side of one, fired. Telling about it afterwards, he said the bear gave a grunt, tumbled over, kicked a log out of the side of the house, got up and decamped with the others, and they never found any trace of the wounded bear.

In that same district bears were plentiful. One day a well known prospector named Kinlock, was run into camp by three of them. They did not act as if they really wanted to hurt him but just enjoyed seeing him run, though **Kinlock** thought every jump would be his last. Fortunately Gilbert Tower, Kinlock's partner, was in camp and saw the end of the chase. He grabbed his gun and killed the three bears with as many shots.

Another man who made quite a killing of bear one day was Gene Aiken. Gene was out over in the neighborhood of Tepee. He was armed with a Winchester and knew how to use it. He had with him a little dog which ran ahead hunting through the brush. Suddenly the dog ran whimpering to Gene and closely following him were four bears. As I said before Gene knew how to use his gun, whether for bear or any other animal. And he killed the four bears without moving from his tracks.

There was the bear that mauled Shorty Landis. Shorty was a prospector in the Queen Bee district. In following a wounded deer one day he stumbled onto an old she bear with two cubs. Just what did happen in the mixup is a matter of some doubt, as Shorty, when he was able to tell about it seemed somewhat confused as to particulars. After a while he did evolve something of a coherent story, but in some particulars it varied so widely from his first statements that his friends did not encourage its repetition. Shorty said the way he made it let go, was he gouged its eyes out with his thumbs. The probability was, that the bear was as much surprised as Shorty, and jumped him in order to protect her cubs and allow them to get away. She knocked him down, probably stunning him and bit him through one knee. She fastened her jaws on his face tearing one cheek and his nose nearly off.

R. B. Hughes.

THE GREAT SNOW STORM

The 7th day of March, 1878, was one of the days never to be forgotten by the early pioneers of the Hills for on that day one of the greatest snowfalls in the history of western South Dakota took place. The day opened up a beautiful, warm day. As the oxen of the freight trains slowly trod along the winding trails leading to the Hills great clouds of dust were thrown into the air, and the bullwhackers as they trod along beside their trains and cracked their whips o'er their backs, became so warm they removed their coats and traveled in their shirt sleeves. It was almost the same as a nice summer day in June. In the afternoon a rain began to fall and soon turned into snow which increased in intensity toward night. One of the freighting outfits, about which we will speak of in this item, was under the command of Jesse Brown and at the close of this day it went into camp in the Hills near Whitewood. In the morning the whole country was covered with a deep blanket of snow with still more rapidly falling. The herders who had been in charge of the oxen were unable to hold them against the drifting snow and the animals drifted away into the canyons. For three days the snow continued to fall and the prairie was covered with seven feet of snow which the strong wind had piled in drifts to the depth of twenty feet. The men in this camp were obliged to procure boards from a nearby saw mill with which to make snow shoes before they could get out to hunt for the oxen they had turned loose several days before. Finally they found where the oxen had drifted into gulches and fifty-four head of the one hundred and fifty oxen were found dead, having been crowded over precipices by those who were behind them driven by the swift blowing snow.

In Deadwood many roofs were broken down and business was at a standstill. Snow shoveling was the order of the day and on the sides of the street the mass of snow was piled to the windows on second story buildings. Horses were led up the gulch so as to break the way for travelers. The quantity of snow falling on a hay scale weighed 3165 pounds. The weather turned out fine and warm and the great snow soon went down the ravines in rivers in a mad rush to the plains. The mud became almost as much of an obstacle as the snow had been and ten yoke of oxen were required to one load while hay was $60.00 per ton.

GREAT FIRE IN DEADWOOD IN 1879

The most destructive fire that had ever occurred in the Territory of Dakota destroyed the greater and all the most valuable portion of the new city of Deadwood, the commercial capital of the Black Hills mining region on the morning of September 26th.

The fire started at twenty minutes past two o'clock in the morning in the Star Bakery on Sherman street, one of the principal business streets. The building was situated in the midst of a block of combustible buildings all constructed of wood. The fire started from a baker upsetting a coal oil lamp. All efforts to extinguish the flames were unavailing and soon spread to either side. When the fire reached Jensen and Bliss' Hardware store three doors south and on the opposite side of the street, eight kegs of blasting powder exploded with a terrific force that seemed to shake the mountains. The blast threw sparks and firearms in all directions, starting fires in many new places. The fire department was promptly on the ground but the building where its apparatus was stored was in flames and was soon destroyed, with hook and ladder, hose and hose carriage all consumed. This situation left the city perfectly helpless to fight the destroyer, fanned as it was by a strong breeze from the south. Scores of tenants were in the upper stories of the business houses and barely escaped with their lives. In the brief time the fire crossed Lee street which runs east and west and was licking up the business houses with their contents. The people seemed to be paralyzed, or half crazed, and hundreds of them climbed the hills on either side of the gulch with a few valuables carried on their backs and watching their dwellings go up in smoke. The fire passed down Main street to Gold and Wall streets and back on the hill for three blocks leveling everything. In the other directions it extended along Sherman street until it was checked by blowing up small buildings, saving some residences of excellent design and finish on Ingleside, and on Cleverland. The area covered by this awful scourge was about twenty-five acres, consuming a total of one hundred business houses, and seventy-five dwellings and entailing a loss on first estimate of three million dollars. The total insurance all told was one hundred thousand dollars. The granaries in the city were filled with wheat and oats, the harvest having been unusually abundant, and the merchants had about all received their winter's supply of goods. All newspaper offices, Masonic, Odd Fellows and Knights of Pythias halls were destroyed. The government signal office and the U. S. military telegraph station lost nearly all of their metorological instruments. The fire consumed everything, but within twenty-four hours the ashes had been raked away in places and tents, borrowed from Fort Meade, were set upon the lots and dispensing liquid refreshments obtained from the fireproof cellars began. Lead City restaurants were supplying the hungry with meals served on pine boards for tables and Deadwood had, like the fabled Phoenix, risen from the ashes. The Deadwood Times managed to issue a small paper on the 28th, two days after the fire, which contained the following: "The old saying that it is an ill wind that blows nobody good, can with reason be applied with much force to our case. Probably in the history of the country there has been no such destruction of property, comprising so many business houses, and the dwellings of so many families, throwing so many people out of business and families out of a habitation, where there is so little suffering and destruction, as there has been or will be to our people from the fire. Of course many have lost their all, their last dollar, and with nothing but the clothing on their persons, saw the accumulations of years wiped out and vanish in smoke, and found themselves without a mouthful to eat nor anything but a pine tree to protect them from the elements. Their character and credit is all they have left, and the only remaining capital upon which to commence anew."

There were many amusing incidents that occurred while the fire was raging, such as throwing looking glasses out of windows and carrying old rugs and scraps out carefully. A printer in the News office put down a hundred dollar's worth of type and grabbed two bottles of Hosteter's Bitters which he carried to safety. After the fire was subdued, women were seen wearing men's coats and hats, and men protected themselves with shawls wrapped around their shoulders.

The total loss of the property was estimated at one million, three hundred ninety thousand, nine hundred dollars and no call was made for outside help. While some lost everything, they had strong arms left and went to work at good wages preparing the new buildings.

Here are some of the advertisements that appeared on the 30th, four days after the fire: "J. Harry Damon, the boss rustler of Elizabethtown, has on hand a large stock of goods, also a fine collection of liquors and cigars, a large bakery in connection where can be obtained, bread, cake and pies at the same old prices. R. D. Kelly is selling flour and bacon at the same old prices. Ruggles, of the Oyster Bay, opened up this morning and is prepared to serve all who call. Joe Gandolfo has opened up his fruit store at the old stand and has a selection of fruits, etc. The well known Wentworth has opened up in the Anthony block where meals and lodging will be furnished at the same old prices. At Chase's where they sell cheap, will be found a large stock of clothing, caps and men's furnishings at the same old prices."

This is what the News had to say of the conditions after the fire: "After the derangement of the general run of business, we have settled down to the regular course of business. In all branches of trade, our merchants, artisans, and laboring men are all as busy as a bee in a tar barrel. There has been no tendency to take advantage of the general necessity and tenders of credit have been extended to all of our principal business men. Some do not need it. The business outlook was never better and this episode is a mere transient loss in the course of trade. While the town was burning, many sad hearts were made glad through the kindness of friends and neighbors, by sharing their home with those less fortunate in losing theirs, and as we stand now, the great heart suffers but survives. The bright star of the west still shines. It was remarkable that no merchant or business man made any effort to try to raise prices on any commodity, although there was a shortage of some necessities. Other towns in the Hills that had a supply of articles needed on hand, graciously responded to all requests and shared with them. Western spirit never showed up in clearer light than now in the time of distress."

THE HUNTING PARTY

Some of the pioneers of the early days varied their experiences of washing gold and fighting Indians with a hunt for buffalo and the trapping of beavers out on the vast plains of the Black Hills. One such party as this was organized in the fall of 1880 consisting of Boone May, Frank Howard, Fred Willard, H. O. Alexander and later Captain Willard. Boone May was the leader of this party as he had been brought up on the frontier and had hunted buffalo before. The party left Deadwood, in November, 1880, crossing the Belle Fourche River about where the city of Belle Fourche now stands and while there Alexander succeeded in purchasing a fine shepherd dog from a man whom he met there, for the sum of $2.00. This purchase proved to be a very valuable investment.

The party finally established a camp at Chalk-butte, now in Carter county, Montana, as the winter was very severe and long. Game was very plentiful as will be realized from the fact that Boone May killed twenty-three buffalo, Alexander and Fred Willard killed fifteen deer in one day. Howard went back to the Hills in December and Captain Willard went out to the camp in January, 1881. The winter was spent in hunting and trapping and going back and forth to the trading stations to obtain supplies. While at the Stoneville station Captain Willard received word that a large party of Indians were leaving the Pine Ridge Agency and going north for the purpose of arresting all hunters and trappers found between the Little Missouri and Yellowstone Rivers. Fred Willard set out to warn all the men in the prescribed area, of the coming of the Indians, for to go upon the Indian reservation was in those days considered as an unfriendly act and the agents upon the reservation supported the Indians in their efforts to prevent the trespassing on the part of the white men. A large body of hunters and trappers had gathered and they set out hunting for the Indians whom they located on Box Elder Creek in Carter County, Montana. The Indians rode after the white men and after a while when a parley had been given a half breed Indian interpreter rode up and was informed that there was a large body of hunters and trappers who were very active for a fight and that the Indians had better strike out for a new territory in order to avoid trouble. This advice was followed by the Indians but in passing to the north of this party they met with a hunters' camp known as the Berry Wilson hunting party and the only one who escaped was Berry Wilson, the other men being killed by the Indians. After the Indians had passed on from the territory the men set to work to hunt game. Captain Willard went back to the Black Hills while the rest of the men still remained in the party. Boone May and Fred Willard went out to hunt and trap contrary to their promises and they went on into the Indian reservation where they proceeded to hunt near their camp in what is now Perkins county, South Dakota, near the present postoffice of Meadow. They met with great success in their hunting and trapping and were just about to decide to turn back to the Black Hills before they might be overtaken by Indians and were lying about their camp fire planning a homeward march when the little shepherd dog began to bark and yell, and sure enough sneaking down upon them, was a large party of Indians not more than three hundred yards away. The Indians immediately charged, Boone May yelled, "Cover boys" and in the fraction of a short minute the camp was in an uproar. One Indian charged up to where Boone was standing with a shell jammed in his rifle and he dropped his rifle, pulled his six shooter and the Indian fell dead near the fire. Fred Willard fired a few rounds and then ran out and caught a couple of ponies that had been used for packing and hurried them over a bank out of the firing line and returned to the fight. By this time the Indians had killed all the white men's horses excepting the two rescued by Willard and the little dog, but none of the hunters were injured. The Indians decided to quit the fight and withdrew carrying with them their wounded men. They left behind them six dead and one wounded Indian close up to the fire whom Boone May soon put out of his misery with a knife. There were also twenty-two dead Indian ponies on the field. May was a fatalist and after the fight was over commented on his favorite subject stating that "A man will not die until his time comes," and in order to prove his argument said to Fred Willard, "Now that Indian shot at me twice when my gun was jammed. Now what would you call that?" Fred Willard replied, "I would call that damn poor shooting," and that ended the argument.

The hunters now immediately packed their goods and hides and struck out for the Hills on foot, arriving at Crook City in good order. Needless to say their friends who had heard of the fight and the roaming band of Indians out on the reservation were delighted to see the hunters return safe and sound.

THE PIERRE TRAIL

The writer well remembers Judge Church's advent into the Hills. It happened to be my run the morning he embarked for Deadwood. I had two coaches that morning, a regular and extra. William Sample, one of the shot gun messengers rode on the extra. The passengers aboard my coach were Judge Church and his family and the wife of the bookkeeper of the Homestake mine at that time. The stage and freight outfits used to cross the river to Fort Pierre on a ferry boat. The weather was stormy and the roads bad. About a mile from Fort Pierre we had to pass through a canyon and came near upsetting. The soil was a sticky clay called gumbo. The old settlers about Pierre know what gumbo is. It took us seven hours to get to Willow Creek. It was pouring rain and the creeks were all high and hard to ford. Mr. Sample and I were obliged to carry the passengers across the creeks, the drivers doubled up, making an eight horse team, and forded all the creeks. Mr. Sample and I had to ride the leaders. We were eighteen hours going from Plum Creek to Mitchell Creek. We all took a spade along for we knew what we had to contend with. Both of the drivers tied their lines to the break staff, took a paddle and got down on one side of the coach and Mr. Sample and I got down on the other side of our respective coaches. The wheels would clog with gumbo with every revolution, and we would have to clean it before we could make another roll.

We were four days getting to the Cheyenne River. The river was still high, although it had stopped raining and the roads had dried up. We loaded the express, mail and passengers on to a scow, and landed them on the other side. The drivers doubled up their teams and forded the stream with the leaders. The water came into the coaches and wet the seats. When we arrived on the other side we reloaded the coaches, satisfied the wants of the inner man and started out again.

When we got to the top of Cheyenne hill the roads were good. The country lying between Pierre and Cheyenne river was an Indian reservation in those days. No liquor could be obtained on the otherside of the Cheyenne river, from which source the drivers would occasionally fall off the "water wagon."

The messengers had no control over the drivers except to keep their time and report them at Deadwood or Pierre. On this occasion one of the drivers got hold of a bottle of liquor. We were riding along at a twelve mile gait, and frequently one of the drivers would drive up alongside and both would take a swig out of the bottle. The drivers' names were George Dean and Kid Ellis. We were going down a gully about 12 o'clock at night and a mule train had been through the day before and cut up the road. The wheels on one side dropped into a deep chuck hole and upset the coach. Fortunately nobody was injured. It took about half an hour to right up the coach. We then resumed our journey to Lone Tree station. We finally arrived at Rapid City when it commenced to snow and on the way from Rapid City to Sturgis Mr. Sample and I became snow blind. This rig was drawn by four horse teams. The meal stations were Lance Creek, Medicine Creek, Cheyenne River, Rapid City, Sturgis City and Deadwood. The rest were way stations professional bullwhackers and mule skinners. The run could be made in 36 hours on good roads.

The drivers would know within five minutes when the coaches would arrive on good roads. They would have their teams harnessed and ready to lead out immediately on the arrival of the coach. The horses were trained like fire horses and knew their respective places. A change could be made in three minutes. Horse was the chief topic of conversation among the drivers. Their off leader and night wheeler were topics of general interest. Their ambition was to swap horses and match up their teams better. When the superintendent, "Old Gid" as he was called, came around on a tour of inspection they would use their power of persuasion for him to make a change. Sometimes he would and then a row would ensue. The names of some the drivers that operated along the route were, Hank Williams, Red Raymond, Ben Gee, Geo. Dean, Jack Matlock, James Callahan, Kid Ellis, Stuttering Dick and W. L. Bronson, who was afterwards agent at Rapid City.

A messenger accompanied every regular coach. A messenger's duty was to time the drivers between station—they having an allotted time to make a station—and to deliver all mail and collect all moneys at meal stations. The messengers had charge of all mail and express and were expected to make themselves generally useful along the route. The names of some of the regular messengers were Nerm Seebold, Joe Slattery, Johnny Hunter and Joe Goss. The writer of this article was also a messenger over this route.

The company had a treasure coach that used to leave Deadwood the first and fifteenth of every month, taking out the bullion from the Homestake.

The bravest men and the best shots the country could produce accompanied this coach. They were heavily armed with Colt revolvers attached to patent leather belts and filled with cartridges, also a shot gun loaded with buckshot. They were called "shot gun messengers." The names of some of them were Scott Davis, William Sample, Johnny Cochran, William Brewer, Eugene Decker and Jesse Brown.

There were many distinguished men that used to ride over the line. Among them were Judge Gaffy, Judge Moody, first United States senator from South Dakota, Judge Church, afterwards governor of Dakota and Alaska territories, and the sheriff of Lawrence county to carry prisoners over the route on their way to Detroit, Michigan. Whenever they made a turn to the left they would pull the line, to the right when they would jerk it. Short turns were made by the wheelers. The mule skinners used shorter whips than the bull whackers. Experts claim they could sever a fly from the leader's ear. Twelve of these teams made up a mule train. Pierre, now the capital of South Dakota, was a wild and woolly town in the early days, and the officer of the law was an unknown quantity. People were not safe to travel at night unless they were heavily armed, and lanterns were used to guide the pedestrians before the days of street improvements. It was a common occurrence for a bull whacker to step out from a low dive and shoot out the lights of a belated pedestrian and then rob and murder him A desperado by the name of Arkansas lived at Fort Pierre. Arkansas had murdered several men and was a frequent visitor to Pierre. The people feared him for he was a dead shot. He and his companions were notorious in their outlawry. The citizens organized a vigilance committee, and ordered Arkansas and his companions to leave Pierre. They became frightened and complied with the request of the committee, but shortly after Arkansas got on a protracted spree and returned to Pierre and started to shoot up the town. The vigilance committee commenced camping on Arkansas' trail. Arkansas ran down the banks and hid in the brush. The vigilance committee followed him and called him by name. Arkansas fired at them. The vigilancers responded with a volley and they riddled him with bullets.

Many of the early settlers met their death over the Pierre route by Indians. The spring following the ice on the river gorged below Pierre. Pierre is located on low bottom lands rising to a higher plateau in the back ground. The business men used boats to transfer goods to the highlands. Many of the bull whackers were hard up that spring. They commenced thieving and the vigilantes rounded them up, loaded them in boats and sent them across the river.

Pat Comfort, the first sheriff of Pierre, protested

but it was of no avail. The Northwestern Stage Express and Transportation Company owned the finest stock and coaches west of the Mississippi river. The stage stations commencing at Pierre were Willow Creek, Lance Creek, Plum Creek, Mitchell Creek, Medicine Creek, Bad River, Box Elder, Rapid City, Spring Valley Ranch, Sturgis City and Deadwood. Two hundred miles over a mostly prairie country. The stations were twelve relays of horses between Deadwood and Pierre. The old time Concord coach, hung on thoroughbraces, with front and hind booth, for mail and heavy luggage was the rig used.

The early settlers of Pierre experienced a typical frontier life. Pierre is situated on the east bank of the Missouri River. The Chicago and Northwestern Railway established a terminal at Pierre in the eighties. The Northwestern Express Stage and Transportation company previously operating at Bismarck moved to Pierre and started a stage and transportation line from Pierre to the Black Hills. Fort Pierre is on the opposite side of the river from the town of Pierre. The freight was shipped via Sioux City and transported up the river to Fort Pierre prior to that time. Yankton was the capital of Dakota Territory at that time. The pioneer freighter controlling freight from Fort Pierre to the Black Hills was Fred T. Evans. The freight was shipped to the Hills by means of bull and mule outfits. The transportation wagons were of the prairie type with square box and canvass top manufactured by Studebaker Brothers of South Bend, Indiana. A large lead and two shorter train wagons were hauled by twelve yoke of Texas cattle constituting a bull team. The trails had short tongues and all three were coupled together. Twelve teams made up a bull outfit under the supervision of a wagon master. The names of some of the wagon masters were Louis Hartzell, Dick Mathieson, Jesse Brown, Mr. Silverthorn and Mr. Schofield, and a man known by the nickname of Tex Hemphill. The teamsters were called bull whackers. They were a rugged class of men and were heavily armed with revolvers attached to patent leather belts. They wore wide brimmed cowboy hats. They used a whip thirty feet long with a buckskin cracker on the end. The stock was three and one-half to four feet long. The crack of the whip was like a shot in battle, and the bull whackers perverted language making a bull team haul through a bad mud hole created discordant bars of music, and the bulls knew they had to go some. A bull team traveled ten miles a day on good roads. They would travel through the cool of day, and when they stopped to satisfy the wants of man and beast they would form a corral, driving one-half of their wagons on one side of the road making an aperature large enough to yoke up the oxen. When they yoked up chains were placed across the gap at each end so as to keep the cattle together. A camp was used to cook meals. The bull whackers' sleeping apartments were their wagons. A herder had charge of the stock at night. In case of an Indian attack they would form a corral by driving the wagons together in a circle. They would drive the cattle inside the enclosure and throw up breast works against the wheels. Texas cattle could do quite a running stunt coming back from the hills empty. The bull whackers and mule skinners on arriving at Deadwood or Pierre would don their war paint and go out on the war path. They put themselves in fighting trim by fire water of an alcoholic nature.

A mule team consisted of eight or ten mule teams driven double. There was a saddle on the nigh team mule for the skinner to ride. A check-line extended from the nigh team mule to the nigh leader and attached by a jockey stick to the off leader and was used to guide the team.

Deadwood was the next station after leaving Sturgis, the end of the route. The roads were bad and the passengers had to walk up all the hills. Mr. Sample and I had to carry the children.

On another occasion while crossing Box Elder

Creek when the water was high the driver got the coach stuck in the creek and we had to get down and cut the horses loose. The driver went on to Box Elder station with his horses but I had to remain on the coach all night wet and shivering and watch the mail. The driver returned in the morning with two four-horse teams and pulled the coach out onto dry land. We then resumed our journey to Box Elder station.

Calamity Jane and Wild Bill were picturesque characters. They were Black Hills pioneers. Calamity usually traveled in male attire. Her costume when on dress parade was a buckskin suit nicely decorated, broad brimmed cowboy hat, patent leather belt filled with cartridges and two Colt navy revolvers attached. She was an expert with the whip and a dead shot with a revolver or rifle. She had a warm heart and a strong love for her friends, which was characteristic of the early settlers of the Hills.

Harry Ashford.

THE DEADWOOD FLOOD

In the month of May, 1883, there was a lot of snow in the hills surrounding the city of Deadwood. The weather had turned out very warm and the deep blanket of snow began to melt and soon became very slushy. About eleven o'clock in the forenoon of a bright day of May a rain began to fall and within a few hours the melting snow began to rush down the hillsides in torrents of water. The creek began to fill with water from the melting snow, and falling rain, and continued to rise as the hours passed on. In the upper part of Deadwood there was a man by the name of Chandler and his wife who kept the toll gate and lived in a house nearby. This house had been built by H. A. McDonald who was a near neighbor of the family. In erecting the building he had placed it upon piling about which the dirt later had been thrown and realized that the foundation of the building was therefore very weak and unsafe. He advised

Mr. Chandler and his wife to get out of the building and go to higher ground. However, they insisted that there was no danger and retired on the night of the day of the rain with full confidence in the stability of their home. In the house at the same time was a man known by the name of Gus Holthusen. The night was passed without any unusual incident, although the water continued on in its torrential course, but about daylight the flood waters had finally succeeded in undermining the foundation of the house and it suddenly tumbled over into the raging water, carrying with it the three human beings. The body of Mrs. Chandler was found a few days later, after the water had subsided, in the sand along the bank of the lower town with every stitch of clothing except a waist, torn from her body and her hair so matted and filled with sand that it was impossible to do more than simply brush the outer strands. The body of Chandler was found some distance from where the house went in, by a little boy who about a week or more afterwards in going along the side of the creek noticed a human hand sticking out from the drift sand. The body of Holthusen was not discovered until long afterwards when people engaged in removing the drift wood and debris that had collected in the lower part of the gulch found it with the feet sticking up and the head down and jammed among the trash. He had been clothed with brand new boots and his other clothing, but so terrible had been the force of the raging water with the timbers and rocks rushing by that there was nothing on his body when found except one boot and a leather belt.

Great property loss also ensued as the torrential waters went rushing down the mountain gulches. Houses and small buildings were carried away and strewn along the banks, bridges were torn out and general havoc done to the city in the sum of $250,000.

THE DEATH DEALING BLIZZARD OF 1896

On the 26th day of November, Thanksgiving Day,

the morning of the day was rather mild, only a few flying clouds were to be seen, and the sky had a hazy appearance, but was as calm as a midsummer day. Joe Le Fors, a stock detective from Wyoming, A. P. Long, a stock detective for South Dakota, and myself had planned to start on a trip of about one hundred miles to the lower Cheyenne River. I did not like the appearance of the weather; neither did any of us for that matter, and was rather reluctant about starting. Finally we agreed to wait for dinner and if it did not grow any worse we would go. So I went to the stable, hitched up my team. Joe LeFors was in the buggy with me and Long on horse back. We had proceeded only a few minutes until the storm broke loose in all its fury. We concluded that as long as the storm was on our backs we could reach Farwell's place, about twenty miles east, which was a favorite stopping place.

The wind increased in velocity, the snow in quantity, and the atmosphere colder and full of electricity. In crossing a gulch only nine miles out the horses in floundering through a drift broke a single tree. We hunted for some wire along a fence near by and fortunately found enough to fix up the break and while doing this became pretty cold from exposure to wind and snow. Continuing we came to a ranch house, and thought to stop there but found that a family had just reached there and was unloading their furniture, so concluded to go on to Roscoe Keene's ranch two miles further. Before reaching there, darkness had settled down, and was so intensely black that we could not see our hands before our eyes. The wind was blowing with hurricane strength and the worst blizzard in the history of the Black Hills was on. Our horses were blinded by the snow packing inside of the blinds, covering their eyes completely, and turn which way we would, it seemed as if the wind was in our faces. We did not succeed in reaching Keene's. After wandering around for some time we gave it up. I believe now that we were going in a circle. At this time we thought to find a school house that should be close so we hunted up and down, back and forth as we supposed, but found no school house. Things began to look serious if not desperate. Our horses were really refusing to move, so we thought the only thing to do was to turn them loose, which we did and started on foot to try and make it back to the farm house which we had passed, the one where the family were just moving into. Fortunately Providence appeared to be on our side, for we had not proceeded far until we ran against the school house fence. We were soon on the inside, but the snow had drifted in at the windows and under the door so as to cover almost the entire floor. There was no wood in the house, but floundering around outside we found a pile of wood under the snow. It was dry and in about an hour the room began to feel a little warm. Then it seemed as if we were getting colder, and did really feel the cold more than previously. After a while we began to take stock of ourselves, and found A. P. Long was pretty badly frozen about his face and neck. My face and nose was frosted considerably but by rubbing with snow it did not give me any serious trouble. The storm kept up all night and until about eight o'clock in the morning, but by noon the sun was shining. The wind ceased and there was not a cloud in the sky. We looked out and there was our buggy about three hundred yards to the east. The snow was drifted in places higher than the wire fences.

There were several lives lost in this storm. Jerry Millin, Scotty and Robert Carson were moving a band of sheep out to the J. D. Hale ranch, camped on a creek where there was plenty of wood, but could not keep up their fire on account of the fierceness of the wind and drifting snow. Scotty froze in bed. Millin and Carson started to reach a ranch house. Millin fell and perished within sight of relief. Carson managed to reach the door and fell exhausted, but had been heard and was taken in and cared for. He lost his toes on both feet. Five others in different parts of the country perished in this storm.

A Dakota blizzard is something that I cannot accurately describe, and no person that has not experienced such storms can really know and understand the immensity and the bewildering effect of a real blizzard. In one home northeast of Sturgis, the son, a young man, went to the barn to care for the stock, and not returning in the expected time his father went to look for the boy. He found him in the haymow snugly covered in the hay. The boy had concluded not to try to make the trip back to the house, but the father thought they had better make an effort to do so rather than take chances in the hay. They made the attempt but never reached the house, for both were found frozen after the storm.

THE STORY OF BLACK HILLS GOLD JEWELRY

Black Hills gold jewelry is always admired by people coming to the Hills and many times questions are asked about the origin of the design. The pattern consists of grape leaves and grapes, and the leaves are always in two colors, red and green, which are obtained by using two alloys. Gold alloyed with copper produces red, and with silver for green color. The same general design is carried out in nearly all articles, such as stick pins, brooches, hair pins, bracelets and rings. Black Hills jewelry is now sent practically to every state in the Union, and even to Europe. A matter of fact story is to the effect that, away back in the early days, when the Indians were still on the war path, at times, a couple of young men were making their way to the famous Eldorado, the Black Hills. They had started from Pierre with a freight outfit, but went out hunting one day, and not being acquainted with the lay of the country, took the wrong direction for camp. They finally managed to get back to the wagon road only to find the outfit gone. At one point they found some bacon and braed, which one of the thoughtful, kind hearted freighters had left for them provided they should happen to come that way. This appeased their appetites for a day, and they forged ahead. But there was nothing else for them to eat. They came to a small stream, and drank their fill, but that was the last of either water or food for nearly two days. They crept on, the awful fear of starving staring them in the face. Finally they saw ahead of them what they hoped might be trees, and if so, water. After hours of painful tramping they realized that they had not been deceived. Trees were ahead of them. They were so weak through lack of food and drink that they could scarcely drag themselves along; and then they feared that Indians might be lurking in the shade of the trees, which, however, seemed to be their only salvation. At last reaching the friendly trees there was shade but no water. When about to give up and resign themselves to their fate, one of them upon looking around espied a low hanging grape vine, and several bunches of lucious ripe grapes. Their lives were saved, for the grapes were both food and drink. After eating enough to partly appease their hunger, they crept by the side of a fallen tree covered with weeds and vines, where they would be hidden from Indians, should they happen to be thereabouts and went to sleep. When they awakened they found more of the grapes, and, much refreshed, started on their way. They learned later that the place of their salvation was the Cheyenne river close to Frank Cottle's ranch. Much to their delight another freight outfit came along, who, upon hearing their story, gave them a square meal and let them work their way into Deadwood, where one of the young men, who was a jeweler, a short time later found work in a jewelry shop. Being something of a genius and original at that, he experimented at times, when not otherwise engaged, and one day showed his employer the result of his work, saying, "The original of that saved my life on my way to the Hills." The jeweler was delighted with the design placed in his hands. It was a gold ring embellished with grapes and grape leaves, in colors as are to be seen now on the beautiful jewelry, the pride of the Hills, and the prized souvenirs of visitors to this section. So popular did the conceit of the young man's brain become that all his time was given to making the articles that have since become known the world over.

Alice Gossage

LANGUAGE OF THE ROUNDUP

The range land is rich in idioms, corruptions, abbreviations and adaptations. The cow puncher's vocabulary is replete with short but expressive terms which should be of interest to all patrons of the roundup. In the early days of the panhandle Joe and Jim Maverick were such constant and persistent rustlers, that any slick ear found on the range and about which there was any dispute would be turned over to the Mavericks and hence the term Maverick.

"Slick ear," a yearling that has escaped the branding iron or being ear marked.

"Roundup," the spring and fall gathering of cattle on the ranges in order to brand the calves and make shipments of beef.

"Remuda," a Mexican word meaning the herd of saddle horses used by the cowboys when on a roundup.

"Chuck wagon," the moving commissary of the roundup.

"Chaperajos," the leather or hairy leggins worn by the cowboys as protection against chapparral or or mesquite brush, or the weather, which in accordance to the cow punchers disinclination for long words has been shortened to "chaps."

"Cayuse," an Indian pony.

"Broncho," or "bronk," Mexican names meaning, rough, wild or mean, being applied to the native or unbroken horses. Wild horses distinguished from the bucking horses. These are horses native to the range which have never been handled.

"The Outlaws," a term applied to a horse whose spirit is unconquerable.

"The Sunfisher," a movement some horses have of twisting in the air, and sunning their sides. A sunfisher is generally very difficult to ride.

"Pulling leahter," a term applied to a bronk rider in grabbing any part of the saddle in riding a bucking horse, in order to steady himself. "Choking the Horn," "Squeezing Lizzie," "Grabbing the Post," "Reaching for the Apple," "Holding the Jug Handle," "Safety First," "Shaking Hands with Grandma," are all synonyms of pulling leather.

"Riding straight up," consists of rider sitting straight up in saddle holding the halter in one hand and the other in the air.

"Riding safe," sitting close to the saddle, legs tightly clinched against the horses sides, and spurs set firmly in the cinch.

"Sloppy riding," sitting loosely in the saddle allowing the body to flop about in response to the pitching of the animal; not considered good form by competent judges.

"Close seat," steady and firm seat in the saddle, otherwise called "sitting close to the plaster."

"Bucking straight away," consists of long jumps straight ahead without any twists, whirling or rearing, an easy horse to ride.

"Swapping ends," a movement peculiar to a bronk where he quickly reverses his position, making a complete half circle in the air.

"A fall back," a bronk which deliberately falls backward with his rider. A very dangerous animal and usually barred out of contests.

"Seeing daylight," a term applied when a rider leaves his seat with each jump of the horse, so that spectators can see between rider and saddle.

CHAPTER X.

The history of the Black Hills Trails is not wholly that of the struggle between right and wrong, nor of the sacrificing of human life upon the altar of gold. True it is that in the numerous gulches of the Hills where men assembled for a time, the star of hope sank for many, never to rise again. Could the rugged peaks but speak and reveal the secrets that they hold, of deeds of man done within their shade, there would be such a tale of wrong, suffering, sorrow and tragedy, as has never been penned by human hand. But sad as was the fate of some, cruel as was the fell clutch of circumstance, yet the conquering force of progress went on and victory was perched upon its banners. While some were falling by the wayside, others were valiantly going forward and accomplishing those things which made for the establishing of the commonwealth. In this chapter, we gladly turn from the pictures of strife, to the more pleasing scenes of the growth of the industrial welfare of the Hills.

TRANSPORTATION

The great rush of fortune hunters to the Black Hills in the early days, soon rolled up a population that made the subject of food supplies and materials an important one. The problem of supplying the people with the articles necessary to enable them to maintain themselves in the mountains, soon grew to be of great concern, and men of wealth soon saw an opportunity for them in the field of freight and passenger transportation.

The first group of men to prepare for this lucrative field of endeavor. was composed of Sioux City capitalists, Fred T. Evans, Judge Hubbard, John H. Clark, and John Hornick, who organized the Sioux City and Black Hills Transportation Company. Their first train left Sioux City in April, 1875, but when near Gordon, Nebraska, the government troops met them and destroyed the entire outfit and left the peo-

Cheyenne and Black Hills Stage

ple afoot. But the company was not to be defeated and as soon as possible took up the work again and became one of the largest transportation companies to the Hills, the main road being from Pierre to the Hills. It employed from 1000 to 1500 men and wagons, 2,000 to 3,000 oxen and 1,500 mules. About the same time, the Witcher Company was organized and prospered for a time, but did not reach the volume of business handled by its competitor. Other freight companies of lesser importance maintained trains and an enormous amount of merchandise was hauled over the various routes to the several mining camps of the territory.

To handle the passenger traffic and express articles, a more rapid system of transportation than that of the ox teams and heavy wagons, was required and the Cheyenne and Black Hills Stage Line was projected by Gilmer, Saulsbury and Patrick, in 1876. The first attempt to open this stage line was made in the spring time, but the Indians were too hostile and the effort failed after the loss of several head of horses and the station houses. In July, 1876, they got through their first four-horse stage coach, but on the return trip from Custer, the Indians made a successful attack upon the coach, killed the driver, and took the horses from the coach, leaving the passengers to shift for themselves. In September, 1876, all obstacles were overcome and the line established to Deadwood.

Over this line was carried the gold bullion from the mines and in order to lessen the chances for robbery, Superintendent Voorhees built the famous "Treasure Coach," lined with heavy iron plates to resist the attack of robbers and protect the guards within. Many of the robberies and holdups related in this book, took place on this line and were made against this company's coaches, on their long journey from Sidney to Deadwood.

From Bismarck, another company, the Northwestern Express, Stage and Transportation Company, of Minnesota, with R. Blakely as president, opened a

THE BLACK HILLS TRAILS

daily run of coaches to Deadwood in May, 1877. In 1880, they changed the line to start from Pierre to Deadwood, and carried some five thousand passengers yearly for several years. When the railroad reached Chadron, Nebraska, in 1886, they also connected up that city with the Hills.

For a few months in 1876, Seymour and Utter maintained a pony express mail service from Ft. Laramie, Wyoming, to Deadwood, the rate being twenty-five cents per letter. Although the number of letters reached several thousand per trip the project was not long continued and more satisfactory service was established.

The year 1886 saw the decline of the freight and transportation business by small companies. On the 5th day of July, 1886, the first railroad train to reach the Black Hills came rolling into Rapid City amid the tooting of whistles and the joyous shouts of the people gathered to witness this most important event. In due course of time, the railroad was extended to the north towns, and then the southern towns were reached by the B. & M. railway. With the two companies, the Elkhorn road on the east and the Burlington in the central, the day of the pioneer transportation companies closed.

THE STORY OF THE CITIES

The early history of the several cities in the Hills is interesting and a short account will be given here. The founding of Custer it will be recalled was narrated in former chapters of this book and will not be repeated here. The first attempt to lay out and name a town was in the spring of 1875, when the Tallent party surveyed a townsite and called it "Harney." The entire party was removed by the soldiers, and the next attempt to lay out a town was in 1875 during the month of August when General Crook was taking out the second band of gold seekers. This time the name first proposed was "Stonewall" but the second proposed name of "Custer" won out and Custer then became

Hill City Before the Stampede to Deadwood

The story of the starting and the decline of many mining camps in the early days of the Black Hills is an interesting one, and that of Hill City lacks nothing in the telling. It is the second oldest mining camp in the Black Hills and the first to have its rise and fall.

the first established and continuous town in the Hills.

In the month of February, 1876, Tom Harvey and John Miller wandered over to the gulches near Hill City and finding promising deposits there organized and laid out a town which they named Hill City. The incoming prospectors finding Custer filled to overflowing and no further opportunity for them there, migrated on to Hill City and soon this new town was a worthy rival to the first city.

However, the roving miners scurried over the hills far and near and soon came the stories of the wealth of a new place in the gulch of the Whitewood, and Hill City became a deserted camp over night. The new town became the most famous city of the west and we will devote more space to it for the reason that the name "Deadwood" stands preeminently as the historic pioneer city of the Hills.

DEADWOOD

The first attempt to lay out a town along Whitewood Creek was in April, 1876. A party of newcomers arrived in the gulch in the fore part of the month, and camped near where the Northwestern freight depot is now located. Here they set their stakes and laid out a town which they named "Elizabeth Town" in honor of Elizabeth Carl, a young girl of the party about sixteen years of age. Craven Lee and Ike Brown did not quite agree with the restrictions laid down in the organizing of the new town and moving up the creek a little farther, proceeded to lay out a townsite according to their own ideas and named it "Deadwood." The second camp soon outstripped its rival and eventually absorbed it and the whole became known as Deadwood. From the files of the Pioneer of October, 1876, we have been able to reproduce a splendid picture of the town in its infancy.

Early in October, 1875, a few adventuresome spirits, discouraged with the results of their labor in the southern portion of the Hills made their way north, prospecting the various creeks on their route, until they struck Deadwood Creek—so named from the vast bodies of dead timber which cover the mountain sides adjacent to the stream. Here they found good prospects, but had hardly commenced work before winter came on so that little was done in the

DEADWOOD, 1876

way of mining. Enough, however, was accomplished to warrant these hardy men to decide to remain here and endure the rigors of a severe winter in an unknown country, exposed to the dangers of starvation and the merciless bullet of the savage. Conflicting rumors of the gold deposits of this section of the

Hills kept floating through the air, and with the softening rays of the March sun the tide of emigration set in toward the north.

About the middle of April mining operations commenced, but were much retarded by the want of lumber to construct the sluice boxes. As there were no mills in the country, the only way of manufacturing lumber was with the whip-saw. But comparatively few claims were fully worked until about the tenth of June, by which time we had three saw mills turning out on an average of about twenty-five thousand feet of lumber per day. Even with this large amount of lumber manufactured daily, the demand exceeded the supply for building and mining purposes. During all this time a steady stream of immigrants kept pouring in.

A headquarters for miners, where they could get supplies was a necessity. About the 20th of April a town company was organized, and on the 25th of the same month a town was laid out at the junction of Whitewood and Deadwood creeks named Deadwood City.

The first house built of pine logs was laid by Lee and Brown, and occupied by them April 30th and by a singular coincidence the first frame house was erected on the adjoining lot by Gardner and Co. Neither of them are remarkable for their fine finish or beauty of architecture, but in those early days of our history was looked upon as a marvel of beauty and stability and as a marked epoch in the growth of of our city.

From the time the first log was cut out for the first house, the growth of Deadwood has been almost marvelous. Only five months ago the town site was a perfect wilderness of pine trees. Today our city contains over three thousand people, stretching along Deadwood and Whitewood Creeks more than a mile. We have nearly two hundred business houses, a municipal government, mayor, board of aldermen, police, and all the other officers necessary for the administration of justice.

Our mining operations have been prosecuted with a vigor and a degree of success unknown in any other mining country, during the first year of its discovery. Experienced miners and practical business men estimate that the amount of gold taken out within twenty-five miles of Deadwood this season will reach nearly or quite $2,000,000.

Such is a brief resume of what has been done by our citizens in the short space of five months. This, too, in the face of murderous Indian war, without the aid or sanction of the government, and without law, except such as we have improvised for our own protection.

There is much room for encouragement. We have it from the highest officials in the land, that ere long we shall have law, government and protection. Give us those, and within one year Deadwood City will contain ten thousand people, and our mines—placer and quartz—instead of yielding $2,000,000 will add to the wealth of the world, at a low estimate $25,000,000. We think we know it to be true, absolutely, that the Black Hills is the richest country in all the natural elements of wealth on the globe, yet discovered.

We may expect a dull, hard winter, but let us work together faithfully and earnestly, helping each other, upholding each other, knowing that the good time will surely come.

DIRECTORY OF 1878 OF DEADWOOD

Nearly half a century has elapsed since the fame of Deadwood as a wild, western mining camp spread around the world. In the late '70's the little county seat of Lawrence county had some very distinguished men engaged in business, men who in later years became a power not only in the community but in the State and Nation. With the passing of the years great changes took place in Deadwood, and one by one the old time business men either died or moved away until today less than half a dozen of the merchants of the early day period are still there. A former resident of Deadwood has run across a directory of the Deadwood business men of 1887 that will make interesting reading over the state today. In the list there are about four names of men who are there today. Henry Frawley, Jacob Goldberg, Charles Zoellner, and Thomas Whittaker. Although the firm names of a couple of others are still preserved under different management.

The list follows:

Forwarding Agents, Cuthbertson & Young; assayers, C. C. Davis, George H. Hewitt, J. F. Sanders, J. Dosenthal & Co., Sander & Engelskirchen, Ed Sieber, and S. A. Wheeler; Attorneys, A. Allen, Atwood & Frank, Chas. E. Barker, Bennett & Wilson, E. C. Bearley, J. H. Burns, Caulfield & Carey, W .H. Claggett, Gaffey & Frazier, Henry Frawley, F. Gantt, Gooding & Graham, R. W. Hamilton, Harney & Watson, Hayden & Bennett, F. W. Knight, W. C. Kingsley, W. L. Kuykendall, Mose Liverman, J. H. McCutcheon, Miller & Hastie, Morgan Corsen, D. T. Potter, Parker & Story, Ed A. Wetmore, B. C. Wheeler, Williams & Simonton, J. M. Young; Auctioneers, W. S. Travis, Leimer & Co., M. N. Levy, Sam Soyster; Bakeries, Charles Elsner, George Eggert, R. M. Johnson, J. A. Wilson, J. M. Stephens; Banks, Brown & Thum, Miller & McPherson, First National Bank; Barbers, A. Bauman, Girard Bros., Thomas Smith, E. R. Simms, and John Worth; Bath, Frank Welch, Billards, Taylor & Riddle; Blacksmiths, Samuel Ickes, Joseph M. Rickel, T. B. Tarpy, E. C. Taul, F. C. Thulen, Walsh & Langdon; Boots and Shoes, D. P. Burnham, Hamilton & Co., Charles Karcher, J. Losekamp, J. D. Sears, Fred Zipp; Hotels and Boarding, Idaho Boarding House, Wentworth House, Merchants Hotel, Wagner Hotel; Breweries, Black Hills Brewery, A. Schuchardt, Mrs. E. A. A. Brown, Fred Heim, Rosenbaum & Decker, Parkhurst & Conk, Downer & Co.; Builders, M. H. Brown; Carpenters, Kidd &

Benn, John Foster, W. Shaw, Stewart & Martin, Joel Seward, S. P. Wyman; Butchers, Butterfield Bros., N. Frank Sherman, R. H. Geary, Steve Geis, Rosenbaum & Co., William Sauer, Jake Shoudy, Smith Coad & Farber; Candy Manufacturers, Geo. Eggert, Clothing & Furnishings, Sol Bloom, I. H. Chase, Chambers & Cohen, Dan Holzman, I. M. Monash & Co., Munter & Lilienthall, Sol Rosenthall, Straus & Whitehead, M. J. Wertheimer; U. C. Commissioner, A. R. Z. Dawson; Commission Merchants, Daugherty Kelly & Co., Lemar & Co., Mattheissen & Goldberg, William McHugh, Sam Soyster, Waiten & Castner; Confectioners, Cella & Hall, H. Gilman & Co., Hillary & Co.; Corrals, Buffalo Corral, R. L. McGuigan, J. Simpson, D. H. Spear; Dentists, J. J. Clark, R R. Buchanan; Dress Making, Mrs. R. A. Clark, Mrs. E. H. Slassen; Drugs, Bent & Deetkin, F. P. Hogue, Hurlburt Bros, Spooner & Co., H. Seim; Dry Goods, F. Poznansky, Straus & Whitehead, Sol Rosenthall, M. Wartheimer, Welf & McDonald; Firearms, McAulland Bros, Gaston & Shankland; Fruits, Cella & Hall, Mike Curcio; Furniture, Graves & Curtis, F. A. Kriegar, Star & Bullock; Rooms, J. L. Bowman, A. O. Kimball, Mrs. L. E. Lynch; Grocers, Hildebrand & Harding, Mathiessen & Goldberg, T. S. Martin & Co., Deffenbach & Hollenbach, Miller & McPherson, Wardner & Bittinger, Adams Bros., W. A. Beard, Browning & Wringrose, Chew & Co., T. T. Cornforth, Ben Holstein, R. D. Kelly, C. H. Lewis, Vaughn & Decker, J. M. Robinson, W. L. Zink.

The files of the Sidney Telegraph of May 22, 1877, complete the picture of future town of Wild Bill and Calamity Jane, as follows:

It is a peculiarity of this mountain region that hundreds of hills in the same are covered with the trunks of decaying trees. The tall sons of the forest seem generally to have been killed by forest fires for in many places the dead trees are still standing with their trunks and branches charred, while others that have been prostrated by storms are gradually rotting away. The large number of dead trees on some of the hills enclosing the Deadwood Creek gave to it that appellation, and the creek gave the name to the city. The name might with equal propriety be applied to scores of other valleys whose mountain sides are covered with the decaying logs of dead trees.

A year ago there was on the site of this town an impenetrable jungle; now it is the center of life and civilization—of a kind. The narrow valley has within the space of twelve months been covered with a thousand homes. I may here repeat that the definition of the word "house" includes in the Black Hills log houses, cabins, shanties, huts, etc.—the majority of the structures being indeed of the most primitive style of architecture.

Deadwood is now the center of business operations in the Black Hills, the market from which all outlying mining camps are supplied with groceries, provisions, miners' supplies, wet groceries, etc. Bankers, brokers, lawyers, doctors, "et hoc genus omne" are as numerous as the stars of the heavens in the tropics; it is also where the miners within the radius of ten miles resort on Sundays to do their trading, to spend their surplus gold dust in a glorious spree, or to deposit it in faro or other banks—in one word Deadwood is the metropolis of the Black Hills, and she knows it, too, and assumes metropolitan airs with becoming modesty. The streets are daily crowded with busy people quite as much as with loafers and idlers. But talking of streets, I might perhaps rather use the word swamps, for their condition is that of first class bogs, and they are a disgrace to the chief town of the Territory. The mud on Main street is knee-deep and to cross over anywhere else but on the two or three plank crossings is almost a matter of life and death. The condition of the streets of Deadwood recalls to my mind a saying of Lord Palmerton's. During the great stench from the Thames river, some thirteen or fourteen years ago, the great premier once received a deputation from "the city;" after listening to the petition read out to him, his Lordship observed, that it seemed to him, that a conservancy nuisance was, "valuable matter in the wrong place." Now it appears to your correspondent, that there is in Deadwood a great deal of valuable matter in wrong places. The mud of the streets would be of great value for brick making purposes, and the huge piles of gravel thrown up by the miners on the back streets (and where they are a nuisance) would make splendid material for Main street, and greatly improve it.

The condition of the streets of Deadwood is, indeed, a matter that deserves the serious consideration not only of the county commissioners, but of all citizens interested in the welfare of their town.

It is difficult to make an exact estimate of the population of Deadwood. If one were to form an estimate from the number of persons one sees on the streets, one would be likely to place it much higher than it really is. There is only one street which in a curve goes over into South Deadwood, and all the traffic of the town is confined to that street. Hundreds in front of the hotels, restaurants and saloons, and in passing up and down the streets one always meets the same faces again. These idlers help to fill the streets and lend to the appearance of containing a large population. Besides a large number of the people one does see are miners from the outlying camps, who don't live in Deadwood. Looking to the number of houses in the town I do not think that Deadwood, together with South Deadwood and Elizabethtown contains over 3,500 souls.

There are many large two story structures, but the majority of the houses are small one story cabins, made either of logs, or of green sawed lumber. The log cabins are by far the most solid, while the latter kind are extremely frail structures. Made of green wood, they soon shrink, and one can always see through the partitions from one room into the other. They are, moreover, so loosely put together, that a person leaning with his back against the wall is very likely to knock a plank out. The fact is, Deadwood is simply a mining camp—people put up their abodes in the quickest possible way, they are built for the present moment only. Nobody thinks it worth while to spend much on buildings they are liable to desert at any time. Should valuable discoveries be made in any other portion of the Hills, a stampede would take place to that region, and Deadwood might, like Custer City, become a town of many houses, but with a few residents. As long as the mines around Deadwood continue to be the best paying, so long will Deadwood remain the metropolis of the Hills. But even if no exodus to any other camp should take place, it is doubtful whether Deadwood will permanently remain the chief town in the Black Hills. It has a most inconvenient and too confined site for a large town; the locality is too unhealthy and the valley affords no room for a central railroad station. The last defect is a serious one, for the future capital of the Hills must also be a railroad center.

Besides the gold mines in and around Deadwood must give out in the course of a few years and no quartz leads of any value have, so far, been discovered in the immediate neighborhood of the town. The most valuable quartz is further up the gulch between Troy and the Golden Gate, or near Lead City. Large towns are building up in those places, and there is every probability that Deadwood will walk over to Troy, Lead City and Galena. The business men of Deadwood are aware of this fact; some may not be willing to admit it, while others say, we will move with the town. This uncertainty as to the future of Deadwood accounts for the unwillingness of many of the merchants to invest in property, they mostly prefer to pay high rent for stores which they could buy for what they pay out in rents in eight or ten months. Whatever the future prospects of Deadwood may be, business at the present time is good in most branches. Grocers especially do a rushing business and can't get up their goods as they sell them. There was not a sack of flour left in Deadwood last week and the price went up to $32. It is still at $16.00 per sack of fifty pounds. Kerosene oil is worth $3.00 per gallon only, with none in the market.

The hotels are all doing a big business and each of the three principal hotels is a genuine gold mine to their proprietors. The "I. X. L." is kept by Messrs. Vandaniker & McHugh of Omaha, the Custer house by Suiter & Ammernan and the Grand Central by Carl Wagner from Salt Lake City. The hotels are crowded nightly, and it is difficult to secure lodgings in any of them—and still more difficult to do so anywhere else. During meal times the dining rooms in each of the hotels afford a lively scene, and in each of the first two places from five hundred to six hundred meals are served daily. The charges are $3.50 at the Grand Central and $3.00 per day at the other two houses.

Of saloons there is an unlimited number; ditto of gambling houses where all the various games are played night and day. The little joker, a species of three card monte or rather three nutshell monte always draws crowds around the table but in spite of all cappers employed there are but few entrapped into betting.

The two saw mills can barely supply the demand for lumber, that of Boughton & Berry in South Deadwood is the oldest in the Hills, barring the little Red Cloud Agency concern, which arrived a few days sooner. It started first in Custer City, but was moved to Deadwood when the exodus took place last year. The mill turns out 10,000 feet of lumber a day, and about 2,000,000 per annum.

Three breweries cannot supply the worshippers of Gambrinus sufficiently and lager beer is sold only in a few places, one brewery manufacturing twenty barrels each week which is disposed of in their own saloon.

There are several banks, but that of Stebbins & Post monopolizes the bulk of the financial business of the town; they buy and sell gold dust at $18.00 per ounce.

The groceries all do a big business, General Cunningham, of Plattsmouth, Nebraska, is now running one in the same store with W. McHugh. Chambers & Cohen are also located in Deadwood and engaged in the clothing and gents' furnishing goods business with a stock of liquors and cigars at wholesale as well as retail.

I am very sorry to report the death of Mr. Featherstun, the popular and efficient division superintendent of the stage line. It seems that he was enroute from Deadwood to Custer City when the horses took fright at something and in running over the stump of a tree was thrown out of the vehicle and broke his neck.

LEAD CITY

In February, 1876, Thomas E. Carey, while prospecting for placer gold in Gold Run Gulch found enough of the particles to convince him that he was in the right place for gold and he accordingly built the first cabin in that gulch. Later, "Smoky Jones" came into the same gulch, and decided that there was a fitting location to build up a town and accordingly he proceeded to use his pocket compass and with the aid of other prospectors, laid out a townsite in the lower part of the gulch which was named "Washington." Among the first business men to come to this new camp was P. A. Gushurst, who laboriously carried his small stock of merchandise on his back up the steep canyon to his little store. But he stuck to his job and in time became one of the most prosperous and influential men of the Hills country. He was one time mayor of the city that once boasted of the second largest city in the state, and he in due time became president of the largest bank in the western part of Dakota.

In the spring of 1877, a new survey was made by J. D. McIntyre further up the gulch toward the head and the name was changed to Lead. We herewith append a newspaper description of the early mining town which is interesting from the historical standpoint.

This smart mining town, situated about four miles southwesterly from Deadwood City, on the Golden Run, a tributary to the Whitewood Creek, was named Lead City on account of the large number of quartz leads discovered in this neighborhood as early as February and March, 1876. The first mine located in this neighborhood was the Golden Terry, discovered by some French boys on the 21st of February, 1876. It is situated on the Bobtail gulch, between Deadwood gulch and the gulch of the north fork of the Golden Run. The Father DeSmet mine is a continuation of this lead on the Deadwood Gulch slope of the hill. Immediately after many other "leads" were discovered and claims located in the neighborhood, all within a belt of about two miles, extending northeasterly from Lead City and about two miles broad. The miners called it the "golden belt" and believed that no good gold bearing quartz could be found outside of the same. A large number of claims were located last summer within the belt, but the majority of the claims were staked out within the last five or six months, some of the best leads having been discovered only within the last thirty days. Now every foot of ground is taken up in the original belt, but the area of this belt is much more extensive than what the pioneers thought, and quartz of a good quality has been discovered in the hills as far as five or six miles south of Lead City, and prospectors have still a chance of locating good quartz claims.

Old timers all declare that the characteristics of the gold bearing quartz in the Black Hills are very different from what they are in other mining regions. In California, Colorado and Montana, the richest gold is found in a hard, white, flinty quartz. There is little of that kind of rock found here; and when met with, it rarely contains any traces of gold. The auriferous quartz here is of a reddish color; either found mixed up in a slate formation, or, as is more common, mixed up in small lumps with a mass of soft dark-colored matter. From the appearance of the formation one would conclude that the stone had at one time been subjected to a great heat, which had vitrified portions of the same, but have since become partially disintegrated. The deposit is comparatively soft and easily crushed in the mills.

Another characteristic of the formation here is that the quartz is not found in "leads" (such the miners style it) as in other mining regions, but is found in "blow-ups." The difference between a "lead" (in the sense used by miners elsewhere) and a "blow-up" is, that a lead is a well defined vein of quartz, of variable thickness between two walls, generally of granite. The quartz in the Black Hills is generally found on the surface. It would seem as if it had during some volcanic eruption been thrown out from the bowels of the earth and settled on the tops and sides of the hills. Old miners express with grave faces doubts as to whether any good could come from such a departure from the rules of other mining regions. They don't deny the gold bearing quality of the deposit, but hint, that because there is no regular "lead" the deposits will and must soon give out. Now your correspondent does not pretend to be an old miner, but he can not comprehend why the deposits here should give out sooner than in leads such as I have seen at the Centennial mine near Laramie City, and in other places. A "lead" may extend further in one direction, but the cubic contents of the gold bearing deposits in this country seem to be much greater. A good many tunnels and shafts have been carried through these "blow-outs," and some of them to great depths, without reaching the limits of the deposits. Indeed in some places the entire mountains seem to be a mass of gold bearing mineral, thus realizing the stories of Father DeSmet's gold mountains.

Sidney Telegraph.

The city grew and prospered and as the Homestake mine forged to the front, Lead became known far and near as the headquarters of the great gold mine and the city a mile above the sea, this being the height of certain points in the streets. The thousands of homes as they rise tier upon tier above each other, present a novel and interesting sight to the many visitors that throng the steep and narrow streets.

TOWNS OF THE PAST

While "Harney" was the name of the first townsite laid out in the Hills nothing more than merely doing the platting and choosing the name was ever done towards this embryo town, for the Tallent party, who proposed the town, were removed bag and baggage by the soldiers. The second attempt to lay out a town was that in which Custer was finally brought into existence in August, 1875. While the prospectors along French Creek in 1875 had fixed upon the park as the location for a town, however, other miners had passed into another pretty park and found it to be a promising place for a city. The miners had been in the main taken out by General Crook in August, 1875, but in October, most of them had returned, and finding prospects good in their valley, laid out a town and called it "Golden" in harmony with their hopes for the valley. This name was later changed to "Sheridan" in honor of the dashing cavalry leader of the Civil war. In course of time Sheridan became the most promising city in the new mining country and was the scene of the first meeting of the commissioners of Pennington County, and also of the first United States Land Office and the First Black Hills District Court, Judge Bennett presiding. Soon, however, Deadwood came to the front and took the land office, Rapid City became the county seat and the district court also convened at Deadwood, and Sheridan gradually disappeared from the map.

Sheridan was not the only town of the Hills that in its youth gave great promise of importance, only to eventually become nothing more than a memory. In 1875, General Crook in his trip through the Hills had camped in a splendid park to the northeast of the hills and later when prospectors in their search for gold along the Whitewood creek, camped there, they decided to lay out a townsite which they named "Crook City." In this town was established the second newspaper to be published in the Black Hills, "The Tribune," which came out a few days later than the "Pioneer" of Deadwood. So rapidly did the new city grow in size and importance since its creation in the spring of 1876, that when the subject of a county seat for Lawrence County arose upon the appointment of county commissioners by the governor of the state, Crook City was the scene of the first session of the newly appointed Board. But Deadwood exerted the greater pull and it became the county seat, after a very warm contest. From that day, the fate of Crook City was sealed, and the once populous mining town, is now the scene of peaceful farm life, with scarcely a mark to indicate the glory of by gone days.

FORT MEADE

The continual attacks by roving bands of Indians in the summer of 1876, caused the settlers to appeal for the protection of the United States army, and accordingly General Sheridan ordered a military force to be stationed in the north Hills. The camp was located at the west foot of Bear Butte on Spring Creek, in August, 1876, and was named "Camp Sturgis" in honor of Lieutenant Sturgis who was killed in the Battle of the Big Horn. General Sheridan then came out to the Hills and leaving Crook City, in the fall of 1877, rode out over the country north and east of the Black Hills to decide upon a permanent location for a military post. He finally selected a site south of Bear Butte and along Bear Butte Creek at the foot of the Hills, and there as he rode about on a gallop, he indicated where the officers' houses and soldiers' quarters should be placed. Lieutenant Scott, later with the aid of a compass surveyed and fixed the general plan for the several buildings and quarters that comprise Ft. Meade. In the month of August, 1878, the work was completed, and by order of the War Department, the post was named Ft. Meade in honor of the hero of Gettysburg.

To this military post have come many distinguished men and many famous soldiers and the vale at the foot of the rugged hills covered with its purplish green woods has been the scene of many memorable and historic events. For a time "Comanche," sole survivor of the disaster of the Little Big Horn, was held there to recover from his wounds. In course of time there has been built up one of the finest military establishments in the nation and many hundreds of thousands of dollars have been spent to maintain the fort.

STURGIS

While the soldiers were encamped near Bear Butte in Camp Sturgis, the usual crowd of camp followers and grafters that always followed the movements of the military in the days of the frontier, flocked to the new camp and established themselves a few miles distant from the soldiers and beyond the immediate jurisdiction of the army. They chose a site near the abundant springs and water supply on land claimed by John Fredrick, widely known as "Grasshopper Jim." In this camp there were gathered the most lawless and immoral elements of the Hills, all bent on relieving the soldiers of their money on pay day and in the most expeditious manner. One thief was as good as another and naturally there existed a gang who sought to prey upon those who became possessed of the army cash and there being no semblance of law or order, this camp soon became the embodiment of all that was beyond the pale of law and earned the very appropriate name of "Scooptown." Calamity Jane and women of her class were much in evidence as well as expert gamblers. But when the military was removed to Ft. Meade, the permanent post, the army of parasites followed their hosts, and took up their pursuit in the new town of Sturgis which soon assumed all of the unsavory reputation accorded to "Scooptown" and was more widely known by that name for many years, than any other.

The first settler in the valley now occupied by Sturgis, was George Bosworth, who built the first log cabin in the valley on a forty acre tract, in the summer of 1877. William McMillan, also was one of the first settlers in the valley, but he took up his land in the eastern part of the vale and along the creek. where he became possessed of several large springs, later sold to the government for use at the Post. While prospecting along the stream one day, the Indians sneaked into his camp and stole everything worth carrying away, among which was a compass. However, the activity of the magnetic needle was an unexplainable phenomenon to the red men, and they carefully deposited the instrument on a large rock some distance away, rather than chance any further association with the nervous needle.

After the establishment of Ft. Meade, a party of men bent on availing themselves of the prospective town boom wealth, proceeded to lay out a townsite, which they named "Sturgis" in honor of Colonel S. D. Sturgis. The party consisted of Major J. C. Wilcox, J. W. Rodebank, B. G. Caulfield, Judge Dudley, Arthur Buckbee, J. W. Caldwell, and Major H. M. Lazelle An original plot of eighty acres was covered by Barney G. Caulfield, under Valentine script on October 25, 1878. Other additions were later made and for a time lots in Sturgis were regarded with great value, but the expected land boom never became a reality and the town became the ordinary frontier place, until the coming of the new century when it grew into an important trade center.

RAPID CITY

In February, 1876, John R. Brennan and a party

480   THE BLACK HILLS TRAILS

of miners became disgusted with the job of shoveling sand in a vain search for gold and struck out for

Scene on Main Street of Rapid City in 1877

Scene in Rapid City in 1880

Rapid Creek with the design of laying out a townsite. After some days of wandering they finally stopped upon the present site of Rapid City, and here with the aid of a compass owned by Sam Scott, who later joined the party, a plat one mile square was laid out and this constituted the original town of Rapid City, a name proposed by W. P. Martin, owing to the name of the creek. The party was composed of the following named persons: John R. Brennan, Wm. P. Martin, Al Brown, Mart Pensinger, Wm. Marston, Tom Ferguson, Dick King, Sam Scott, John W. Allen, James Carney, Wm. Nuttal, Major Hutchinson.

After many fights with Indians and numerous depressing incidents, Rapid City began to grow and today has become the metropolis of western South Dakota, and by reason of its growing manufacturing interests and the advantageous location, bids fair to become the leading city of the state.

SPEARFISH

In the month of May, 1876, the party of disappointed gold seekers known as the Montana Party, upon their arrival in the north Hills, scattered over a beautiful valley along the banks of the Spearfish Creek, and many of them took up the task of winning their fortunes from the tilling of the soil. H. R. Evans took up the first ranch and Joseph Ramsdell squatted upon a site near the proposed town, his land now being a part of the city. On May 29, 1876, the town was surveyed and Spearfish began its existence in the most beautiful valley and location for a city in the Hills. Here in course of time was established a State Normal school that has developed into one of the best institutions of its kind in the state.

We will not devote further space to the story of the cities in the Hills, for there are many of them, and each has its quota of interesting stories of the past, but to dwell upon them all and give justice to the story would prolong this volume beyond the scope desired. A list of some of the leading towns in their chronological order may be of interest and is as follows: Custer, August 11, 1875; Sheridan, October, 1875; Hill City, February, 1876; Rapid City, February

25, 1876; Deadwood, April 25, 1876; Lead City, spring of 1876; Crook City, spring of 1876; Spearfish, May 29, 1876; Central, January 20, 1877; Sturgis, October, 1878; Piedmont, 1887; Tilford, January, 1888; Hot Springs, December, 1882; Belle Fourche and Edgemont, 1891.

THE LIVESTOCK INDUSTRY

The abundant and luxuriant grasses that grew upon the foot hills and valleys of the Black Hills country, together with the creeks and numerous springs, soon attracted the attention of those pioneers who saw in them an ideal territory for livestock. Accordingly many of them forsook the pan and shovel and followed the more certain trail of wealth through the medium of stock raising.

M. V. Boughton is said to have been the first man to drive a herd of cattle into the Hills. He located on the False Bottom and Red River creek valleys in the northeastern part of the county. However, he was not permitted to carry out his work unmolested, and in one of the attacks by Indians, a herder was killed. Before the summer of 1876 was over, the red thieves succeeded in running off his entire herd and he never recovered any of them. Another herd of some four hundred belonging to Captain Dodson near Crook City fell a prey to the marauding Indians who swooped down upon them and before assistance could be had, the entire herd was slaughtered and the parts desired by the Indians, carried away. Shortly after this, the herd of "Skew Johnson" was driven off by the Indians, and help was sent to his ranch, under the command of Lieutenant Cummings, who had been detailed with a body of cavalry to help guard the settlers of the north hills. He followed the trail of the Indians out to their rendezvous northeast, but when near enough to their camp to hear the lowing of the cattle, he decided that he had better not follow further because of the danger of ambush and left the band with their booty.

The first band of sheep was taken in by a man named Ames, but it was not long before the red thieves had taken possession of the entire herd and proceeded to trail it to their camp. However, sheep do not travel as rapidly as cattle, and fortunately, Lieutenant Cummings in returning from a scouting trip, came upon them as they were being urged onward by the robbers, and the Indians beat a hasty retreat. Ames had given his flock up as lost and was greatly surprised to find the troops returning with the stolen animals.

The miners who rode into the Hills were generally supplied with horses, and from the first days of the new gold fields, we find horses in varying numbers brought into the Hills. An animal so valuable to the pioneers, and to the Indians as well, proved to be a fruitful source of trouble for the owners. It will be recalled that in 1876, so great had been the number of horses, that the price of feed was almost prohibitive in the mining camps, and accordingly herds were established out on the prairies. Such a one was first attempted by Joe Cook and Mike Burton at the head of Centennial Prairie, but soon ended in failure in the big Montana stampede on the 20th day of August, 1876, when Preacher Smith and three other men fell victims to the bullets of the red men. However, John and Rasse Deffebach, were more fortunate in their efforts with stock raising in the seventies. They brought in a herd of cattle and horses from Colorado in 1876, and moved the stock over to the Spearfish valley. They made a business of supplying beef for the miners in the north hills.. Later they established a ranch on the Belle Fourche river which became known as the VVV ranch, which they sold to Clark and Plum. The brothers decided to locate on Sweet Water, Wyoming. John Deffebach, started out with the herd of some three hundred head of horses and cattle, but when he had arrived near a point west of the Bear Lodge Mountains, the Indians were lying in wait for them and the whole herd of horses and cattle was captured and run off by the savages. John Deffebach was shot and killed in the fight, and his body thrown in a washout by the warriors. Rasse Deffebach was in the hospital in Deadwood, suffering from a broken leg, but he arranged for a rescue party, who in charge of Dan Deffebach rode after the robbers, and engaged them in a battle further west of the Bear Lodge Mountains. In the fight, a man named Rhodes was killed and a number of Indians, but few of the horses were recovered.

In 1878, John D. Hale, on his second trip to the Hills, brought with him a large herd of hogs, which he readily disposed of to the miners. He was then employed to help move the Indians to Spotted Tail agency, but returned to the Hills in 1879 with a herd of two hundred and fifty hogs. In 1880, he drove in a third herd of some four hundred hogs and also a band of sheep, from which time he continued successfully to conduct sheep and cattle ranches.

Despite the troubles with Indians and cattle rustlers, the livestock industry thrived, until near the close of the last century, there were over three hundred thousand head of cattle feeding upon the prairies about the foot hills, and Belle Fourche became a great shipping point for the thousands of cattle sent to market each year.

And those fertile prairies that called forth such glowing words of praise from General Custer as he rode over them in 1874 for which he had foretold their future value to the livestock industry, were destined not alone to feed hundreds of thousands of beef stock, but also to place the Black Hills country in the lead as a dairy country. For in the Belle Fourche country not far from the line of Custer's march, was developed the wonderful dairy cow, Hester Aaltje Korndyke, owned by M. J. Smiley. This cow in her time held the world's record over all breeds of cattle, at the then unheard of figure of 46.786 pounds of butter in seven days.

BLACK HILLS NEWSPAPERS

It is an old saying that "The pen is mightier than the sword." The truth of this adage is proved by the story of the knights of the pen in the pioneer days of the Hills. With the first adventurers there came the pencil pushers who sent out accounts of the life in the mountains and kept the world informed as to the wonders of the new territory. Their glowing pictures kept a steady and growing stream of volunteers for the front ranks until the conquest was completed. The dawn of the newspaper industry in the Black Hills may present items of interest to some of our readers.

In the winter of 1876 W. A. Laughlin and A. W. Merrick, purchased a complete printing outfit in Denver, Colorado, and had it transported to the Black Hills, a distance of over four hundred miles. Part of the outfit arrived in Custer in May, 1876, just as the glory of that camp was fading and the fame of Deadwood was sending its splendors far out beyond the hills. However, through the medium of the press and the type on hand, the energetic owners got out a small half sheet, which they called the Black Hills Weekly Pioneer, and then decided to join the throng that was turning their steps to Deadwood. But they were out of funds and stranded.

When the hour of despair seemed to be the darkest, there came to their rescue, a fellow printer and leader of men, who opened to them the door of opportunity that had seemingly closed. Captain C. V. Gardner, who arrived in Custer for the second time on May 14, 1876, and had been in the newspaper game in Iowa, learned of the presence of the embryo journal and sought out the owners. He found Merrick and Laughlin and was informed that they were stranded and anxious to go with the crowd to the new gold fields. Laughlin was suffering from tuberculosis and was lying on a blanket spread over pine boughs. Gardner was informed that they needed two hundred and five dollars to reach the new camp. He said to them, "Will you go to Deadwood, if I will guarantee the payment of that amount on the arrival of the outfit?" the afflicted man, raising up from his pine bough couch, said between coughs, "We surely will."

Captain Gardner went on his way, and true to his promise, when he arrived in Deadwood, prepared and circulated a petition asking for funds to bring the newspaper to camp, heading the list himself with twenty-five dollars. Then there followed Curtis & Graves, Lee & Brown, Judge Kuykendall, Bent & Deetkin, Judge Miller, Wagner of the Grand Central, and Al Swaringen, each twenty-five dollars. The balance of the money necessary to get the plant into camp was paid by Gardner himself when it arrived in Deadwood. Mr. Laughlin was quite sick and asked Captain Gardner to purchase his interest in the paper, which he did and wrote some of the items that went into the first issue of the paper, which was run off on June 8th, 1876. Joe Kubler presided at the press in this first issue as he had also aided in the first half sheet that was sent out in Custer, the month before. The work was done in an unfinished log cabin, but the advent of a real newspaper was hailed with delight and proved a success from the beginning.

The second number was written entirely by Captain Gardner, and at the third issue he became half owner and publisher. His partner, Mr. Merrick, was an able mechanic, but did not attempt to do any writing while Gardner was connected with the paper. He also found that he had a real task on his hands as may be understood from the Captain's account of one of his experiences, which he states as follows: "One hot evening in August, 1876, I was busy turning off copy for the Pioneer. One of my two compositors was off on a 'jamboree' and my partner was out bucking the only weakness he had, 'Faro.' I was wondering how I ever could get the paper out on time, when in came a young man dressed in overalls, and introduced himself by saying: 'My name is Dick Hughes. Do you want a compositor?' I said, 'Yes, if you know your business.' He said, 'Try me.' From that day to this, I have considered Dick Hughes as a friend. This same Dick Hughes is Richard B. Hughes, for years editor of the Rapid City Journal, and the most finished writer that ever wrote a paragraph for a Black Hills paper."

Gardner continued with the newspaper for six months and then sold out his interest to Merrick who handled it alone. On May 15, 1877, the Pioneer came out as a daily newspaper, and on December 1st, 1887, the name was changed to the Deadwood Pioneer.

The first daily newspaper published in the Black Hills was established in Deadwood by Porter Warner, who shipped a complete outfit from Denver, in March, 1877. On the 7th day of April, 1877, the first issue of the first daily appeared on the streets of the western mining town and the enterprise continued under the able management of Mr. Warner until in 1897, when it was sold to the Pioneer and the Deadwood Daily Pioneer-Times was published, under the management of W. H. Bonham and Porter Warner.

During the pioneer days, although not printing in the Hills, a young newspaper man from Sidney, Nebraska, Joseph Gossage, kept the world informed of the progress in the gold camps, through able correspondents that he secured from time to time for publication in his paper, "The Sidney Telegraph." But the appeal of the Hills that touched him in 1876 on his first visit, impelled him to make them his home and in 1877 he opened up a print shop in the new town of Rapid City, a mere camp at the time, and on January 5th, 1878, issued the first copy of the Black Hills Journal. Success crowned his efforts and in 1886 he established the Rapid City Daily Journal, which has grown to be the largest and best newspaper west of the Missouri River in South Dakota. Its great perfecting press that rolls its thousands of copies out per hour for the newsboys to supply their customers, is a monument to his successful management. In ·later years, the bulk of the work has fallen to the shoulders of his most efficient help meet, Mrs. Alice Gossage, whose unlimited energy and commanding ability as a journalist, has kept the daily in the lead of all competitors.

The other daily newspapers now published in the Hills, the Lead Daily Call and the Deadwood Telegram do not belong to the pioneer class, although they have for many years held forth under the varying fortunes of the lives of daily newspapers. Throughout the Hills there are numerous weekly newspapers that enjoy good patronage and supply the readers of their neighborhood with excellent service. But the rich country of the famous region has not been found to be a land of milk and honey for the man who would wrest a fortune from the residents through the medium of the pencil. Ninety-six newspapers have come and gone in the brief period of the development of the Black Hills and we here submit a list of the names and locations of the several defunct publications that have passed to the happy hunting ground of all good newspapers.

Belle Fourche—The Times. Buffalo Gap—Republican, News, Globe. Conata—Herald. Custer City—Black Hills Herald, Custer City Mail. Central City—The Daily Herald, Black Hills Champion, Mining Record, The Index, The Register, The Enterprise. Crook City—The Tribune. Cascade Springs—The Geyser, State Advance. Deadwood—Black Hills Miner, Western Enterprise, Deadwood Press, Evening News, Mining Journal, Deadwood Post, Deadwood Journal, Black Hills Champion, by Chas. Collins, The Weekly Herald, Mining Review, Independent, The Equality, The Evening News. Edgemont—The Kicker, Enterprise. Farmingdale—The Clarion. Galena—The Star. Hermosa—The Pilot, The Hustler. Hill City—Tin Miner, The Mining Review. Hot Springs—The Hatchet, The Hesperian, The Signet. Hat Creek—The Frontier. Keystone—Tin Miner, The Keystone Nugget. • Lead City—The Telegraph, Belt Herald, Lead City Herald, The World, The Daily Tribune, The Daily

Register, The Fairplay, Enterprise, Black Hills Democrat. Minnelusa—Butte County Star, The Boomer. Nemo—Inter Mountain Globe. Oelrichs—The Times, The Advocate. Rockerville—Black Hills Miner. Rochford—Black Hills Central, Rochford Miner, Rochford Homesteader. Rapid City—The Black Hills Index, Black Hills World, Black Hills Democrat, Black Hills Stockman, Northwestern Stockman, The Republican, The Daily and Weekly Union, Evening Herald, Daily News, Stock Review, Flaming Sword, The Daily Guide, The Black Hills Booster. Spearfish—Evening Bulletin, Enterprise, Spearfish Register. Scenic—Observer. Smithwick—Sentinel. Sturgis—Champion, Advertiser, Standard. Sulphur—Match. Terry—Bald Mountain News. Tilford—Meade County News, The Reformer. Vale—Register. Viewfield—Meade County Review. Whitewood—The Sentinel, The Plaindealer.

THE TIN INDUSTRY

While making his geological survey of the Hills in 1875, Professor Jenny reported that indications of tin were found in the country about Harney Peak, but the miners were so absorbed in their search for gold that no attention was paid to the possible existence of this mineral, which had hitherto been imported from Europe. However, in March, 1883, Dr. S. H. Ferguson, was working his "Etta" mine for mica six miles east of the Harney Peak, when he noticed a strange mineral in the ore. A piece of it was placed in a common forge and when melted it looked like silver. A later chemical test of the material disclosed the fact that it was tin and in June, 1883, Major A. J. Simmons wrote an article that was published in the "Rapid City Journal" in which he indicated that an extensive deposit of the mineral would be found.

Further development was made and interest in the new mineral became intense and much prospecting took place. In the fall of 1883 English capitalists had the deposits examined and received a glowing report from their geologists. The Harney Peak Consolidated Tin Company was then organized and proceeded to buy up every claim of value, and plants were erected and several millions of dollars spent in the development of the concern. When the whole control of the tin bearing area in the Hills was had and signs pointed to that country becoming a serious competitor to the big foreign interests, trouble arose between the American and English stockholders, the mines were shut down, and today, the tin industry in the Black Hills is strangled. However, it is safe to state that untold millions of dollars worth of tin are safely locked within the granite hills of the Harney country, until such time as the stockholders see fit to turn the keys in the doors and let the white metal glisten in the kitchens of the world. It is now some thirty years since the engines were stilled but the property and buildings are not allowed to decay or fall to ruin.

THE STORY OF GOLD

The Great Plains of the Northwest extend for hundreds of miles in the vast oceans of rolling prairies. But in their broad expanses there rises the emerald island of the Black Hills whose rugged peaks would pierce the azure vaults of the skies. In this land of enchantment there reigned for untold centuries, the siren whose voice held enthralled the hardy voyagers who had sailed thither from homes afar. For the lure of gold in all times has moved men to deeds of daring, adventure and achievement.

The stories related in this book, were the result of the power of this golden charmer, as it called men from their firesides to its domain, and although many left their bones to bleach upon the shores, yet there were those who survived and became masters of the situation. That the reader may have some conception of the magnitude of the golden stream and the bewitching sway it held over the pioneers, we herewith set forth a sketch of the development of the gold industry.

The first gold in the Black Hills was found by the Indians who noticed the yellow nuggets from time to time, appearing along the banks of the streams, as they sought out the sprightly trout that disported along the stony brooks, rushing down the gulches. Traders and trappers in turn became the owners of the golden pebbles, and from time to time curious and daring trappers ventured into the silent depths of the far away hills. In due course reports were made to the United States government at Washington, as to the existence of gold in the Hills, but the land belonged to the Indians, and the government officials filed the reports and made no further mention of the story.

As years went by, greater numbers of nuggets and stories of gold, trickled past the barriers, out into the general public knowledge and grew in the imagination of the people. So persistent became the rumors, and so great became the pressure upon the officials at Washington, that it was decided to send an expedition of exploration to the region and gain definite information as to the extent of the deposits. Accordingly, General Custer was ordered to carry out this task, as has been heretofore described in the first chapter of this book. The glowing account of the wonderland with its golden streams, so fired the imagination of the people, that there was no restraining the miners, and the gates were loosed.

Then there first came the brave and noble Annie D. Tallent with her little band of companions who landed in Custer valley on the 23rd day of December, 1874, and there at once they found gold in the prospect holes of Ross and McKay on French Creek. After building a stockade for protection against the Indians, they did a little prospecting and sent two of their number, Gordon and Witcher, with specimens of the gold taken from French Creek, back to Sioux City, where they arrived after a long, cold journey, beset with great hardships and privations.

The arrival of the two men with precious metal created a furore among the townspeople and the news spread far and wide. Men everywhere were planning on rushing to the new gold fields, but the opposition of the government kept a restraining hand upon most of them. In the meantime, detachments of the army were sent out to fetch the trespassers back from the Hills. One of the expeditions from Red Cloud very nearly perished in a blizzard that overtook them on their return from a point thirty miles from where the miners were encamped. Hands, feet and faces were frozen and some men permanently crippled from the biting blasts of the howling wind that hurled the icy darts against them at a temperature forty degrees below zero. A third force under the command of Captain Mix, with the aid of several deserters from the new camp, found the unlucky band in their camp, near where they had laid out a new town and called it "Harney." They were given twenty-four hours to prepare to leave and at the end of that time, after secreting their tools and gathering what little of their personal stuff they could carry, the whole band was taken out under escort, and brought to Fort Laramie, from whence they were given transportation to Cheyenne. They learned that they had been fortunate indeed, for the Indians were preparing in force to come upon them in their mountain camp and destroy them utterly. The forced march of the army saved them.

But the miners from all parts of the country turned their steps towards the new gold fields, and despite the watchfulness of the military, flocked to the Hills. Professor Jenny was later sent to the mountains and made a second exploration of the mountains and found the yellow metal widely diffused along the streams. He found miners already along the streams and more still coming into the country. General Crook had taken out a great number of the trespassing prospectors, and later Captain Pollock annoyed, hunted and harassed the gold seekers, but finally, the government withdrew the military opposition and soon the country was dotted with the tents of fortune hunters. The winter of '75 to '76 saw Custer grow into a city of 1400 houses and a constant stream of new comers arriving each day. French Creek and all its tributaries were shoveled and washed from end to end and gulch after gulch was prospected for the yellow particles. It was impossible for all of the throng of gold seekers to find streams and places for prospect in the country about Custer, and as all prospecting at that time was for placer mines, the later comers were compelled to seek new creeks and gulches. Hence the canyons of the northern hills were soon echoing with the tramp of eager searchers and revealing the hidden wealth.

Frank Bryant and a party with him washed out the first gold in Whitewood and lower Deadwood gulches in August, 1875, but found nothing to satisfy them. However, William Lardner and a party of men with him while camping on Little Rapid Creek, heard that prospects for gold were promising in Deadwood gulch and soon were on their way. In November, 1875, he staked out his discovery claim at the mouth of Blacktail in Deadwood gulch and the great Bonanza gulch was soon to be known. Soon the creek was dotted with locations and below "Discovery" at a point where the family of industrious beavers had dammed the stream and made it difficult to prospect, later miners located their claims that proved to be fabulously rich, yielding $27,000.00 in three months. Here also came the Wheeler brothers, experienced miners, and by the fall of 1876 had washed out in their two claims, about one hundred fifty thousand dollars in glittering dust. They sold out their claims together and prepared to turn their backs upon the Hills of fortune. Accordingly, they picked a body of brave men at a salary of twenty-five dollars per day each, and heavily armed, sent them forth to guard their fortunes. Other lucky miners sent along their piles and when they arrived in Cheyenne, the gold on a pair of wagon scales tipped the beam at 1964 pounds, the largest shipment of gold dust to be made from the Hills|

The rumors of the rich gold diggings found in the Deadwood gulch created a stampede to the new field and in an incredibly short time, every available foot of the gravel along the creeks was occupied by prospectors who diligently shoveled and washed the sands. Naturally there was not enough ground to accommodate each gold seeker, and trouble over the claims arose. The most serious controversy that arose and one fraught with potential ruin and death for many, occurred in April, 1876, under the leadership of three men, McNabb, Smith and O'Leary, who gathered a force of one hundred men and advanced the proposition of reducing the size of a placer claim from three hundred feet up and down the stream to half that distance in order to accommodate the later arrivals and give more men a chance. With this body of desperate and disappointed men, the three intriguers, came to the busy toilers in the gulch and served their ultimatum upon them. It was like stirring up a hornet's nest, for it meant taking from the first comers, thousands of dollars, and rights that had been heretofore recognized as inviolate. A miners' meeting was promptly called, which was attended by five hundred excited and determined men. They unanimously voted to each hold fast to the original amount claimed and to fight at the word of command of either of three leaders chosen at the time, among whom was V. P. Shoun. Accordingly the locaters repaired to their several diggings along the stream, armed and ready for the fray, while the leaders stood ready for any overt act on the part of the would-be claim jumpers. And when McNabb and his covetous followers came down the gulches and looked into the angry and grim faces of the indignant miners, they decided that discretion was the better part of valor, and reluctantly sought other scenes of operation But for a few hours Deadwood gulch saw the most tense and nerve racking time of its history. One rash move on the part of those who sought to overturn the law of the miners, and there would have been five hundred maddened men hurling leaden missiles into the ranks of the robbers, and not a one of the hundred trespassers would have remained to tell the story.

The original gold hunting in the Hills was what is known as placer mining. In this process, a trough is made of boards through which the water is allowed to run from the streams. In the bottom of the trough or long sluice box, are placed cleats and into this newly made channel are dumped the shovels full of gravel and sand taken from the creek bed. The water rushing down through the wooden trough, washes the dirt and gravel away, but the gold being heavy, falls to the bottom and rests along the cleats in the trough, where later the miner taking it up with the sand and fine stuff, places it in his gold pan, a large round bowl-like tool about eighteen inches in diameter and two and one-half inches deep, and by careful rocking and washing, removes the sand and leaves the gold dust to be placed away in the buckskin bags, cloth bags being too porous. This later part is called "Panning" and requires great skill to get the proper motion and remove the sand and dirt and at the same time not wash away the small particles of gold.

One other method of mining the gold was used in the early days and that was hydraulic mining, where a stream of water was taken by flume from a source far above the claim and ran through pipes and nozzles directed against the gold bearing gravel and sand and carried the material over the large sluice boxes, where the gold later was removed as in placer mining with the shovel. This process requires capital to start with and was not used by the small prospectors. However, there was a large hydraulic mining industry at Rockerville, commenced in 1878 that ran the water of Spring Creek to the dry placer locations in Rockerville, a distance of seventeen miles, along mountain sides and across gulches, which cost about $300,000.00. The cleanup, however, proved the effort well spent for in five years, there was over a half million dollars in gold taken from the gravels.

With the thousands of gold seekers rushing into

the Hills from all directions, it was not long until all of the gulches and creek beds had been prospected and all desirable claims located. But the old miners well knew that the gold that was found so plentiful in the creek beds, had been washed down from a higher point in the mountains and soon the hill sides were being scratched and dug into by the quartz seeking prospector. The most fortunate of these quartz miners were the Manuel brothers, who on April 9, 1876, located the large vein that was the starter of the great mine, which they named the Homestake. They dug and found a piece of quartz weighing two hundred pounds, which was the richest ever found in that mine. They continued to develop their claim and removed $5000.00 worth of ore the next winter. Senator Hearst of California became interested in the property and upon receiving a favorable report from his mining expert purchased it for the sum of $70,000.00. The Old Abe was also sold for $45,000.00 and the Terra for $35,000.00. And the foundation of the Great Homestake Mining Company was laid.

The turning of the mining industry to the gathering of ore, necessitated a more complicated process than that of the placer method. More capital was required and we find mining companies were soon organized. The first mining company was the "Black Hills Gold Mining Company" organized by Captain C. V. Gardner and other men in Cheyenne. They then went to Denver, where Gardner purchased a ball pulverizer and had it shipped to Deadwood, where it was erected on August 15, 1876, under the charge of Jabez Chase. This was the first quartz crushing mill to be erected in the Hills, but did not prove to be very satisfactory and was soon abandoned. Milton E. Penny, in November, 1876, brought in and had erected, the first stamp mill in the Hills. The stamp mill process of working gold bearing rocks proved much more satisfactory and is used in all the mills.

THE GOLD INDUSTRY IN 1877

With the thousands of miners in the Hills in the early seventies, it was a time when the air teemed with stories of gold production and discoveries. And due to the courtesy of Joseph Gossage, we are enabled herewith to submit an interesting page from the long ago, that brings one back to the days of the gold pan and high topped boots. Let one not think that those were listless times.

September 20, 1877.

Over five thousand dollars' worth of retort from Lead City, was yesterday received at the assay office of Chambers C. Davis. This is the result of one week's work by fifty stamps.

It is the intention of the Father DeSmet Company to erect a sixty-stamp mill a short distance from their arastra before winter. Messrs. Elliott and Parker have ordered the machinery for the addition of ten stamps, which will be run on ore from the Father DeSmet mine.

At a meeting held on Saturday, September 15, a town was laid out one-half mile above South Bend, named Lancaster City, after Mr. Lancaster, one of the owners of the Gustin mine. There are about 200 lots, 25x100 with sixty days allowed after date of location for building thereon. The future of the town is bright at present. There are two ten-stamp mills running on the Gustin and Laura ore; the firm of Spring, Lancaster and Frost are putting up fifteen stamps more, which will make twenty-five in all, and more mills will soon be erected at this place. Black Tail Gulch is well suited for milling purposes, being plentifully supplied with water all the year round, sufficient to run from 400 to 500 stamps. A road is extended from the Laura, Fairview, Keets and Aurora mines. The road will be a good one, 60,000 pounds of ore can be easily hauled over it by a single team. On the Gustin extension mine, Jack Parrot has twenty men getting out ore and having it crushed in the Cunningham mill. There are two boarding houses owned by Mrs. Parrot and Mrs. Springer, which have between forty and sixty boarders. Phillips Bros. are doing a good mercantile business, and a new saloon is in course of erection. The quartz on Black Tail is unsurpassed in quantity and quality, therefore it is only a question of time for this place to rise in importance.

The Keets mine has a daily yield of fifty tons, furnishing constant employment to thirty-five men.

A recent run made from ore from the Homestake No. 1, at Lead City, averaged $16.00 per ton.

Messrs. S. Edwards and company of Central City, have their mill up, and are rapidly pushing the work to completion.

A. P. Moore & Co.'s five stamp mill at Central City, will be ready for operation in about two weeks. It is likely they will commence work on the Keets ore.

Professor Cherry was looking round Gayville, Central City and Golden Gate yesterday for a site for his new sixty-stamp mill. Twenty stamps are now on the road, which, with the accompanying machinery, weigh about 110,000. The stamps for this mammoth mill weigh 850 pounds each. This equals anything outside of the famous Comstock, Nevada.

The Patten mine is located near Keets in Hidden Treasure Gulch. The tunnel is being driven into the hill a distance of 150 feet. The company is working three eight-hour shifts, consisting of six men each. Ten stamps of their new thirty stamp mill are ready for work. When the remaining twenty stamps are in order, they can extract and crush sixty tons of ore per day.

The Father DeSmet Company made a clean-up yesterday from one hundred tons or ore, crushed in the Elliott & Parker's ten-stamp mill. The work was accomplished in eight days, and gave a return of $3,500. The new tramway is a great addition to the works on this mine, as ore can be transported from the lode to the mill at the small cost of twenty-five cents per ton

THE BLACK HILLS TRAILS 499

A clean-up was also made from the Arastra owned by this company, but we have not learned the amount realized.

There are more people in Deadwood today, than there were three weeks ago, and from appearances, we should judge that the immigration to the Hills will be heavy. Of course, there is a large number leaving the Hills every day who are either afraid to winter here or else have not the means, or have reached that stage of homesickness which calls imperatively on them to return to their native heath. In our judgment, we shall never feel the loss of such men as these from our midst. They are only obstacles to the development of a new country, and ought not leave the country they were born in.

The Girdler Ore and Milling Company, at Poorman's Gulch, made a clean-up a few days since on Eureka ore yielded $900. The retort was at $19 per ounce.

Cunningham & Dorrington who up to last week have been crushing the Keets ore at their mill in Central City, are running this week ten stamps on the Eureka ore, and ten on the Gustin Extension. A clean-up on the latter has been made which yielded $12 to the ton.

Prickett, Hayes & Philpott's new mill in Hidden Treasure Gulch is rapidly nearing completion.

Considerable excitement has been caused within the past few days by the discovery of a rich deposit of gold bearing quartz in the Rhoderick Dhu mine in Sawpit Gulch, which has, until the past few days, been considered but of little value. The ore in appearance resembles very much that taken from the Father DeSmet.

Edward Florada estimates the yield of the principal placer claims in the Hills up the first instant, as follows:

No. 1, above, Allen Florada & Co., $65,000.
No. 2, above, Johnson & Co., $70,000.
No. 3. above, Pierce & Co., $80,000.

No. 4, above, Scott & Co., $30,000.
No. 5, above, Thompson & Co., $40,000.
No. 6, above, McIleer & Pierce, $75,000.
The other claims above will average about $30,000 each.
No. 1, below, Hilderbrandt & Co., $50,000.
No. 2, below, Simpson & Co., $75,000.
No. 3, below, Neal & Co., $25,000.
Nos. 4 and 5, below, Neal & Co., $30,000.
No. 6, below, Spencer & Morton, $25,000.
Nos. 7 and 8, below, John Kane, $30,000.
No. 9, below, Jack McAleer, $30,000.
No. 10, above, George Stokes, $20,000.
Nos. 11, 12 and 13, above, Gilmer, Saulsbury & Co., $40,000.

The last clean-up at the Hidden Treasure mill from 225 tons of ore realized $10,500. As a clean-up from the batteries had not been made for a month, it increased the amount to this figure, making an average of nearly $50 per ton.

The twenty-stamp mill of Pinney Bros., is crushing ore from the Alpha mine.

McLaughlin & Company's mill at Central City, is running ten stamps on ore from the Keets mine, and ten stamps on ore from the Pecachor.

A very large quantity of first quality ore is on the dump at the Hoodlebug lode, Poorman Gulch. This is one of the most valuable discoveries in the Hills.

Gold Run presents a very animated appearance. The Golden Star and Homestake numbers one and two, each employs a large number of men who are constantly employed getting out ore for the mills at Lead City.

The Cinnabar mine which was discovered some time ago near Elizabethtown is said to be panning out big.

The owners of the plumbago mine on Whitewood, a half mile from the postoffice, are taking out a quantity and shipping it east in order to have it thoroughly tested.

Messrs. McIntyre & Clapp, mining engineers, have just completed the work of the survey of the Golden Star, Old Abe, Homestake, Prince Oscar and Homestake No. two, the Bonanza mines of Lead City and are now making the map for the same.

THE HOMESTAKE MINE

The first year of gold operations saw over two millions in gold removed from the hills. Since that time hundreds of mining companies have come and gone and many millions in gold have been extracted. The total figure will run over two hundred thirty millions of dollars since the first prospector on French Creek saw the golden gleam in his pan. And today there is being produced each year, out of low grade ore, about six millions in gold by the Homestake Mining Company alone. This mine is one of the greatest gold mines in the world. The main shaft in Lead, the city a mile above the sea, sinks to about twenty two hundred feet below the surface and passes eighteen working levels, ranging from one hundred to one hundred fifty feet apart. The tunnels that radiate out from the mine shafts extend over a distance of sixty miles equipped with a narrow gauge railroad over which are shunted the ore cars by compressed air engines, whose tanks have been charged with the powerful air compresser. Electric lights glisten in the dismal depths with the power sent through them from the generators miles away on the Spearfish hydroplant. Huge and powerful pumps throb and rumble as they lift great streams of water from the underground brooks and send it up to the surface to rush down the mountain gulches, from whence perhaps it had seeped ages ago. Ponderous fans from above drive the bracing mountain air from the hillsides, down to the hithermost burrows of the men. Mammoth steam hoists snatch the ore broken from its rocky caverns unlocked for millions of years in the eternal darkness, and rush it to the surface where it is hauled to the stamp mills. Here the broken rocks are crushed and hurled to their fate beneath nine hundred twenty stamps, which with the roar of an unending thunder storm, pound and crush the mass into tiny fragments that are washed out over large plates covered with quick silver, which quickly seize upon the particles of gold and hold them fast as they would hurry away to seek the bed from whence its fellows years ago had been taken by the eager miner as he rocked his gold pan to and fro. Some particles do escape and are not entirely removed from the grasp

of the sand and rock that has so long claimed them as their own. These escaping bits of sand and gold are called tailings, and after settling in huge dams, are placed in immense tanks containing solutions of cyanide, and here after being treated with this process, twenty-two per cent more are saved to man. Seventy-two per cent was gathered in by the amalgamation plates as the precious metal began its journey under the light of day, and twenty per cent more was rescued by the cyanide process. But six per cent of the beautiful metal outwits the hands of men and goes skipping down the mountain rills to thenceforth rest untroubled by human touch. Thirty thousand dollars is the ransom that would be gained every month by the delivery of these millions of particles from their captors, but engineering and chemical skill has not as yet learned the word that when spoken, shall unloose the doors that hold the golden treasure locked within.

Nevertheless, there has been taken out by the Homestake Mining Company in the forty-four years of its existence, the enormous sum of over one hundred eighty-one million dollars in gold. They have paid out for labor in this task over forty-four millions of dollars. The output in gold each year will approximate six millions of dollars at this time. And in the sixty miles of underground railway there is enough gold ore in sight to keep the huge machinery of the company running full blast for the next twenty years to handle alone. And yet the end of the great vein of gold is not found. The mountain upon which the city of Lead is built is honeycombed like a huge ant hill, and at all times, there is about one-fourth of the population digging, blasting and burrowing away beneath the hills, while above, their comrades, enjoy the splendid recreation rooms, baths, hospitals and libraries furnished to them for their sole benefit by the great corporation.

Some idea of the magnitude of the operations carried on by this powerful company, with its two thousand employees, can be gained when we learn that each year, 1,750,000 tons of ore are hammered into gold, 1,554,117 pounds of dynamite are used, which were each stick laid end for end, would reach almost three hundred twenty-nine and a half miles, that enough caps to explode the dynamite are used, if laid end to end would reach almost thirty-two miles, and fuse needed, would extend almost seven hundred twenty-three miles. To furnish the cable used on the "Old Abe" hoist where the ore is lifted, there is required two hundred thirty-two miles of number 15 wire, weighing about seventeen thousand, two hundred eleven pounds. To furnish coal for the huge operations, most of which comes from the coal mines owned by the company in Wyoming, one hundred thousand tons of coal are used. To supply the electric current necessary, two hydro-electric plants are maintained, of five thousand horse power each. For miles the water of the river is carried through underground flumes so large that the caretakers from time to time, row along in their boats over the stream. A steam plant of four thousand horse power also is in operation.

To erect the enormous buildings, to prop up and sustain the gigantic mass of rock above the tunnels, demands a stupendous supply of lumber and we find that the company owns twenty-seven thousand acres of fine timber and there are several saw mills in constant operation, with several hundred men engaged in the lumbering department. A general merchandise and department store is maintained by the company where all supplies for the citizens of the city may be had. A recreation building for the free use of its employees is furnished, a hospital to care for the employees and their families and supply them with the best of medical care and attention without charge, an old age pension system, insurance against accident and death, and many other aids to charity come within the attention of the company. At the head of this broadminded organization is Bruce Yates, superintendent, who by his masterful executive ability has held the company in the forefront as the model industrial organization in the world, where the welfare and living conditions of its employees are not excelled anywhere.

To tell the complete story of the Homestake Mine would require a volume in itself and is beyond the scope of this book. There were days when great disasters threatened the company, and the future looked dark. Two fierce mine fires put the management to a severe test, but the efficiency of the organization rose to the occasion, and great mountain streams were diverted into the mines until the fires were drowned out in the oceans of water that came roaring upon them.

Then came the arduous task of unwatering the mines and placing them in working order again.

However, enough has been shown to reveal the thrilling story of gold and the latent power that was hidden beneath the pine clad hills. Great as has been the wealth and prosperity of the Homestake, yet untouched billions of mineral wealth still remain hidden in the rock ribbed gulches and fortresses of Nature awaiting the conquering hand of men. Other mines there are in the Hills, many other mines there shall come in the fulness of time.

THE ROMANCE OF ALFALFA

Throughout the far reaching territory over which the Black Hills Trails were blazed, there are now thousands of fertile fields that for a time in the summer, wave like vast oceans of green to be soon followed by the beautiful purple of the blooming plant as it fills the balmy air with the fragrance of its perfume. There live the oldest pioneers of the Hills, the everlasting alfalfa, one of the most valuable forage crops grown in the west. The story of this world-wide wanderer, is quite unique and may prove of interest.

Through the long research work of Charles C. Haas, of Whitewood, South Dakota, who has become an expert and specialist in the cultivation of this thrifty plant, he was successful in determining who was the first men to introduce alfalfa growing into the Black Hills and from whence the seeds came to America. He learned that his friend, William Quigley, trapper, miner and scout of the west in the late sixties, had, in 1881, fed alfalfa hay to his horse on the Bullock ranch near Belle Fourche. From Seth Bullock, he found that the seed for this hay had been obtained by him from Captain Tom Russell from the Cache Valley in Utah, where he had seen the plant grow so luxuriantly. He planted it in the spring of 1881, and it grew and prospered. Bullock, finding it a success, gave seed from the crop to his neighbors in the north hills and in this manner the acreage grew rapidly. Several years later, Samuel Moore from the Piedmont valley secured seed from the same source in Utah, and from his farm, the plant spread over the southeastern part of the Hills. To Seth Bullock, then belongs the honor of having first introduced the alfalfa plant to the Black Hills, and thereby established one of the most historical grasses to be found on the continent today, by reason of the romantic story of the little plant in its long and steady march.

Over two thousand five hundred years ago, there romped upon the great valleys and mountains of the Himalayas in Asia, a pretty girl who grew to be a princess renowned for her beauty. Far to the west of her country, there reigned a most powerful king of a great nation, who upon hearing the story of the beauty of the eastern princess, demanded her as his queen. His wish was the law of the world in those days and the princess became Queen Amuhia of the Babylonian king, Nebuchadnezzar. But the mountain princess from the wilds of the Himilayas, was not content among the teeming millions of the great city on the plains and her loving husband sought to please her by building wonderful gardens for her like unto those of her childhood, wherein were placed trees, flowers and grasses from her homeland. The hardy, purple flowered alfalfa plant was among them, and in time proved to be of value to the king himself who ate of this wonderful grass to cure his digestive troubles.

Then by a turn of the wheel of fortune, we find the haughty dynasty of Babylonian kings crumbling into dust and the Persian armies ravaging the country, and marching forward, feeding their vast herds of livestock upon the enduring alfalfa grass until they came to the Grecian Republics. Here, for seven long years, Xerxes wages the war, and upon the conquered plains, grows alfalfa as forage for his thousands of cattle and horses. And then, through the defile in the mountains at Thermopolae, he drives his millions of slaves whipped to the battle front, until Leonidas and his band of Spartans fall, to be trampled under foot by the

Persian hordes as they flow out over the fertile fields of Greece.

Centuries roll on and Alexander the Great rises from the western front to be master of the known world. In the fiery time of restless youth he ravages the nations, and carries the war across the desert, against the Phoenicians, and in Egypt, still bouyed up with the produce of the wonderful forage grass, alfalfa. Then he cries for more worlds to conquer and dies. But the humble plant that sustained the steeds

Seth Bullock

of his victorious legions as they galloped across the deserts, knew no halt and found new worlds to win.

In its onward march, alfalfa fell into alliance with the Phoenicians, who carried their sturdy ally across the Mediterranean Sea to the City of Carthage and the north coast of Africa, about the dawn of the Christian era. Here it grew and prospered, until its tillers, in the height of their glory and power seven hundred years after the coming of Christ, conquered the land of Spain, and there, in the shade of the beautiful Alhambra, famed for its magnificent splendors, the wanderer from Asia came to feed the Moorish cavalry.

Time with his great levelling scythe humbled the conqueror, exalted the vanquished, and we find the Spanish ships, proud masters of the oceans, sailing the seas to a new world. Pizarro in 1526 lands upon the domain of the Incas, and with him, the conquering ally of his cavalry, alfalfa. Soon in the Peruvian mountains, the purple blossoms perfume the air, as their ancestors did in their far eastern home of Asia, centuries before.

Pizarro and De Soto in their turn play their little part and having played, pass on from the stage of human effort, but the humble grass went marching on through the centuries. Up along the western coast of the continent went the restless throng of treasure seekers and adventurers, and to the land of flowers, California. Here the Franciscans, bent not upon the quest of gold, but the winning of the souls of men, founded their missions and taught the natives the arts of civilization. Here they planted the fruits and grasses of the old world, and here they grew the ever present ally of the conquerors of the past, alfalfa.

From the good fathers of the Pacific missions were sent afar the seeds of the wonderful plant and to the land of the Mormons in Utah came the fame of the enduring grass that made the desert bloom. Here the pioneers found the ally that assured the winning of the plains and its march went steadily forward until the year 1881, saw it form the battle line for its last victory, the Black Hills frontier.

Thus, today, upon the slopes of the Black Hills, there thrive the descendants of the plants that grew in the Hanging Gardens of Babylon and saw the Persian hordes as they razed the most magnificent city of its time; that saw Alexander the Great in the prime of his ravaging and world destroying youth; that heard the agonized cries of the Inca, tortured at the hands of the treacherous Pizarro; that perfumed the incense of the Spanish padres before their western altars, with the fragrance of their purple blossoms.

THE TALE OF THE HILLS

With this picture of peace reigning over the hills and dales, clothed in the royal purple of the sturdy alfalfa plant and the dark green of the noble pines, kind reader, we will close the story of the Black Hills Trails. The memory of the sacrifices, struggles and privations of the men who wended the weary miles of their way, must in the years to come, kindle anew the fires of patriotism and lead men to give full honor to the winners of the west. To know the story of the pioneers is to feel the power of the Hills and the enchantment of the mighty canyons. With the kind permission of Charles Badger Clark, poet laureate of the Black Hills, eloquent singer of mountain and plain, we are pleased to give to our readers, his splendid poem first read at the dedication of the monument commemorating the discovery of gold in Custer valley, had on the 27th day of July, 1922.

THE TALE OF THE HILLS

God made our Black Hills country toward the last.
The plains were spread like mighty tapestries,
Green, brown or white, as changing seasons passed,
Shadeless and flat and endless as the seas.
Fair was the prairie; fair it still appears,
But, tiring of those endless, flat domains,
God built this island in the sea of plains
And kept it for himself ten thousand years.

He built the sculptured peaks and canyon walls
And painted them in red and brown and gray;
And sent the clear creeks glistening on their way.
He planned a thousand creeks and waterfalls
He sowed the red-barked pine trees everywhere,
With aspen, birch and spruce along the streams,
And flower-flecked mountain meadows here and there
Such as an old saint pictured in his dreams.

God made this island in the sea of plains
And kept it for himself ten thousand years,
Free of man's labor scars and battle stains,
And clean of human blood and human tears.
The lazy eagle circled in the blue;
The rough bear dozed in peace before his den;
The dainty deer stepped through the morning dew,
But never was there sight or sound of men.

The prairie red men watched the far blue peaks
Where often storm clouds gathered fold on fold
And lightning laced the gloom in darting streaks
And down the echoing canyons thunder rolled.
"The Thunder Hawk lives there!" the red men cried,
And fled away across the prairie sod.
So through the ages on the mountain side,
The pine trees sang their song alone to God.

Then from the eastern land the white man came,
Driven by high desire and restless blood.
He to the prairie laid his lordly claim
And fought the red man there to make it good.
Far on the plains the dust cloud and the fire
Marked long trails the conquering white men made,
But still no iron hoof or wagon tire
Rang on the rocks within the canyon's shade.

Yet in the end the chosen time came round
And then up Castle Creek, one summer day,
An eager line of blue clad troopers wound,
While gallant, fated Custer led the way.
And soon upon the site of Custer town
The gray past of the lonely mountain land
Changed to a shining future of renown
Bright as the golden grains in Ross's hand.

THE BLACK HILLS TRAILS

Gold! our great blessing, curse, or what you will,
But, curse or blessing, ever most desired,
Gold! the word seemed to leap from hill to hill
And down the plains, like signal cannon fired.
God built our mountain land in love and pride,
And kept it to himself ten thousand years,
Then with that word He flung His bars aside
And inward stormed the Black Hills pioneers.

They were a breed that feared no thunder bird,
Nor ghost, nor imp, nor thing of mortal breath.
Wild with the music of that magic word,
They laughed at Sioux and soldier, storm and death.
Gold! and the timber wolf at close of day
Sniffed the new camp smoke with uneasy whines;
Gold! and the mountain lion dropped his prey
To hear the axes ring among the pines.

And so its ancient ways were changed for new—
This mountain island under prairie skies,
The dread throne of the Indian's Manitou,
The daring white man's last and dearest prize.
Then from the Hills a new stream took its course;
In waves of golden wealth it richly ran,
Millions of gold from that first tiny source—
The doubtful yellow gleam in Ross's pan.

For more than forty years that stream has rolled—
Strange flood tha tstarted here in Ross's pan!
Feeding our country's wealth with yellow gold,
Swelling at last the world-wide wealth of man.
And here in Custer's city we are met
To dedicate these stones that tell the tale,
Lest coming generation should forget
Ross and the men that followed on his trail.

Hail to our pioneers, who played the game
In sweat and blood until they won the stake—
A land worth winning for its golden fame,
A home worth holding for its own sweet sake.
Yes, to the true Black Hiller of today
The gleam of Black Hills sunlight through the pines
Or on the towering rim rock will assay
As high as any metal from the mines!

Hail to these stately Hills we now possess,
Their towns and ranches stored with worldly goods,
Their gulches full of holy quietness
Where God still walks among the piney woods!
Proudly we call them South Dakota's crown,
But when we leave their blessed shades to roam,
And homesick longing dogs us up and down,
We name them in our hearts—the Hills of Home!

Scott Davis, Jesse Brown and A. M. Willard
at Canyon Springs

APPENDIX

BIOGRAPHICAL SKETCHES

Some readers may wish to know a little more of the life history of some of the actors mentioned in the preceding pages, and accordingly we herewith present intimate sketches of a few of the pioneers, trusting that they may prove of interest. A biography of the many pioneers who have nobly done their part in the history of the Black Hills would require too much labor to prepare and would be beyond the purpose of this volume.

CAPTAIN WILLARD

A. M. Willard was born in the Territory of Wisconsin on December 14th, 1847, where his parents had settled in the year 1839 after moving from the State of New York. His early playmates were Indians and the few white boys who were in the neighborhood. As a small boy he hunted and trapped to earn the money with which to buy the school books to be used in the school house that was built in the woods nearby. The chief occupation in those days was the clearing of land and everybody from young and old was busy chopping trees and grubbing out the stumps. His life was spent this way with a few months of school in the winter time of each year until the breaking out of the Civil War in 1861, when his father, older brother and uncle enlisted in the new army. Willard at the time was too young but in 1864 he enlisted in Company A 43rd Regiment Wisconsin Volunteers in which organization he served as a private until the end of the war. After his discharge from the army the monotony of the old home backwoods life was too great for him and after a short visit he obtained employment in the Green Bay Lumber Country where he worked in the winter and sailed on the Great Lakes in the summer time. After nine years of this kind of life he obtained his Master's License and then proceeded for the west.

In the year 1875 he drifted into Cheyenne, Wyoming, and in 1876 he joined some of the parties who were rushing to the Black Hills in search of gold. On this trip out from Fort Laramie the party came across the bodies of two men who had been killed by Indians. Near the hand of one of the dead men was a piece of board covered with writing but they were unable to read it. He arrived in the southern Hills in July and spent most of the summer prospecting along different streams. After making several trips to Deadwood he finally, in the month of September, decided to remain there and became interested in several claims on Bear Butte Creek near Galena. He built a little cabin in Deadwood where he made his home. In those days most of his time was spent mining and prospecting but when the people of the Hills organized for enforcement of the law and preservation of order and Seth Bullock was appointed sheriff he appointed Willard as one of his deputies and from thenceforth Willard became a persistent upholder of the law and his life from then on became a constant occurrence of fights with desperate characters and struggle to preserve law and order. Many of the instances which are related in this book are ones in which he was one of the men whose arm was lifted in behalf of the law. He also served a term as Deputy United States Marshal and his work carried him through the western part of the then Dakota Territory. After serving as an officer of the law in the northern hills, he moved to Custer county, where his ability was soon recognized and he was elected to the office of sheriff of the county. He continued to uphold his past reputation and proved to be a most efficient officer.

After tiring of the work of supporting various sheriffs in their work, he homesteaded land in the Slim Buttes country where he acquired large land holdings and conducted the live stock business. His son, Boone Willard, was associated with him in the business and as old age began to press upon the father, Captain Willard took up a residence in Belle Fourche, where he resided while engaged in the task of collecting material for the writing of this history. His wide acquaintance and active participation in many of the stirring events of the pioneer days, enabled him to ferret out the truth in many of the stories and gave him a broad view of the field to be covered. He soon associated with himself, Jesse Brown, who likewise had long planned upon preserving the story of the pioneers.

After the material was all assembled and given over to the editor for preparation for publishing and the long sought day for the realization of his dream seemed about to dawn, on Friday, July 22, 1921, the palsied hand of Death pressed down upon him, and Captain Willard crossed the Great Divide. He had been sick but a very short time and his death came as a surprise to his many friends who could scarcely realize that the genial and big hearted pioneer had obeyed the final summons. On Sunday afternoon funeral services were held in the Masonic Temple, attended by friends and pioneers who gathered from far and near. Interment was had in Mount Moriah Cemetery beneath the pines and overlooking the streets of Deadwood, where he had spent the prime of his life in the cause of preserving law and order.

The sole ambition of Captain Willard in his later years was to see "The Black Hills Trails" in print and he often said to the editor, "John, hurry the work along. I want to see it printed before I cash in." He seemed to feel the approach of the messenger whose withering touch ends all. However, his son, Boone Willard, agreed that the work should not stop and permitted Jesse Brown to carry out the plans as agreed upon before the passing of the fellow pioneer and historian.

JESSE BROWN

Upon request I will endeavor to write a brief outline of a few experiences of my life, although upon glancing back over the path that I have traveled things appear so insignificant that I am almost persuaded to stop right here. Nevertheless, I will make an effort and let it go for what it is worth.

I was born in Washington County, Tennessee, August 24th, 1844; moved to Clark County, Missouri, in 1848; lived there until the outbreak of the war. My parents were poor, and my brother, older than I, having died in 1860, it was necessary for me to remain at home as one of the mainstays of the family. I was not old enough to be drafted, and my mother did not want me to volunteer. I left home and went to Ottumwa, Iowa, little thinking I would never see those familiar scenes again. A gentleman for whom I worked in Ottumwa had a nephew visiting him from Delaware, a brilliant young lawyer who was anxious to see the West, and with him I went to Nebraska City in 1865. Here we had an offer to drive teams, "whacking bulls" is what they called it, which we accepted. Our employer was a splendid fellow named Theodore Comstock, who had been a lieutenant in the volunteer army, and stationed at Plum Creek, Nebraska. When his term of service expired he bought a small freight outfit, and loaded for Fort Kearney. He told us so many frightful tales of bloodthirsty savages that we two tenderfeet were nearly frightened to death. Having a small outfit, the drivers were compelled to take turn about in the night herding the stock. I cannot describe my feelings the night I stood guard on Plum Creek, which was said to be the worst place on the road for Indians. I never expected to see another day. I walked the entire night through, carrying an old muzzle loading shotgun, and if anything in human shape had shown up I know I would have dropped that old gun, and struck for camp.

Next trip we made was to Fort Laramie, where we were pressed into service to haul wood for the post. I worked for the government one hundred days, and then took a four mule team with supplies and twenty-two men, and started for Nebraska City, reaching there the last day of December, '65, with

THE BLACK HILLS TRAILS 517

more money than I had ever possessed before in my life. Next year I drove team and hauled freight west of Omaha. In '67 we loaded at North Platte for Fort Phil Kearney. I was promoted to assistant wagonmaster that year. We were attacked five times during the summer by Indians. The first time was on the Cheyenne River. Just as we corraled for the night a band of Sioux charged on us. I was working at the lead wagon on the right wing, and saw them coming within three hundred yards of us. I yelled "Indians," and grabbed my gun. In an instant every man was shooting. The Indians checked up and circled away, and we ran out of the corral and poured lead into them so fast that they did not return. The wagonmaster gave us great praise, and we felt so jubilant over the easy victory that we thought we could whip the whole Sioux nation; but wait! A few days after that we crossed Powder River, and camped on Crazy Woman Creek. The day was fine, and we were still talking and laughing about the way we chased the Indians down on the Cheyenne, and were foolish enough to imagine that they were afraid to tackle us again. After breaking camp we had proceeded about two miles to where the road entered a canyon. We had twenty-six teams and seventy-five men, including forty soldiers, and had not heard a sound or caught a glimpse of anything unusual, but just as the seventeenth team was passing into the canyon suddenly the reds were on all sides of us, shooting, yelling and screeching like so many devils turned loose. Surprised! Well, that was no name for it. We were stampeded, paralyzed, demoralized for an instant, until we drew our second breath. The Indians charged on the rear of the train and cut off nine teams. The other seventeen were in the canyon where the wagonmaster had bunched them for defense the best he could considering the room he had. The Indians drove the nine drivers from the rear teams and they ran to the front. We got them together and went to the rear to save the teams that had been cut off from the main outfit. There was a squad of soldiers in the rear guard, but they were not strong enough to hold the Indians at bay, so they left the wagons and had taken shelter in ditches and behind rocks I went with twenty-five men from the front to help get these rear teams. We found three soldiers down, wounded, and several of the steers shot dead in the yoke. We got the wounded men into the wagons, and then had to get right into the open and take the yoke from the dead cattle, and roll them out of the way before we could move. While part of the men were doing this, the rest of us were behind the wagons shooting at everything in the shape of an Indian, and they were keeping up a constant rain of bullets and arrows on us. We killed several of them, and wounded others, and quite a number of ponies were killed. Finally they fell back a little, and took shelter behind rocks, and behind a hill on the north side of the road. That gave us a chance to move the teams up to the front, which we did without any further mishaps. A sergeant by the name of Day and myself were standing a little ways from the wagons. when one of their big medicine fakirs left the main body, and came charging right at us. We both fired and killed him and his horse. I wanted to go out and scalp him, but I knew the risk, and the sergeant advised me not to try it. After everything was bunched up in the canyon to protect the stock to the best advantage, the Indians divided their forces, and part of them went almost to the creek, and got into and followed a big washout that brought them within about one hundred yards of the corral, giving them a clear view to shoot under the wagons. We laid flat on the ground and watched for their heads when they would peep above the bank, and thus we forced them to quit that game. Their next move was to fire the grass. Although it was June the grass was dry and burned fiercely. Major Freeman, in command of our escort, ordered a charge on the ditch, while we fought the fire. It was necessary that this should be extinguished as some of our wagons were loaded with powder, which made a somewhat desperate situation. Besides, if the fire had reached the cattle there would have been a stampede. The Indians kept us there until eight o'clock that night, and perhaps some of us would have been there yet if it had not happened that there was another large outfit immediately ahead of us, and when they heard the shooting they corraled. Charley Clay, who was traveling with us, heard the Indians yelling and looked back and saw that we were surrounded, put spurs to his horse, and rode on and notified the outfit ahead of ours of our danger. They had an escort of forty soldiers. After three or four hours had elapsed and they could still hear the reports of our firing, Clay prevailed on the officer in charge to send us help. They had a piece of artillery, which was sent with twenty-five men. When the Indians saw them coming they left us and attacked the soldiers. Sheltered behind three wagons loaded with corn which would stop a bullet, the way the soldiers dropped the redskins was a caution. This re-inforcement finally reached us, and after throwing a few shells over the hill, they succeeded in forcing the Indians to retire. We got things straightened up and pulled out, travelled all night and stopped at Buffalo Springs for breakfast. This is the first water east of Clear Creek, where the town of Buffalo is now located. We unloaded at Fort Phil Kearney, where I took charge of an outfit of twenty-four teams and hauled saw logs for the government. That was the worst place I ever saw for Indians. They were determined to drive the soldiers and other whites from that territory, and they did as the next year the government made a treaty with the Sioux and vacated that country. Many nights we could see Indians dancing and pow wowing around their campfires, only a short distance away. They hovered around the post all the time, and if anyone dared to venture a short distance from the stockade alone the chances were that he would be scalped. An outfit from Fort C. F. Smith camped on the creek just below us one day was attacked by Indians, and we responded to their call for help. We saw the men running from the outfit toward the herd. I went down there and they had just carried in one of the day herders who had been shot and three scalps taken from his head which was entirely clear of hair except a little fringe on the back part. He was a light haired, blue eyed boy from Des Moines, Iowa. I have forgotten his name, not having written it down. The old freight road from Fort Phil Kearney to Fort Fetterman is lined with graves without any identification mark, and many a mother has wept for a long lost son that never returned; neither will their names ever be mentioned in history. Don't you believe that these men that sleep in unmarked graves deserve some little credit for what they did in civilizing this country? The troops had to have supplies or they could not remain at their stations, and these men virtually took their lives in their hands when they engaged in the business of carrying these supplies.

I left Kearney in September, having finished my contract, and you can rest assured we were glad to find ourselves alive. On our way out we were attacked twice by Indians, but nothing serious happened as we were on our guard. I loaded supplies at Julesburg for Fort Fetterman, which I reached in January, '68. The weather was very cold with snow, and the men suffered many hardships on account of not having proper clothing, as we had not expected to be so long in making the trip. We wintered on the Sabile the balance of the winter, about sixty miles west and south of old Fort Laramie. I believe it was the prettiest place I ever saw in the west, bunch grass a foot high, spring water that did not freeze, and plenty of timber and shelter for stock. Our cattle went into camp poor but came out fat enough for beef. Besides the country was full of deer, antelope and elk. We had more than we could possibly consume, and salted and cured a lot of deer and antelope hams. I never enjoyed a winter anywhere as I did that winter.

Jesse Brown.

THE BLACK HILLS TRAILS 521

With the coming of the gold rush to the Black Hills, Brown was drawn to the new country in his work with freight trains and guarding. His quiet bravery, absolute trustworthiness and careful attention to his duties, soon won the respect of his employers, and it was not long before he became one of the famous shot gun messengers of the Treasure Coach as it carried its golden burden from the Hills. Several of the incidents that occurred in this work have been recorded in the preceding pages.

After the passing of the treasure coach and the long freight trains, Brown came to Meade county, where he has made his home ever since. His reputation for respect for law and order and his sturdy fearlessness was so widely known, that he was chosen to serve as sheriff of Meade county for four terms and later he served as deputy sheriff. He was then called upon to serve his county as commissioner while residing in Sturgis, where he was engaged in the coal and feed business. And today, after a long life of activity, the people of the county have drafted him to serve them as register of deeds.

The hard struggle of the boy from Missouri, the stirring scenes through which he passed, and his natural love for honest and fearless devotion to duty, prompted him to give heed to the men of action in his day, and moved him to a desire to preserve the record of their deeds. And when he and Captain Willard joined forces in the mutual ambition to write the story of the early days, the creation of this book became a real possibility. He has given it time and money without stint, making many sacrifices to assure the successful ending of the efforts begun many years ago. He, like Willard, was awake to the early coming of the Grim Reaper, but has been fortunate enough to live to see the printed page as the climax of a long and useful life well spent.

SCOTT DAVIS

Scott Davis was born in Kinsman, Ohio, October 2, 1854. His father died when he was two years old. His mother remarried to R. W. Hazen and four years later the family immigrated to the west where they located on a road farm on the Platte River near Columbas, Nebraska, and operated a tavern where Hazen built a large log house, barns and sheds for immigrants, travelers and stage coaches and prospered in this work.

When Scott was fifteen years of age he struck out to make his own way in the world and went to Nebraska City where he got employment in a big freighting outfit which crossed the plains to Denver with government supplies. He continued in the freighting business for some time and drifted out farther west to Utah and Idaho, finally landing on the Union Pacific railroad which he helped to build. Mr. R. Hall was in charge of the outfit at that time and was doing work of the rough class that could not be contracted and had about two hundred men and fifty teams. From this place Davis drifted into Texas where he continued to work on various railroad lines that were being built and thus he was employed until 1874, until the rush was made to the Black Hills when he again took up his work with freighting crews hauling supplies into the Black Hills. After a while he changed from freighting work and became a guard on the Treasure Coach running out from Deadwood to Cheyenne and from Sidney to Fort Pierre, and in this work his most notable achievement in the great task of preserving law and order and protecting parties in the west was done. A number of his exploits as the reader will recall have been set forth in this volume. After the Black Hills had been won and the exciting days had passed Davis became engaged in stock detective work for the Union Pacific railroad.

Jesse Brown and Scott Davis

GEORGE V. AYRES

George Vincent Ayres was born on a farm in Pennsylvania, in 1852. He lived in Missouri, Kansas and Nebraska, obtaining his education in Beatrice, Neb. Came to the Black Hills in March, 1876, and settled in Deadwood on May 23rd of that year, since which time he has been a prominent resident of the Black Hills and the state of South Dakota.

A Republican in politics, a prominent Freemason

George V. Ayres

and Elk, member of the Black Hills Society of Pioneers, also State Historical Society. Mr. Ayres was married twice and was the father of six children.

Besides engaging in mining and general merchandising he has for years been a member of the Ayres & Wardman Hardware Company of Deadwood. Elsewhere in this book many incidents of his life have been mentioned in connection with the stirring happenings of pioneer days.

WILLIAM J. THORNBY

New York was the birthplace of W. J. Thornby in 1856, and he arrived in Deadwood in April, 1877, where he worked on the Pioneer for two years. In 1879 he, in company with Prof. W. P. Jenney, located the hot springs where is now the city of Hot Springs. Graduated from the State School of Mines in 1896, was one of the judges in the mining department of the World's Columbian Exposition in Chicago, and later

W. J. Thornby

was for several years assayer in the government assay office in Deadwood.

Mr. Thornby was the first county assessor of Custer county, state senator from Custer and Fall River counties, and was a member of several secret orders.

On the 26th of July, 1894, he was united in marriage to Miss Bertha Youmans. He died while still in active pursuit of the duties of life.

C. V. GARDNER

C. V. Gardner was born in Morrow County, Ohio, on August 13, 1836. He received a common school education and when fifteen years of age, he came to Iowa, and at Cornell College he attended school during the years of 1856-57 and 1858. He then took up the study of law in the Cincinnati Law School from which he graduated a few days after the bombardment of Ft. Sumpter. However, he never practiced his profession, for having gone out to Colorado, right after his graduation, he was employed in the management of a saw mill. One day he overheard a sympathizer of the rebel cause boast of the prowess of the Confederacy in the opening days of the war, which so stirred his patriotism, that he then and there walked into the office of the company, handed over his keys and stated that he was going to enlist in the Union army. With all his earthly riches in his carpet bag and a blanket to sleep in, this young lawyer walked the entire distance from Central City, Colorado, to Council Bluffs, Iowa, a distance of five hundred miles to seek a recruiting station. Sleeping under the stars at night in hidden places from Indians, he arrived in August, 1862, and while eating in a restaurant after having had most of the dust and grime of the prairies removed from his person, he heard another person speaking of the plan of arranging for a recruiting station and learned that the man was a recruiting officer about to open a place for new men. Gardner immediately offered his services, was taken in as number one in what afterwards became known as Company A, 29th Infantry Volunteers, drilled a few minutes by the sergeant and was ready for business. Soon other men came and he was told to show them how to handle the gun and became at once a drill sergeant, and when the regiment was mobilized, was appointed first sergeant. In January, 1863, the captain of the company resigned,

company except two and was promoted to the rank of captain over the two lieutenants. After the battle of Helena, Arkansas, he was offered the rank of captain in the regular army, but refused as he thought his work was already regular enough. In 1867, President Grant appointed him to the grade of First Lieutenant in the regular army, but the loss of part of his left hand, prevented him from receiving the commission. His last military service was on the Rio Grande River, near Brownsville, Texas, where for a time, he was in command of the regiment.

Capt. C. V. Gardner

After the war, he took up his residence in Iowa, where he was elected to the office of register of deeds of Iowa county, was marshal and secretary successively of the Grand Lodge of Good Templars, assistant secretary of Iowa State Senate for three sessions, and a member of the State Immigration Commission for two years. He also engaged in the real estate, loan and insurance business. The thrill of adventure again called to him and on February 24, 1876, he struck out for the Black Hills, and arrived in Custer on the 20th day of March, 1876.

The Hills thenceforth became his home and held him chained with their enchantment. Here his life continued to be filled with achievement and he continued his leadership as in the years of his youth. He built the first frame building in Deadwood, was the first editor of the first newspaper in the Black Hills and later part owner, brought in the first quartz mill to the Hills, in which the first gold quartz was crushed, was in partnership with Porter Warner in the first flour mill located at Spearfish. He was instrumental in the organizing of the Black Hills Soldiers and Sailors Association, which once had more than four hundred members, and of which association, during its existence of twenty-one years, he was five years its president, and seven years its secretary. He served nine years on the Board of Trustees of the State School of Mines, four years of which time was filled with the duties of the secretaryship. He carried off the honors as member of the South Dakota Chicago World Fair Commission, and as secretary, secured an appropriation from Pierre to finance this work. He has been post commander of Harney Post G. A. R. of Rapid City, a member and president of the Society of Black Hills Pioneers, and Junior Vice-Commander of the Grand Army of the Republic, of which his brother, Washington, was once Commander in Chief.

And now after almost eighty years, this grand old man of the Black Hills, hero of the Civil war, pioneer Indian fighter, enthusiastic lover of the Hills, tireless optimist of the great days to come, is busily engaged in the task of raising funds to erect a fitting monument to the memory of the first white woman to stand upon the green vales of the Black Hills, Mrs. Annie D. Tallent. And he shall succeed, and in that work he shall pay tribute to the nobility of true womanhood and at the same time, enroll his own name upon the eternal page of chivalrous manhood that shineth ever brighter.

RICHARD B. HUGHES

A charter member of the Society of Black Hills Pioneers, was born in Somerest County, Pennsylvania, on April 14th, 1856. His parents moved to Cumberland, Maryland, in the spring of 1860, where they resided until late in 1864, moving thence to Illinois. In the spring of 1867, the family continued westward to Nebraska, settling at West Point, in the Elkhorn val-

R. B. Hughes

ley. Between that time and the spring of '76 the subject of this sketch attended school for two years in Chicago and served an apprenticeship at the printer's trade on the West Point Republican. He also taught two or three terms of school. In April of '76, he, with M. D. Rochford and William Van Fleet, came west of Sidney and joined a party of ten men with three wagons from Kansas bound for the Black Hills. This party became a part of a large wagon train, but left it a short distance from Red Cloud Agency when the captain, who had been elected, decided to wait for re-enforcements before proceeding farther. From here the party of thirteen pushed on to the Hills, reaching Custer on the eighth of May and Deadwood Gulch on the twelfth. From this time until December, 1880, Mr. Hughes alternated prospecting with working on various Deadwood papers, as he himself says, the former from choice, the latter from necessity.

With his partners he located Hidden Treasure and Pocket Gulches for placers. These proved disappointing. The partners also acquired an interest by location in the Justice Fraction of the DeSmet group. This they sold to Captain Nichols in the winter of '76 for five ounces of gold dust, value $100, to outfit Rochford for the Wolf Mountain Stampede. In '77 he and Rochford made the first quartz locations in what is now known as Rochford district. Between times he did some hunting and packing of game from the Central Hills to the Deadwood market.

In December of 1880, he became editor of the Rapid City Journal, then a weekly, and when later the daily was established remained as its editor until the fall of 1889.

During those years he served as Rapid City's first city treasurer, one term as county treasurer of Pennington County, a term of chief of the fire department, two years as president of the Commercial Club and four years as member of the Board of Trustees of the School of Mines.

In March of 1884 he was united in marriage to Mattie A., daughter of Mr. and Mrs. William Lewis, of Rapid City. They have two sons, Richard L., and Clarence W. Hughes, also two grandchildren.

With the organization of the State of South Dakota. Mr. Hughes was elected a member of the first state legislature. In 1894 he was appointed by President Cleveland as U. S. Surveyor General for the federal district of South Dakota, and filled that position for four years with offices at Huron.

Returning to the Hills at the expiration of his term of office he interested himself in mining, making his residence in Spearfish. He was for several years superintendent of mining property in the Northern Hills, and later president of the Holy Terror Mining Company. In 1912, he with his family returned to Rapid City where they owned some real estate, and acquired an interest in the Merchants Bank, later merged in the Citizen's Bank.

His home is in Rapid City ,where he is trying to take such ease as a somewhat severe case of rheumatism allows, as he looks back over the years that have passed and the changes that have been wrought in his dearly beloved Black Hills since he entered them as a boy, and recalls the experiences of his not inactive life.

W. H. BONHAM

The massacre of brave Custer and his heroic soldiers by the Indians on the Little Big Horn, north of the Black Hills in 1876 did not deter immigration to that region, in fact it helped to stimulate it by advertising the place. The moment it was learned that gold had been discovered along the gravel beds of the shallow babbling brooks of the Hills, people began to flock to the territory by the thousands from every direction, regardless of the Indians or hardships to be encountered. There people had to be fed, clothed and sheltered. Freighters with teams of all descriptions and even pack trains were called into service. One of these men, the proprietor of the old Black Hills Outfitters store at Cheyenne, Wyoming, traded his homestead for 130 Mexican burros preparatory to taking up this work. These burros were heavily loaded with supplies for the miners, and started for the Hills in 1877. A young painter and paper hanger who had drifted over from Denver and who had been working in the Old Outfitters store during the winter, was selected and placed in charge of the outfit. He was strong, lithe, cool headed and adventuresome, just the kind of a man needed to make the initial trip. Be it said to his credit that he got this outfit through without the loss of a burro or pack. He made the trip in eighteen days and July 17, 1877, this young adventurer, Willis H. Bonham, today editor and proprietor of the Pioneer Times, landed in Deadwood, Dakota Territory, where he has since made his home. When he arrived he found Deadwood a city of 15,000 people living in log houses, tents, dugouts, everywhere, anywhere spread out over the hills in all directions. They had fairly gone gold crazy, every mother's son of them imagined that he had a fortune hid away in his little gravel bed and was looking forward to the happy day when he would return to his family with his treasure. But listen to the Poet, he says—

The lust of gold succeeds the rage of conquest,
The lust of gold unfeeling and remorseless
The last corruption of degenerated man.

And yet with all due respects to these classical gentlemen of a bygone age let it be recorded that out of this motley array of gold seekers came much of the sturdy citizenry of our state. Thus the rough characters of frontier days were there also. When Bonham arrived at Deadwood, Wild Bill (Hickok) had been slain, but Calamity Jane, Tende Brown, the famous gambler, Doc Boggs, the confidence man who operated a lottery, Dirty Shirt Brown, who never washed his clothes, Socks, a street fakir, Shirt Collar Jewett, who wore a very large collar and operated a restaurant, and old Jim Levy, the gunman who had slain a number of people, were all in evidence those days. Today they are all off the stage of action and gone. Calamity Jane and Wild Bill are sleeping in calm repose up on the hill that fronts Deadwood from the east, called Mount Moriah Cemetery; but William Bonham is with us still. A man of quiet demeanor, aged 77, standing at his post of duty serving his generation to the last with a spicy, well balanced newspaper built up through his own industry from humble origin to one of the leading dailies of the state.

Early career: Common to most men who have won distinction in our state through their own heroic endeavor and sticktoitveness, Bonham was born on a farm and remained there until he reached his majority. He came into being in Jasper County, Illinois, on January 13, 1847. He attended rural school and spent one year at Abington College. This constituted his scholastic preparation for life, the remainder of his education being acquired through systematic reading and in the hard but vital school of experience. In 1873 he went to Denver where he worked for three years at painting and paper hanging, a trade he had learned after he was of age in Illinois. While in Colorado he got his first experience in politics, while the state was seeking admission to the Union in 1876. The Republicans and Democrats were both seeking to control it. Young Bonham was an officer of the Grand Lodge of Good Templars. The Republicans sent him to visit every lodge of this organization in the state. From Denver he went to Cheyenne, thence to Deadwood. After arriving in the latter place he worked for two years at his trade, then he worked for three years on the Deadwood Times, learning the printing business. In 1883 he purchased the Pioneer and in 1897 he acquired the Times, and consolidated them under the head of the Deadwood Pioneer Times, which name the paper bears today. Under his direction the paper has become a power in politics, as well as social life in the Black Hills and especially in Lawrence County. In the early days Bonham was active in amusements. He organized the South Deadwood Hose Company, helped organize the city's fire department, and was its chief engineer. He also served as city clerk of Deadwood for six years under three different mayors. Governor Mellette appointed him a trustee of the State School of Mines at Rapid City, under the old law, and President Roosevelt appointed him Postmaster of Deadwood. The flood of years are upon him, in calm content he can say, "I performed my duty as I saw it." He was always kind, and courteous to all and was a true, reliable friend to those he thought worthy of receiving it. In the language of the poet—

> I hear the muffled tramp of years,
> Come stealing up the slope of time,
> They bear a train of smiles and tears,
> Of burning homes, and dreams sublime.
>
> O. W. Coursey.

CAPTAIN JACK CRAWFORD

One of the pioneer leaders that distinguished themselves in the early days of the Black Hills was John W. Crawford, commonly known as the "Poet Scout." Captain Jack was born in County Donegal, Ireland, of Irish and Scotch parentage, his mother being a lineal descendant of Sir William Wallace. The family emigrated to New York where his father, a tailor, worked at his trade, but being addicted to the use of intoxicants the home life was very miserable. The young boy, Jack, was compelled to help support his family, and thus he was deprived of all opportunity for an education and when at the age of fifteen he joined the 48th Regiment of Pennsylvania Volunteers, he was only able to make his cross. In the battle of Spotsylvania the young soldier was wounded, and was taken to the hospital, where under the kind assistance of the Sisters of Charity, who nursed him back to life, he was taught the rudiments of reading and writing. In this war his father was wounded and finally died. After Jack recovered from his first wound he returned to his regiment but in April, 1865, he was again wounded and thus he closed his experience in the Civil War. While home, his mother died and on her death bed she had him promise in the presence of his brothers and sisters to never touch a drop of intoxicating liquor and this vow he kept faithfully through all the temptations of the subsequent years spent among the pioneers, in the army and in the big cities.

After the death of his mother he wandered out to the wild west and began scouting for the army. He was captain of the first company of "Minute Men" organized in Custer City to protect the new comers from the ravages of the Indians. He was one of the founders of Custer City, Deadwood, Crook City, Gayville and Spearfish. During the Indian campaign of 1876 he superceded Buffalo Bill as chief of scouts under General Crook. Captain Jack was a man of highest integrity, of the greatest honor and one of the noblest characters that ever took part in the winning of the west. From the standpoint of honor, citizenship and worth while bravery and successful deeds he was far above Wild Bill, Buffalo Bill and others of the various scouts of the pioneer days. Despite his lack of education he wrote many interesting rhymes of frontier days and some of them we have reproduced herein. He was a friend of Wild Bill and Buffalo Bill as well as the trusted scout of General Custer.

JEAN P. DECKER

Jean P. Decker, for more than a quarter of a century recognized as one of the leading editorial and news writers of the great west, has forsaken the Fourth Estate and gone into mercantile pursuits, having purchased the Curio store on Montana Avenue from Lee Warren.

Few newspaper men in Montana are better known than Mr. Decker and his retirement from active newspaper work will come as a surprise to the profession and to his many friends and admirers who have follow his writings for years. Yet he is not going into a business with which he is unfamiliar, for he has long been considered one of the best informed men in the country on Indian relics and curios, having at one time owned in the city of Butte one of the finest collections of the kind in the country.

He brings to the work an intimate knowledge of the west. He knows what is real and what is unreal in Indian and pioneer workmanship, a knowledge se-

cured from a life among the Indians and the pioneers.
When a boy, before the advent of the railroad in this
great valley when the Indians roamed the Dakotas
and Montana plains, Jean Decker walked from the
Missouri river to the Black Hills, where he was one
of the best known residents in the early days. For a
long time he was the guard of the treasure box to and
from the famous Homestake mine. He has been express messenger, deputy sheriff, miner, Indian fighter,

Jean P. Decker

cowboy, pioneer editor, one of the men who really paved the path of progress and aided in the early development of the west. He was in Montana before the railroad. He is one of the few men now living who really saw one of the famous Indian sun dances. His story upon that has been pronounced one of the most realistic ever written. It was his life, before the days of the tourist to whom he will not cater, before he entered into the newspaper field gained him knowledge about Indian relics and trophies, a knowledge that especially fits him for the profession which he has now entered. His stock of curios is as fine as has ever been gathered here. In it are some real treasures. Upon going over the stock he found some mighty fine specimens whose history and whose significance he delights in telling to those who call on him at his new place.

"You never saw anything like this before," said Mr. Decker to one of his old newspaper friends who dropped in yesterday, as he held up a beautifully tanned Elks hide robe on which were drawn a large number of Indian pictures, buffalo, etc., in the natural colors, such as only the Indian medicine man used. "It is a real sun dance robe. It depicts the story of a buffalo hunt from the starting at the camp fire to the bringing in of the meat. I have never seen one like it before and have only heard of one other in existence. It was painted by a medicine man before the days of the shot gun or the rifle for only bows and arrows are shown. It is older than the oldest of us.. Some day some museum will give a lot to get it as a sample of handicraft and a folk lore that has long been gone. I found it in the stock here, probably purchased from some Indian to whom its real value was unknown."

The newspaper man would not have known its value or its rareness, but by the old Indian fighter, the pioneer of the west, who possessed an intimate knowledge of such things, it was immediately recognized as a rare treasure of Indian art.

There are scores of such things in his store, among which he likes to work. He seems just as perfectly contented as when in the old days he ground out the editorial or hustled after the festive news item, when he swayed the political beliefs of his readers or portrayed the everyday happenings.

In the retirement of Mr. Decker to the more quiet life of a curio merchant the newspaper profession loses one of its brightest stars—whose brilliancy has dazzled the Fourth Estate and charmed his auditors for years, one of the brightest editorial writers of the treasure state.

His first experience in the newspaper business was gained in Deadwood after leaving the pioneer life. From there he traveled considerably. He worked in San Francisco, in Seattle, in Omaha, and in the principal cities of the west. He was city editor and one of the staunch Clark supporters on the Butte Miner during the stirring days of the Clark-Daly fight. He was on the Anaconda Standard when Daly gathered together a brilliant corps of newspaper men determined to make it the great paper of the west.

For years he was assistant to Colonel Sam Gordon, the vitriolic pen artist of the Yellowstone, the only man Colonel Sam was willing to admit could wield the pen equal to himself. From Miles City he came to Billings and was for seven years editor of the Billings Daily Gazette. Much of the early prestige of this paper is due to the faithful work of Mr. Decker. In 1907 he retired temporarily from the newspaper field to become secretary of the Billings Chamber of Commerce.

He deserves the title of "Father of the Lake Basin" for he induced the first dry land farmers to settle in that part of the country. The men he first sent into that district have brought more than 600 families to the country tributary to Broadview. He had no criterions on the job, but he showed his versatility by the excellent work he did, the results he accomplished. In 1909 he started a magazine, retiring from which he went to Big Timber and purchased the Pioneer, which he built into one of the foremost papers of the state, selling out early this year.

During the past six months he, with Mrs. Decker, has been in California for the benefit of her health, but the possibilities of Billings, so inculcated during his editorship of the Gazette and his secretaryship of the Chamber of Commerce, were so strong he has decided to return to the Magic City and engage in the Curio business, a pursuit which his early training in the great west especially fitted him to follow.

Daily Gazette, Billings, Mont.. 1913.

MAJOR A. J. SIMMONS

Major Simmons died December 23, 1920, aged 86 years. Obeying the summons to which all must harken Major Andrew Jackson Simmons, yesterday stepped across the line of life and death to repose in eternity. His life on earth had been a big one. It is not possible within the compass of this story to relate in detail more than a small part of the large part played by him during the 86 years of usefulness he spent on earth. Born in 1834 his early youth was spent in Indiana, where in 1851, fired with the spirit of adventure which survived within him as long as the breath of life, he joined a caravan, having as its destination the gold fields of California. Indiana at that time itself a frontier, had created and fostered a desire for the greater and more wonderful experiences only to be had by listening to the call of the west. The trip across the plains and mountains between the starting point and goal was full of incidents, including hair breadth escapes by field and flood, besides more or less conflicts with the hostile tribes of Indians as well as numerous bands of outlaws and marauders, which preyed and sought to prey upon the hardy, indomitable men and women who blazed the way across the continent.

The route followed by Simmons and his party, with whom he traveled took him through Council Bluffs, Iowa, and there he first met the late Sol Bloom, already a pioneer merchant, then proprietor of a little store and doing a thriving trade with the Indians. Other stops on the long trail were upon or near the sites now occupied by such large and flourishing communities as Cheyenne, and Casper, Wyoming. Salt Lake City, Utah, and other cities and towns located where then not a human being had permanent habitation within a distance of several hundred miles:

Though prospering in California, incited by the wondrous tales from Nevada, Jack Simmons was later found in the hurry, bustle and activity of the Comstock. He took an active part in the organization of the Territory of Nevada, and upon its admission to the Union, was elected a member of the first legislature, and became the speaker of the first house of representatives. Among his intimates of this time were the late Samuel L. Clemens, (Mark Twain) who was a roommate for several months. The late former United States Senator of Nevada, Stewart and Simmons were of about the same age and having had experiences along the same lines of life, naturally became fast friends. Simmons contributed in no small degree to the election of his friend to the U. S. senate, and then advised and labored with him in framing the chapters of the federal laws on mines and mining which still control the location, appropriation and acquisition of lode and placer claims in the United States today.

Having acquired fortune as well as fame in Nevada, he returned to California, remaining in San Francisco until a series of unfortunate investments wiped out his fortune. The story of the process by which his financial downfall was accomplished by the manipulation of the ring of bonanza kings is itself a romance. From California he went to Idaho and then to Montana, in the latter he accepted the appointment of Indian agent for one of the reservations. Though the occupation in those days was attended by a great deal more excitement than is incident to it now, it still did not appeal strongly enough to Simmons, and before long he resigned to again enter the mining game in Montana. Shortly after this the Black Hills were opened to settlement, and Major Simmons arrived in Deadwood, to at once take a prominent place in the building up of the community and the development of its resources. Always an optimist he was most enthusiastic concerning Black Hills mines, and had an abiding conviction from the very first that nature had here established for mankind a vast and inexhaustible storehouse of treasure, From date of his early day arrival here, until his migration to Denver only some eighteen months ago, to make his home with his son, Jesse, he had been a resident of the Hills, most of the time of this city. During all these years he was active in promoting and endeavoring to promote and establish upon a profitable basis one mining enterprise after another, the last one with which he was connected was the Echo, now developing a group of claims near Maitland in Lawrence County. While a resident of Rapid City Major Simmons served both as member of the City Council, and as mayor of the city,. worked with characteristic energy for the upbuilding of the city and it was due largely to his efforts that the School of Mines and other important educational institutions were located there.

Before coming to the Hills, Major Simmons married Miss Kate Chumasero. Mrs. Simmons died in 1905. Jesse, born in Deadwood, the only child of this union, now resides with his family in Denver, Colorado. A complete story of Major Simmons would necessarily include a large part of the history of the development of the western part of the United States, in the making of which development he played an important part. Of a most kindly, genial, loving and loveable disposition, he had few if any enemies, and practically numbered his friends by the number of his acquaintances. His long, useful and honorable career cannot be better summed up than by saying: His life was gentle, and the elements so mixed in him, that nature might stand up and say to all the world, This was a man.

Newspaper Article, December 24, 1920.

JOSEPH B. GOSSAGE

Joseph B. Gossage was born at Ottumwa, Iowa, May 19th, 1852. When a young boy he began his apprenticeship in the office of the Courier at Ottumwa where he commenced his training in the printer's trade. At sixteen years of age he went to Chicago where he worked for a number of different printing concerns and was engaged for a time in the office of the Chicago Republican. After the big Chicago fire he returned to his old home in Ottumwa and again took up his work with the Courier. In 1870 he assisted in getting out the first issue on the 19th day of April of the Sioux City Journal. He was also em-

Joseph B. Gossage

ployed for a time in the office of the Pekin Register, of Pekin, Illinois. In the early 70's we find him after his various experiences in the newspaper offices through the middle west, settled in Sidney, Nebraska, where he assumed control of the Sidney Telegraph. This newspaper he owned and published for five years and had correspondents writing for him from the Black Hills, and although he did not sell the paper until May, 1878, he soon joined the rush to the Black Hills where he landed in the winter of '77-78, and established the Rapid City Journal at Rapid City, South Dakota. The first issue of this newspaper was printed by him on the 5th day of January, 1878. The many articles that have been republished in this book taken from the Sidney Telegraph are due to the care and attention of Mr. Gossage who made note of many important and now almost priceless records of those days.

The establishing of the Rapid City Journal marked the thirteenth paper and newspaper office in which Mr. Gossage had received his newspaper experience. This venture proved to be his lucky number and the little Weekly Journal established in the beginning of 1878 in a small log cabin town has grown and added a morning and evening daily, with one of the best equipped printing plants in the west, this book being a product of the job printing plant. A $20,000.00 Goss printing press now rolls off the newspapers by the thousands and three lineotype machines keep the now thriving and populous metropolis of the Black Hills informed of the world's progress right up to the minute. In addition to his work in the newspaper field Mr. Gossage was a member of the Territorial Board of Trustees of the School of Mines to which he was appointed by Governor Pierce and this institution likewise has grown to be a very successful and influential organization.

A few years ago, while attending one of the annual meetings of the Society of Black Hills Pioneers, Mr. Gossage in reviewing early days with Jesse Brown, discovered that he was the same Jesse Brown whom he had known as a young man in the early sixties at Ottumwa, Iowa. The two young men had drifted apart, had forgotten their boyhood playmates, then came together again in the Hills, little dreaming of the days before the spell of the Hills had seized upon them. And when it came to the work of publishing the story of the pioneers, these two playmates of long ago, were pals again, mutually assisting one another to play the game to a finish.

LEE R. BAXTER

More than fifty former residents of the Black Hills sojourning in the San Francisco Bay cities paid their tribute of respect Sunday, March 4th, at the funeral services for Lee R. Baxter, personal friend of Abraham Lincoln, scholar and one of the early Deadwood settlers. His death occurred at an Oakland hospital March 2. The last rites were read in Oakland by the rector of St. Mark's Episcopal church of Berkelye, Rev. W. R. H. Hodgin. Practically every community in the Black Hills was represented in the attendance, with old friends finding expression in a wealth of floral offerings.

Cremation of the body took place the following day, the ashes being strewn on the Berkeley hills back of the Greek Theatre, on the grounds of the University of California, where Leander Robinson Baxter had found delight in sitting at the close of day to view the bay, the Golden Gate and the sunsets up to the time he was stricken by his fatal attack last autumn. This disposition of his ashes was in accord with one of his last requests to his daughter, Edna Baxter Lawson, native of Deadwood, who is now connected with the University of California in the purchasing department.

He made his home with Mrs. Lawson during the last year or so of his life. Mrs. Lawson's address is 1545 LeRoy Avenue, Berkeley. He often said to friends that he found in Berkeley the greatest enjoyment he had ever known, blessed as he was here with the ministrations of his daughter as well as the associations and surroundings that suited his nature. He was essentially an aristrocrat and here in his retirement from activities lived and dressed the part. A college man, a graduate of Beloit and the University of Wisconsin, he was devoted to his books, a student of world affairs, and he could indulge that inclination here.

The vein of sentiment in him was illustrated by his desire to have his ashes scattered on the Berkeley hills in manifestation of his attachment for them. Those who knew him are aware of the basis for the romanticism in him, for he came from patrician lineage, a descendant of British nobility, kin of the Duke of Salisbury, and scion of a family that came to North America on the Mayflower. A pilgrim settlement in one of the original thirteen colonies was named for the Baxters.

Baxter was 79 years old. As a youth he served as an aide on the staff of President Lincoln during the Civil War. In the seventies actuated by his fondness for romance and adventure, he left his home in Wisconsin for the Black Hills where for almost half a century he was known for his education and poise, lending a distinguished presence even in the rough surroundings of the early days.

The fastidiousness in the matter of dress and appearance that always characterized him remained with him to the close of his life, indeed, some of him friends aver it grew on him. For a year, he was a familiar figure in Berkeley, always groomed impeccably, his snow-white beard close trimmed, the personification of dignity and culture. Those who looked upon the body as it lay in state will always carry that picture of him.

JACK LANGRISHE

Langrishe's theatre was one of the well known institutions of early Deadwood. Langrishe himself was well known in every mining camp of the west of sufficient importance to boast a playhouse. He was one of the most versatile of men. A printer by trade and a good one, he usually set up all his own advertising matter, posters, etc., at the Pioneer office. He was a fine comedian, and had his desires not kept him all his life on the frontiers of civilization he must have made himself a place high among the famous lights of the drama. As a writer he had a quick wit and a ready pen. His generosity was unbounded and no old time stranded actor could call upon it in vain. His heart was over large for his purse and his response to the calls of impecunious friends kept him always in straightened circumstances. He brought with him to Deadwood or assembled soon after coming, a company in which were such old time reliables as Groos, Jimmy Martin, and Jimmy Griffith with others of equal talent whose names have passed from memory. It is as a writer, however, that Langrishe will longest be remembered. He had a way of dashing off rhyming narrative of current events, that made interesting reading and during the winter of 1876 he contributed much to the columns of the Pioneer, and even for a year or two later, when he left the Hills, did more or less work on that paper. For there was no place that he felt more at home than with the newspaper boys. A few of Langrishe's "Jingles" linger still in memory. In one he treated of the vicissitudes of the miner who had gone out on the ill fated Wolf Mountain stampede, describing his appearance on his return. This stampede, it was charged and probably with truth, was started by a number of men who had horses for sale and who succeeded in disposing of them at high prices asked of the prospectors. Indeed it was stated that a special raid was made by several dare-devils to the Sioux Reservation and a large number of Indian ponies were stolen and brought into the Hills to supply the demand. Prospectors flocked into Deadwood from every quarter, bought horses, and outfits and started off pell mell with the most indefinite idea of whither they were bound. As a result great hardships were endured and many of these stampeders were killed by Indians, and of those who finally reached Deadwood on their return more than one fully justified by his appearance and condition the picture drawn by Langrishe, as follows:

> This is the man of whom we read,
>   Who left Deadwood on the big stampede;
> He's now returned all tattered and torn
>   From looking for gold on the Big Horn.

He has no malt, he has no cap,
  He has no coat, he has no hat,
His trousers are patched with an old flour sack
  With "For Daily Use" to be seen on the back.

His beard is shaggy, his hair is long,
  And this is the burden of his song;
If ever I hear, or if ever I read
  Of another great or big stampede
I'll listen but I'll pay no heed,
  But stay in my little cabin in Deadwood.

When the notoriously bad Indian, Crazy Horse, was killed on the reservation by Lame Deer, Langrishe wrote a historically correct account of the affray in the following brief epitaph:

> The happy grounds are found at last
> And Crazy Horse's days are past,
> On earth he struck a poor Lame Deer
> Who sent him to another sphere.

One cold snowy, blustery day in the winter of '76, Langrishe came in to the Pioneer office which was then housed in a log cabin, on the alley west of Main street. His somewhat prominent nose was white with the frost, and he immediately sought the grateful warmth of the red-hot stove in the rear end of the room. He was inspired by the incident to devote ten minutes to writing the following lines:

Oh, the stove, the beautiful stove
  Heating the room below and above.
Broiling, roasting and keeping warm—
  Beautiful stove you can do no harm.

Fill her up to thaw your toes
  Fill her to thaw the end of your nose
Open the damper and let her go
  She'll soon knock h--- out of the beautiful snow.

THOMAS COOPER

The bronzed, weather beaten, kindly countenance of "Uncle Tom" Cooper, who in the course of fifteen years' service as day depot master on the Union Pacific passenger station, assisted thousands to and from trains, endearing himself to railroad employees and frequent travelers, will be seen no more in his accustomed place. Monday, January 18, while posting train schedules on the blackboard, Cooper suffered a

Tom Cooper

stroke of paralysis and was taken to his home where he died the following night. The veteran Indian scout, stage driver and depot master did not recover his power of speech after the accident, although as late as Tuesday afternoon he nodded his head in recognition of members of his family and intimate friends who visited at his bedside.

Cooper was born in 1850, therefore was 64 years old, at the time of his passing away, January 19, 1915. He was married in 1875. There was one son, James

six horses to a Concord coach equal to the best known in the Rocky Mountain country. Mr. Voorhees considers Tom Cooper his most reliable driver on the Black Hills line."

It is generally known all over the west that Tom was the preferred man to ride with. General Crook would telegraph to the Cheyenne office to secure the driver's seat on Cooper's run. He had the utmost confidence in Cooper, and many times has consulted Tom on subjects of importance, for the latter had been one of the General's most capable and efficient scouts in the Sioux war of '76. At the State Fair at Douglas in October, 1914, Mr. Cooper was given an ovation by the old timers gathered there, among whom were Luke Voorhees, Scott Davis, Jesse Brown, Mizzou Hinds, Ed Patrick, John Higby and others. On this occasion a reproduction was given of the Canyon Springs holdup that had taken place on September 29, 1878. Davis, Brown and Cooper took a very active part in helping to exterminate the robbers, and road agents that infested the line in those days. Cooper was considered one of the best scouts in the campaign from '73 to '76. General Crook and Colonel Stanton both said that they preferred the old reliable Cooper to Colonel Cody with all his show of buckskin beaded coat and trousers. Cooper was always modest. Frequently he would find men or women and children in want at the depot. He would do for them what he could and assist them in finding what they wanted. Frequently he would ask a reporter for the Leader to put a little item in the paper concerning some missing person sought by friends or relatives, or some family in distress. And would generally say "Now don't mention me, but let's do something to help them out." I doubt if his equal will ever be found for he was the only Tom Cooper. I have listened to him telling his experiences and escapades many times. It would require a great deal more space than I have here to repeat a small portion.

Jesse Brown.

F. Cooper, who is assistant chief clerk in the office of the United States railway service at Cheyenne, Wyoming. For forty-two years "Uncle Tom" was a resident of Wyoming, and he knew and had a part in much of the early thrilling history of the state, when pioneers fearless and hardy were combating with the savages, road agents and outlaws, and the hard conditions that accompany the existence of first settlers in a virgin country. He followed up a splendid service as Indian scout, and stage driver on the Black Hills line by entering the employ of the Union Pacific before that railroad began the practice of keeping employment records. Later in 1889 the record shows that he was employed as train guard and then in another department of the system, and yet later he became depot master, where hundreds learned to know and love him because of his quiet kindness, unassuming ways and efficiency at all times in the discharge of his duties. In his neat uniform of gray prescribed by the rules of the railroad corporation, Cooper looked very unlike the rugged young man who faced danger and death as an Indian scout, stage driver and soldier in Wyoming in the early days of its history.

Robert S. Strahon who rode on the driver's seat over the stage line many times with Cooper when the latter drove for Luke Voorhees between Cheyenne and Deadwood wrote: "For six months ending June 30, 1877, the Cheyenne and Deadwood stage company, the finest organization of its kind in the whole west, and of which every citizen was proud, carried 3,128 first class passengers for which fares amounting to $48,766 was collected. This company has $200,000 invested in its elegant coaches, fine stock, etc. It requires 600 head of horses which are the finest and best that can be had, to run this broad gauge line, which is only second to a narrow gauge railway. Luke Voorhees, one of the owners and general manager, takes great pains to secure the very best men as his employees. Thomas Cooper is one who can handle

JOHN MANNING

No one ever called him John. It was "Johnny" to his dying day. He was born in Ireland in March, 1841, and came to the Black Hills from Montana on March 16, 1875. From the first he was known for his bravery and at the same time desire for law and order to take the place of outlawry. As sheriff of Law-

John Manning

rence county he did his duty as an officer of the law. It was in 1879 that he was sheriff when the famous "Pagan Jury" was so roundly scored by Judge G. C. Moody.

Mr. Manning is one of the "old timers" who was "gathered to his fathers" some time ago, before the advent of the present day advantages and comfortable surroundings. Read about him in "The Black Hills Trails."

H. O. ALEXANDER

Among the few who came to the Black Hills in the early days and have remained to enjoy the comforts of civilization is H. O. Alexander, who took part in many of the stirring scenes of the early settlement of the Hills. Among other things he delighted in

H. O. Alexander

hunting the buffalo and deer, and as far back as 1879 we find him killing as many as fifteen deer in one day.

After the peaceful pursuits became the custom Mr. Alexander took up the work of a traveling salesman, and at present is in the mercantile business in Blle Fourche, South Dakota. His name appears several times in this book in connection with important happenings.

ELLIS T. PEIRCE

"Doc" Peirce came to the Black Hills in February, 1876, and settled on French Creek. Born in Pennsylvania in 1846, he was thirty years old when he entered upon an exciting career in the Hills country. Previous to this he had been in the Civil War, a member of the 39th Missouri Mounted Infantry, and was one of

E. T. Peirce

the four who escaped at the time of the Quantrell Massacre at Centralia, Mo.

Mr. Peirce loved fair play as will be seen in the many incidents in which his name is mentioned in this book. He was fearless and performed many deeds of valor during the early days of the settlement of the Black Hills. At present he resides in Hot Springs, South Dakota.

JOHN D. HALE

A history of the stock interests in the early days of the Black Hills territory would not be complete without a sketch of the life of John D. Hale, or "Jack" Hale, as he is known all over the west. Jack has undoubtedly done more towards the driving in and raising of all kinds of stock than any other one man in the Hills country. I will give a brief sketch of his life and of his business and political activities. Although born in the old South, he went west early in life and became identified with the west and grew up there. He is called a typical western man. Jack Hale was born in Grayson County, Virginia, in the year 1847, but the life in the old home did not appeal to Jack. The "spirit of adventure" took possession of him and he struck out for the west. He arrived in Omaha, Nebraska, in 1867, drifted into Cheyenne, Wyoming, the same year and went to work on the Union Pacific railroad. When this road was finished he drifted into Montana, the "El Dorado" of the west, where he tried his hand at mining. He cast his first vote in Bannock City, Montana. His mining ventures did not prove to be a good move so he soon left Montana and went to Salt Lake City, Utah, where he had the pleasure of hearing the great Mormon leader, Brigham Young, preach. The next year we hear of Jack in Madison County, Nebraska, there he filed on some land and was elected sheriff of that county. He came into the Black Hills with a freight train (commonly called bull whackers) in 1877. In the fall of this year he was employed by the government to move the Indians from Camp Sheridan. In 1878 he came into the Black Hills with an outfit and drove in a large band of hogs. This year he was employed by the government again to move the Indians back to Spotted Tail Agency. Here he met the famous Sioux Indion, Chief Spotted Tail, and a lasting friendship was formed. "Old Spot" invited Jack to come to a dog feast. Now that is the highest honor that an Indian can offer any man, but Jack, who is a born diplomat, managed to decline this honor without offending the old chief. "Old Spot" then offered his daughter's hand in marriage to Jack, but, with even more diplomacy, he declined that honor also.

In 1879 Hale came in with an outfit of seventeen wagons. He brought in another herd of 250 hogs. In the year of 1880 he brought in another herd of over 400 hogs and a large band of sheep. At this time he owned the "Pleasant Valley Stock Farm," now in

John D. Hale

Meade county, South Dakota. This is one of the finest farms in the county, and is now owned by O. J. Hanson. In the fall of 1880 Jack Hale was nominated by the Democrats for the legislature and was elected by a good majority. There were only two Democrats elected that year in the whole Territory of Dakota. Jack Hale has served four terms in the lower house of the legislature and three terms in the senate. He was beaten once by Sam Mortimer of Belle Fourche, South Dakota. This district is now and always has been Republican in politics by a large majority, and it shows the esteem in which he is held by all the different parties, regardless of politics. At this writing Jack is still an active man. He owns a large tract of land on the Belle Fourche river just below the Devils Tower in Crook County, Wyoming, a very fine body of highly cultivated land consisting of 5400 acres all in one body. It is one of the most valuable stock ranches in the west. Besides laying out the town site of Battle Creek he drove several bands of horses into the Black Hills from Oregon and Montana. Take it all around he has been a very enerrgetic and public spirited man all his life. He still resides in Sturgis Meade County, South Dakota, near the scenes of his former business and political activities, and takes an active part in all the local and state politics but refuses to hold office again. He is taking life easy and enjoying life fully. He has done his share towards developing the resources of the West.

Jesse Brown.

GALEN E. HILL

I suppose that I enjoyed the acquaintance of Galen E. Hill longer than any other person in the Black Hills country. I first met Galen in Cheyenne, Wyoming, along about 1873. He was in charge of a freight outfit belonging to Joe Small. I was in charge of another outfit belonging to James D. May, and we were sent to Fort Laramie to haul hay to the Fort on a contract awarded to May & Small. We worked together all that summer, and wintered together on Pumpkin Creek, north of Sidney, Nebraska, the winter of '73 and '74. We separated after this until 1878 when we met again on the old Iron Side Treasure Coach, carrying the gold bullion from Deadwood to Cheyenne. We rode together, and scouted for signs of road agents, up until September when the fight occured at Canyon Springs between robbers and guards on the Treasure Coach, in which battle Galen was shot twice through the lungs and one arm. The next morning I prepared a bunk in a cabin that was close to the stage barn, and moved Galen to it, and took care of him until he recovered from his wounds.

Galen E. Hill was a likeable fellow, was always cheerful and jolly, even during his affliction he never complained. He looked on the bright side of things as they appeared and seemed to see sunshine through the clouds. Galen was ambitious, and as the saying is here in the west, he had the sand. There was no yellow in his makeup, he was game, from first to last, and deserves to be classed with the heroes of the west. He was the right man in the right place. Necessity demanded men of his stripe, at the time when the Black Hills were being settled and was overrun with outlaws, thieves and murderers. Galen came to the front as one to combat this class of law violators, and he did it with all his might.

And we who are here at this time can thank Galen E. Hill for his part in dispersing the Indian, the outlaw, and road agents, and making these beautiful Black Hills a fit dwelling place for honest men and women.

JOE E. COOK

By request of Mr. Willard, I shall attempt to jot down some of the incidents of my life since 1863. In that year I drove an ox team to Denver, Colorado, and on my way back I met my brother driving a team, one of twenty-six big Murphy wagons loaded with corn for Fort Laramie. As one of the drivers had quit a day or two before, I got a job to drive to Fort Laramie. In both instances our starting point was from Plattsmouth, Nebraska. The winter of 1863 was an exceptionally cold winter and a great many cattle froze or starved to death.

It may be of some interest to a great many to know that the Sioux Indians were not hostile to the whites at that time until the fall of 1864. In the fall of 1863 we visited their tepees that were strung all along the Platte Valley from Fort Kearney to the mouth of the Cache La Powdre River. In August, 1864, eleven four-mule teams loaded with freight for Denver were quietly driving up the Platte Valley, and when within three miles of Plum Creek station they noticed a band of Indians coming from the south in a leisurely way on horse back, and when the Indians got within 250 yards of the train they set up their blood curdling yell and whipping their ponies they surrounded the wagons and began shooting the drivers. I never heard what caused them to turn hostile. In the spring of 1865 when I went to Montana all that was left of the stage stations was the metal that would not burn, such as heating and cooking stoves, the irons off wagons and other metal. They cut open sacks of flour and poured the flour on the prairie. Two feather beds that were a part of families freight who had gone to Denver on the stage coach were cut open for the ticks. In the spring of 1865 when I again went over the road the feathers were still hanging to the sage brush. We arrived in Virginia City, Montana, on the 25th of August, 1865. From there I went to the Gallatin Valley and farmed it for ten years. The Indians (Sioux) made raids into the Gallatin Valley nearly every fall, always driving off a lot of horses and killing one or two men that they would catch on the outskirts of the valley. In the summer of 1873 the Northern Pacific railway route was surveyed. General Stanley with 2000 men started from St. Paul and surveyed west and Colonel Baker with 800 men started from Tacoma, Washington, and surveyed east. They met at a point on the Yellowstone River they called Pompey's Pillar on a small island in the Yellowstone River.

A straggler by the name of Vernon came up the Yellowstone with Stanley. He claimed to be a prospector and that he washed out one dollar and twenty-five cents to the pan and that he drove an iron picket pin into a cedar tree at the mouth of the gulch, and that he could take us right to the spot. This created quite a furore all over Montana, and in the early spring of 1874 one hundred and forty-eight of us went down into that country to get a gold mine, Vernon agreeing to pilot us to the El Dorado on Goose Creek. He and three other men left Bozeman three or four days before we all got together on the Yellowstone. The day before we got to his camp he said he would wait for us on the Yellowstone River. The day before we arrived at his camp he met two of his men going back to Bozeman after a supply of flour, as they said they were about out of flour. The next day at noon we got to his camp, and in the afternoon he made us a nice long speech, telling how to go on and that as soon as his men got back from Bozeman he would overtake us. Our outfit consisted of twenty wagons and nearly all of our provisions were donated by the citizens of Montana. Colonel Story, a wealthy man of Bozeman, donated a big Murphy wagon and six yoke of oxen to haul it. We had some teams. Fort Ellis gave us a six powder cannon and ammunition to go with it. Colonel Bozeman brought an iron piece of four inch calibre. We had to make the ammunition for this piece. We got some blue flannel and made sacks to fit the muzzle, and about ten inches long to hold the powder, and for shells we went to the tin shop and had cans made to fit the bore of the gun. For projectiles, we went to the blacksmith shop and got all the old scraps of iron horse shoes and cut them up to fill the cans. I want to record that when we fired this gun, the cans bursted when they left the muzzle of the gun, the pieces of iron not being the same shape or size, each and every one of them had a tune of its own, as it passed through the air. We organized on the Yellowstone River, on the 12th of February, electing Frank Grounds, captain; William Wright, lieutenant, and Eli Way, adjutant. Way's duties were to detail the guard night and morning. The guards stood six hours on and then six off. We traveled down the north side of the Yellowstone until we got to Goose Creek, this being the creek that Vernon said that he found the gold on. We prospected this creek from its mouth to its source and did not find even a hat full of gravel, as it runs through a gumbo soil all the way. After finding Vernon's statement all a hoax, we crossed to the south side of the river with the view of prospecting the streams on the south side.

The morning we left the Yellowstone to go across lots to the Rosebud, we encountered thirteen Indians. As we were going up a draw, a young fellow, I think his name was Davis, who rode a buckskin horse, was a half mile ahead of the train, was the first to see them. He had gone over the ridge out of sight of the train. The Indians had seen him first and had stripped their horses of everything, such as provisions, blankets and other things. I think they intended to take him alive, for they never shot at him during the race. Davis' horse was a plug race horse and he rode away from them. As soon as the Indians got to the top of the ridge, and saw the train they stampeded up the mountain, and we got their pile of stuff. This little band of Indians harassed us every day by shooting at us from behind ridges and trees and then getting out of the way. Right here I will give the reader an idea of their strategy. We were camped in a gulch, and just in the gray of the morning they fired several shots at us before we were out of bed. About sun up we put out pickets and turned the horses out of the wagon corral to feed. About one-half mile from camp we had four horsemen on a ridge, about another half mile still further out a lone Indian who was riding a good looking sorrel horse, came out in the open, and flashed a small mirror, thereby expressing a desire to talk to one of the pickets. There was a ridge extending out to where he was. One of the pickets said he would ride out there and kill this Indian and get his horse. The three other guards remonstrated and tried to keep him from going. He would go, and as the lay of the land was uneven he did not see the Indian disappear. He rode on out to where the Indian had been, when he started back six Indians that were secreted, surrounded him. As they ran he emptied his

Winchester at them, but did not hit any of them. The Indians rode so close to him that they struck him several times with their quirts in the face. He was shot through the upper part of the shoulder and once through the right foot, the bullet going in at the instep and coming out through the sole. The next day's travel after this brought us to the Rosebud. The first thing that engaged our attention was the wide road that the Indians' travois made going up the creek just a day or two before we got there. Right here I want to describe their mode of transportation. Their tepee poles are from sixteen to eighteen feet long. They bore one-half inch holes in the little end of each pole through which they pass a stout piece of buckskin or elk skin. They drag these tepee poles by tying the little ends to their pack saddles, and the big ends drag on the ground, six or eight feet on each side of the pony. Behind the pony they tie a couple of cross pieces, on which they have a wicker work made of willows for a platform, on which they carry their goods and small children. From the size of the tracks they had made we concluded that the whole Sioux tribe had gone up the valley, so we expected an attack that night and at midnight we were surrounded by them.

I am going to describe this fight more definitely as it was our longest and the most disastrous to the Indians We camped in the bottom about 400 yards from the creek. Our corral was about sixty yards from a hay draw that ran from the foothills to the stream. It was about fifty or sixty feet wide. Sage brush about 18 inches high grew between the corral and the draw. We had dug a trench about two feet wide and two feet deep on both sides of the corral for breastworks for the protection of our pickets. We dug holes out from two to three hundred yards from the camp. Each man cut a head log from eight to ten inches in diameter and about three feet long. We laid this on the embankment and dug a little post hole under the log, so that the Indians could not shoot us in the head while we were shooting. Our rule was that whenever any of the pickets fired a shot all the other pickets were to come into camp as soon as they could. Near midnight on the 4th of April the pickets next to the creek saw something they took for Indians, and they fired on them. All the pickets came rushing in and the entire camp was routed out of bed. All of us stood around shivering and finally went back to bed and the pickets were sent out to their posts. My bedfellow was on picket on the bank of the draw. He did not quite get to his picket hole when there were a dozen shots fired at him, but he was not hit by any of them. By this time there was a constant stream of fire from the draw which lasted until after sun up. Several horses were killed, but only one man was wounded. His head log was rotten and in adjusting it a bullet went through it and made a flesh wound in his arm between the wrist and the elbow. After sunrise we charged on the draw and killed ten Indians. One old buck, who must have been eighty years old and weighed at least three hundred pounds, had his right foot shot off just above the ankle, and his foot was hanging on by the skin on the inside of his leg. He was trying to get away, by jabbing the bones of his leg in the ground every step he took. Some one put an end to his misery by shooting him in the back with a 50 calibre needle gun. Another young Indian about thirty years old, was found in a little patch of brush, apparently dead. A fellow by the name of Bill Coffee, after looking at the Indian a while said, "I think I will shoot him once more for luck." He understood what Bill said, and he raised up to a sitting position and commenced to beg for his life, when Bill stuck his Colts 45 in his face and fired, blowing some of the Indian's teeth out, the bullet coming out of the back of his head. We stayed in this camp one more day. We had two big fat Newfoundland dogs that must have run to the bank of the draw to bark at the Indians for after the fight was over, the dogs' bones were lying about the fire where they were cooked. For the benefit of some of the readers of this I must tell them that a fat dog is one of the greatest luxuries that a Sioux Indian enjoys.

We stayed in camp expecting the Indians to come and get their dead, but they failed to make any appearance. We drove off the next day, leaving the bodies where they fell. About four days afterwards, they tried to get our horses, we had just turned them out to graze in the morning, and just as they began to feed the Indians came out of the mountains north of us, and tried to stampede the herd. They are great bluffers. As soon as they came in sight, they began yelling and shooting, thereby thinking to intimidate our herders. In the melee one of our boys shot one of the Indians off his horse, and the horse came into camp with our horses. About ten of us started out to scalp the Indian, and when we were about half way an Indian about five hundred yards up the creek fired at the bunch of us, killing Zach Yates. Zach was walking behind me and a little to the left. Some one said, "Zach is shot." I looked around and he was lying on his back with his legs drawn up against his stomach and his hands clasping his stomach. I stooped down and asked him where he was hit, but he made no reply, and in three or four seconds he began to straighten out his limbs and with a quiver of his body, life was extinct. Four of us picked him up and started to the camp. I presume the Indians wanted us to leave him where he fell so they could get his scalp, for they poured their bullets around us like hail until we got out of gun shot. We hauled his body that day, and after dark we buried him. We filled his grave that was dug right along side of a rifle pit, so that the mound over his grave was a part of the breastworks on that side of the corral. We had to do this to keep the Indians from digging him up and scalping him. Mr. Yates was the only man that was killed, and only two were wounded.

When we were traveling we had a front and rear guard of twenty men in each squad, and a right and left flank guard of the same number that moved with the train, from a quarter to a half mile distance from the train all owing to the lay of the country through which we were traveling. The next and last general battle we had was on a stream called Rotten Grass. It was about 10 o'clock in the morning when one of our left flank guards came to the train and reported the timber along the creek full of Indians. As we were in the middle of the valley the captain ordered us to move over to the foothills, thereby preventing the Indians from having the timber and foothills both to shoot from. The Indians seeing what we were going to do, started in to checkmate us. About three hundred of them came out of the timber on horse back and on the dead run started for the train, thinking our left flank would stampede for the train. But the men dismounted and kneeling down they sent such a storm of lead into them that the Indians turned off and went into the foot hills. About eighty of them left their horses behind, and crawled up behind a ridge, and were killing our horses. Eli Way called for a detachment to charge the ridge, and here I got my Indian. About twenty-five of our boys ran across a plateau and Eli Way and I were in the bottom. The Indians seeing us coming, got to their horses and made a get away, excepting one. He came out of a little gulch about forty yards from us, and was running away from us. He had on a brand new shirt made of white domestic sewed with black thread and his pants were black woolen stuff. I had a 50 calibre needle gun and Way said, "Is your gun loaded? Shoot the son of a gun." Thinking that I would not miss, I drew a bead on his body just where his pants and shirt met. I hit him in the right hip joint and the bullet came out in his groin. This charge ended the last fight we had with them. We soon came to the old Fort Fetterman and Fort Smith road. After we crossed the Big Horn River we fell in with the Crows, Black Foot being the chief of this band. We traveled with them until we came to their agency on the Little Rosebud. The Crows boast that they have always been friendly with the Whites. We got back to Bozeman on the 12th of May, having been out just three months.

ANNA DONNA TALLENT

The chapter on biographical sketches will be closed with a short survey of the long and useful life of one of the most heroic and most widely admired characters of the pioneer days, Mrs. Annie D. Tallent, whose full name was Anna Donna Tallent. She was born in York, New York, about April 27, 1827, and spent her childhood days in the Empire state. She received an excellent education and graduated from a course of study in the schools of Fort Edward, New York. This early training proved to be of great value to her in the long years to come when adverse circumstances compelled her to sustain herself and family.

Her life was uneventful until in the year 1874 when with her husband and young son, she embarked from Sioux City, Iowa, on the long and perilous trip that brought her to the Black Hills of Dakota. On the 6th day of October, 1874, the expedition composed of twenty-six men, one woman and her young son, and six canvas covered wagons each drawn by two pairs of cattle, began the long march across the prairies. The progress was slow and the loads heavy, and behind this small train, the woman trudged along bravely bearing her part of the burden of the undertaking and by her kindly manner and hopeful words, sustaining many of the men who would have turned back long before the end of the journey.

In the splendid history of the Black Hills with which Mrs. Tallent crowned her long life of achievement, she gave a very interesting account of the many incidents occurring along the route. The hardships of the journey, the sorrows and worries along the way, and the fears and doubts born in the minds of the adventurers as they looked into the unknown, future, are pictured in a most accurate and able manner. There was the opposition of the government, besides the cer-

Anna Donna Tallent

tain hostility of the Indians, to be considered. In addition to these most serious difficulties, there were added the hardships and sufferings incident to the slow ox team transportation across a wilderness. The undertaking was indeed one of unusual importance and one that called for real bravery of the highest order and a spirit of determination seldom found among men even of this day. Through it all there gleamed the noble courage and kindly spirit of the lone wife and mother, as she tramped the weary miles of sand, rocks, or prairie grass, and later, the snow covered trails.

The journey was not without its grim tragedies and the most trying one is described by Mrs. Tallent in the following words, which reveal the gentle and Christian character of the brave woman, when one of the men of the expedition became sick and died: "All that day I walked along on foot by the side of the wagon, with the long agonizing wails of the dying man ringing in my ears, every cry piercing my heart like a two-edged sword. He begging to be shot, and thus relieved from his terrible suffering. This thought no doubt was suggested to his mind by the sight of a gun strapped to the canvas above his head, which was soon removed. About one hour before arriving at our camping ground, his cries ceased, and we all fervently hoped he had fallen asleep. Upon reaching camp and looking into the wagon it was seen that, indeed, he was peacefully sleeping the sleep that knows no awakening. 'Ah, pity 'tis, 'tis true;' that the poor pilgrim had fought the supreme battle alone, with no tender hand to wipe away death's gathering teardrops, or smooth his dying pillow—but yes, did not the pitying angels hover above and around him, even 'neath that coarse canvas?

"Gloom, like a dark pall, hung over our little camp on the dreary, lonely prairie that night. Death was in our midst and every gust of wind that blew adown the valley seemed laden with the wails and groans of our departed companion.

"A coffin of small hewn timbers, strongly pinned together with wooden pins, was constructed, in which the body was recently laid, then a cover, also of hewn timbers, was pinned down in like manner. Surely no prowling wolves or coyotes could ever reach him in his impregnable bed. A grave was then dug on a little grassy eminence overlooking the lonely valley, then sadly and tenderly his comrades lowered him into his final resting place, there to await the call of the trumpet on resurrection morn.

"A cross also of small, smooth, hewn timber was erected over his grave. On the pedestal of the cross was written the following inscription: :'Died on the 27th day of November, 1874, on his way to the Black Hills, Moses Aaron, aged 32 years. May he rest in peace.'

"No audible prayer was uttered, no funeral dirge was sung; each one stood reverently with bowed, uncovered head, around the grave until the first earth fell upon his rude coffin, then turned sadly away. I would give much to know whether that solitary grave has remained undisturbed all the long years since then.

"At 3 o'clock p. m., November 28th, the simple ceremonies being over, our train moved on leaving our late companion in that desolate spot, far from home and friends, where the summer's breezes and winter's blast would wail a perpetual requeim athwart his lone grave."

The surviving adventurers continued on their way with the varying incidents of a trip through the outlying plains and hills near the Black Hills region, and on December 9th, 1874, at about noon, in a howling snow storm, they first stepped upon the soil of the Black Hills at a point four miles below the present city of Sturgis. Here their hearts were gladdened for they met the heavy trail made in August as General Custer turned down the valley and bade farewell to the Hills. On the night of the same day, they camped in the canyon about two miles below the site of Piedmont and here took their first sleep within the precincts of the lofty hills. On through storms and snows, up hill and down, through forests and canyons they slowly drove their foot sore and starved oxen until they finally reached their destination about two miles below the present site of Custer. Here on December 23rd, 1874, they pitched their tents, and at once sought and found the prospect holes of Ross and McKay, where they obtained specimens of gold.

In describing the Hills of those days, Mrs. Tallent writes: "We found the Black Hills a profound solitude, with peace, like a guardian angel, reigning over the whole wide expanse, and without a single vestige of civilization; and as we marched along the shadows of the lofty hills, I remember how greatly I was impressed with their vastness, and our own comparative insignificance and littleness........All along the route could be seen in places, on one hand, huge rocks piled high one upon the other, with almost mechanical regularity and precision, as if placed there by the hand of a master workman—a great wall of natural masonry; on the other the everlasting hills, with majestic pines, that looked like sentinels guarding the valleys below, towering far, far above our heads; then anon low lying ranges of hills, clothed with dense forests of pine, and away in the hazy distance, other ranges rising up like great banks of clouds against the horizon."

When the camp for the permanent location was selected, a stockade was built that in point of efficiency was perfect for its purpose of resisting attacks by the Indians. Inside the heavy timbered stockade fence, were erected substantial log houses, and the severe and stormy winter was spent in the effort to endure the heavy charges of the artillery of the snows. There were some desertions from the camp by parties who could not endure the intense homesickness that came upon them in the trying ordeal, but Mrs. Tallent went bravely on with her tasks and displayed a wonderful courage and optimism that put to shame the sturdy men of the party. But all her early dreams were soon to be shattered, for the army detachment sent out to get the trespassers, finally located them in their camp and within twenty-four hours, Mrs. Tallent was seated for the first time in her life, upon the back of a government mule and was on her way out of the Hills. Upon arriving at Ft. Laramie, she had good cause for rejoicing for it was seen that in a short time, the Indians would have wiped the little band of adventurers from the face of the earth.

Nothing daunted by this turn of events, Mrs. Tallent again returned to the Hills in the spring of 1876 and there remained for the rest of her life. For a time she taught school in several of the small towns of the Hills and for four years she served as the efficient superintendent of schools of Pennington County. She also served for several years as the president of the Rapid City School Board, and was active in the religious life of the city. The last years of her life were devoted to the great task of writing her splendid history, "The Black Hills, or Last Hunting Grounds of the Dakotahs," which was completed while she resided in Sturgis, with her son, Robert Tallent.

Mrs. Tallent was not destined to long enjoy the popularity of her literary efforts, for on the 13th day of February, 1901, at the close of day, the grand woman pioneer and historian set sail on the sea of eternity. The report of her death spread far and near and so great was the admiration of men throughout the Hills for the kindly and noble womanhood of the departed, that on the day of her funeral in Sturgis, when the remains were forwarded to Elgin, Illinois, the Circuit Court was adjourned in Deadwood and a special train was chartered by the Society of Black Hills Pioneers, who attended in a body and bade farewell to the form of one whose sublime faith and courage had often inspired many with new hope.

Almost a half century has rolled around since the day when the foot sore and weary pilgrim, the first white woman to tread upon the slopes of the Black Hills, trudged through the snows of early winter and stood awed and humbled at the feet of the majestic mountains that had beckoned to her for days and weeks across the toilsome prairie trail. The years that followed, held for her life's bitterest trials and sorrows, and the fond dreams of her youth were destined to be mere phantoms of hope. Yet, through it all, the noble and pure womanhood of Mrs. Tallent shone with the light of untarnished faith and firm purpose.

Anna D. Tallent builded better than she thought. The kind and cheering words of long ago, the gentle ministrations to her fellows in the hour of sorrow, her purity of thought and action, the unflinching courage that smiled while the heart was bleeding under the cruel blows of unkind fate, have won for her memory so deep an admiration that those who knew her in the days of the past, will erect to her memory, a fitting and splendid monument. It will perpetuate the name of a true and noble wife and mother, a heoric and intrepid woman pioneer.

And beneath the monument the boys of long ago will gently lay to rest the remains of the first white woman to wake the echo of the Hills. From the far off prairies of Illinois, will be brought the ashes of their comrade to once for all, mingle with the earth of the Black Hills. Here, each springtime shall see strewn upon her mound, the wild flowers of the vales whose perfume shall be wafted as a sweet incense to the memory of the noblest pioneer of them all.

HORATIO N. ROSS

Horatio N. Ross and William T. McKay were two members of the Custer expedition, miners, and to them has been accorded the honor of first discovering gold in the Black Hills. Mr. Ross fixed the date as July 27, 1874, and the place where Custer is located as the spot. As will be seen elsewhere in this book there is some discrepancy as to dates and place, but there is no doubt as to Mr. Ross being the miner who first discovered the gold that was to make the Black Hills famous. Very little is known about him. He was a miner and that seems to be about all history has to offer, but to have found gold in the Black Hills and thus pave the way for the settlement of this beautiful garden and recreation spot of the United States is glory enough for one man. As the tourist travel increases and the Black Hills become known more and more the name of Horatio N Ross will not be forgotten.

General Custer's expedition, of which Messrs Ross

Horatio N. Ross
First Discoverer of Gold in the Black Hills in 1874

and McKay were members, had with it as botanist Prof. A. B. Donaldson of the University of Minnesota, and in his report he said, "Neither gold nor silver have been found, but the miners (Ross and McKay) report indications." Mr. Ross always felt aggrieved over that report of Prof. Donaldson, claiming that it greatly retarded the development of the Hills. The failure of the officers of the expedition to note this place and date, may be due to the fact that Prof. Winchell had not been called upon to decide the nature of the metals supposed by the privates in the command to be gold, and felt somewhat piqued. Prof. N. H. Winchell was the official geologist of the Custer expedition.

MID-AMERICAN FRONTIER
An Arno Press Collection

Andreas, A[lfred] T[heodore]. **History of Chicago.** 3 volumes. 1884-1886

Andrews, C[hristopher] C[olumbus]. **Minnesota and Dacotah.** 1857

Atwater, Caleb. **Remarks Made on a Tour to Prairie du Chien: Thence to Washington City, in 1829.** 1831

Beck, Lewis C[aleb]. **A Gazetteer of the States of Illinois and Missouri.** 1823

Beckwith, Hiram W[illiams]. **The Illinois and Indiana Indians.** 1884

Blois, John T. **Gazetteer of the State of Michigan, in Three Parts.** 1838

Brown, Jesse and A. M. Willard. **The Black Hills Trails.** 1924

Brunson, Alfred. **A Western Pioneer: Or, Incidents of the Life and Times of Rev. Alfred Brunson.** 2 volumes in one. 1872

Burnet, Jacob. **Notes on the Early Settlement of the North-Western Territory.** 1847

Cass, Lewis. **Considerations on the Present State of the Indians, and their Removal to the West of the Mississippi.** 1828

Coggeshall, William T[urner]. **The Poets and Poetry of the West.** 1860

Darby, John F[letcher]. **Personal Recollections of Many Prominent People Whom I Have Known.** 1880

Eastman, Mary. **Dahcotah: Or, Life and Legends of the Sioux Around Fort Snelling.** 1849

Ebbutt, Percy G. **Emigrant Life in Kansas.** 1886

Edwards, Ninian W[irt]. **History of Illinois, From 1778 to 1833: And Life and Times of Ninian Edwards.** 1870

Ellsworth, Henry William. **Valley of the Upper Wabash, Indiana.** 1838

Esarey, Logan, ed. **Messages and Letters of William Henry Harrison.** 2 volumes. 1922

Flower, George. **The Errors of Emigrants.** [1841]

Hall, Baynard Rush (Robert Carlton, pseud.). **The New Purchase: Or Seven and a Half Years in the Far West.** 2 volumes in one. 1843

Haynes, Fred[erick] Emory. **James Baird Weaver.** 1919

Heilbron, Bertha L., ed. **With Pen and Pencil on the Frontier in 1851: The Diary and Sketches of Frank Blackwell Mayer.** 1932

Hinsdale, B[urke] A[aron]. **The Old Northwest: The Beginnings of Our Colonial System.** [1899]

Johnson, Harrison. **Johnson's History of Nebraska.** 1880

Lapham, I[ncrease] A[llen]. **Wisconsin: Its Geography and Topography, History, Geology, and Mineralogy.** 1846

Mansfield, Edward D. **Memoirs of the Life and Services of Daniel Drake.** 1855

Marshall, Thomas Maitland, ed. **The Life and Papers of Frederick Bates.** 2 volumes in one. 1926

McConnel, J[ohn] L[udlum.] **Western Characters: Or, Types of Border Life in the Western States.** 1853

Miller, Benjamin S. **Ranch Life in Southern Kansas and the Indian Territory.** 1896

Neill, Edward Duffield. **The History of Minnesota.** 1858

Parker, Nathan H[owe]. **The Minnesota Handbook, For 1856-7.** 1857

Peck, J[ohn] M[ason]. **A Guide for Emigrants.** 1831

Pelzer, Louis. **Marches of the Dragoons in the Mississippi Valley.** 1917

Perkins, William Rufus and Barthinius L. Wick. **History of the Amana Society.** 1891

Rister, Carl Coke. **Land Hunger: David L. Payne and the Oklahoma Boomers.** 1942

Schoolcraft, Henry R[owe]. **Personal Memoirs of a Residence of Thirty Years With the Indian Tribes on the American Frontiers.** 1851

Smalley, Eugene V. **History of the Northern Pacific Railroad.** 1883

[Smith, William Rudolph]. **Observations on the Wisconsin Territory.** 1838

Steele, [Eliza R.] **A Summer Journey in the West.** 1841

Streeter, Floyd Benjamin. **The Kaw: The Heart of a Nation.** 1941

[Switzler, William F.] **Switzler's Illustrated History of Missouri, From 1541 to 1877.** 1879

Tallent, Annie D. **The Black Hills.** 1899

Thwaites, Reuben Gold. **On the Storied Ohio.** 1903

Todd, Charles S[tewart] and Benjamin Drake. **Sketches of the Civil and Military Services of William Henry Harrison.** 1840

Wetmore, Alphonso, compiler. **Gazetteer of the State of Missouri.** 1837

Wilder, D[aniel] W[ebster]. **The Annals of Kansas.** 1886

Woollen, William Wesley. **Biographical and Historical Sketches of Early Indiana.** 1883

Wright, Robert M[arr]. **Dodge City.** 1913